American Foundations

American Foundations

An Investigative History

Mark Dowie

The MIT Press
Cambridge, Massachusetts
London, England

Library of Congress Cataloging-in-Publication Data

Dowie, Mark.
    American foundations : an investigative history / Mark Dowie.
        p. cm.
    Includes bibliographical references and index.
    ISBN 0-262-04189-8 (hc : alk. paper)
    1. Endowments—United States—History. 2. Charities—United States—History. I. Title.
    HV97.A3 D68 2001
    361.7′632′0973—dc21

                                                                00-054627

To Daniel, Rachel, Mark, Peter, Katina, Riley, and their children.

Contents

Preface

A foundation is a large amount of money completely surrounded by people who want some.

—Dwight MacDonald

No one can say for certain what portion of the enormous sums of money economists predict will transfer from one generation to the next over the next twenty-five to fifty years will wind up in the treasuries of philanthropies.[1] But even a tenth of the most conservative estimate of that wealth transfer—recently projected at somewhere between $41 and $136 trillion—will create a financial tsunami for foundation endowments. However, many of the same economists have discovered that when wealth transfers increase relative to GNP and personal income, the proportion flowing into philanthropic resources also tends to rise. So if the economy remains strong and the tax code amenable, as much as two-tenths of the total transfer of private wealth could end up in foundation endowments.

Twenty percent of $41 trillion, along with a strong securities market, would swell foundation assets by nine or tenfold—to over three or four trillion dollars—by sometime in the second quarter of the century. That combination could well make organized philanthropy the fastest growing financial sector in the economy for the next fifty years; by 2050, foundations could be granting well over $200 billion every year, ten times their $22.8 billion 1999 total. If that happens, the so-called golden age of philanthropy, as the 1990s is sometimes known, will be seen as but a bare beginning.

It is important to keep in mind, however, that as large as it seems on the page, that $200 billion a year will still pale compared to the total given by individuals, if they continue to give at their present level of generosity. In the United States today almost 80 percent of all money provided to various nonprofit organizations is donated by living individuals. Add bequests and individuals, living and dead, account for 88 percent of all philanthropy.

Even then, we should note, the hundreds of billions of dollars received from all nongovernmental sources will not come close to compensating nonprofit social service institutions for the sums lost to them through the devolution of state and federal governments. Nevertheless, conservatives will continue to hold up the growth of private philanthropy as an argument against any redistribution of wealth through taxation. Meanwhile, if poverty persists, foundations will be pressed to abandon all but their charitable activities—which won't come close to solving the problem.

Though philanthropic organizations in America have larger assets than those in any other developed nation, proportionately less of the nation's wealth or income finds its way to the lowest 20 to 30 percent of its population, which possesses an average net worth well under zero. Foundation giving is minuscule compared to the income adjustment that would be required to bring the United States up to the income- and wealth-distribution levels of Europe. In fact, as foundation assets and the charitable sector have grown, so, paradoxically, has the gap between rich and poor.

Whatever the size of the forthcoming wealth transfer, in the foreseeable future foundations will continue their impressive growth. And they will remain at the epicenter of an emerging national debate over the meaning, legitimacy, and purpose of private philanthropy. As government shrinks and a fiscally starved nonprofit sector looks to private philanthropy for relief, foundations—which have historically seen their function as the identification of root causes rather than outright charity—have become a subject of public controversy. In this book I examine their history, explore the debate over their character, and propose a number of ways to preserve foundations' unique role as seekers of root causes.

Much of the contemporary literature on philanthropy—by writers like Waldemar Nielsen, Frederick Keppel, Ellen Condliffe Lagemann, Ben Whitaker, James Smith, Judith Sealander, Barry Karl, Teresa Odendahl, Michael Lerner, Dennis McIlnay, Stanley Katz, and F. Emerson Andrews, to name only a few—focuses principally on the grantmakers. It describes the inner workings of large foundations, the intentions of donors, the role of trustees, and the evolution of a field sometimes called *philanthropic science.*

While I have learned much from this literature, my own approach is quite different. I examine foundations from the public perspective, describing how their large-scale philanthropy has affected the fields of human endeavor they have supported over the past century. Although foundations and their subculture are intriguing, and not well understood, it is their impact on the rest of American society that demands our attention. I therefore leave study of the internal operation and mores of organized philanthropy to the anthropologists and focus my inquiry principally on the foundations' impact on several of the intractable challenges facing America at the end of the "American century."

The archives of philanthropy that are being opened to public view, slowly, one foundation at a time, are treasures of unrecorded history. Although ponderously boring, and carefully screened and edited before release (usually twenty years after the date of a given document), they contain exciting nuggets of information, even an occasional smoking gun. Many of the documents I examined had never been read by outsiders, though they had been sitting in open files for ten years or more.

It is from these documents, along with over two hundred interviews I conducted with foundation officers, critics, and recipients of their largess, that I created the heart of this book. That is its investigative component. The rest is essay.

Acknowledgments

My special personal thanks go to Alan Abramson, Nelson Aldridge, Judy Austermiller, Peter Bahouth, Harriet Barlow, Peter Barnes, Judith Bell, Lucy Bernholtz, Gwenda Blair, Bob Bothwell, Wendell Breuner, Claudia Callender, Connie Casey, Michael Caudel-Feagan, Ralph Cavanagh, Roberta Clark, Sally Covington, Gene Coyle, Sophie Craighead, Claire Cummings, Jodi Curtis, Alan Divak, Bill Domhoff, Pat Dondonoli, Leonard Duhl, Alvin Duskin, Sharon Dynak, Pablo Eisenberg, Jed Emerson, Diane Feeney, Carol Ferry, Michael Fischer, Frances Fitzgerald, Chryseis O. Fox, Tracy Gary, Arlene Goldblatt, Peter Goldmark, Jane Gordy, Jonathan Green, Elizabeth Guheen, Herb Gunther, Ellen Gurzhinsky, Carol Guyer, Charles Halpern, Hal Harvey, Winona Hauter, Nancy Hechinger, Robert Herdt, Anne Hess, David Himmelstein, David Hunter, Warren Ilchman, Craig Jenkins, Daniel Kevles, Mark Kramer, Marty Krasny, John Kreidler, Anne Krumboltz, Arun Kashyap, Herb Kutchins, Tom Layton, Bokara Legendre, Helaine Lerner, Michael Lerner, Lance Lindblom, Dick Magat, Jerry Mander, Rob McKay, Bill Mergener, Ellen Miller, Sandra Minkkinen, Clay Morgan, David Morris, David Mortimer, Bill Moyers, John Moyers, Brian Murphy, Pete Myers, Waldemar Nielsen, Michael Northrop, Terry Odendahl, David Olsen, Todd Oppenheimer, Louise Ottinger, Stacey Palmer, Richard Parker, John Perkins, Raymond Plank, Nancy Rader, Betsy Reed, Mark Ritchie, George Roberts, Wally Roberts, Tom Rosenbaum, Peter Rosset, Rusty Russell, J. A. Savage, Tom Schlesinger, Wendy Schwartz, Peter Shifter, Bill Shutkin, Tom Silk, Ed Skloot, Jim Smith, George Spencer, Vince Stehle, David Stern, Francis X. Sutton, Betsy Taylor, Marty Teitel, Gary Toenniessen, Tom Van Dyck, Enza Vescera, Steve Viederman, Tobiah Waldron, Marian Webber, Albie Wells, Curtis Wilkie, and Sid Wolfe. Will those whom I have forgotten please forgive me?

A Note on Semantics

Accountability   One of the hottest buzzwords and a virtual obsession of contemporary philanthropy, *accountability* can refer to the obligations of any number of persons or groups: a foundation's responsibility to the public, the government, its trustees, or its grantees; grantees' responsibilities to foundations, the public, government, and their own trustees; the responsibility of trustees of nonprofits to their own organizations, the public, and the foundations; and foundation trustees' responsibility to the foundation and its investments.

A more recent obsession with accountability applies the standards of venture capitalism to philanthropy. It demands a measurable "return on investment" in a sort of Harvard Business School bang-for-the-buck mentality that fails to take into account the subjective, unquantifiable nature of much philanthropic work. The principles of *venture philanthropy* have much to offer the nonprofit sector (as explored, for example, in chapter 10), but not when its proponents insist that everything of value can and should be quantified. Such venture philanthropists want grant recipients and foundations to be held fiscally accountable for the money they spend, as if shareholders somewhere—aged pensioners or widows and orphans—would suffer if they used it for poetry, or "wasted" it on an experimental project that ultimately failed.

Civil Society   You may have noticed that I devote chapter 9 of this book to "Civility." Using that title should not imply respect for the term *civil society*, which has become the captive of academic "experts" and conservative essayists who limit its application in ways that are anything but civil. In this chapter I attempt to broaden this overused term to include concepts, like civil rights and citizen activism, that these writers too often exclude from their definition of civil society.

Independent Sector   I believe this term, when used to describe the non-profit or third sector of society—institutions separate from government and industry—is a misnomer. It misleadingly implies that the third sector relies solely on its own economic resources. This, of course, is nonsense. While some institutions in the sector are genuinely self-sufficient, or acquire all their funds from within the nonprofit world itself, most non-profit organizations rely heavily on government, on private support (including corporations), or on both.

Therefore, while we can fairly describe this group of institutions as either the *third* or the *nonprofit sector* of American civilization, it is far from independent—nor should it be. So I will not use the term *independent sector* in this book, except to refer to an inappropriately named national membership organization, Independent Sector, which provides research and organizational assistance to nonprofit organizations.

Philanthropy   If we attempt to define *philanthropy* (literally "love of humanity") in accordance with the varied spectrum of organizations and foundations that operate under its rubric, it will remain a word without definition. The list of things done in America in the name of philanthropy is simply too varied and conflicting. Unless otherwise defined, in this book I use the word to mean the process of using money to create change, whether for the betterment of humanity or not, depending on the project in question.

Plutocracy (the rule of wealth)   In the course of an interview with a politically liberal and intellectually brilliant president of a major American foundation, I was advised to avoid using the word *plutocrat* or any of its forms. I would not be taken seriously if I did, he promised, "particularly by people in the foundation world." I should also, he added, avoid the use of *oligarchy*.

"But how can one write a book about foundations that make a strategic decision to influence public policy," I asked, "and avoid discussing the power of wealth?"

You can't," he answered. Admitting that the influence of wealth can be insidious, even destructive, he then advised me: "By all means describe the ways that private philanthropy can compromise democracy. Just don't use the *p*-word." I took his advice and use it sparingly.

Progressive "People use the word *progressive* to avoid thinking," a Ford Foundation executive remarked dismissively when I used the word during a conversation. He was right; I was guilty as charged.

I seriously considered writing this book without using this overworked and frequently misunderstood word. Its meaning, like so many others in our popular discourse—*paradigm, sustainability, entrepreneurial, sacred,* to mention only a few—has grown ambiguous and turbid through overuse. Despite the wide variety of interests and objectives they represent, most philanthropists and philanthrocrats consider themselves progressive, if only because they expect their grantmaking to produce progress.

However, when used in a historical context *progressive* can mean very different things, depending on the era it refers to. Early–twentieth-century Progressivism was in many respects the opposite of late–twentieth-century progressivism. In fact, it was to some degree a response to trends and tendencies we now consider progressive. Since the McCarthy era, however, the word has been derided by conservatives, who associate it with the welfare state, and employed by 1960s leftists seeking respectable euphemisms for *liberal* or *socialist,* words that have been branded on everything to the left of center.

So, in my quest to define *progressive philanthropy,* I try to restrict the word to ideas and causes anyone to the left of Attila the Hun would consider progress: better education, improved public health, stronger democratic institutions, equal opportunity, international peace, civil and human rights, lively creative arts and humanities, science in the public interest, and equal justice for all. As the Cold War subsides into history, we can only hope that Americans across the political spectrum will come to a new consensus about what *progress* really means and will find enough common ground to accept *progressive philanthropy* as an essentially good thing.

Introduction

Leveraged Influence

Foundations are America's passing gear.
—Paul Ylvisaker (1921–1992)

Paul Ylvisaker, a life-long public servant and legendary public affairs director of the Ford Foundation, believed in 1987 that, "viewed in the aggregate, foundations do not emerge as a force out in front of, and certainly not at odds with American society and its institutions." That was true when he said it. It is true no longer.

Shortly after Ylvisaker made that remark America's private foundations began to change in fundamental ways. Today the complexion and quality of the nation's life are profoundly affected every day, for better and for worse, by the trustees and staffs of a few hundred private and community foundations. Their influence is far greater than it was in the century Ylvisaker worked in philanthropy and, in spite of the foundations' increasing visibility, far greater than the public recognizes. That too is about to change.

Until quite recently philanthropic foundations were shielded from public oversight. They operated behind a veil of privacy long defended by founders, their families, and the fiduciaries appointed to oversee them. Foundation trustees regarded the endowments as their private domain for which they were accountable to no one. Over the past forty years, however, that veil has been gradually lifted, an inch or so at a time, sometimes voluntarily and occasionally under threat of government regulation. Foundations are now so close to being considered public institutions that many of them advertise their existence and promote their work in the mass media.

Yet even as these active residues of great wealth are openly "branding" themselves, the essence of their work and the impact of their benevolence remain shrouded in self-generated mythology. The ambiguous public/private nature of their existence, which confuses people on both sides of the veil, has prompted more than one observer to describe foundations as "privately organized public institutions."[1] This ambiguity has afforded foundations a chameleonlike existence: they can appear to be one thing in public while acting quite differently in private. That too is changing, and it will soon end.

Although American philanthropy continued to evolve in form and substance throughout the twentieth century, the shift it is currently undergoing is more fundamental. New elements that are transforming foundations from covert to overt arbiters of knowledge and culture will further expand their traditional vocation as mediators of public policy and magnify their role as creators of new social orthodoxies. Instead of wielding their influence in private darkness, as they did in their first century of existence, they will have to act in the broad daylight of public scrutiny.

Of course, the shaping of public and social policy is not an entirely new pursuit for foundations, which from their earliest days have been prime contributors to American social philosophy. Over the twentieth century as the institutions they created grew in size and number, philanthropists have concentrated their power, developed a prominent professional cadre, and significantly advanced the fine art of leveraging influence. The areas in which these private organizations have exercised that leverage, the role they have played in twentieth-century American life, and the very different role they could play in the twenty-first century are the subjects of this book. I focus in particular on the imagination that has driven foundation officials to pursue so many different goals, and I provide a historical critique of their efforts. Brilliant and constructive as some of their work has been, much of it has also been fruitless, uninspired, and designed to do little more than perpetuate the economic and social systems that allow foundations to exist.

At the turn of a new century—and a new millennium—it is time for our allegedly open society to ask whether placing so much power, covert or overt, at the disposal of an existentially bewildered, nondemocratic institution is a entirely wholesome development. If foundations are indeed "America's passing gear," we need to ask what, or whom, are they passing, and where are they taking the country? Do we need to go there? Do we want to go there? Is the foundations' imagined America the one we seek? And who will decide? These are the central questions of this book.

My intention in asking them is not to undermine America's private foundations. Indeed, I hope that they survive; not because they deserve to for any historical, moral, or legal reason but because through exposure, criticism, and democratic reform they could become truly vital institutions of American civilization. One alternative, the confiscation of private wealth by a government beholden to the interests of too few, is not at the moment either desirable or feasible. Would it not be better to put excess wealth to work de-corrupting government?

Philanthocracy

Those who have the gold rule.
—Anonymous twist on the Golden Rule

Philanthropy grows with our increasing disparity of wealth, and muffles systemic efforts at political reform.
—Michael Lerner, President, Jennifer Altman Foundation

As American wealth expanded, private foundations established in the early decades of the twentieth century—foundations with familiar names like Ford, Carnegie, Rockefeller, Mott, Pew, and MacArthur—have grown exponentially. Meanwhile their endowments have been far surpassed by newer trusts created by such later entrepreneurs as Johnson, Packard, Kellogg, Lilly, Hughes, Annenberg, Wallace, Hewlitt, Duke, and Gates. The latter, by adding tens of billions of dollars to foundation endowments, have raised the total of philanthropic assets to well over $420 billion.

Yet these endowments are insignificant compared to the sums in corporate and government treasuries, which are measured in the trillions. And their financial contributions amount to less than a tenth of what is donated by individual philanthropists. Nonetheless, philanthropic foundations exercise great power in American life, power far beyond their wealth, and influence that extends beyond their founders' imaginations.

That influence derives directly from the proactive nature of their grantmaking and their methods of leveraging money. It represents the concerted efforts of innumerable officers at the nation's largest foundations, most of whom have been consistently bent on developing an agenda for the nation.

The "science," if not the art of philanthropy is an indisputably American invention. No other civilization has been designed by the imagination of its organized philanthropists to quite the same degree as the United States. And nowhere else in the world have so many foundations been so heavily staffed with *philanthrocrats*—the approximately ten thousand foundation professionals who, though not wealthy on their own account, often refer to themselves as philanthropists. Nowhere else have such vast national organizations and trade associations been created to serve the foundation "industry." And nowhere else have private trusts assumed so large a role as educators, researchers, and pollinators of policy think tanks.

The increasing prominence of that role has received surprisingly little public attention. Not that the foundations entirely shun publicity. They seek it, but very selectively. Many foundation officials have a rather naive public relations sense that their work is somehow fascinating to the public and the media. In fact, in 1999 the theme of the fiftieth anniversary convention of the Council on Foundations was "Communicating Philanthropy." It featured highly professional workshops on methods of attracting media attention and informing the public about their activities. Colleagues encouraged each other to lift their veils of secrecy ever higher.

But hosting press conferences, lifting veils, and pumping out press releases does not inform the public about the true nature and power of the foundations. Given their very substantial policy influence, they seem remarkably free from oversight. Currently much that is published about these powerful institutions is written by foundation alumni working in foundation-supported universities and think tanks. This captive literature of philanthropy is informative, and occasionally insightful, but it is rarely expository or critical of the foundations' programs or grant decisions.

And although government has displayed an unwelcomed interest in foundations from time to time—most recently during the late 1960s—the media has rarely done so. In spite of their number and vast influence, there isn't a single mass media journalist assigned to the foundation beat.

While a few general assignment reporters cover philanthropy on the side, they seldom write about the foundations, whose privacy thus remains inviolable.

I am not suggesting that foundations deserve or need a classic exposé. They are not evil institutions, as critics from both the right and the left have sometimes asserted. There is barely a scandal a year in the entire industry worthy of more than a few lines on page 14 of a local daily. Nor are all of them ineffectual, incompetent, or slow.

But they are indisputably plutocratic. As great wealth will undoubtedly continue to be concentrated in the hands of a few fortunate Americans— and as foundations will remain one of the best places offered by the tax code for squirreling away excess wealth—perhaps the best that we can hope for is that these enormous trusts will be gradually democratized. The vital question is, then, will that democratization come about voluntarily or will it be forced on the foundations by regulatory legislation?

Drag Anchors

If you wait long enough the weather will change.
—Mark Twain

As the second century of American organized philanthropy opens, trustees, managers, and program officers are meeting discreetly with academicians, policy analysts, and business leaders in countless seminars and conferences, exploring ways to increase the impact and influence of foundation philanthropy. A host of rather bland, self-congratulatory manifestos and interminable white papers on the role of philanthropy in civilization will be churned out, written in a vague, indecipherable language I call *philanthropese* (see box insert). All will promise to meet imprecisely defined programmatic challenges, exercise new forms of restraint, and ensure that grantees comply with various standards of accountability. And all will include the obligatory commitment to the public welfare.

If historical precedent were to hold, foundations would act on many of the recommendations in their own reports, though not necessarily the best ones. The courses taken would be safe and uncontroversial, succeeding in some endeavors and failing in others. Achievements would

Philanthropese

In the chapters to follow the reader will come upon baffling phrases and passages quoted, for the most part, directly from foundation reports and memoranda. It may be necessary to read and reread what appear to be ordinary sentences and paragraphs as many as three times before they begin to make sense. When their meanings finally becomes clear, they will often seem utterly banal. Why, then, weren't they expressed in simpler terms?

Such passages appear to be written in English but are in fact expressed in an obscure dialect known as *philanthropese,* the lingua franca of organized philanthropy. It should not, incidentally, be confused with *proposalese,* a crude subdialect used by fundraisers attempting to mimic *philanthropese* in order to impress philanthrocrats. Very few grant seekers ever become fluent in *philanthropese,* which is essentially a clandestine language kept in constant flux to disguise the intelligence of its users, whom Dennis McIlnay describes as "masters of the obvious, who believe that ideas not worth stating bear repeating."

Social commentator Dwight MacDonald describes *philanthropese*—he calls it *foundationese*—as "a dead language, like Latin, written rather than spoken, designed for ceremony rather than utility, its function magical and incantatory, not to give information, communicate ideas or express feelings, but to reassure the reader that the situation is well in hand." Editor Neva Beach simply calls it "verbal flatulence."

To prepare the reader for passages with no coherent alternatives, I offer the following samples of *philanthropese,* each one followed by a translation.[2]

• "This initiative intends to identify and disseminate methods of development and new techniques which will demonstrate and improve the efficiency of existing models in making available cost effective systems."
Translation: Here are some cost-saving ideas.
• "The major risks inherent in this undertaking stem from factors of uncertainty and unpredictability that can typically be expected in an initiative of this kind."
Translation: In projects like this, uncertainty can create risks.
• ". . . struggles over power and accountability that can serve to diminish effectiveness and dilute the learning that the experience might otherwise generate."
Translation: . . . squabbles that inhibit understanding.
• "A similar inquiry focused on the steps community partners might take to enhance working relationships could be profitable."
Translation: Another study focused on community relations might work.
• "Germinal concepts as ongoing seminal opportunities". . . "Trailblazing demonstration projects."
Translation: New ideas . . . new projects.

We could interject the following buzzwords almost anywhere in the above phrases without substantially changing their meaning: *inclusively, responsiveness, collaborative, seminal, community, empowerment, community empowerment, urgent immediacy, global importance, partnering, entrepreneurial, entrepreneurial partnering,* and (my personal favorites) *paradigm* and *paradigmatic.*

be flaunted and failures euphemized into neutrality. Over time, ever so gradually, philanthrocrats would reform their institutions and preserve their own status and influence by inventing new ways to leverage money.

But the second century of American organized philanthropy will not be like the first. Signs of a more fundamental reform are in the air. The foundations face a host of challenges to their influence and their very existence—from the public, the government, and even the community they support financially, the nonprofit sector.

America has entered the third millennium in something of a crisis— or, perhaps better, in a crisis of small crises. This is not a new or unique situation, for any complex society is bound to face an abundance of seemingly intractable dilemmas and impending catastrophes. In the past, foundations have eventually addressed, one way or another, most of America's obvious national crises. Some have played central roles in their solutions, while many others took the credit.

However, a good generalization about organized philanthropy's reaction to crisis is that it is slow to see problems coming, slow to respond, and quick to justify every decision. Thus, with the best of intentions, its remedies are often late and occasionally entirely futile. In the context of the additional stress brought about by government devolution, the new century's challenges will test as never before the foundations' abilities to use their endowments for the public good.

The challenges facing the nation are multifarious. Public educational systems are in various states of disarray; decent health care is virtually unavailable to tens of millions of Americans; the environment is under assault; the arts and humanities are debased and devalued; and the treasured institutions of civil society—cultural, religious, and democratic— are in dire straits. Quite naturally, organized philanthropy approaches all of these challenges with a sense of urgency. But can we predict the foundations' grantmaking activities in relevant fields from history? Can we assume that, as in the past, urgency will be tempered by caution? Will they provide too little, too late, funding safe and uncontroversial projects while ignoring or avoiding proposals advocating fundamental change?

Or will the imagination of an emerging new philanthropic class be energized by this grim state of affairs to invent a new philanthropy for troubled times? If the trends described in this book continue, we should assume, though not without some hesitation, that they will. For while foundations have risen to the occasion when faced with some national crises, they have just as often faltered. Moreover, the heroic role that these trusts have allegedly played at earlier times of national crises has been largely a self-generated legend. The truth is that most foundation trustees and executives have been well aware of impending disasters but reluctant to adopt a crisis mentality and hesitant to respond with innovative solutions.

Moreover, as the large twentieth-century foundations became more established, more professionalized, and more bureaucratic, they tended to become sclerotic. Sadly, as their size and potential influence increased, the imagination that sparked their creation often waned. With some remarkable exceptions, older foundations became, and have for too long remained, drag anchors on American social, political, and scientific progress, choosing, it seems, to slow forward motion in order to avoid some perceived obstacle.

Known to veteran sailors as a *drogue,* a drag-anchor is a device carried aboard oceangoing sailboats. Made of canvas and shaped like an oversized megaphone, the anchor is thrown overboard in heavy seas and dragged, large end forward, though the water. By slowing the boat's movement and using undercurrents to counteract the effects of strong winds, a drag-anchor can prevent a large vessel from being blown off course during a storm. If the device works as intended, the vessel is kept as near as possible to its course, though forward progress is noticeably slowed.

A defender of drag-anchor philanthropy might say that arriving later is better than being shipwrecked—a reasonable enough remark. But a drag anchor is neither designed nor employed to prevent shipwrecks, and it will not always do so. It is used primarily to keep a boat on or close to its intended course. In philanthropy the drag anchor is an appropriate metaphor when a foundation reduces or eliminates funding of a beneficial project that is well on it sway to a goal but encountering resistance—so delaying progress or moderating an outcome in order to assuage conservative currents. Drag-anchor philanthropy is not a bad thing per se; it is simply counterprogressive. In the chapters that follow I document how the timing and structure of notable philanthropic initiatives intended to ameliorate national and international challenges in public education, environmental health, civil rights, energy deregulation, and food production have had the effect, sometimes intentionally, of slowing down rather than accelerating progress.

History does reveal that foundations *can* be creators of a better world. Nonetheless, as historian Waldemar Nielsen notes, "the profile of their activity is largely conventional, not reformist. They are overwhelmingly institutions of social continuity, not change."[3] It is the argument of this essay that the aim of the next generation of foundation leaders should be to challenge this indictment, eschew drag-anchor funding, and find ways to make philanthropy work faster and more consistently for social progress. Moreover, there are already some indications in the initiatives of a new group of philanthropists—people like George Soros, Irene Diamond, Ted Turner, Tracy Gary, Paul Brainerd, Marian Rockefeller Weber, and George Roberts—that a new and imaginative era of philanthropy may be upon us.

Intractable Challenges

Philanthropy may be a subject too dangerous to touch, precisely because it is so revealing of individual motives and social preferences.
—Stephen Graubard, *Daedalus*

Of all the seemingly intractable challenges facing America in the new century, none is greater, I believe, than that of public education. Despite enormous public and private investments and a long-standing national commitment to maintaining an informed citizenry, the overall quality of American public schools, the basic skills of its graduates, and erudition of the electorate are all alarmingly low. Democracy is thus challenged. Yet education, as a funding category, has historically been the leading recipient of philanthropic largesse in the United States. Will that pre-eminence continue? And if it does, will the foundations pay adequate attention to improving elementary and secondary public schools, where the vast majority of Americans learn most of what they know? Or will private philanthropy continue its historical pattern of favoring elite private schools and research universities?

A few massive philanthropic initiatives aimed at improving public education are presently under way in the United States. I focus on one such endeavor in chapter 2. The impressive investments of the Annenberg Foundation and several other institutions, which are devoting billions of dollars to school reform and substantial amounts to promoting their stratagems, seem to promise major improvement. Veteran observers of education philanthropy, however, are beginning to wonder whether private philanthropy can ever reform public education, particularly in the absence of a democratic decision-making process. But it's definitely worth a try.

American science has long been another major focus of philanthropic concern. In fact, no other field of endeavor has been as strongly influenced by foundation support. And science, though it rarely faces a crisis of its own, is consistently called upon to produce solutions to modern crises. In chapter 3 I describe how, through foundations' early desire to make the United States competitive, and eventually preeminent, in the fields of science essential to industry, they supported, and in some cases created, the research universities where most advanced scientific development takes place. Until the federal government became the major funder of scientific research in the 1950s—mostly for purposes related to national defense—private foundations were the sole support of programs in basic science and the technological application of scientific discoveries. That preeminence was particularly important in interdisciplinary sciences and in the development of fields such as molecular biology and cognitive science.

As the federal government became increasingly interested in science and created huge funding sources through the Department of Defense, the National Science Foundation, and the National Institutes of Health, the foundations were marginalized in many fields of science. For fifty years or more, their influence over basic research diminished along with their grantmaking, waning almost to zero. In recent years, however, the foundations have dedicated major funds to scientific research, mostly in fields whose lack of military potential or immediate application to public health attract minimal support from the federal government. Foundation funding of science provides an exception to my drag-anchor assessment of organized philanthropy and an excellent example of how effective bold and innovative private philanthropy can be.

American foundations' second-largest area of financial support is health, a broad category that includes medical institutions (mostly hospitals), biomedical research, public health, health policy studies, and design of health care delivery systems. Although by many measures, America is the world's healthiest nation, there are disturbing trends that reflect major failings in public health—notably high infant mortality rates and a gradual but persistent rise since 1950 in the overall incidence of cancer.[4]

Moreover, although America's medical researchers (often supported by private philanthropy) have produced more remarkable medical technologies than any other nation's, those developments are available to a rapidly shrinking proportion of the population. In categories where the United States once led the world, national health statistics compare less and less favorably with those of other developed nations. In some areas they even approach the level of the Third World.

Over the last century, American foundations initiated and supported some legendary medical breakthroughs and channeled millions of dollars into the construction of teaching hospitals and medical schools. Yet the primary focus of most foundation-supported research has been specific diseases and technological development. I conclude in chapter 4 that the foundations' enthusiasm for high-tech diagnostic systems, pharmacology, and the disease model of medicine has not only inhibited the development of preventative and holistic approaches but has also retarded public health and fostered the evolution of an essentially unjust health care system.

The prognosis for a U.S. health care system driven by for-profit insurance carriers and the disease lobby has been considered by only a few philanthropic organizations, most notably the Commonwealth, Kellogg, and Robert Wood Johnson foundations. Whether others will follow their lead remains to be seen. Until there is greater equity in health care delivery, funding new medical technologies and breakthroughs seems futile. In the meantime, conversion foundations created from the assets of nonprofit hospitals and health plans that convert to for-profit services offer the best hope for philanthropic support of public health.

Until quite recently the public health effects of environmental pollution have been virtually ignored by the large foundations. While environmentalists and their adversaries debate their achievements, assays of human and wildlife adipose (fatty) tissue continue to find increasing residues of recognized carcinogens, mutagens, teratagenic agents, and, more recently, endocrine disrupters. By any measure of environmentalism's success or failure, this finding must be the most significant, although the aforementioned 55 percent rise in cancer incidence is also a worthy candidate.

As I indicate in chapter 5, the environment has been an historically low priority for organized philanthropy. Less than 3 percent of all foundation grants went for environmental research in 1998. And even the minor amounts flowing to environmental protection and advocacy have been highly controversial among active environmentalists. Many of them believe that the foundations have squandered resources on expanding environmental bureaucracies that have long been hobbled by the crushing power of a better-financed industrial lobby.

Under the broader rubric of environmentalism, I focus in chapters 6 and 7 on two other very large, long-term foundation initiatives. Both have been regarded as major triumphs of American philanthropy, and each has had major, unanticipated environmental and social consequences. I selected these initiatives for special attention to demonstrate how even the most laudable philanthropic intentions can go awry, how the aforementioned drag-anchor effect works in practice, and what happens when proactive philanthropy is pursued without the participation of the people most affected by it.

The fifty-year Green Revolution, an ambitious, foundation-driven attempt to feed the world (chapter 6), and the creation of the Energy Foundation by three larger foundations (chapter 7) illuminate the pitfalls of misguided proactive philanthropy. Though both initiatives are frequently touted as exemplars of dynamic grantsmanship, the Green Revolution has fostered unforeseen social dislocation and environmental damage, and the Energy Foundation has virtually undermined the original intentions of its founders. Any objective assessment of their results must invite the question: Is this good philanthropy?

Meanwhile, a younger and "greener" cohort of "biophilic" donors and professionals are entering the philanthropic domain, and observers expect foundations to provide increased attention and support to environmental causes in the future. Will that expanded support strengthen the movement, improve the environment, and guide national policy toward critical solutions to environmental degradation? Or will it simply purchase more conservation easements and bloat the bureaucracy of mainstream, Washington-based environmental organizations? These two projects make it all too clear that saving the world's environment requires, like so many other crucial concerns, creativity on the part of foundation officers and grantees.

The creative force itself is being devalued in America, where the arts and humanities are increasingly regarded as either elitist pursuits or market commodities. As legislators shift their discourse on arts support from "how much?" to whether to fund them at all, cultural arbiters bemoan the state of American humanities and foundations seem reluctant to step into the gap. Many of those who do fund arts projects see them as little more than a civic adjunct, a utilitarian catalyst of urban renewal, rather than the cultural expression of a complex civilization. In chapter 8 I ask whether foundations intent on strengthening democracy will change course to look upon robust arts and humanities as essential to a civilized nation, as they did in the 1960s and 1970s. Will contemporary discourse on cultural philanthropy rise above seeing the arts as a commercial magnet to provide a competitive advantage for one tourist market over another? And will the foundations come to understand that the arts, far from being the mere window dressing of a commercial culture, can be a creative force for community?

Like many other liberal and conservative observers concerned about the community in which they live, I contend that the glue that holds any civilization together is not healthy in America. In chapter 9 I describe how organized philanthropy's long-time goal of supporting and strengthening the assemblage of social organizations and institutions outside commerce and government has become the poster child of conservative scholars and philanthropists. These social critics carefully select certain institutions to be part of "civil society" while excluding a myriad of others. They seem bent on narrowing the definition of civil society and wresting its support from the state.

I argue that if moderate foundations allow such observers to limit the boundaries of civil society to family, neighborhood, church, and palliative charities, American society will become far from civil. It will be interesting to see whether mainstream foundations come to share the conservatives' commitment to civil society but redefine it, through their grantmaking, in broader, more progressive terms that see social and economic democracy as essential to an advanced civilization.

Such a redefinition is particularly crucial in an era of government devolution and concurrent decline in support for social services of all kinds. The crisis in the human services sector brought about by disastrous cutbacks can never be completely offset by private philanthropy—despite assertions to the contrary from conservative think tanks, politicians, and the countless commissions created and funded by foundations.

Yet, though individual and institutional philanthropists are incapable of writing enough checks to cover the deficits in the nonprofit sector, foundations are not helpless to address the crisis. The situation does not prevent the foundations from traveling a path they have followed for the past half century: inventing improved systems and policies to address poverty and social injustice. If there was ever a time for philanthropic pioneering, or for creating opportunities to leverage foundation influence through proactive, imaginative grantmaking, it is now in the area of human services. Will the foundations rise to the occasion? Will the philanthropic imagination create new, democratic ways to improve the world? The ingenious initiatives examined in chapter 10 suggest that there is hope. However, the inventive efforts I describe may be complicated by differences in the funding priorities of conservative and liberal foundations, for in no other area have the disagreements been more pronounced or more intense than in the matter of social policy.

Every year, at every level of government, public policy is determined less and less through democratic processes. And when it is, the constitutionally elected officials responsible for it are all too often the virtual handmaidens of powerful economic interests opposing the very policy that is needed. Yet you can count on one hand the American foundations that have taken even a tangential interest in campaign finance reform, or in other obvious crises of electoral democracy. Where are the foundations that fostered voting rights in the 1960s and the emerging social movements of the 1970s?

During the last twenty years of the twentieth century, it was conservatives who prevailed in the war of political ideas, financed the Reagan revolution, and provisioned the Republican recapture of Congress. A dozen or so medium-sized, uncharacteristically patient foundations can take a good deal of credit for the rise and endurance of America's conservative revolution. They systematically fostered their own intellectual cadre and strategically lent support to a host of effective policy think tanks. Through these institutions conservative foundations have remained intensely proactive in the planning of government social policy.

More recently, following this bold twenty-five-year foray into public policy by right-wing foundations, the Left has stepped timidly into the fray with a few programs in economic and political justice. Will mainstream foundations, too, learn from the conservative foundations' triumph of leveraged influence? Or will they continue their minimal, unimaginative funding of safe and soft institutions proposing weak, incremental solutions to urgent and undeniable crises?

One way or another, competition among foundations seems unlikely to abate, and organized philanthropy is certain to play an ever-increasing role in the creation and direction of new public policy. With the foundations structured and governed as they are, however, that is hardly a step toward democratic decisionmaking. Perhaps, in fact, they will not move strongly toward fostering political democracy until they themselves have become genuinely democratic institutions. I take up that final issue in chapter 11.

Ultimately, any treatise on private foundations must examine the terribly sensitive matter of plutocracy—the rule of wealth. As I mentioned in "A Note on Semantics," I was warned against using the p-word (*plutocrat*) or any of its derivatives in this book—lest I be written off as a Marxist crank. Yet any serious writer about philanthropy must risk such a fate, for private wealth creates foundations, and the leverage of private wealth is what organized philanthropy is all about.

For a century the Left has argued that American foundations are not genuine expressions of philanthropy and human compassion but, rather, extensions of economic power and elite privilege. One critic, Robert Arnove, asserts that they have "a corrosive influence on democratic society. . . . They represent relatively unregulated and unaccountable concentrations of power and wealth which buy talent, promote causes, and, in effect, establish an agenda of what merits society's attention. They serve as 'cooling-out' agencies, delaying and preventing more radical, structural change."[5] Arnove is not entirely wrong.

Founded, as so many of them were, by men and women of enormous wealth who clearly intended to further their own and their families' influence, foundations are not solely engines of philanthropy. This is not to suggest that original donors, their trustees, and their professional staffs have no affection for humanity, or lack the ability to imagine a world made better with money. It is just that much of what many foundations do and fund seems principally designed to protect and strengthen the professional and scientific classes and the institutions that produce wealth for future philanthropists.

Most philanthropists are not deeply troubled by that characterization. Nor does it seem to bother the American public. We tend to notice the rule of wealth only when it directly affects legislation. When they aren't attempting overtly to buy political influence, we admire and honor our billionaires. Fascinated by their lifestyles, we are mostly oblivious to the less visible ways they affect our lives—through the institutions that made them wealthy and those they create with their wealth, particularly their foundations.

Why, then, should we notice or be concerned about the impact of their philanthropy, or ask ourselves whether private wealth should have such extraordinary influence in a democracy? Would it help if democracy were somehow a constituent element of philanthropy? If so, how do we think that democracy should be expressed? Through elections? Should we require more direct grassroots participation in the grantmaking processes? Those questions all lead inexorably to the topic of regulation, and to one last question: What hand should the government play in organized philanthropy?

If Congress assumed a role (as John D. Rockefeller originally intended it should), would philanthropy become just another unimaginative adjunct of the federal budgeting process? Would philanthropic endowments become a shadow treasury subject to all the parochial political and economic pressures that compete for other government resources? Would Congress and the executive branch raid the endowments to balance budgets or otherwise cook the books, as they have with Social Security and other allegedly inviolable trusts? Would congressional and White House staffers become grantmakers, and grant seekers become lobbyists? In the answer to these questions lies, I believe, the most convincing defense of unregulated private philanthropy.

But there the defense rests. For, as I argue in chapter 11, unless democratic processes exercise some form of influence over the foundations, the latter's activities, and their very existence, will become harder and harder to justify.

Success and Failure

Why are we doing better than ever and our grantees are doing worse?
—Franklin Thomas, Former President, Ford Foundation

Foundation mythology is replete with claims of triumph: "We conquered this or that disease. . . ." "Our Project X lowered crime in the inner city. . . ." "Strategic grantmaking in media led to. . . ." Of course, like most myths, there is some truth in such claims. But we need to apply two caveats to the literature describing the work of the foundations. The first is to ascertain the origin and sponsorship of each report. In-house foundation histories, besides being terminally boring, tend to create what historian Ellen Condliffe Lagemann characterizes as "a false facade behind which trustees and foundation officers and staff can feel securely proud of their apparent altruistic, apolitical contributions to knowledge, culture and humankind."[6]

The second caveat is to examine carefully all information about the origins of a given philanthropic idea or project. Sometimes we find—as in the cases of Rockefeller and the yellow fever eradication project, and Ford's early arts funding—that the project was cooked up by imaginative foundation staffers. But all too often foundation communications people claim creative credit for projects they were merely the first to fund, or the largest grantor. The true innovators and risk takers, if mentioned at all, appear as mere footnotes in the history of philanthropy. Such is the fate of a Newton, Massachusetts, mother who was so revolted with

Credit Where Credit Is Due

One could easily conclude from reading the literature of philanthropy, that most of the good things done in America are either generated or supported by foundations and that philanthropists themselves accomplished many of the twentieth century's major breakthroughs in medicine, education, science, and race relations. The legendary figures of modern philanthropy—Warren Weaver, Abraham Flexner, Alan Pifer, Mary Lasker, John Gardner, MacNeal Lowry, Irene Diamond—are frequently credited with advances they merely underwrote. Too often forgotten are the grantees who really made it all happen, men and women of science or the arts who could as easily have accomplished what they did with a grant from Ford as one from Rockefeller—or from the federal treasury for that matter.

Of course, American foundations have initiated some remarkable advances. This book is full of them. However, philanthropic historians too often credit philanthropists with the triumphs of their beneficiaries, and foundations willingly accept the praise. Though there is no lasting harm in misplaced credit, the desire to receive it has too often led professional philanthropists to ignore the ideas and proposals of nonprofit functionaries. At times they have initiated projects of their own, at times even keeping them inside the foundation and under their personal control.

children's television that she started the Children's Television Workshop, creator of *Sesame Street;* foundation literature credits the Carnegie Corporation, which did write the first check for it, with originating the program. (See box insert "Credit Where Credit Is Due.")

In the chapters that follow I attempt to identify and credit the innovators, inventors, and movers whose work was largely supported by foundations but who could have produced the same results with support from any source. Taking questionable credit reveals one of organized philanthropy's least appealing motives—self-justification. As they mature in their second century of existence, we can only hope that foundations will confront their insecurities and motives, historical and contemporary, and stop behaving as if they were at risk of annihilation.

Such an examination would reveal that American foundations were created for many purposes. One, of course, was to protect industrial capitalism, as many critics have alleged. But philanthropists have also initiated sincere efforts to reform the system, while a very small number have employed their surplus capital against capitalism itself. Thus the age-old debate about the hegemony of capital is carried on, though sotto voce, inside as well as outside the world of philanthropy. And that world is not, as some leftists would have us believe, a monolithic conspiratorial bulwark of capitalism created by robber barons solely to protect the system that made them rich. That motive was, of course, present in greater or lesser degree. Nonetheless, preserving capitalism is not, nor ever was, the primary stimulus of organized philanthropy.

Nor is foundation philanthropy, as one rightist describes it, "a Trojan horse dragged into the camp of capitalism intent upon destroying the system that allowed it to flourish." As we shall see, the philanthropic imagination is not consistent, nor is it singular in design. Many impulses created American philanthropy—religious fervor, guilt, narcissism, paternalism, greed, the wish for immortality, and as its name implies, love of humanity. Thus the word *philanthropy* (as I noted in "A Note on Semantics") defies clear definition. We should probably only use it with a modifier like *organized, Judeo-Christian, reform, conservative, responsive,* or *charitable.*

Nonetheless, because most of America's original philanthropists were capitalists or heirs of capitalists, the culture of capitalism has quite naturally permeated the philanthropic imagination. Some capitalists do value private philanthropy because it creates a countervailing force against socialism; others because it quells social dissent. And those who favor an enlightened philanthropy fear that without it government will step in and the infrastructure of civil society will be absorbed by the state. Many believe that such a takeover would lead inexorably to the nationalization of industry and the death knell of free enterprise.

Social democrats and democratic socialists, too, value a third sector as independent of government and industry as possible—a protected space in which social movements, particularly those that challenge powerful economic and political interests, can flourish. Whether from the right or the left, the critics of foundation philanthropy bring their own, quite predictable political and social values to the dialogue. The result is an ongoing debate. At times it is heated, but rarely does it question openly the desirability, effectiveness, and legitimacy of foundations—issues I address in the following chapters.

The Ridiculous and the Sublime

All generalizations are false, including this one.
—Anonymous

Those who have the gold rule.
—Anonymous twist on the Golden Rule

In the course of assessing the crises and challenges facing American civilization, foundation staffs and trustees spend thousands of working hours struggling to define values and concepts such as *democracy, compassion, community, justice,* and *inclusion.* They do so in hopes of identifying a social need or problem that fits both the intention of their original donors and their own preconceptions of how to use money to enhance the public good.

Their collective imagination has created some of the best and worst institutions in American society, funded the most sublime and the most ridiculous projects, wasted money and spent it wisely. In this regard, both boosters and critics of foundations are correct, though never for the same reasons, and never by invoking the same grants.

Ironically, many of the institutions and projects funded or created by organized philanthropy are found on both "best" and "worst" lists, one writer's triumph being another's catastrophe. Most of the social development programs of the Ford, Rockefeller, and Carnegie foundations, for example, while widely regarded by philanthropists, academics, and historians as notable achievements of American philanthropy, are seen by pundits like Pat Buchanan, Heather MacDonald, and Chester Finn as shipwrecked social engineering.

In fact, the ultimate benefits of organized philanthropy are very much in the eye of the beholder, and the politics behind those eyes are a pretty good predictor of an individual's assessment of a specific grant or initiative. In the introduction to his landmark book *Philanthropy in Action,* Brian O'Connell former president of Independent Sector, holds up the Rockefeller Foundation's Green Revolution as "inspirational," an example of sublime philanthropy. But he brands Emma Robinson's Christmas Dinner Trust for Horses as "silly" and condemns Garrett Smith's funding of John Brown's raid on Harper's Ferry as "dangerous" philanthropy.

More important, even if they *could* agree on the nature and priority of the crises this book addresses, all fifty thousand foundations operating in unison could not resolve all the social, scientific, and cultural challenges to American civilization. Money is only a lubricant, a catalyst, a fertilizer. Those empowered to make grants should not assume that they have the wisdom to solve such serious problems simply because they control the money.

Nor should they take or accept credit for working out solutions that are successful. Or presume to use their wealth to impose such massive systemic reforms as the Green Revolution or the restructuring of the American electric energy industry.

This assertion, of course, raises the issue of accountability addressed briefly in "A Note on Semantics." What is the responsibility of private wealth protected by law from taxation? To whom are foundations accountable? How should their work be evaluated? And by whom, with what criteria, what standards, what goals, and with what sanctions? These are all questions with which foundation trustees, executives, and their trade organizations torment themselves every day, knowing full well that the public, the media, and the government will eventually get around to asking them.

The fact is that many other institutions of American society are already taking a long look at organized philanthropy and asking themselves: Is this experiment paying off? Could it be delivering more? What is required to make foundations more effective? A few, more-adventurous thinkers even ask: Do foundations deserve to exist?

Unjust Desserts

If men are to remain civilized, the art of association must develop and improve among them at the same speed as the equality of conditions spreads.
—Alexis de Tocqueville, *Democracy in America* (1835)

The central thesis of this book is that foundations do deserve to exist; but only if they evolve swiftly from an essentially private to unremittingly public institution of American life. As I have already intimated, I believe they will.

The shift I foresee will be driven not only by the questions and concerns of the American public, but also by social forces arising from the crises in education, public health, environment, culture, government, and civil society discussed in this book. Changes in organized philanthropy will also be mediated by compelling criticisms (from left and right), immanent tax reform, government devolution, massive twenty-first century wealth transfers, and structural realignments that are forcing the whole nonprofit sector to become both more transparent and more accountable to the public.

In the last chapter I propose three simple reforms to democratize the foundations through fiscal restructuring and widened participation in decisionmaking. None of these reforms will endear me to foundation trustees or their staffs, but together they would help organized philanthropy become a far more productive and legitimate institution of American civil society. As more taxpayers realize that approximately half of foundation assets—which would have flowed into state and federal treasuries if not protected by trusts—in effect belongs to the public, the pressure to implement reforms will accelerate. So too will the demand for openness and public accountability, transforming foundations from elite, secretive trusts into high-profile "public" institutions.

In short, democracy is discovering the foundations, and vice versa. An opportunity for organized philanthropy to break with its elitist past and become a vital instrument of American civilization is in sight. A new foundation model is already emerging among, mostly, community and conversion foundations and smaller experimental cooperative foundations. Their citizen trustees, grantee advisory boards, and strong social agendas signal a new covenant between society and philanthropy. Very soon the traditional private, corporate, and operating foundations will feel the impact of the new covenant. The only question is whether they will transform themselves voluntarily or be pushed into reform, as they have in the past, by threats of government intervention.

1

History

Anticipate charity by preventing poverty.
—Maimonides

The system that makes the foundation possible is probably worth preserving.
—Henry Ford II, Former Chairman, Ford Foundation

Although from its earliest days organized philanthropy has been integral to American culture, foundations are not an American invention. In fact, many civilizations whose inhabitants accumulated private wealth eventually developed institutional ways to put excess profit to work for society—though not always in ways that we would today call "philanthropic." In fifteenth-century England, for example, the Week's Charity was created to purchase firewood for burning heretics.

In ancient Persia the practice of establishing small trust funds called *vaqfs* (pronounced *waffs*) for charitable purposes has existed for a thousand years or more. In pre-revolutionary France there were also numerous large foundations; they were eliminated after 1789, however, by a regime that repudiated plutocracy and envisioned a state far better able to serve the interests of charity. The foundations of modern Europe, while larger than vaqfs and more like their American counterparts in structure and practice, are comparatively few and far between.

Massive trusts numbering in the thousands, some with $10- and $20-billion dollar endowments growing ever larger as new wealth is created, are a uniquely American institution. They arose in the late nineteenth and early twentieth centuries as a few fabulously rich American industrialists began casting about for a means to avoid taxes and put their wealth to use in new and imaginative ways. Throughout the twentieth century

American foundations, with their elite, self-perpetuating boards and large professional staffs, exerted subtle but profound influence over key sectors of government and civil society.

We can conceive of that first century of American foundation history as three, somewhat indistinct waves or periods of development, each with its own overriding purpose The waves overlap and are only imprecisely bounded by particular historical events. Although many common themes endure through all three periods, they are differentiated by significant shifts in emphasis and in the priority placed on particular initiatives.

The first wave, which began around the turn of the twentieth century, lasted for about forty years and focused principally on the advancement of formal knowledge. In the second wave, starting around 1945, the foundations began to see themselves as mediators in the formulation of public policy. And in the third wave, which began in the 1960s and is still with us, they sought to promote, quite cautiously, their own conceptions of social justice. The binding theme of all three waves has been the foundations' shared commitment to building a better society. Thus, the common goal of American organized philanthropy throughout its first century of existence has been *change*.

During each wave, the size and number of foundations grew steadily, from the eighteen that existed before 1910—only one of which (Russell Sage) held assets over $10 million—to today's almost fifty thousand private, corporate, community, and operating foundations whose combined assets approach $425 billion. (About forty foundations each boast endowments greater than $1 billion.) As one wave followed another and their numbers increased, the foundations learned to multiply the impact of their fast-growing wealth through leverage (see box insert). Thus the growth of their social influence has outpaced even the increase in their number and assets.

While many foundations were originally formed to pursue such singular goals as advancement of a particular branch of science, promotion of a religious denomination, or cure of a rare disease, behind these explicit intentions lay an implicit concern for human welfare—deeper in some founders than in others. In that light, the adjective *philanthropic* (loving humanity) was appropriate. But as change, not charity, became the driving force behind these institutions, the word *philanthropy* gradually took on a different meaning. Though philanthropists, their survivors, trustees,

Leverage

The philanthropic imagination not only envisions better worlds, it also contrives new ways of giving money—flow funding, community foundations, intermediaries, passthrough foundations, challenge grants, charitable gift funds. The motivation behind most of such contrivances is *leverage*—parlaying a limited grant into a large institution, project, building, change, or endowment. In dollar terms, foundations play a relatively minor role in supporting the nonprofit sector but a major role in structuring, defining, leading, guiding, directing, and managing the sector. Thus their leverage is large.

The classic example of leverage is, of course, Andrew Carnegie's creation of a public library system throughout the United States and Canada. Carnegie knew that even his own enormous wealth could not support twenty-eight hundred libraries in perpetuity. But he could create the infrastructure (the bricks and mortar) in return for which each community would commit its full faith and credit to the stocking, staffing, and running of a library, in perpetuity. Thus, with the philanthropic outlay of a few million dollars, Carnegie created a public institution—one that has since spent many, many billions more than that making books available to the public free of charge—with leverage.

Leverage has since been achieved in many ways. Funding a direct mail campaign that costs $50,000 and raises $100,000 is leverage. Paying the $100,000 salary, benefits, and expenses for a fundraiser who raises $1 million is leverage. Progressive philanthropist Philip Stern rarely gave anyone everything they asked for. Instead he would say, "I'll give you $50,000 if Foundation A gives you $50,000." Or "After you have raised half your budget I'll give you the rest." Challenge grants were not, however, Stern's invention. In fact, his grandfather, Julius Rosenwald, offered them routinely. The motive, as Stern explained it to me years later, was to force grantees to establish a wide base of foundation support.

Without leverage, foundations would be far less significant, influential, and powerful; for they provide but 7 percent of all charitable resources. As funders of nonprofit activity they are relative pipsqueaks, providing less than 10 percent of the independent sector's overall budget. Nonetheless, large grants speak louder than small ones. So the five million people who support a large national organization with a $25 annual donation have far less influence over its direction or policy than a foundation that grants it $50,000 for a specific purpose or program. Clearly, leverage applies to power as well as to wealth.

In philanthropy, it should be emphasized, leverage can be a negative as well as a positive force.

employees, historians, and other observers argue endlessly over the definition of the word and the effectiveness of specific philanthropic programs and strategies, they generally agree that the purpose of their work is to imagine a better society and help bring it into existence by fostering change with money.

From Ripple to Tidal Wave

History can be a tricky and unreliable teacher, its lessons elusive and contested.
—George Herring

Although a few small foundations were created during the late nineteenth century, the first noticeable wave of organized philanthropy began in the early twentieth century with America's two wealthiest industrialists. John D. Rockefeller (JDR) and Andrew Carnegie decided, almost simultaneously, to do something unusual with their fortunes—become reformers.

Carnegie and JDR were unique in their time. Most American robber barons were ruthlessly parsimonious men. Some even devised elaborate schemes to keep heirs from using their estates for philanthropic endeavors. It seems, unfortunately, that the ratio between the philanthropic and nonphilanthropic super-rich has changed very little since that era. In fact, recent studies of individual giving suggest that low- and middle-income donors became more generous as the twentieth century progressed, while the wealthy decreased their giving. Nonetheless, as wealth expanded, enough millionaires and billionaires chose the path of Carnegie and JDR to make foundations one of the defining institutions of American society.

The founders of that first wave of American foundations shared a conviction that society was advanced by the generation and sharing of knowledge. They believed that new learning would create progress, expand wealth, and advance civilization and human welfare. And it would prevent reoccurrence of the enormous social unrest that had marked the late nineteenth century and brought the specter of socialism to the attention of America's capitalists.

Early donors and their advisers recognized that the advancement of knowledge called for massive investments in education, science, and technology; they were eager to build systems and institutions for both furthering knowledge and distributing it as widely as possible. What came to be known as "scientific philanthropy" would, they felt sure, allow society as a whole to benefit fully from knowledge. According to historian Judith Sealander, the early philanthropists "were seekers of system," not—as so many critics have described them since—"defenders of system."[1] The impulse to use philanthropic resources to defend capitalism came later and, strangely enough, was more often initiated by foundation trustees than by original donors.

In dividing foundation history into three waves I do not, however, suggest that foundation grants during the first thirty years of the twentieth century went primarily to the creation of knowledge and only secondarily to policy studies. The founders' interest in public policy emerged early in the first wave and overlapped with their dedication to science and other forms of knowledge. Today, two waves later, projects in public policy still receive about a third of the money all foundations provide.

In the early decades of the century questions of public policy and social reform in America were debated primarily by private foundations, which immersed themselves in issues such as affordable housing, working conditions, and race relations. While other western societies sought to solve such social problems through their central governments, American foundations and nonprofit institutions created privately supported and directed systems of social reform and welfare. When, during the Great Depression, the federal government was finally forced by market disruptions and poverty beyond the reach of private charity to accept roles it had previously rejected, it embraced systems that had been designed, tested, and promoted by private philanthropy.

The second wave of American philanthropy began soon after World War II. American military technology had proven that, at least in science and engineering, America was no longer a second-rate power. However, social problems and inequities persisted. It was time, philanthropists believed, to shift focus. Foundation leaders developed a new theory of change arguing that the best return on the philanthropic dollar would come from investing in the formulation of progressive public policy. The resources devoted to policy analysis and public advocacy were increased as foundations used the power of grantsmanship to create links among nonprofit organizations, social science researchers, reformers, and government agencies.

During the early 1950s foundation leaders became the mediators between academic experts and government. Research institutes established at the margins of government enormously increased the prestige of an emerging national elite of scholars in every field of interest vital to industrial advancement, particularly the social sciences.

Second-wave foundations used the knowledge gained during the first wave of their existence to promote formation of a national society. The responsibility of the federal government to assure equal opportunity, enforce civil rights, and protect the environment now taken for granted by most Americans was originally supported and promoted by private philanthropy during this period. It was time, foundation trustees were persuaded, for the government to "scale up" and implement nationally the models of human welfare developed with foundation support in various smaller communities. It was also time, they believed, for the federal government to invest directly in the advancement of knowledge, which it eventually did through the National Science Foundation, the National Institutes of Health, and the National Academy of Science. Foundation officers saw their own organizations' task as researching and proposing ways to use science to formulate progressive public policy and pave the way to the modern state.

This quest resulted in various strategies aimed at establishing or strengthening large, quasi-public institutions like the Social Science Research Council, the National Bureau of Economic Research, and the Brookings Institution. These organizations, which were modeled on such earlier private organizations as the Rockefeller Institute of Medical Research and the Carnegie Institution of Washington, operated alongside a host of smaller, private research institutes we now call "think tanks."

Although the medical and physical sciences continued to receive major foundation support, grants were also awarded for purposes that went far beyond simply uncovering new knowledge. Brilliant strategists of an earlier era like Warren Weaver, the godfather of interdisciplinary science, became revered figures as the search for knowledge was subsumed by the age of policy and applied science.

Eventually, the involvement of private wealth in creating and staffing institutions with the power to generate, communicate, and design public policy drew the attention of critics inside and outside government. But by then a small cadre of large foundations had already become indispensable financiers of policy research.

The third wave of American philanthropists emerged in the early 1960s. Having watched second-wave foundations struggle with politicians and bureaucrats, the new class of *philanthrocrats* (the professional foundation officers who by then ran the major foundations) believed that the next stage of national progress could not be reached by relying solely on government policy and initiatives. Social movements, they concluded, were necessary catalysts to such changes. The foundations thus emerged as noticeable, though cautious, advocates and financial champions of civil rights; a little later they lent their support to environmentalism and, eventually, to moderate feminism. By the end of the twentieth century the only American social movement overlooked by organized philanthropy was, quite understandably, organized labor. (Why would captains of industry and their heirs support a movement that increased their cost of doing business and, by its very existence, challenged the primacy and authority of capital?)

Early in the third wave politics became a philanthropic issue, and ideological differences between conservative and liberal foundations became discernible. The debate over funding social movements precipitated organized philanthropy's first schism. The split has since become so acrimonious that conservative foundations spend millions of dollars on research attempting to prove that social-movement philanthropy and the activism it encourages is destructive to American civilization. Their findings, however, have done little to stem the tide of liberal philanthropy's social advocacy, or to stifle conservative foundations' own support for groups on the opposite side.

The Life Cycle of Foundations

I want to be a great philanthropist.
—Charlie Brown

But you have to have a lot of money to be a great philanthropist.
—Linus

I want to be a great philanthropist with someone else's money.
—Charlie Brown

Individual foundations have a life cycle of their own that in many ways reflects the historical evolution of organized philanthropy as a whole. Both begin with charity (L., *caritas:* love of other). John D. Rockefeller, a devout Baptist, gave 10 percent of his first paycheck to the church; he continued the practice for many years before he thought of creating a foundation. Like JDR, other early creators of America's great foundations tithed themselves long before they institutionalized their charity. Like him, they established foundations simply because personally managing the X percent of their income they devoted to charitable purposes became burdensome. Moreover, as word of their generosity spread, representatives of every church and organization serving the dispossessed appeared at their doors, hat in hand. Industrialists were simply making money faster than they could give it away, and as their fortunes grew their eleemosynary affairs became unwieldy. Thus, charitable organizations were organized, and organized charity evolved into philanthropy.

The early foundations that gave shape to the whole venture of organized philanthropy were, with occasional exceptions, founded by industrialists committed to organization, efficiency, and rationality. Convinced that the same scientific principles that led to industrial success could solve social problems, these men structured and operated their foundations much as they did their business organizations. Today many graduate schools of business accept that premise and offer courses and degrees in nonprofit management (including the management of foundations) that diverge somewhat from the corporate model, though they preserve the principle of applying business standards of investment and accountability to organized philanthropy. Whether the corporate (or Harvard Business School) model of nonprofit management has increased charitable activities or produced more desirable results is a question implicit in any study of foundations. I discuss the answer, a variation of sometimes-but-not-always, in subsequent chapters. In any case, corporate culture remains firmly entrenched in American foundations, and one hears few proposals to institute anything noticeably different.

For the possessor of great wealth the impulse to create a foundation is only the first step toward abandoning control and ownership. As the founder weakens and dies control of the foundation usually passes to family members, a few trusted business associates, and perhaps a lawyer or trust officer. In the second phase of its existence, authority is generally vested in a few wealthy or accomplished patricians, mostly men somehow connected to the founder or his family. Most of these men believe that they understand the domestic and international challenges facing the nation and the world and, moreover, possess the wisdom to solve them. A few wives, and even fewer daughters, may sit quietly at the table as the patriarchs in their midst haggle, often acrimoniously, over strategy and priorities. At this point in their development, many foundations are paralyzed by disagreements among trustees and remain so for months, sometimes years; in the worst cases, they are unable to reach agreement for whole generations. Regardless of their uncertainty about the foundation's purpose and management, trustees during this phase often plant the seeds of institutional arrogance; in larger foundations this stage can last for another generation or two. Indeed, *arrogant* is the most common characterization of foundations used by others in the nonprofit world.

By a full generation after the death of the original donor (twenty-five to thirty years) most foundations are in the hands of complete strangers. A family member or two may still sit on the board of trustees, and perhaps a young partner from the founder's favorite law firm. But as a general rule the foundation is on its way to becoming a quasi-public institution. This is the third of many steps that lead toward becoming a democratic institution—a status that only a handful of America's fifty thousand or so foundations has yet attained.

During this third stage, patrician trustees are replaced on the board by experts, generally highly accomplished professionals and educators in fields of particular interest to the foundation and consistent with the founder's original intent. During this phase university presidents, Nobel laureates, and eminent scientists and scholars find their way onto foundation boards, where—as one would expect—their presence does little to diminish organizational arrogance.

The fourth phase occurs gradually, as the staff of a large foundation grows and becomes increasingly more professional and bureaucratized. Preoccupied with their individual interests and institutions, the trustees increasingly defer in their decisions to the studies and recommendations of professional philanthrocrats. The latter spend much of the foundation's time and money documenting social crises and designing programs to alleviate them with money. Unfortunately, there tends to be no decline in arrogance during this phase, only a slight shift in its expression from board members to professional staff.

The history of the Ford Foundation provides a good example of the kind of internal disputes that emerge as a foundation evolves from a family trust to a staff bureaucracy. During the presidencies of George Kennan, Robert Hutchins, and Paul Hoffman in the 1970s and 1980s, competing camps dueled over, first, international development; second, the foundation's role in assuring world peace; and, somewhat later, the proper relationship between foundations and social movements. The whole spectrum of thought on these international and domestic issues was represented on the board. All three presidents became targets of the public's growing public distrust of large foundations and of private philanthropy's most vocal critics on the Right and Left.

Hoffman, who was president of the foundation in the late 1970s, was burdened with the additional challenge of having to "devote my life to the education of a young ignoramus." He was referring, of course, to Henry Ford II, the last member of the family dynasty to chair the board of trustees. Early in 1977 conservative attacks on the foundation reached a fever pitch, and Ford joined the chorus. He resigned his position in a huff, leaving behind a letter that is still widely quoted by free-market ideologues and defenders of original intent. Their favorite passage is well worth quoting. "I'm not playing the role of the hard-nosed tycoon who thinks all philanthropists are socialists and all university professors are communists," Ford wrote. "I am just suggesting to the trustees and the staff that the system that makes the foundation possible is probably worth preserving."[2]

It is unlikely that any of Ford's fellow trustees had lost sight of the fact that private foundations operate within the context of capitalism. But they may have agreed with him that they had lost control of the staff. Since then, many others have come to believe that the grant decisions made by philanthrocrats, even foundation presidents, too often challenge the mother lode.

As control over foundation assets and grant making shifts from founder, to family, to patrician trustees, to expert trustees, and to professional staff, a concurrent evolution in the organization's purpose—from relief to improvement to reform—occurs within most foundations.[3] The operating principle of the early era is compassion, a holdover of the original donors' intentions to provide short-term relief. During the second phase, as the founder's descendants and unrelated trustees gain influence, the emphasis shifts toward improvement in particular areas of the social and intellectual environment. The overriding goal of the foundations in this phase becomes progress, and the purpose of grant making the maximization of human potential.

In the transition from the second to third phase, as the third or fourth generation of trustees comes on board and the office is staffed increasingly by experts, foundations define and express their political positions. At this point most, but by no means all, foundations take an active interest in major social reform. Justice, vaguely defined, becomes a guiding principle for decision making, and the foundation's aim is identified as the support of research, program development, and implementation of solutions to major social problems.

We can discern the political diversity of foundations in their identification and prioritizing of social problems and in the solutions they advocate. The trustees and staffs of the Ford Foundation and the Bradley Foundation, for example, both express grave concern about the deterioration of civil society in America. But they define *civil society* quite differently and express widely disparate views about how to heal it. In chapter 9 I describe the breadth of foundations' disparities, the depth of their disagreements, and the intensity of the emotions that surface during their internal debates over the future of civil society.

Criticism

Foundations have freed large parts of the world from the curse of diseases such as malaria and yellow fever; have brought enjoyment of the arts to millions of people; have created and helped support universities and research institutes; have clarified and otherwise served the law; have in many practical ways promoted international understanding and have encouraged the cause of peace; have shown how population can be controlled and people fed; have helped develop broadly trained leadership for business and government; have significantly aided the emerging nations; have importantly contributed to our growing knowledge of physical and living nature; have been alert in aiding new fields of activity; have helped to clarify the goals of present day humanistic scholarship; have made possible the development of important new scientific instruments for studying the atom, the cell and the star; have in language and areas studies, anticipated and

provided for some of the pressing needs of our country in its new worldwide responsibility; have created multi-million dollar funds for basic research; have developed and supported projects to extend the opportunity of higher education to qualified Negroes; and have liberated thousands of gifted individuals from the limitations of inadequate education, thus freeing them for greater service to society.
—Warren Weaver, Vice President, Rockefeller Foundation

In shaping the great changes that have taken place in my lifetime, foundations have been about as consequential as drug stores.
—Waldemar Nielsen

Nearly all foundations are influenced by those who seek to destroy our country.
—H. L. Hunt

The glare of publicity can be uncomfortable for grantmakers long used to acting publicly in a private manner
—Susan Beresford, President, Ford Foundation

As the above quotes suggest, observers of philanthropy are capable of examining the same creature and drawing very different conclusions about its nature. Many philanthrocrats react with indignation to challenges of their views. Foundations are fountains of good and evil, promoters and obstacles to progress, or agents and enemies of wealth; the choice in each case depends on the observer's political perspective. As Robert Payton, dean of the University of Indiana School of Philanthropy, so cleverly put it, "The ideological right (left) has charged that the ideological left (right) has seized control of philanthropic foundations." The only thing observers and critics of foundation agree about, it seems, is that foundations are powerful. "While foundations and their critics acknowledge their vast power," notes historian Joan Roelofs, "they disagree over whether it's benevolent."[4]

Since the turn of the century, criticism of foundations has been fairly constant, though rarely loud. Generally populist in tone, it has come from the Right and the Left—often simultaneously—and been aimed mostly at the same target: large centrist foundations like Ford. Left-wing critics castigate them as elitist engines of plutocracy, and rightists attack them as promoters of socialist agendas. In fact, the same foundations, according to historian Barry Karl, are often viewed as both "conservative supporters of reactionary capitalism, and Trojan horses carrying left-wing ideology into the camp of American free enterprise."

Arguments to sustain both views are available, for the grant lists of Ford and most other large foundations include donations to radical activist organizations as well as to relatively conservative institutions. Thus critics can describe the same trustee as a raving liberal or a raving conservative. Probably closer to the truth, however, is the assertion of Florence Foundation manager John Moyer that most "large foundations are raving moderates."[5] Of course, adjectives like *moderate, liberal,* and *conservative* do not neutralize the more general populist charge: that foundations invest society's excess wealth in the framing of public policy through nondemocratic processes. And that fact bothers American conservatives as deeply as it does liberals.

Foundation historian Stanley Katz reduces the long-running social critique of foundation to four indictments.

• Right: "It is inappropriate to use private funds to influence public policy."
• Left: "Foundation money is 'dirty', and thus an insincere way to curry public favor in an effort to rehabilitate robber baron images."
• Right: "Foundation activities interfere with the democratic process."
• Left: "The tycoons who started them would do better to raise worker's wages."[6]

Katz overlooks, of course, the persistent and embittered drone of the nonprofit community, which generally finds foundations "insular," "elitist," "secretive," "rigid," "bureaucratic," "risk averse," "intellectually bereft," "insensitive," and, as previously mentioned, "arrogant." Although in many cases these are valid characterizations, they are driven mostly by grant applicants' own disappointing experiences: they hear the word "no" nineteen times for every time they hear "yes."[7] Understandably, they are peeved, deeply and inexorably peeved.

In certain periods, usually coinciding with larger majoritarian political trends (who's in the White House, which party controls Congress), pressure from one side of the political spectrum is most pronounced. Congressional objections to foundations—the only kind philanthropists take seriously—tend to appear in twenty-year cycles and to alternate between Left and Right. The earliest expression of congressional wrath came from the Left around 1915, a year after the Ludlow Massacre.[8] The attack was aimed at industrialists like John D. Rockefeller, whom progressives accused of using foundations to protect monopolies and cleanse their robber baron images. "The huge philanthropic trusts, known as foundations, appear to be a menace to the welfare of society," proclaimed Frank

Walsh, chairman of the U.S. Commission on Industrial Relations. Hearings on the foundations prompted him to "challenge the wisdom of giving public sanction and approval to the spending of huge fortunes through such philanthropies as the Rockefeller Foundation." These organizations, he warned, were "becoming molders of public thought."[9]

In a 1981 article for the British journal *Minerva*, two later observers, Barry Karl and Stanley Katz, paraphrased the early left-wing critique of foundations this way:

Money which ought to be in the hands of the public is being retained by aristocrats for purposes beyond the control of democratic institutions; the academic freedom of universities is being subverted by the control of academic budgets by foundations; public policy is being determined by private groups; the scientific and scholarly research and the artistic creativity of individuals are being stifled by the emphasis of foundations on group research; smallness and individual effort are thwarted by materialistic and business-oriented demands of foundation management; foundations are bastions of elite Anglo-Saxon managers holding out against the normal development of a pluralistic and ethnic society.[10]

Similar indictments were repeated many times throughout the twentieth century and are still heard from leftists and others who regard private foundations as a threat to democracy and intellectual freedom. "The most ominous product of giant foundations," historian Roelofs states," is their translation of wealth into power. They can create, sustain and disseminate an ideology protective of capitalism; they can deflect criticism and mask or actually correct damaging abuses of the system; they can hire the best brains, popular heroines, even left-wing political leaders to do their work."[11]

Predictably, the early twentieth-century attacks on foundations subsided, and the institutions survived. "Nothing succeeds like longevity," Karl and Katz observe wryly." By 1929 foundations had come to appear traditional, inevitable and acceptable."[12]

After World War II, however, as tensions with the Soviet bloc heated up, the attacks were renewed. Spokespersons for the Right became obsessed with foundations, which they chastised for funding civil rights and voting rights programs proposed by "Communists and their dupes." Foundation support of equal rights, integrated education, and minority suffrage was, according to Republican Congressman B. Carroll Reese (Tenn.), "undermining our American way of life."[13]

During the McCarthy era the House of Representatives formed a special committee chaired by another foundation critic, Representative Eugene Cox (D-Ga.). The Cox Committee's mandate was to probe "subversive and Communist penetration" of philanthropic foundations. When the Ford Foundation became a prime target of Cox's polemics they inspired boycotts of Ford products in the South.

The right-wing assault on foundations continues, chiefly through the initiative of the Washington-based Capital Research Center (CRC). Founded in 1984 by Willa Johnson, a former senior vice president of the Heritage Foundation and associate director of personnel in the Reagan White House, CRC was fertilized with seed grants from the Richard Mellon Scaife, John Olin, and Adolph Coors foundations. "A unified, sophisticated and well-funded philanthropic elite is dedicated to imposing on us the doctrines of 'progressive' philanthropy, doctrines that would reorder our political, economic and cultural priorities." wrote Johnson in 1991. "This movement, driven by a bankrupt ideology, long since disproved by history, would impose its own standards of 'social justice' based on more involvement of government in philanthropy and more involvement of charities in politics. It has lost faith in the traditional American values of individual responsibility and free choice, to say nothing of the diversity in the marketplace of ideas."[14] CRC has since published voluminous research attempting to prove Johnson's thesis about traditional foundations. She has even accused some corporate foundations of deliberately subverting free-enterprise capitalism.

Populists on the other side also weighed in during the 1960s. Representative Wright Patman, a Texas Democrat, led a ten-year jihad against the abusive tax practices of the rich, whom he accused of using foundations as shields for self-dealing (i.e., using a foundation's tax status to enrich oneself without taxation). "Philanthropy, one of mankind's nobler instincts," Patman testified, "has been perverted into a vehicle for institutionalized, deliberate evasion of fiscal and moral responsibility to the nation."[15] Although Patman's investigators uncovered some self-dealing and other abuses, he was unable to convince many of his congressional colleagues that foundations were committing major crimes. His quest was effectively stifled by Treasury Secretary Douglas Dillon, a former Rockefeller Foundation trustee, who managed to place a young colleague named Tom Troyer in a critical committee position. Troyer saw to it that the interests of foundations were protected, particularly from Patman and Senator Albert Gore Sr., both of whom thought it would be a good thing if all foundations spent themselves out of existence in twenty-five years or less. This sentiment did not please the partisans of perpetuity who directed and worked in most foundations.

When Patman tired of the battle, the crusade was continued by a less-zealous, but nevertheless concerned, representative, Wilbur Mills of Arkansas. Mills successfully wrote some moderate regulations into the omnibus Tax Reform Act of 1969. It requires foundations to divest themselves of all but a small portion of shares in their founding corporation, thus ending the practice of allowing huge corporations to operate behind the protective shield of a private foundation. The act also required foundations to give away at least 6 percent of their assets every year (later lowered to 5 percent) and to file an annual tax return with the IRS. (I discuss the adequacy of a 5-percent payout in chapter 11.)

In the 1970s congressional debate on philanthropic abuses led to creation of the Commission on Private Philanthropy and Public Needs, better known as the Filer Commission after its chair, John Filer (an insurance executive from Aetna Life and Casualty). When Filer recommended establishment of a permanent national commission on nonprofits, President Jimmy Carter rejected the idea. In 1979, however, Independent Sector (I.S.), an umbrella council empowered to facilitate research on the entire nonprofit community (including the foundations) was formed.

By 1988 I.S. had created or otherwise supported the creation at American universities of twenty centers to conduct research on nonprofit organizations. Ironically, these centers were themselves funded by foundation grants and were therefore unlikely to provide objective assessments of foundations' role in the nonprofit sector.

Overall, far too much of the research literature on American philanthropy is uncritical and celebratory in tone. In fact, the general impression gained from published discussions of the foundations is that they are the crucial bedrock of civil society. This implicit claim ignores the fact that more than 88 percent of charitable revenues come from individuals, not foundations, and that over a third of funds for nonprofit organizations flow from state and federal treasuries.

The lack of tough criticism from the academy has not stopped the Right and the Left from railing against the foundations, particularly those that support the universities. According to Olin Foundation President William Simon, foundations and conservative philanthropists should "cease the mindless subsidizing of colleges and universities whose departments of economy, government, politics and history are hostile to capitalism."[16] The Left, for its part, complains that foundations too often join hands with their corporate brethren to stifle intellectual freedom.

One independent critic of organized philanthropy, Michael Lerner, contends in a profound essay that "as direct beneficiaries of the extraordinary disparity of income distribution that American society tolerates, which contribute to many if not most of the pathologies of civil society, foundations have a stake in soft-pedaling structural corrections of the inequalities. Indeed the habits of thought that they encourage in response—model programs for treating the victims of family abuse and the like—distract citizens from thinking clearly about government initiatives that would ameliorate inequities, as so many European industrial societies have."[17]

Very few of the philanthrocrats with whom I discussed foundation history seem bothered by this sort of analysis, although one or two admitted that they were troubled by the idea that the institution that employed them arose from economic injustice and would soon disappear if it were eliminated. "Criticism has been largely ignored by foundations," says Katz, "unless it has come from Capitol Hill." As only government can substantially affect the lives of philanthropists and their employees—whose accountability to the rest of society is minimal and symbolic—they largely disregard criticism from the rest of the nonprofit sector or from the media. Even when a *Philadelphia Inquirer* op-ed piece indicted foundation endowments for "sucking wealth out of the nation's tax base," as it did in April of 1993, few philanthrocrats responded. "Like the judiciary, we are trained to ignore it," says Gara LaMarche, who after a long career with the foundation-dependent Human Rights Watch, leapt over the funding barrier to work for one of George Soros's foundations, the Open Society Institute.[18]

LaMarche laments the lack of tough criticism and blames it on both the foundations and the media: "There is not enough funding of efforts to reframe the debates that influence and mediate philanthropy," he says. "I don't think the press is doing the job of keeping an eye on this group of powerful institutions . . . whose power over dependent grantees mutes most of the voices that might be raised in protest. Foundations receive little credible scrutiny and reporting on how they carry out influential policy initiatives." [19]

The mass media's sparse coverage of organized philanthropy also baffles philanthrocrats, who believe they have an exciting story to tell. Only occasionally do journalists like the *Philadelphia Inquirer* writer fire a shot across the bow of foundations. From time to time, but still infrequently, journals of opinion attack the foundations from one side or another. In the September 1995 *New Republic,* for example, David Samuels chastised the large foundations for shifting their philanthropy from universities and social research to advocacy groups for the poor and disenfranchised.

That's a common complaint from the Right, which seems unfazed by the millions that flow from conservative foundations into adversarial think tanks such as Heritage Foundation, the American Enterprise Institute, and the Manhattan Institute—which promote reduced taxation, less regulation, and other policies of interest to the rich. On the other hand, conservative essayists have long felt free to attack any foundation that departs from what they perceive as legitimate philanthropy. Heather MacDonald, writing in the *City Journal,* scolds the Ford Foundation for "eschewing medical research and public health in favor of social issues such as first amendment restrictions and undemocratic concentrations of power, economic problems, world peace and social science." She deplores former Ford Foundation executive Richard Magat's call for a more "radical vision" and his demand for (in his words) "action oriented, rather than research oriented," grantmaking that would "test the outer edges of advocacy and citizen participation." No, retorts MacDonald, "the megafoundations should repress their yearning for activism once and for all." [20]

In 1995 a voice from the Left, Daniel Callahan, described the central role played by some foundations in the Reagan revolution. "Thirty years ago, in the wake of Barry Goldwater, conservatives wandered in a political wilderness from which some observers predicted they would never emerge," Callahan wrote in *The Nation.* "They did, of course, and well-funded intellectuals were instrumental in leading the conservative movement onto the prairie of power. Today liberal foundations should insure that policy thinkers on the left have everything they need to undertake a similar task." In a later *Nation* article, Michael Shuman agreed heartily, praising liberal foundations for funding advocacy groups but complaining that far too much money went to grassroots organizations and not enough to "progressive" think tanks.[21] (I consider this controversy in more detail in chapter 9.)

Pablo Eisenberg, whose former employer, the Center for Community Change (CCC), is a significant recipient of foundation support, wrote in 1996 that "many foundations know what is needed, but are unwilling to take appropriate steps. They do not like supporting organizing, activism, public policy activities and advocacy. They are much more comfortable with research and services." He pointed out that "with the exception of a small number of conservative foundations like Bradley and Scaife, which have a clear vision and know what they want to do, many of our large and midsize foundations fret about appearing balanced and nonpartisan."[22]

Eisenberg, who before he retired from the CCC relied heavily on progressive funders to support his projects, is strangely complimentary toward foundations that would never have financed his work. Right-wing funders, he asserts, are "model grantmakers." They deal with issues and are "strategic, visionary, and intellectually rigorous, capacity builders who stand by solid organizations and foster leadership on the Right."

This position, which is echoed by Shuman and others, is supported by the extensive research of Sally Covington at the National Committee for Responsive Philanthropy. After studying the grant-making practices of twelve conservative foundations, she described their "impressively clear, coherent and concerted effort to undermine what political conservatives have regarded as the institutional strongholds of modern American liberalism—academia, Congress, the judiciary, major media and even philanthropy." Covington found that the policy changes advocated and funded by the conservative foundations—most notably deregulation, reductions in government spending, and the privatization of public institutions and services—have been so aggressively marketed that they have "transformed the parameters of national policy debate."[23]

Of the approximately $300 million granted by the twelve foundations during the period of her study, over $200 million went to political think tanks, conservative media, public interest law firms, academic programs, and advocacy groups bent on moving public policy to the Right. No comparable foundation initiatives, Covington noted, were being exercised on the Left.

Conclusion

Foundations will no doubt continue for many years to be targets of attack from those who see them as protectors of conservative power or as fomenters of radical change. As they have for a century or more, foundation advocates will continue to insist that they are neither, but rather private institutions engaged in private efforts to improve human existence and civil society. Nonetheless, as the assets, leverage, and influence of foundations continue to increase at accelerated rates, the debate will rage on. What forces and institutions should have the power to change society? What role should money play in the process? And who should control that money?

And, almost certainly, the ambiguity about whether foundations are public or private institutions will persist. "'Private philanthropy' remains the distinctive phrase it always has been," observe Karl and Katz. "'Private' began as a legitimating modifier, but as the meaning of the term was changed so has it's political force."[24] As foundations continue to press for policies that affect the public, the ambiguity will live on—fed by theories from both sides about "invisible governments" and conspiracies by the holders of private wealth to influence public policy in ways critics believe should be reserved for ordinary citizens acting through traditional democratic processes.

The confusion of the words *public* and *private*, whether used to describe foundations' status or their powers, has been endemic in foundation history. If anything, the ambiguity surrounding the terms has grown more acute, because private institutions are playing increasingly public roles in American society; and because conservative forces are pressing government to privatize so many activities and functions that have for half a century been essentially public responsibilities. Organized philanthropies themselves thus remain lodged in the public mind—and perhaps even in the minds of philanthrocrats—somewhere between public and private, terms that themselves remain vague and ill-defined.

Meanwhile, the central theory of organized philanthropy insists that the public interest is well served by the existence of private charitable trusts. Confiscating surplus wealth and letting it sink without trace into the morass of state and federal treasuries is not only politically unfeasible, it's an option doomed to failure. The hundred-year American experiment with foundation philanthropy has produced mixed results, as the rest of this book attests. But given the growing tendency of legislators and the executive branch to reject the welfare state and gradually abdicate the authority of the central government to protect the environment, workers' safety, and consumer health, there seems to be no choice but to continue the experiment.

2

Knowledge

Let there be light . . .
—God . . . and Andrew Carnegie

. . . to illuminate, as far as practicable, the minds of the people at large.
—Thomas Jefferson

It is as if Thomas Jefferson had guided the pens of American benefactors as they drafted the charters of new foundations. So many of them perceived, to one degree or another, the vital link between education and public welfare, between a discerning electorate and a lasting democracy. They seemed to concur with Jefferson that "an enlightened citizenry is indispensable to the proper functioning of a republic."

Whatever our complaints about the quality of American schools or the depth of public knowledge, we cannot fault the foundations created by those benefactors for lack of effort in improving education. Throughout the entire history of organized philanthropy, education has been the highest priority, and remains the most elusive challenge. Even in the midst of war and depression, foundations have been catalysts, pollinators, and leavening agents in the arduous process of building and reforming educational systems and institutions.

Nonetheless, despite thousands of grants targeted by foundations at every level and system of American education—particularly during the last fifty years of the twentieth century—two issues remain debatable: (1) whether private philanthropy has contributed significantly to the Jeffersonian imperative; and (2) whether, in the final analysis, foundation trustees and program officers are the appropriate agents of reform in basic education.

Certainly, they have played a major role in higher education. Foundations have supported, and even helped create, some impressive private institutions of higher learning, such as the University of Chicago and the Carnegie Institute of Technology (now Carnegie Mellon University). The latter was spawned at the turn of the century with a Carnegie grant and is still reliant for much of its leading-edge research on foundation support. As the next chapter attests, American technology could not have advanced as far or as fast as it has without the early start foundations provided such private universities in basic and interdisciplinary science. But, as results demonstrate, the foundations' role in public education has been quite another matter.

It is evident that, with a few notable exceptions, American philanthropists and foundation trustees have placed inordinate faith in the faculty and curricula of colleges and universities. They seem to have forgotten, or never known, that what in the final analysis makes universities great is not the brilliance of well-paid staffs, the magnificence of their campuses, or the size of their endowments but the raw material sent to them from the secondary schools.

Moreover, although they have recently laid out billions of dollars in search of "excellence" and other lofty goals for public schools, the foundations' role in public education remains ambiguous. Are they the best agents to promote real change in education? Might they better confine themselves either to funding the design of a few innovative programs or to organizing key constituencies to pressure the government for better education? Reforming the pedagogy of a multicultural nation may simply be a mission too large, too complex, and too demanding of democratic processes for private philanthropy as it is currently structured to undertake. Later in the book I consider the overwhelming nondemocratic nature of modern foundations, and I argue that for foundations to become effective agents of change the public participation required to reform public institutions also needs to be applied to them. But in this chapter I look at the pursuit of knowledge and the role that private wealth has already played in selecting its priorities.

Priority One

The ineffectiveness in teaching reading skills to so many young people, whether black or white, poor or rich, strongly indicts foundations and government for not spending funds effectively.
—Martin Luther King Jr.

During the 1920s 43 percent of the grants from America's largest hundred foundations went directly to the advancement of knowledge, though far more to basic research than to pedagogy. The share of foundation grants given for knowledge research has fallen sharply since then, but it remains the top funding priority of organized philanthropy. Twenty-four percent of all foundation funding in 1997 went to education, followed by health and medical at 17 percent, human services at 15 percent, and arts and humanities at 13 percent.

Jefferson would clearly approve the fact that education remains number one. But were he to return, visit a few public schools, read a random sample of college applications, and observe the myriad reform initiatives attempted and abandoned, would he find the billions granted to improve education over the past century money entirely well spent? And, if he stayed long enough to observe the state of the electoral democracy he helped design, would either the citizenry or their representatives meet his standards of enlightenment? One can only wonder.

Surely he would be impressed by our philanthropic commitment to education. Billions of dollars are granted to schools, academics, and think tanks by foundations motivated by the goal of an enlightened citizenry. Yet the quarry seems elusive. The attainments of American high school students as a whole compare less and less favorably with their counterparts overseas, while children in the bottom quartile remain trapped in an infrastructure where it seems virtually impossible for them to learn anything of lasting value.

Blame for the situation can hardly be laid at the feet of foundations. But a grant or two to assess the consequence of favoring bricks and mortar and prestigious faculty chairs might indicate that, in the end, universities rely for their achievement, not these accoutrements, but on attracting impressive students. Such students, sadly, seem more likely to be spawned by the schools of a dozen or more foreign countries than by those in most American school districts.

Higher Education?

Not even God himself can stop me from giving my money to the University of Chicago.
—John D. Rockefeller

Foundations are held captive and blinded by modern research universities.
—Charles Halpern, President, Cummings Foundation

Over a twenty-year period from 1949 to 1969 foundations led all other private funding sources as supporters of higher education. Today about 20 percent of all voluntary support for higher education still comes from foundations, which in 1998 contributed $3.8 billion. Foundations now rank third after alumni, who donated $5.5 billion (30 percent), and friends, who gave $4.5 billion (24 percent). Foundations only slightly out-granted corporations, which the same year donated $3.25 billion.[1] Observers attribute the gradual decline of foundation support to universities to many factors: low asset growth, reduced number of new foundations during the 1980s, reassessment of mission, changing views of higher education, and some foundations' growing realization that primary and secondary education stand in dire need of attention.

Nevertheless, while it has declined from 20 percent to about 10 percent of overall foundation giving, support of colleges and universities remains the favored education category among foundation trustees. In 1995 almost 60 percent of the foundations' educational grants went to institutions that offer undergraduate and graduate degrees to the 24 percent of American high school students who enroll in college or university. That same year 27 percent of foundation investment in education went to public elementary and secondary school projects.

More curious imbalances are embedded within the higher education grant category itself. Only about 8 percent of American college students attend the private research universities that receive 31 percent of the charitable contributions. And, although endowments are not a direct result of foundation philanthropy, they reflect a similar disparity; most of the nation's educational investment capital is held by a handful of highly favored institutions. Private universities, which enroll less than 25 percent of all college students, receive three-quarters of all earnings from endowment. And it is to those very institutions that the bulk of foundation funding goes.

Five prominent universities—Harvard, Yale, Stanford, Princeton, and the University of Texas—together enroll less than 1 percent of American college students, but they hold 20 percent of the total American endowment in higher education. These five institutions, plus Columbia and the University of Chicago, also excel in fields like science, engineering, and business management, which are most likely to attract foundation support.

As the offspring of industrial wealth, it is not surprising that foundations have, from their earliest days, been eager to advance academic disciplines and departments that fill industry's ongoing needs. That hasn't changed.

Both John D. Rockefeller and Andrew Carnegie had these needs in mind in establishing their trusts. Although Carnegie's foundation was launched with a loftier intention—"to promote the advancement and diffusion of knowledge and understanding among the people of the United States"—until very recently most of it's education funding went to grantees who better fulfilled the purposes of the Rockefeller Foundation. In a recent annual report the latter described its mission as "the development of institutions to train professional people, scientists and scholars in the applied disciplines, who in turn will train succeeding generations of students, advance the state of knowledge in their fields, and respond to their country's needs."

That statement is consistent with both founders' abiding faith that knowledge is a special power when applied not only to private enterprise but also to public policy. The Rockefeller report continues: "The Foundation's faith in knowledge as the first step toward realizing man's potential, its faith that man himself is ultimately a rational creature, runs deep. It has survived undimmed the past six decades."[2] Andrew Carnegie would certainly have agreed, though he began his own education philanthropy in somewhat different ways.

Carnegie, a descendent of Scottish radicals intent upon "destroying every vestige of privilege in England," began his philanthropy with deep concern for "the education and improvement of the poorer classes." He funded thousands of scholarships for working-class children in Scotland and donated generously to the education of African Americans. But eventually both he and his foundation shifted to favor toward more elite pursuits.

Like Rockefeller, whose General Education Board sought "to promote a comprehensive system of higher education in the United States," Carnegie developed elaborate plans to restructure America's entire system of higher education. Before he died, $118 million of his money was invested in the plan, most of it through his Foundation for the Advancement of Teaching, formed in 1903 to provide pensions to college-level teachers.

His foundation became a strategic catalyst for higher educational reform, for in order to qualify for pension grants colleges had to conform to rigid standards set by the founder: admit only the best students, maintain a strong faculty, have a healthy endowment, and remain completely free of sectarian control. The latter condition did little to endear the old man to American churches. "The Carnegie Foundation tried to weaken and kill off denominational colleges," according to education historian Frederick Rudolph.[3]

When a nationwide faculty pension system became more than it could support, the foundation created the Teacher's Insurance and Annuity Association (TIAA) to pick up the slack and assure faculty mobility from one institution to another. After the creation of an independent TIAA, the Carnegie lost much of its leverage over the structure and content of higher education; but by then it had inaugurated lasting reforms, severely limiting the influence of the clergy and leaving a curricular imprint that persists to this day.

As American corporations began their global reach after World War II, the large foundations, joined by a new giant, Ford, began to fund higher education overseas, particularly in Latin America, where they put the emphasis on agriculture, economics, and the social sciences. Collaboration, particularly between Ford and Rockefeller, became a common practice. By the mid-1950s (and for the next decade) the Ford Foundation was the preeminent education funder among U.S. foundations. And, as we shall see, its interest in education came to diverge widely from that of other foundations.

Pebbles in the Mississippi

Public education is as radical an idea as Americans have embraced.
—Lawrence Cremin

"Elementary education appears to be well provided for," Abbott Lawrence remarked upon making a fifty-thousand-dollar contribution to Harvard University in 1850. He was responding to Horace Mann, himself a college president, who was attempting to persuade Lawrence that Harvard had enough money and that his donation would be more productively invested in public education. Mann pointed out public school teachers in Massachusetts were paid $68.40 for an entire school term and that the average number of books in public school libraries was twenty-five.

A century later, with two notable exceptions, private philanthropists and their foundations had still given close to nothing to institutions of public education or to programs for designing innovations that would affect public primary or secondary schools. The exceptions were the Spelman Foundation (a Rockefeller Foundation named after John D. Sr.'s wife, Laura Spelman) and the Rosenwald Fund, which in the early century built over five thousand rural schools in the South for the education of black Americans. This focus ignored the fact that well over 80 percent of American students never went beyond the twelfth grade and that most were educated in public schools. This huge block of students would not only, upon reaching adulthood, comprise the bulk of the nation's work force, it would also constitute the majority of the electorate.

Nonetheless, cultivation of an intelligent voting public seems not to have been factored into early philanthropic decisions. Public schools, according to the prevalent view, existed to Americanize immigrants, not to enlighten voters. Only universities could provide essential leadership for American society and keep the country competitive in the international economy. The politics of knowledge, at least as perceived by philanthropists and foundation staffs, thus clearly favored the education of experts over the creation of an enlightened citizenry. Moreover, public schools were perceived as black holes into which unlimited private money could be poured without producing favorable results.

However, around the middle of the twentieth century, a few foundation trustees, principally at the Ford Foundation, began to consider the costs of this approach. They realized that as most Americans were educated in public schools the quality of public education affected not only the preparation of college freshmen and the entry-level skills of workers but also the very fiber of American democracy. If public schools were "dumbed down" (in our current vernacular), so would the electorate and so, inexorably, would the elected. There were (and still are) clear signs of this process in the nation's legislatures.

Midcentury census data added fuel to the argument. By the mid-1950s it was evident that public schools were facing a demographic, as well as a pedagogical, challenge. Between 1950 and 1960 the nation's primary and secondary school enrollments would increase from under thirty million to over forty million. Such a sudden growth would sorely strain the existing infrastructure and resources of the system.

Ford Foundation researchers also observed a wide disparity of skills and knowledge among secondary school students, which reflected an even wider disparity of educational opportunity. They came to believe that by addressing these differences public schools could ameliorate such related social problems as racial discrimination, intergroup violence, and economic inequity. By moving full force into public education, Ford sparked an era characterized by what education historian Lawrence Cremin describes as "the increasingly direct harnessing of education to social ends" in an effort to "solve certain social problems indirectly through education instead of directly through politics."[4]

It remains for historians to decide whether Ford initiated a trend in educational reform or merely responded to a growing American tendency to rely on their schools as cures for every conceivable ill. As Cremin points out, there is considerable evidence for the latter view.

Americans want their schools and colleges to teach the fundamental skills of reading, writing, and arithmetic; to nurture critical thinking; to convey a general fund of knowledge; to develop creativity and aesthetic perception; to assist students in choosing and preparing for vocations in a highly complex economy; to inculcate ethical character and good citizenship; to develop physical and emotional well-being; and to nurture the ability, intelligence and will to continue with education as far as any individual wants to go. . . . And this catalogue does not even mention such Herculean tasks as taking the initiative in racial desegregation and informing [students] about the dangers of drug abuse and AIDS.

Public education, then, "is as radical an idea as Americans have embraced. It is by its very nature fraught with difficulty, and the institutions we have established to achieve it are undeniably flawed."[5]

It was at the undeniable flaws in American public education that the Ford Foundation aimed its philanthropy during the 1950s, through its now-legendary Fund for the Republic. Every year , in addition to giving hundreds of millions of dollars to universities and hospitals, the fund made five hundred smaller grants totaling $50 million to short-term pilot projects aimed at reforming K through 12 education nationwide. Although many educational innovations were also funded, the main thrust of Ford's separate Fund for the Advancement of Education was to recruit and train competent liberal arts graduates as teachers. And, along with the Fund for the Republic, it was designed to make the Ford Foundation "better and more favorably known."[6]

This public relations goal was the natural response of an institution that had been subpoenaed by congressional committees twice within the preceding two years: in 1952 by the Cox Committee investigating "subversive and Communist penetration" in philanthropic foundations and, in 1954, by the Reese Committee. The latter inquiry, chaired by Representative B. Carroll Reese (Tenn.-R), was intent on proving that foundations were part of a "diabolical conspiracy" to undermine American values. It created an aura of caution among Ford's trustees, who feared the wrath of an increasingly aggravated right-wing bloc in Congress. René Wormser, general counsel of the Reese Committee, charged that foundations were producing an elite

in control of gigantic financial resources, operating outside of our democratic processes, which is willing and able to shape the future of this nation in the image of its own value concepts. An unparalleled amount of power is concentrated increasingly in the hands of an interlocking and self-perpetuating group. Unlike the power of corporate management, it is unchecked by stockholders, unlike the power government, it is unchecked by the people.[7]

Although Reese's committee found no evidence of subversion or wrongdoing, its very existence had a chilling effect on social pioneering for several years.

By the end of the 1950s, Cold War hysteria had subsided in Washington, and Ford published Decade of Experiment, a report citing the unfinished business of educational reform. It was a time when nearly everyone thought that "with more money, more buildings, and more teachers, our nation's schools could indeed make a few adjustments and changes to produce a better society."[8] With that sentiment in mind, Ford launched its ambitious and controversial Comprehensive School Improvement Program (CSIP).

Over the following decade CSIP provided $30 million to twenty-five separate education reform programs in as many communities. By the mid-1960s funding emphasis had shifted from pedagogic innovation to using schools to address social and economic inequities. Ford's "Partnership for change," though not regarded as a notable success (even by foundation officers), did heighten private foundation interest in both public education and civil rights. And it generated yet another angry attack, this time from conservative foundations and other institutions of the Right. That assault continues.

In a 1996 article describing America's large foundations as "liberal leviathans," conservative critic Heather MacDonald singled out the Ford Foundation for leading the entire philanthropic community into a world where foundations no longer "improved the lot of mankind by building lasting institutions but by challenging existing ones. . . . Once an agent for social good," she writes, "the biggest U.S. foundations have become a political battering ram targeted at American society." Through its "activist" funding of educational reform, most notably in the Bedford-Stuyvesant school district of New York, MacDonald asserts, Ford promoted black militancy, exacerbated racial tension, and "debased curriculum [*sic*] into divisive victimology" (through women's studies). By supporting multiculturalism in higher education, she argues, foundations have devalued Western culture, "whose transmission is any university's principal reason for existence."[9]

A year earlier *New Republic* essayist David Samuels had exploited the same theme: "That poverty in America is caused by racism and can be eliminated through education is one of the fundamental assumptions of liberal politics that American foundations effectively promoted during the 1950s and 60s." During the 1960s, Samuels argues, foundations willfully set the social agenda for America. Like MacDonald, he deplores the philanthrocrats' penchant for activism, their funding of agitators, and their respect for multiculturalism: "The preponderance of grants to advocacy groups," he says, "suggests that foundations are less devoted to the reasoned pursuit of the public good than to the multi-culturalist dogmas propounded by their staffs."[10] In fact, no such preponderance existed, nor does it exist today; foundations were then, and remain, staunch supporters of the reasoned pursuit of incremental change.

Funding for education took a dramatic drop during the 1980s, as foundations shifted their grantmaking to human services left bare by the Reagan administration's withdrawal of support. From an annual average of over 30 percent of the total grants made in the early 1970s education funding dropped to 16 percent in 1983, and remained near that level for the rest of the decade. A revised coding by the Foundation Center, which added library science, medical, and professional education to the category, bumped education up to 20 percent in 1989. Since then it has risen gradually to around 25 percent.

In the 1990s a host of new funders, principally the Annenberg, Hewlett, William Penn, Annie Casey, Gund, Edna McConnell Clark, and Robert W. Woodruff foundations (and an even larger number of community foundations), perceived a further decline in the basic skills of American high school students. They directed their attention to the reform of public primary and secondary education, particularly at inner city schools where less than half the eleven million students were achieving even minimal learning standards. Programs like Brown University's Coalition for Central Schools, Stanford's Accelerated Schools, Johns Hopkins' Success For All, and Yale's Full Development Project received generous support from foundations but accomplished very little. "Tossing a pebble into the Mississippi," is how one funder described her work.

Several constructive projects for local school districts are funded by these foundations—particularly in large cities like Chicago and Cleveland. Most of the money, however, stimulated by Walter Annenberg's 1993 $500-million challenge grant, goes to huge regional reform projects like the Los Angeles Metropolitan Project (LAMP), the Chicago Annenberg Challenge, the New York Network for School Renewal, the Bay Area School Reform Collaborative, and similar initiatives in Detroit, Miami, Houston, Boston, and a host of smaller communities in almost every state of the union. The Annenberg challenge, which has created a magnet for $550 million in additional corporate and foundation funding for K through 12 reform, illuminates both the value and the follies of large-scale proactive philanthropy.

Dropping a Bomb

Life is not about orthodoxy, it's about heterodoxy.
—Vartan Gregorian, President, Carnegie Corporation

When Vartan Gregorian was provost at the University of Pennsylvania in the late 1970s, Walter Annenberg was on the board of trustees. According to people who knew them both, they were like son and father. They talked constantly about education, particularly public education and the problems it faced throughout the country. When Annenberg cashed out of the Triangle Corporation and decided to invest the bulk of his wealth in educational reform, he called on his former protégé for advice. Gregorian told him that urban schools were the toughest educational challenge facing the nation. And nothing short of a Marshall Plan was required, particularly if the almost lost, bottom quartile of the country's students were to be saved.

Annenberg is a conservative Republican whose working-class father served a prison sentence before he launched the *National Racing Form.* The paper and the publishing empire it spawned grew fast and made the family rich, but young Walter never forgot the hard times. Although he dines today with queens and presidents, at some level he identifies with the underdog roots from which his father rose. Thus equal educational opportunity and the improvement of schools in working-class neighborhoods makes a lot of sense to him—enough sense to design and fund a Marshall Plan." "I wanted to elevate precollegiate education as a national priority," Annenberg told his biographer, Christopher Ogden. "To do that I felt I had to drop a bomb."[11]

When Gregorian told him that conservative reform programs promoting vouchers and privatized schooling would sacrifice an unacceptable number of students, mostly poor, inner city minorities, Annenberg believed him. At a White House banquet a few days later he committed $500 million to the broad reform of public education. He would fund no fancy experiments, no privatization, no magic bullets, single panaceas, or New Age visions—just basic reform of existing systems conducted so that no student could be ignored. "I do not believe that $500 million will do the job," he told the president and his guests. "This must be a challenge to the nation. Those who control sizable funds should feel an obligation to join this crusade for the betterment of our country."[12]

Annenberg made twenty-one eight-figure grants to American cities with seriously failing educational systems and challenged local foundations and corporations to match them. By the end of 1998, about $375 million had been added to Annenberg's $500 million. The result, known in some cities graced with his funding as the Annenberg Initiative was—until Bill Gates made his foray into education reform—the largest individual attempt in history to improve public education. The controversy surrounding it is predictably fierce.

Annenberg insists that his money be spent "as close as possible to the kids." From the start he feared that the funds would never reach the classroom. In the year 2000 the initiative encompasses twenty-seven hundred schools in three hundred districts teaching 1.8 million students. It represents a natural step in a long process of public school reform that began in the 1960s with an emphasis on specific subjects—most frequently math and science. Early on, educators developed experimental classroom models that they hoped to replicate and, if successful, implement throughout the country. Subsequent efforts, however, shifted the base of operations to individual schools, then to districts, then to large cities. Now education problems and policy are addressed on a regional, or even statewide, basis.

The Bay Area School Reform Collaborative (BASRC), for example, involves over twelve hundred schools in 118 separate school districts and affects seven hundred and forty thousand students in the nine counties surrounding San Francisco Bay. There, Annenberg's $25-million grant was matched by William Hewlett and the Hewlett Foundation, who together leveraged the total budget—by obtaining additional matching funds—to over $100 million. While BASRC's focus is on changing the "whole school" learning environment, administrators clearly hope that the systemic innovations being applied throughout the Bay Area region will result in improved performance by individual students. True to the ambitious nature of his initiative, Walter Annenberg wants to reform all public education, K through 12, for every student in the United States. Most objective observers believe that his dream is unlikely to be realized. But Annenberg and Gregorian are hopeful. And hope is a vital ingredient of the philanthropic imagination.

So, of course, is money, and Vartan Gregorian is sitting on a large pot of it. So it came as no surprise when, fifteen months after assuming the presidency of the Carnegie Corporation, Gregorian shifted the priorities of that foundation strongly toward education. The Carnegie had not, of course, previously abandoned the field; education has always been a major part of its grant mix. But at a board of trustees meeting held in January of 1999, Gregorian proposed cutting programs in African health care, drug education, and teen violence and placing the funds in American public education. The board concurred.

Carnegie money thus followed Annenberg's into the nationwide cottage industry that has bloomed since the 1983 publication of *Nation at Risk* and the almost-unchallenged supposition that American public schools are very badly off.[13] Since then, educational think tanks and reform programs have competed for funding with lamentations about the parlous state of education. The more despairing their descriptions of the future of public schools, the more the money seems to flow. How bad things really are is a matter of constant debate among foundation program officers and their grantees. Some sensible independent observers with no interest in foundation funding seem to believe that the schools aren't quite as badly off as the reform mercenaries claim.

"The debate is driven by myths," according to essayist Peter Schrag, who writes in the *Atlantic Monthly* of the belief that "there was once a golden era when schools maintained rigorous standards, when all children learned, few dropped out and most graduated on time." That era never existed, says Schrag, who proposes a more realistic assessment of public education than the one offered by "a growing number of people, who in the name of world class standards, would abandon, through vouchers, privatization, and other means, the idea of the common school altogether. Before we do that, we'd better be sure that things are really as bad as we assume. The dumbest thing we could do is scrap what we are doing right."[14] Few paid heed to Schrag's advice.

What seems incontrovertible is that the American public education system provides an excellent education to an impressive number of students, and that the SAT and other test scores of formerly marginal population groups are rising (albeit slowly). Nonetheless, the system as a whole still fails to provide an equal educational opportunity to a significant minority of American children. Though they differ about the depth and degree of the "crisis in education," reformers of all persuasions seem to agree that about 25 percent of American public school students are not learning enough to survive in the twenty-first century. And, sadly, a growing number of them each year "graduate" directly from school to prison.

By steadily funding institutions that perpetuate a negative assessment of American public education, private philanthropy has inadvertently spawned two rings of Cassandras who profit from documenting the worst qualities and problems of education while ignoring indicators of success and improvement. One ring, exemplified by the Annenberg initiative, is intent on reforming existing public school systems. The other wants to toss the whole experiment out and start over.

Challenging the Annenberg approach are conservative critics of contemporary education like Milton Friedman, William Bennett, Jennifer Grossman, Chester Finn, and Dianne Ravitch. Much of their work is supported by a handful of small- to medium-sized conservative foundations. Invoking studies that demonstrate the declining academic attainments of American students, they argue in widely published essays and op-ed pieces that the government's "education monopoly" should be replaced by a new model based on educational vouchers and private contracting. Finn attributes to "retail complacency" the fact that 70 percent of Americans reject the rhetoric of failure and consider public schools adequate. He and his followers remain frustrated by the public's reservoir of affection for public education and their own inability to supply enough education through free-market systems.

Largely in response to the critique of Finn and Ravitch, conservative foundations intent upon dismantling all social entitlements joined the drive to reform public education. Perhaps *restructure* would be a better word, or *reformulate,* as both they and Bill Bennett seek not simply to reform but to redefine everything about contemporary education: public schools, teachers, local control, students, and curricula.[15] Redefinition, in their formulation, is the prelude to privatization.

The conservatives talk the usual talk about parent participation, teacher preparation, school choice, competition, and charter schools. They point out, quite correctly, that as long as inner city schools are supported by residential property taxes their students will not receive an equal education. The conservative solution, however, is not a more equitable tax structure or state and federal subsidies for inner city schools. It is what Milton Friedman calls "the dismantling of the public monopoly," which "can only be achieved by privatizing a major segment of the education system, allowing a private, for-profit industry to develop and offer effective competition to public schools."[16]

Conservative foundations of the late-1990s rose to the call and designed what Wall Street now calls EMOs—Education Maintenance Organizations. Privately owned and operated EMOs like the Edison Project, EduVentures, and Michael Milken's Knowledge Universe offer to take over individual schools, school districts, or entire urban school systems and run them on contract as for-profit ventures. The New American School Development Corporation, which began as a government venture and offers a wide variety of educational systems and philosophies, from right to left, is now an EMO. EduVentures, a Boston-based investment banking firm, estimates the total value of the education industry at between $630 and $680 billion, about $6 billion of which represents the investments of venture capitalists in publicly traded educational companies. Although education stocks are currently trailing the larger market, there was a point in

1997 when the stocks of thirty publicly traded education corporations were growing at twice the rate of the Dow Jones Industrial Average.

Supporting the free-market movement, alongside a host of corporate funders like Walmart, Amway, and the Gap, are the Olin and Bradley foundations, both of which fund the Indiana-based Hudson Institute and the Heritage Foundation's public education reform project.[17] In 1996 corporate foundations donated $1.3 billion to K through 12 programs, most of them privatization ventures This sum is three times the amount of the Annenberg initiative and represents about 20 percent of total corporate giving (up from 5 percent a decade ago).

Chester Finn Jr., a John Olin fellow at the Hudson Institute and president of the Thomas B. Fordham Foundation (a conservative Washington think tank), is a favorite of conservative and corporate foundations. Finn worked as an assistant secretary under Lamar Alexander in the Reagan Department of Education (which was programmed by the White House to self-destruct but never did). He is also a founding partner of the Edison Project, which is more of a franchise chain than an educational project. Edison was started by Whittle Communications, designer of Channel One, a closed-circuit educational television network beamed directly into selected public schools; its programming includes advertising commercials of consumer goods popular with school-age children. The channel was recently purchased from Whittle in a leveraged buyout by Kolberg, Kravis, and Roberts, which also owns a firm called Lifetime Learning Systems and PETV, which produces corporate-sponsored television for schools. In the year ending June 30, 1999, Edison announced a loss of $50.5 million on sales of $132 million and has yet to turn a profit.

From a separate think tank called the Educational Excellence Network, housed inside the Hudson Institute, Chester Finn assails "a rigid, governmentalist monopoly centered on an archaic concept of schooling, developed for a 19th century agrarian society with little technology and scant awareness of how children learn." Few educators of any persuasion would challenge that assertion. However, Finn also characterizes as "faddish innovations" such modern methods for addressing the crisis as whole-language reading, constructivist math, mixed ability grouping, and—that bugaboo of the contemporary Right—multiculturalism.[18]

Finn's way out of the mess is to smash the "bureaucratic monopoly" that controls American public education and turn the schools over, one by one, not to parents or elected school boards, but to the Edison Project, Knowledge Universe, or to the New American School Development Corporation. (The latter franchises a prototype school package labeled "The Modern Red School House.") With the profit potential in mind, Finn takes every opportunity to attack alternative reforms, such as the Clinton administration's plan to raise the standards for teacher certification, a system that would apply standards to teachers in the voucher-funded Edison Project as well as those in public schools.

Liberal fears that privatization will further degrade the already abominable condition of inner-city public schools is dismissed by Finn and Ravitch as trade union propaganda. They point to charter schools where minority children are either excelling or improving their skills and compare them to traditional public schools in the same district, neglecting to mention that many charter schools are massively subsidized by corporate and community foundations. (A scientifically sound experiment would give proportionally equal subsidies to a nearby regular school and study the performance of both student bodies.)

Among foundation officials who question the privatization of public schools, few are as outspoken as the MacArthur Foundation's Peter Martinez, who oversees a $40-million school-improvement program in Chicago. "The problem is that there is not a strategy aimed at meeting the needs of a broad-based urban population," Martinez says. "The major concern here is that we have a growing education gap, and a skill gap in the U.S. between the disadvantaged communities and the middle to upper middle income communities—and it's all based around education."[19]

Martinez observes that very few inner-city youths are reaping the benefits of charter schools, or of any other notable reforms, and that American public school students in the bottom quartile of American public school students are, from an educational standpoint, in worse straits than ever. Of all the national foundations that concern themselves to one degree or another with education—and most do—the only one dedicated exclusively to the education of disadvantaged children, most of them in that bottom quartile, is the Annie Casey Foundation in Baltimore. In 1999 it contributed just over $3 million to public education. The other foundations appear to maintain a the-poor-are-always-with-us attitude about a system that fails to educate so many students.

Finn and his followers contend that Casey, Annenberg, and all foundations that attempt to reform public education are wasting their money (much as, they say, taxpayers have done for years). Holding up a handful of successful charter schools that are educating a few nonwhite students, Finn argues that the whole system can be made to work with vouchers and franchised contractors. Though he clearly respects Walter Annenberg for his loyalty to Ronald Reagan, Finn believes that the former ambassador to the Court of St James "has allowed his affection for public education to blind him to its realities. For all the improvement his generosity has wrought, he might as well have joined Ted Turner and poured his money into the sea."[20]

In the next decade, the Finn and Annenberg models of primary and secondary education will compete for national recognition and philanthropic support. They may both survive, leaving the country with a bifurcated system in which public and private systems will match results and compete for public and private support.

Yet, regardless of the outcome of that contest, the amount of private philanthropy pumped into public school reform, even if it were increased by a factor of three or four, would remain minuscule compared to the budgets of existing school systems. The $110-million investment of the Los Angeles Metropolitan Project (LAMP) sounds impressive, but it is negligible compared to the $6.5 billion overall budget of the Los Angeles School District. Another pebble in the Mississippi.

"Philanthropic money is not going to make a difference until public money is used more effectively," asserts Tony Ciopolone of the Annie Casey Foundation. "And even then," he adds, "it will take a very long time to bring innovations to scale. Public education is the most complex system in our society, with more moving parts than any other. The best role that foundations can hope to play in the ongoing quest for better schools is as catalysts of reform."[21] In the process, of course, they must also foot the bill for persuading the public that implementing new systems will be worth the price.

Given these enormous costs and the limitations they impose, what is the proper role of philanthropy? Are grants to think tanks that create models of reform sufficient? Or should foundations also be funding community organizations that demand more of public schools, while providing for carefully targeted research to support their arguments?

Unfortunately, as we shall see in the following chapters, foundations are generally reluctant to support such forms of public advocacy.

So What Works?

The problem is old, the solution unfound.
—Roger Benjamin, The Rand Corporation

Understandably, there is strong competition and disagreement among practitioners in the vast and varied world of education about reform, and about the role that foundations should play in the process. What works? What doesn't work? Who's doing the right thing, and who is wasting time? Did Walter Annenberg get good or bad advice from Vartan Gregorian? Is he or is he not pouring half a billion dollars down a rat hole? Is reforming practice and organization enough, or should policy be altered as well? Are foundations on the leading edge or the trailing edge of school reform? And can reform possibly work in the absence of well-organized community pressure? These are the questions haunting reform practitioners. And they are the quandaries that keep education grantmakers awake at night, torn between the crying need for higher quality and their own obsessive interest in policy research.

Exacerbating that dilemma is the unproven, but widely accepted belief that spending more money on public schools will not improve student achievement. There are compelling studies supporting both sides of that assertion, but none that are conclusive. So the common wisdom remains an unproven assumption. What seems more certain, more beyond debate—in California at least—is the opposite: that is, less money *does* affect student performance. In 1978 passage of Proposition 13 devastated public school treasuries throughout California. In the twenty-two years since then, the state's education expenditure per student has dropped to $1,000 below the national average and California students' national rankings have fallen gradually from number one to number forty-six.[22] Nationally, urban school districts spend about $600 less per child than nonurban districts; and internationally the United States spends far less per student than most other developed nations. The differences in both cases tend to correlate closely with student achievement.

Educational philanthropists, of course, believe that money can improve performance—if it is invested in the right place. They realize, however, that in order for their relatively small investments to pay off in meaningful improvement, and for reforms to be brought to scale, foundation grants must either be leveraged into massive government appropriations or into community organizations that advocate vigorously for those appropriations. "Foundation money is [merely] the leavening agent for change," Susan Eagan, associate director for education at the Cleveland Foundation, reminds her peers. The trick is "to examine how it can leaven most effectively."

At the root of the foundations' dilemma is a curious reluctance to fund independent evaluation of their initiatives. They spend billions designing and experimenting with reforms but virtually nothing assessing their efficacy. While the Annenberg initiatives, for example, make a small provision for self-examination, they provide even less money for independent trials or research. "Foundations are simply not as interested in accomplishments as they are with being associated with aspirations," according to Theodore Lobman director of the Stuart Foundation in San Francisco, one of the few American foundations that grants virtually all its money to education.[23] The result is a patchwork quilt of donations to innovative projects, with virtually no replication of those that seem to work and scant research to test those that are taken to scale.

"The Food and Drug Administration requires scientific testing before new drugs are prescribed," observes Princeton University economist Alan Krueger, who bemoans the plethora of educational reforms that are introduced without supporting research. "Why should we treat children's minds differently from their bodies? Just as the FDA has created an impressive body of medical knowledge, the Education Department can lead the way to a greater understanding of what works and what doesn't by requiring experimental evaluations before federal dollars are thrown to the philosophical and political winds."[24] Foundations could heed the same advice, as they too are major funders of unproven reforms.

Roger Benjamin, a political economist at the Rand Corporation, concurs. "There is virtually no field evaluation or assessment being done of vast nationwide projects like the Annenberg initiatives," he asserts. "There needs to be beta test sites created in San Francisco and Los Angeles to assess the impact of LAMP and BASRC on their large at-risk populations." Until those tests are performed, Benjamin remains "disappointed" in the Annenberg initiatives, which, he says, are "unfocused."

"Good intentions are not good enough." Benjamin and Rand would, of course, be delighted to conduct the research.[25]

In response to advocates of unbiased research, the Annenberg Initiative recently began contracting with independent evaluators. Perhaps suspecting that they would not be invited back for a second round if they were too rough on the initiative, most have been as positive about the program as Annenberg's internal assessors. Herein lies a major dilemma for all organized philanthropy—rigorous evaluation and open accountability—two persistent themes of subsequent chapters.

The fear expressed by so many observers of educational reform, that 25 to 30 percent of American students are being left behind is, according to Benjamin, "legitimate." "We are in deep trouble," he says. "Large schools are not educating new immigrants and the urban poor. This is the challenge." And he repeats the advice Vartan Gregorian offered to Walter Annenberg: "We are going to need a Marshall Plan."[26]

Impatience

Education may be the one area of the non-profit sector where the rigidity of thought is worse than it is in philanthropy itself.
—Robert Bothwell, president emeritus, National Committee on Responsive Philanthropy

American educational philanthropy has been motivated by many impulses, ranging from the sublime Jeffersonian quest for an enlightened citizenry to the ridiculous train-the-kids-in-math-to-compete-with-the-Russians response to Sputnik. As they have in so many fields of endeavor, foundations have been mercurial and unpredictable, flitting in and out of the education field like moths on a light bulb, befuddled by jargon like "reculturing," "higher-order thinking," "child-centered pedagogy," "problem-based learning," and "brain-based instruction." (Is there any other kind?).

Foundations that take an interest in education are likely to fund massive three-year pilot projects or "boutique" reviews of higher education, then just as abruptly abandon the entire field. The Packard Foundation recently did just that after a few years of frustrated educational grantmaking during which they became the third-largest foundation funding American education.

Few foundation trustees seem to realize that restructuring public education is not like inventing a heart valve or opening an orphanage. It requires a full generation of patience, as the glacial process of reform proceeds, innovation by innovation, district by district, school by school, classroom by classroom—constrained at every step by poverty, race, class, and the attendant challenges they impose. Each step needs field testing, followed by persistent lobbying and, of course, more money. And above all, there must be a willingness to fail, a quality for which American foundations are not famous. Though program officers persistently use the language of venture capitalism, they are generally as risk-averse as they are impatient.

"There can be no systematic reform in schools unless donors and grantees take risks," Theodore Lobman reminds his peers. "High risk in search of high return is what venture capital is all about."[27] He might also have counseled patience. Twenty-five-year commitments are clearly required, but three-years-and-you're-out remains common practice. And, Lobman might have added, the unintended consequences of philanthropic failure rarely fall upon the foundations. It is generally their grantees and the communities that feel the brunt of misguided grantmaking. In the case of education, most of the communities involved cannot endure much more failure.

Patience appears to be a quality more common to conservative foundations and other proponents of privatization than to those of liberal bent. "Privatization serves as both an ends and a means," wrote Sally Covington, while working at the National Committee for Responsive Philanthropy. "As an 'end' it reflects conservatism's belief that the market is the most efficient mechanism for the delivery of services. As a 'means' conservatives advocate privatization as a mechanism to distribute power from the government to the private sector," a process they know will take many years, if not decades, to complete.[28]

Conclusion

There can be no education without controversy.
—Rowan Gaither, former president, Ford Foundation

The eternal question regarding the collective intent of educational philanthropy is whether wealth is being employed to create an intellectual vanguard trained to protect the interests (industrial and familial) of their class, or whether the intentions of philanthropists are purely philanthropic—that is, enacted for "the love of humanity." Is the Jeffersonian imperative or the selfish gene at work here? This is not an easy question to answer. The probable answer is—both.

Foundation trustees do seem to favor the spawning of an elite intellectual force over the principle of equal educational opportunity. The great preponderance of educational grants made since Carnegie and Rockefeller created the first great education trusts, have, after all, found their way to institutions of higher education where scientists and other experts are educated. Were love of humanity the primary motive of educational philanthropy wouldn't the ratio between lower and higher education be reversed?

Andrew Carnegie, the individual, certainly saw the value of an enlightened citizenry. Otherwise he would not have created twenty-eight hundred public libraries. And he obviously valued equal opportunity, or he would have not have provided scholarships to the working-class children of Scottish veterans of the Boer War. Yet the grants made by Carnegie's foundations, even while he was alive, seem much less motivated by a desire for social equity than by an impulse to strengthen the social and scientific contexts of industrial capitalism.

Like Rockefeller's, and perhaps most original donors', Carnegie's philanthropic motives and intentions seemed mixed and at times conflicted—not only between expertise and democracy but also between charity and philanthropy. Religion was certainly at work in that dichotomy, alongside expediency. But it also seems clear that in the minds of both men, protection of economic interests went hand in hand with human welfare.

The struggle within the philanthropic community between the impulses to create a scientific elite and to foster an educated electorate persists to this day. "Expertise is necessary in a modern society," Columbia University historian Ellen Lagemann wrote in 1989, "but efforts to nurture expertise without correlated efforts to promote education will erode the basis of democracy. Education is therefore the only way out of an impossible choice between unacceptable alternatives—on the one hand expertise, on the other democracy."[29]

It is reasonable to assume, when examining philanthropic choices, that each grant, whether made by an individual or a board of trustees, embodies its own exclusive set of motives. There is, and always will be, a tension between motives of fostering knowledge for instrumental purposes and for human welfare. Overlaying that tension, of course, is the age-old clash between traditionalism and progressivism, between the followers of John Calvin and those of John Dewey.

Beneath the idealism that continues to drive American educational philanthropy lies the utilitarian impulse of those earliest philanthropists, men who saw an educated work force as the sine qua non of a productive economy fit to compete with the great commercial states of Europe. For them, the vital priority of education was to provide industry with both an educated cadre of brilliant scientists and engineers in every field of technology and a disciplined, factory-ready work force. Thomas Jefferson might, with very great reluctance, have concurred with that goal—for his own ideal was a citizenry of independent agriculturalists—but he might also have questioned the industrialists' policy of favoring elite private institutions of higher learning over public schools. And he would certainly have asked how that priority strengthened and served the institutions of democracy.

What educational philanthropists seem to have learned after a century of cautious grantmaking is that the Jeffersonian dream is a vision with many components. To be attained, every level of education, every class of student, and every school district in the country would have to be nurtured. We ignore one branch or level of education at the peril of the rest. If money pours into private research universities while the quality of entering students declines, what purpose is served? If Wall Street's education corporations turn the corner and make a profit for shareholders, what purpose is served? If suburban children receive excellent education while inner-city youngsters struggle with illiteracy, what purpose is served? And if money is showered upon schools and school districts without attending to the social systems in which they are embedded, how can educational reform succeed?

3

Science

All important fields of activity, from the breeding of bees to the administration of an empire, call for an understanding of the spirit and techniques of modern science. It is the key to [such] dominion as man may exercise over his physical environment.
—Wickliffe Rose, President, General Education Board, 1923

The world would be a very different place if the American government or the corporate sector had seen fit to fund science, particularly the social sciences, before early–twentieth-century philanthropists asserted their influence and shaped research priorities for the next thirty years or more. Although in more recent times they have remained far in the background of science funding, foundations are beginning once again to support basic research and to exert influence over the direction of scientific discovery.

With government support for many sciences either at a standstill or in decline, and corporate philanthropy guided primarily by competitive self-interest, visionary scientists are looking with renewed interest toward private philanthropy. And, as luck would have it, foundations that have previously paid no attention to matters scientific are reconsidering their guidelines and supporting research—most of it biological, all of it leading edge, and a lot of it very controversial.

Thus it is a good time to reexamine the last century of science philanthropy. Although paltry compared with both America's total investment in science and overall private philanthropy (it constitutes less than 5 percent of the latter), historically foundation funding has played a major role in shaping modern scientific disciplines, especially interdisciplinary fields. Moreover, science philanthropy has had a profound influence on education and on educational philanthropy as a whole.

"To understand the history of research," according to Princeton University Professor Stanley Katz, "we must analyze the systematic behavior of funding agencies [because] major trends in research are ordinarily the result of funding decisions, [which] constitute intellectual policies."[1] "Follow the money" is the way a journalist might say the same thing. Either way, it is instructive to compare privately funded scientific research with projects supported by government agencies and corporations, both of which have had their own agendas for science and have sought to mediate intellectual policy through research funding. Foundation interests, however, tend to be more complex.

In the late nineteenth and early twentieth centuries research scientists received little or no support from either government or corporate funders. They turned, quite naturally, to private philanthropists, three of whom responded with great enthusiasm and generosity. John D. Rockefeller Sr. and Andrew Carnegie took a particular interest in the physical and life sciences, while Margaret Olivia Slocum Sage, widow of Russell Sage and then the wealthiest woman in America, favored the social sciences. Later, when Rockefeller and Carnegie saw the wisdom of her preference, the three foundations joined together to shape the future of American social science.

Before then, a handful of large foundations led by Rockefeller brought scientific research into the American university—simply by deciding that the academy was a more appropriate setting for research than hospitals, private laboratories, or government agencies. Even more significant than their creation of the research university was the direction in which the early foundations quite deliberately steered American scientists—away from speculation and theory and toward empiricism, utilitarianism, and problems of immediate public urgency. And in this era of rapid industrialization it is not surprising that to foundation trustees business urgency was synonymous with public urgency.

As most secrets of the rich and famous went with them to their graves, it is difficult to discern their deepest philanthropic motives. Observers have attributed the actions of the early philanthropists in funding scientific and medical research to everything from love of humanity to rank imperialistic self-interest; and, though based on pure conjecture, there is probably some truth to most of their theories (see box insert "Class and Philanthropy").

Class and Philanthropy

American philanthropists are a "class" in economic terms only. Socially and politically, millionaires and billionaires reflect the broad spectrum of American society. In our trailer courts live cads and princes, geniuses and idiots, saints and sinners—just as they do in our executive suites and country clubs. Most philanthropists are well educated, but a few are illiterate. Parvenus outnumber (but rarely outlast) the cotillion polo-pony set; and there are enough socialist millionaires around the country to create a sizable private club. Some of them become significant philanthropists, though they seldom make serious trouble for the system that made them rich.

The same broad assortment of social caste and politics can be found in foundation founders, who range in philosophy and philanthropic purpose from John Olin and Richard Mellon Scaife on the Right to Adam Hochschild and the Stern family on the Left. In between are the less-political mainstreamers, including those whose large foundations are household-names. And foundations themselves contain trustees and staff with a detectable span of ideas and social philosophies. This variety, of course, leads to endless debates about whether Ford, MacArthur, Rockefeller, Pew, and Carnegie are liberal or conservative, progressive or retrogressive foundations. They are all of the above, of course; which, as with individual philanthropists, makes classifying them a pointless pastime.

John D. Rockefeller Sr. and his trusted associate, Frederick Gates, agreed with Carnegie's view, as expressed in *Gospel of Wealth,* that strategically applied philanthropy could shape educational curricula, influence government, and—perhaps most important of all—make science the handmaiden of industry. Moreover, although Rockefeller, Carnegie, and Olivia Sage were the first to realize the potential of science philanthropy for public policy, many others soon followed suit.

As noted in the last chapter, Rockefeller and Carnegie saw knowledge as vital to the advancement of civilization and considered its production just as essential to an industrial nation as the production of steel and oil. For them science was the most important university discipline, and the well-educated engineer its most essential product. In addition, the two men shared the fear, repeatedly expressed in their letters, essays, and memoranda, that if the champions of industry didn't set the agenda for science, "the wordy Socialists" would do it for them. If that happened, they were convinced, all their investments would perish.[2]

Olivia Sage saw things a bit differently. While her hard-driving, parsi-monious husband Russell was making millions in New York real estate, she was teaching school and doing charity work. When he died in 1906 she was eighty years old but determined to start a new life centered on philanthropy. In 1907, at last unrestrained from her stingy, uncharitable mate, she drafted a charter calling for the "permanent improvement of social conditions." She named her new foundation, perversely, after her husband, who would surely have turned violently in his grave at the very idea that social conditions needed to be improved.

The Russell Sage Foundation was, and remains today, a hybrid grantmaking and operating foundation dedicated almost solely to social research. And, unlike the Rockefeller and Carnegie foundations, the Sage has never shied away from public advocacy. The titles of its first depart-ments—in particular, "Child Helping," "Child Hygiene," "Recreation," and "Women's Work"—reflect that motivation. For the next thirty years Sage, which was staffed largely by sociologists and social workers, pub-lished scores of well-documented reports on social problems and distrib-uted them to reformers across the country. It drafted model legislation, not only for child welfare and improved working conditions for women but also for anti-loan shark statutes and reform of the juvenile courts.

In 1933 Sage Foundation staffers arrived in Washington to assist in drafting New Deal legislation that created thousands of federal jobs for social workers and social scientists and created a whole new class of gov-ernment experts. At the time, Rockefeller and Carnegie trustees seemed suspicious of "social engineering" and were convinced that the depression was proving the futility of social science. From early in the century, their funding had leaned heavily toward the safe, utilitarian work of physics and chemistry. Grants for economic and social research were unusual. Although their interests had always gone beyond the creation of pure knowledge, in an era of troubling social change the ultimate quarry of Rockefeller and Carnegie science funding remained new technologies and products to strengthen private industry and bolster a faltering corporate capitalism.

Not until the 1930s, when social conditions and turmoil threatened their economic interests, did the Rockefeller and Carnegie foundations pay attention to the work and priorities of Olivia Sage. Before then, the closest either came to support for social science was Rockefeller's interest in medical research; and even there his interests were utilitarian. Whereas traditional medical charity supports nonprofit hospitals, cancer clinics, and hospice centers, utilitarian medical philanthropy like Rockefeller's builds medical schools, research laboratories, and public health institutions. While the rhetoric was humanitarian, the purpose was utilitarian: to improve the health and maximize the functional efficiency of "human resources."

Disease-specific research oriented toward public health was, in fact, aimed explicitly at ensuring a productive labor force. Even the Rockefeller Commission's eradication of hookworm in the opening years of the century, regarded by medical historians as a triumph of humanitarian philanthropy, was not a purely compassionate initiative. Economic interest in combating "cotton mill anemia," later identified as "the germ of laziness," was openly expressed by Rockefeller Foundation President Frederick Gates. He observed that "it takes by actual count, about 25 percent more laborers to secure the same result in counties where the [hookworm] infection is heavier. . . . This is why the stocks of such mills are lower and the profits lighter."[3] Even Charles Wardell Stiles, the brilliant Department of Agriculture zoologist who persuaded Rockefeller's "medicine men" that the labor-debilitating hookworm disease was epidemic in the South, in 1904 beseeched his fellow scientists not to "leave out of consideration the economic effect which [our] theories and hypotheses may produce."[4]

For the first quarter of the twentieth century, Rockefeller was the largest single source of support for medical research in the United States. The Rockefeller Sanitary Commission for the Eradication of Hookworm Disease alone provided $65 million. Hookworm was almost completely eliminated, and the industrial work force of the South became noticeably more productive.[5] Systems developed by Stiles and the Sanitary Commission to combat the disease, a convergence of scientific medicine and public education, became a model for public health programs around the world.

In 1909 Andrew Carnegie's first grant to science—$10 million to the Carnegie Institution of Washington—was larger than the entire endowment of Harvard University. In fact, it matched the combined research endowments of all the universities in the country.[6] Carnegie believed that philanthropy should support basic science research in order to develop exceptional scientists. The consequence, he believed, would be a more powerful and wealthier nation. And the fastest route to power and wealth for America, he was convinced, was through chemistry. "If there is a millionaire in the land who is at a loss for what to do with the surplus that has been committed to him as trustee," he wrote in 1889, "let him investigate the good that is flowing from chemical laboratories."[7]

Rockefeller, on the other hand, seemed to prefer physics. In 1891, when he created the University of Chicago, he set aside a special fund for scientific research; the university used it to lure to its faculty Albert Michelson, the first American to win a Nobel Prize in physics. Gates also persuaded Rockefeller to support medical research on a long-term basis. "Disease with its attendant evils is undoubtedly the main single source of human misery," Gates wrote his boss, who was already intrigued by the immunological advances of Louis Pasteur.[8] In 1901 JDR created the Rockefeller Institute for Medical Research in New York, modeling it directly on the Pasteur Institute. He pledged the institute $20,000 a year for ten years. Within six years it had identified the cause of several diseases and Rockefeller was granting it millions of dollars. By then he was convinced that organized philanthropy itself should be "a search for cause, an attempt to cure evils at their source."[9]

Meanwhile the Carnegie Institution was supporting and controlling ten major scientific laboratories, principally for basic research in astronomy, geophysical sciences, evolutionary biology, and plant genetics. In 1911 Andrew Carnegie was so pleased with the results that he endowed the institution with an additional $10 million. Not to be outgranted, Rockefeller poured even more money into his own institute, where Simon Flexner pursued research based on the belief that combining physical and chemical research would lead to vital discoveries in medicine.

It was quite natural for Carnegie and Rockefeller to place science at the center of their philanthropy, for science was at the center of their businesses. The chemical and geological sciences were particularly vital to oil and steel production, which were at the forefront of all nineteenth-century, science-based industries. Their mutual interests grew out of a deep respect for what science could do: generating knowledge meant making money. And for both men advancing science meant advancing American prestige in the world. Carnegie often complained of "our national poverty in science" and sought, by funding scientific endeavor and harnessing science to industry, to "change our position among nations."[10] And it worked.

In the opening decades of the century, major American corporations, realizing the value of scientific development, began establishing their own research laboratories modeled on those of the Rockefeller and Carnegie institutes. However, as their research was directed toward specific corporate interests, it was shrouded in secrecy. Corporate scientists did not announce their discoveries until they were patented inventions; nor did they publish their work in peer-reviewed journals. Thus research in the basic physical, biological, and social sciences was dominated by a few retiring titans of business like Carnegie and JDR, unusual men who had risen slightly above their industrial domains and seen that the public interest was inseparable from their own corporate interests.

Once established as arbiters of science, leaders of the two largest American foundations were able to convince state and federal governments that funding science was sound policy, and, in terms of national defense, good strategy. State governments, too, had begun supporting scientific research at state universities, and presidents of public universities became masterful fundraisers for science. Finding that corporations were initially unwilling to support any research that could be shared with competitors, universities focused their fundraising mostly on foundations, the freer offsprings of corporate wealth, which were eager to support innovative research.

Although Carnegie and Rockefeller's early science philanthropy went largely to their own institutes, they gradually extended it to support basic research at major universities. In twenty years they had created an American scientific elite, two-thirds of whom taught and conducted research at the California Institute of Technology (Caltech), Princeton, Cornell, Vanderbilt, Harvard, Stanford, Rochester, and the University of Chicago. In 1919 the Carnegie Corporation looked beyond the university grant-shed and presented $5 million to the National Academy of Sciences to construct a headquarters building in Washington. That same year another $5-million check went to the National Research Council (NRC). Although foundation president Raymond Fosdick heralded the grant as "the beginning of Carnegie aid to natural sciences," the NRC promoted principally research in engineering and the industrial applications of science.[11] In the interwar years six- and seven-figure contributions to such institutions became increasingly common.

The grants to the NRC and similar institutions established a practice that organized philanthropy has followed since: investment of private money in the private sector for the purpose of creating public policy. Trustees believed that "governing would be improved if impartial science were brought to bear in an advisory capacity," writes Ken Prewitt, a former vice president of the Rockefeller Foundation, now a prominent scholar of philanthropy.[12]

Hard Science

We are sometimes called elitist. We gladly accept.
—Albert Rees, President, Alfred P. Sloan Foundation

World War I had stimulated research in radio communication, chemistry, aviation, and meteorology and heightened the foundations' interest in science philanthropy. Observing German military mobilization, Carnegie Corporation trustee and former secretary of war Elihu Root predicted that "the prizes of industrial and commercial leadership will fall to the nation which organizes its scientific forces most effectively."[13] Columbia University economist Wesley C. Mitchell, who had served on the War Industries Board, was convinced that limitations of knowledge were hampering American industrial progress. "Are we not intelligent enough," he asked. "to devise a steadier and more certain method of progress?"[14] Wickliffe Rose heard the call.

In 1923 Rose was chosen head of the General Education Board, by then the largest of Rockefeller's seven foundations. Rose believed that "the promotion of the development of science in a country is germinal; it affects the entire system of education and carries with it the remaking of a civilization."[15] Convinced that American scientists needed to work side by side with their superior European peers, Rose proposed creation of the International Education Board. In 1924 Rockefeller trustees voted the new board $28 million for transatlantic collaborative research.

The board quickly became the central bank of Western science. It made generous grants to universities in thirty-five nations and enabled European scientists like Niels Bohr and Werner Heisenberg to become household names in the American academy. Through the General Education Board, American researchers at Harvard, Stanford, Princeton, the University of Chicago, and Caltech received millions of dollars in research grants. "Make the peaks higher" was Wickliffe Rose's repeated battle cry. By the late 1920s the United States had become preeminent in quantum mechanics, nuclear physics, and aeronautics and was rapidly gaining ground over Europe in other sciences.

A handful of social critics were concerned that the dominance of applied science would lead to the "degradation of learning," and some feared that a few large trusts located in the East were dictating scholarship nationally. But on the whole there was little resistance to the Rockefeller/Carnegie initiatives until the depression, when reformers began to call for applying the tools of science to social problems.

Warren Weaver, director of natural sciences at the Rockefeller Foundation in the 1930s, agreed. "Science," he argued, should contribute to the welfare of mankind, not solely to the economic interests of industry and a few philanthropists. "The past fifty or one hundred years have seen a marvelous development in physics and chemistry," he wrote, "but hope for the future of mankind depends in a basic way on the development in the next fifty years of a new biology and a new psychology."[16] He called for a shift to what he called "vital processes," traveling the country and sending scouts around the world to find worthy grantees. Chemists were prompted to study physics, and physicists were encouraged to apply for biology grants.

Thus began an era when the private support of hard science shifted from self-interested utilitarian initiatives to the funding of science for the sake of knowledge about life itself. At the same time, foundation trustees and executives were developing a cautious interest in the burgeoning social sciences.

Strategic Benevolence

Philanthropy is not about building science. Its about building a better society.
—Ken Prewitt, Social Science Research Council

According to historian Barry Karl, social science was "given its special character for much this century by common values shared with those who created and managed the first foundations."[17] As a consequence, Ken Prewitt believes, early social scientists "had ambitions that reached far beyond knowledge seeking. The social sciences [they came to believe] could and should provide the systematic intelligence that a twentieth century industrial democracy required if it were to cope with the flood of new social problems that followed in the wake of the industrial revolution."[18]

This conviction was in part a reaction to ideas that were floating around the social scientific community, ideas that were deeply disturbing to early philanthropists. The wisest response to the notion that social pathologies were created by economic conditions, they decided, was to fund social science; through the grantmaking process, philanthropists could guide practitioners away from cures for social ills that threatened corporate interests. Thus a kind of scientism that dictated political and value neutrality came to prevail in the academic social sciences.

Foundation trustees encouraged program officers to create a new scientific orthodoxy in which poverty, criminality, and other social problems were seen as the result of specific individual dysfunctions. Such problems could then be treated by social workers trained at selected institutes of social research and service. Social ills, the new dogma preached, could be cured by science. The approved model was the aforementioned Rockefeller hookworm project, which had discovered, through objective research, the disease germ causing a social and economic problem and combated it directly, through public policy.

Germ theory, in fact, became the guiding metaphor for social ills. "Social diseases," like medical diseases, were linked to specific causal agents. Medical disease led to human misery, and so did social disease. According to this logic, poverty, violence, and juvenile delinquency could be eliminated by finding their causes and eliminating them. Just as scientific medicine healed the body, so social science would heal the body politic, obviating the need for advocacy and political action.

"Social research could be disinterested and nonpartisan," writes Prewitt, "that is, free of the corrupting influence of political parties and from populist pressures."[19] The core disciplines of social science—anthropology, economics, political science, psychology, and sociology—if privately funded—could also provide an antidote to the leftist ideas that had entered the American political discourse in the late nineteenth and early twentieth centuries, principally) in the minds of immigrant radicals. Thus, in the opening years of the twentieth century, and again during the depression of the 1930s when capitalism once more came under attack, the foundations quite deliberately employed the social sciences to quell revolutionary fervor.

The private funding of social science also became a quest for the authority to address the intractable social problems that attended the decline of family farming, heavy industrialization, boom-bust economic cycles, immigration, and urbanization. Funders favored social scientists whose explanations of poverty, labor violence, and such social evils as prostitution and juvenile crime were articulated in terms of prudent social reform. If the voices of moderation were not encouraged and published, then, almost certainly, radicals crying out for a new political order and collectivist economic doctrines would prevail.

In the early years of the century, this compromise between the voices of reform and laissez-faire capitalist values had taken the form of Progressivism, an incrementalist strategy promoted by journalists, judges, antimonopolists, social reformers, and centrist national leaders like presidents Theodore Roosevelt and Woodrow Wilson. Its ideas were cautiously supported by philanthropists like Carnegie and Rockefeller, whose own interests were under attack. The philanthropists, however, remained optimistic that even the most intractable national problems could be solved through science. With its emphasis on public administration and municipal reform, Progressivism mediated social change gradually, at a pace fast enough to stabilize political structures and slow enough to preserve the status quo. Best of all, it was accomplished without a major redistribution of wealth. Quite naturally, Progressivism was unpopular with social critics of the Left and Right. Both blamed the foundations for its undesirable consequences, as if philanthropy had created the movement.

Unlike such European countries as Germany and England, where the social sciences (and social services) were often supported by the state, early American social scientists and reformers were virtual wards of private charity. From early in the century and through the depression and World War II—indeed until the 1950s' founding of the National Science Foundation (the first federal agency to fund social science research)—foundation grants provided leading-edge social scientists independence from government control or influence. That independence did not mean, of course, that they were free to design their own research and create their own protocols. Foundation trustees' own private biases were reflected in their funding decisions, and restrictions were often placed on research.

Even much later, after creation of the NSF, the combined social science grants of the Rockefeller, Carnegie, and Ford foundations still equaled the federal government's appropriation for such research. In the first twelve years after World War II the Ford Foundation alone gave $14 million to Harvard University, $10 million to the University of Chicago, and $3 million to Stanford University to foster carefully selected social science research in areas not supported by the government. Ford's approach has been called "strategic benevolence," as it deliberately sought ways to address dislocations in society without challenging "basic political and moral principles." In the post–World War II era any such challenge would almost certainly have raised the ire of Congressman B. Carroll Reese and Senator Joseph McCarthy.

"The tacit goals of social science in the early Cold War were prediction, not prescription; social adjustment, not social change," according to historian Rebecca Lowen, whose recent *Creating the Cold War University* (1997) documents how behavorism became the social science paradigm favored by private philanthropists. The "behavioral revolution," an attempt to make social science research hard and exact enough to be considered true science, was, Lowen believes, "the intellectual fallout of McCarthyism."[20]

Ford-funded social scientists pursued the study of behavior, quite deliberately avoiding political philosophy, ideology, psychoanalysis, organizational analysis, and studies related to class and race. In fact, two scientists hired to advise Ford trustees on how best to "improve scientific knowledge of individual behavior and human relations" were recruited directly from the Rand Corporation, where they had worked on Project Troy, a top secret study of psychological warfare.[21] At Ford, the two social scientists proposed and conducted studies on the stability of totalitarian governments.[22] Once again, scientism had prevailed, although this time it was motivated not by the perceived expediencies of corporate capitalism but out of fear of political red-baiting. That was not, of course, the first time that political pressures had influenced science philanthropy, nor would it be the last.

In the early decades of the century, for example, John D. Rockefeller's eagerness to support social science had been strongly tempered by recent personal experience. The Supreme Court was threatening to break up his Standard Oil Trust (it did so in 1911). And in 1913 the Ludlow massacre, in which eleven women and two children were burned to death in an antistrike action by the Colorado Fuel and Iron Company (a Rockefeller holding) was met with national outrage. Shortly after, the U.S. Commission on Industrial Relations under Congressman Frank Walsh commenced its investigation into "philanthropic trusts," which Walsh saw as serious threats to democracy that held "arbitrary power over the destinies of other men." Foundations, he averred, were a potential shadow government of plutocrats and a threat to the objectivity of science. Walsh's research director, Basil Manly, warned that the "domination of men in whose hands the final control of a large part of American industry rests is not limited to their employees, but is being rapidly extended to control the education and social service of the nation."[23] In Walsh's opinion, "research workers and teachers cannot be subsidized with money obtained from the exploitation of workers without being profoundly influenced in their points of view and in the energy and enthusiasm with which they might otherwise attack economic abuses."[24]

Walsh clearly distrusted Rockefeller's answers to questions about the Ludlow episode. So did American Federation of Labor President Samuel Gompers, who argued that JDR Jr.'s positions on the boards of both the foundation and the corporation made an objective assessment of the incident, or of labor relations in general, impossible. Walsh described the Rockefeller charitable trusts as "a menace to the welfare of society" and as mere attempts "to present to the world, a handsome and admirable economic and industrial regime that draws its substance from the sweat, blood and tears of exploited and dispossessed humanity."[25] He looked askance at the foundation's social science funding, which the Rockefellers promptly suspended for ten years.

However, the Laura Spelman Memorial Fund (a subsidiary Rockefeller foundation cleverly given the maiden name of Rockefeller's wife) remained actively engaged in social science research. Under the leadership of sociologist Beardsley Ruml, the Spelman funded scholars exploring learning theories, gestalt psychology, intelligence testing, and community dynamics. During the 1920s Ruml granted over $20 million to social scientists. It was the only decade in which more Rockefeller funds were spent on social science than on any other field. And, although it was the decade in which Progressivism waned politically, its influence in the social sciences persisted. According to Prewitt, "approximately 80 percent of the scholars who dominated the research agenda of social sciences in the 1920s and 1930s appear in the files of the Spelman and Rockefeller Foundations."[26]

After Ruml left the Spelman Fund in 1933, it was merged completely into the Rockefeller Foundation, and Raymond Fosdick assumed responsibility for social science grantmaking. Fosdick was as convinced as Ruml that support for social sciences should be "based on the belief that the understanding and control of human phenomena lie in the scientific analysis and appraisal of facts." He lamented that social studies had fallen behind the natural and laboratory sciences and wanted to "give impetus to a new kind of realism in social science."[27]

Fosdick also agreed with Warren Weaver about the value of biology and pushed his trustees to support a policy of funding only physics and chemistry projects that addressed biological problems—particularly the biological determinants of mental health. Fosdick was worried that "the physical sciences [had] outstripped man's capacity to absorb them" and that "a serious lag had developed between our rapid scientific advance and our stationary ethical development."[28] He also believed that "this titanic tool of science "could "bring into fresh focus the enigma of the universe, its apparent order, its beauty, its power" as an antidote to the rampant nationalism that was again sweeping through Europe. Finally, Fosdick was confident that the social sciences were mature enough to be used to combat specific social problems. It was time, he urged, to place twenty-five years of social research at the service of America. By 1938, according to the U.S. Civil Service Commission, seventy-eight hundred social scientists were working in various branches of the federal government.

While in the interwar period social science was considered suspect by right-wing politicians and pundits (and remains so today), the scholars supported by Ruml and Fosdick were, within the context of their professions, quite conservative. The preponderance of Spelman and Rockefeller social science grants went to such institutes of higher education as the University of Chicago. Very little was provided to independent scientists, unless they were employed by foundation-created think tanks like the Social Science Research Council or the National Bureau of Economic Research. Not one grant was made to the decidedly liberal New School for Social Research in New York.

As they had in the physical sciences, Ruml and other funders encouraged interdisciplinary social research, pressing psychologists, anthropologists, and sociologists to collaborate in their studies of social problems. Like the supporters of the exact sciences, the funders of social sciences were utilitarian pragmatists displaying "no interest in the promotion of scientific research as an end in itself"; their motive "was not sheer curiosity as to how various social and human phenomenon came to be . . . but as a means to an end . . . the advancement of human welfare."[29] Their aim was to support the "systematic social intelligence" that should inform human affairs.

The most overt, though belated, public expression of Progressivism came during the presidency of Herbert Hoover. Unlike the presidents who preceded him, Hoover thought that scientific and engineering experts could temper business cycles and that social research could provide government policymakers with rational guidance. He also had no reservations about using private philanthropy to prove his point. With a five-hundred-thousand-dollar grant he personally requested from the Rockefeller Foundation he retained Wesley Mitchell and University of Chicago political scientist Charles Merriam to survey social trends in America and report their findings directly to the government. Hoover planned to use the data to guide the nation out of the depression. The survey would be, Hoover promised, "the first thorough statement of social fact ever presented as a guide to public policy."

However, while Merriam and Mitchell and their researchers toiled, Hoover lost his bid for a second term. Their two-volume report, *Recent Social Trends in the United States,* released in January of 1933, came too late; the global scope of the depression had made social trends of far less interest than economic data. Yet the very act of asking a philanthropic foundation to fund a government study established a formal link between privately funded social experts and government offices. Eventually it led to the proliferation of think tanks—the thousand or more foundation-supported research institutes that now abound in America's state and federal capitals.

Scientists at these think tanks quickly discovered, to the joy of their foundation benefactors, that statistics were often enough to advance progress in a desired direction. Document a problem with sound numbers, perhaps backed up by a survey or two, present them to Congress in credibly packaged reports, and peaceful reform would often follow.

Labor union organizers, too, found that statistics on employment and wages could help them press effectively for laws and regulations on working conditions and union organizing. Statistics documenting poverty led gradually to acceptance of the idea of a social safety net and, eventually, to the creation of state and national welfare systems. Increasingly, statistically based economic indicators were used to formulate federal monetary and fiscal policy.

When their trustees and officers realized the persuasive power of numbers, the Rockefeller philanthropies deliberately detached the social sciences from law and moral philosophy and grounded them in statistical quantification and empirical research. Their aim was twofold: first, to give social sciences institutional legitimacy; second, to link them directly to matters of government policy. Thus social science was separated from social advocacy (just as, earlier, social science had been separated from social work). In later years, of course, the Rockefeller Foundation joined with many others in the advocating public policies that flowed directly from the social research they funded.

This reliance on social statistics to inform public policy was the second great shift in American philanthropic thinking. The first was expressed in Carnegie's repudiation of charity in favor of a philanthropy that sought to identify and eradicate the root causes of poverty and other social problems. Rockefeller, who also eschewed charity as the motive for wholesale philanthropy, said of his choice in 1909: "The best philanthropy is constantly in search of finalities—a search for cause, an attempt to cure evils at their source."[30] That statement signaled a sharp departure from the common charitable practice of treating symptoms. Approximately thirty years later, using statistics and indices as tools of quantitative analysis led foundation-funded social scientists to advocate complex social programs they thought would prevent depression and misery. Such progress would also, of course, assure national prosperity.

The Carnegie grants for statistical research to the National Research Council, and Rockefeller's to the Social Science Research Council and the National Bureau of Economic Research, culminated in the 1927 creation of the Brookings Institution. Brookings, a bastion of statistical analysis that has since evolved into a private-public hybrid, provides frequent economic and social guidance to both political parties.

During its first ten years of existence, Carnegie granted the Brookings Institution $1.65 million. Founder Robert Somers Brookings, a St. Louis businessman, sought to balance the board of his new think tank with a mixture of "conservatives and capitalists" (as if there were some distinction). Bankers predominated. Although the institution drew immediate fire from populist politicians suspicious of private bankers' advisory role over government policy, Brookings grew into a Washington fixture and remains one today.

The establishment of Brookings consummated what Prewitt describes as "a marriage of philanthropy to a theory of government that needed to be steered by rational, empirical, disinterested scientific advice."[31] Brookings continues to be a favorite of the large foundations. Between 1955 and 1967 the Ford Foundation gave the institute almost $40 million.

In the years since, social science has attracted the interest of more and more foundations. It has even become the central focus of philanthropists like George Soros, who is intent on constructing vibrant civil societies in emerging democracies, particularly in Eastern Europe. Following the lead of Soros's Open Society Institute, the Ford, Carnegie, Rockefeller, Olin, MacArthur, Bradley, Merck, McKnight, and Mellon foundations have all made substantial grants to social scientists in that region.

"Was this philanthropic concern for efficiency and improved social policy not itself motivated by the desire to control the state on behalf of the capitalist class?" asks Prewitt. Although he doesn't answer the question, he does allow that there were alternatives to the strategy adopted by philanthropists, "the most obvious being to adopt an operations method of attack on social problems." Such a method would be similar to Rockefeller's early approach to public health in which "the purpose was not to study diseases like hookworm and yellow fever so much as to eradicate them." Later Rockefeller officers and trustees, however, clearly feared that "a staff directed, field-based operational attack on social issues would have invited the accusation that those in change of the vast private wealth of the Rockefellers were meddling in politics."[32] It was better, they decided, to remain neutral, objective, nonpartisan, and, above all, avoid public advocacy. The statistical approach conveys just such an appearance of neutrality.

This is not to suggest that foundation-supported scientists were themselves neutral or indifferent to social crisis—often quite the contrary. But their language was laced with facts, not prescriptions, partly because placing facts before policymakers yielded better results than advocacy but also because their benefactors would have it no other way. The legacy of foundation-funded social sciences was thus to create, concludes Prewitt, "an infrastructure for research and training that permanently altered their role in American society."[33] As we see in chapter 9 (Civility), America would be well into the civil rights era of the 1960s before a handful of small, virtually unknown foundations began to support advocacy based on social science.

From Biology to National Defense

We're not an oxygen tank, we're an incubator of ideas.
—Vartan Gregorian, President, Carnegie Corporation

Warren Weaver's persistent encouragement of the synthesis of physics and biology at Rockefeller eventually led to the formation of the new field of molecular biology, which has produced our current, deeper understanding of the structure and chemical bond of proteins and the biochemistry of genetics. Some historians credit Weaver with inventing both the field and the term *molecular biology*, though Weaver, displaying a modesty uncharacteristic of philanthrocrats, made no such claim. He did accept credit for fostering the new discipline, which pushed the nuclear cyclotron into biological laboratories and placed radioactive isotopes at the service of medicine.

Throughout the 1930s Weaver funded the development of the centrifuge, X-ray defraction, and electrophoresis and the invention of electron microscopy. Nuclear physics flourished, not for its military or energy values but because Weaver had faith in its medical benefits. By 1940 twenty-two cyclotrons had been built or were under construction—all of them used for biomedical, not physical, research.

Weaver prodded scientists onto paths they might never have taken if left to their own devices. University of California physicist Ernest Lawrence, creator of the Berkeley Radiation Lab and namesake of the Lawrence Livermore Laboratory (where much of America's nuclear weaponry was designed), confessed to his colleague Niels Bohr that "one reason we have undertaken biological work is that we thereby have been able to get support for all of the work in the laboratory. As you know it is much easier to get funds for medical research."[34]

However, as war raged again through Europe in the 1940s, government-supported scientists shifted their talents to military systems. Scores of physicists who had being applying their knowledge to biological problems were recruited into Pentagon "skunk works"—most notably the Manhattan Project, which developed the first thermonuclear weapon. "Physicists won the second World War," according to science historian Daniel Kevles, "with microwave radar, proximity fuses, and solid fuel rockets. And they ended it with the atomic bomb. So the history of war was instantly understood by physicists and policy makers in the United States."[35]

In the postwar years the lesson was lost on few in Washington. Before the war, scientific research had comprised about 2 percent of the federal budget. Within months of the Japanese armistice, the federal government became America's leading patron of science: first through the Atomic Energy Commission (1946), then through the National Institutes of Health (NIH, 1948), and, finally, through the National Science Foundation (1950).

While national security research received the highest priority, consuming up to 90 percent of the federal R&D budget in the early 1950s, overall research was spread thinly in all the physical and life sciences as foundations gradually diminished their science funding. The Korean War intensified the demand for new weaponry and tripled defense research spending. And, along with nuclear warheads, radar, rockets, and missiles, the Department of Defense continued to fund research in basic science, much of it, strangely enough, through the Office of Naval Research.

The foundations did not long remain on the sidelines. Throughout the late-1940s and 1950s, Rockefeller pursued its concern for international health, funding virological research in tropical diseases and, through its various institutes, continuing to support domestic medical research. It was soon joined by the Alfred P. Sloan Foundation, which was formed just before the war and became an aggressive science funder soon afterwards.

As for social science, the federal government showed little interest. Thus sociologists, anthropologists, and psychologists continued to rely on foundations for research support. Between 1939 and 1950 the Social Science Division of the Rockefeller Foundation granted $21 million to American social scientists to study political democracy, economics and economic history, and interpersonal relations. During the same period it provided $1.7 million to social scientists in Europe.

Then, in 1949, the Ford Foundation was created. Over the next ten years it granted $60 million to social science research, half of it to Harvard, Columbia, and the University of Chicago. The foundation's early interests, voting patterns and behavioral psychology, were eventually expanded to include poverty (urban and rural), human rights, education, governance, and public policy.

Other foundations continued to encourage the development of interdisciplinary fields. In 1949 the Rockefeller funded the Institute for the Unity of Science, the creation of Harvard University physicist Philip Frank. The institute was among the first scientific think tanks to search seriously for a unified field theory—as much an attempt to reform philosophy as it was to advance science.

Meanwhile, philanthropic support of the physical sciences paled in the shadow of massive government funding at all levels. Foundations were prompted to pursue new roles in science and to create new research institutions, most notably the National Foundation for Infantile Paralysis. This organization, an operating foundation dedicated solely to fighting poliomyelitis, had been established in 1938 by Franklin Roosevelt's law partner and friend, Basil O'Connor. Unable to raise adequate foundation support for research, O'Connor went directly to the people. Through his brilliant March of Dimes program, he raised millions of dollars for research and treatment—$3 million in 1940, $50 million in 1953. The polio epidemic of the early 1950s made it an opportune time to study the mechanisms of this particular disease, which was known to be caused by a virus. And O'Connor's campaign was a reminder to fundraisers addicted to foundations that there was a massive reserve of philanthropy in the general public. By the end of the twentieth century almost every major disease had its own publicly supported organization.

Polio research could not, however, have begun without foundation support. And when Rockefeller's international virology research created a domestic payoff by identifying its organism, O'Connor and others succeeded in convincing Congress that biological science was worth a major national investment. Soon foundation philanthropy was dwarfed by federal outlays for basic and applied research. In 1951 the National Institutes of Health budget was $50 million; by 1960 it had climbed to $400 million; and by 1967 to $1.4 billion. These numbers made it increasingly difficult for foundations to make a significant contribution to biomedical science.

Thus, by the late 1960s, the government had become the central bank of science in America. Foundation trustees responded by maintaining their elitist tradition. They stepped into areas of basic science that federal agencies were for one reason or another reluctant to support. "The government eventually preempts the popular activities—those which have immediate general appeal," wrote a distressed Neils Wessell, then president of the Sloan Foundation. "It preempts them moreover with a weight of financial resources which make foundation resources seem almost minuscule. What is left to the private foundation, if it is to carve out its own place and play any kind of vital role, is just those philanthropic activities which are not yet manifestly popular, which are venturesome, and which may possibly fail."[36]

Although Wessell appears to lament this consequence of government funding, most contemporary foundation executives would say it points clearly to the basic purpose of foundations: to pursue the "venturesome" projects while government supports the tested and proven.

The Sloan Foundation, created in 1937 by General Motors chief executive officer Alfred P. Sloan, distinguished itself by undertaking a number of such projects. In the mid-1950s Sloan, who had by then retired from GM and was personally running the foundation, created a research fellowship program and shifted from institution building to investment "in talent rather than projects." In the years since, Sloan has granted $59 million to twenty-six hundred scientists, sixteen of whom have won Nobel prizes.[37] It has also built such high-profile institutions as the Sloan-Kettering Center for Cancer Research, the Sloan School for Industrial Management at the Massachusetts Institute of Technology, and the Sloan Program for Basic Research in the Physical Sciences.

In 1970 Sloan began funding minority medical researchers and made its first grant in the nascent field of neuroscience, where "returns from small investments can be far greater than those in well established areas of science such as particle physics or space exploration that now receive substantial federal support."[38] In the next six years Sloan committed $10 to $15 million to neuroscience research. In 1980 he took the next natural step and began funding the cognitive sciences, an interdisciplinary blend of neurology and computer technology, thus fostering the new field of molecular evolution. The techniques developed make "it possible to unravel the millions of years of evolutionary history that are encoded in the genetic complement of living species."[39] Since then, Sloan has granted $5.5 million to evolutionary genetics.

During the 1970s much of the federal government's research, particularly military research, came under intense political pressure. Both houses of Congress took a greater interest overall in the government's R&D budgets, particularly those related to politically sensitive areas like environment, occupational safety, consumer protection, and public health. And economic competition, particularly from Japanese technologies, motivated politicians to increase research budgets in areas (like robotics and computers) related to industrial production. *Competitiveness* became a buzzword on the Hill, high-tech competitiveness being a particular obsession. Technological development, suddenly, was deemed "socially purposeful research."

During the Reagan administration this trend intensified, although even more of the research budget was devoted to military technology, leaving the development of more speculative areas of research to the foundations. This trend further illustrates many philanthropists' belief that "a private foundation can do for science what the federal government has not found its way to do." These words of Sloan president Albert Rees also reflect their conviction that "a total reliance on government would render the support, however lavish, imperfect in many ways. There is a sense in which foundation support, however paltry in its share of the scientific dollar, is more essential than ever to the health of science."[40]

Shifting Leverage

In the decades since World War II, as the federal government has increased its funding of science the vocation and purpose of private philanthropy has shifted too—away from attempting to influence government scientific policy and toward funding innovative and speculative research. Of course, the days of public influence are not over for science philanthropy, nor have the foundations given up trying to target scientific research and guide social policy. But it is undeniable that foundation influence over the physical and biological sciences has greatly diminished. Program officers know that if the fifty largest foundations donated all their annual outlay to science, the total would still be dwarfed by federal spending—by a factor of six. So foundation strategy has shifted yet again, from pursuing direct influence to moving their small investments to scale by persuading federal agencies to invest in venturesome fields like neuroscience and molecular embryology.

The current goal of most science-oriented foundations, then, is to find neglected or underfunded leverage points at the boundaries of science: interfaces between theoretical and biological disciplines that have fallen through the cracks of federal agencies, areas in which a few small grants can make a big difference.

Jonas Salk describes such areas as "fertile territory."[41] As a trustee of the John D. and Catherine T. MacArthur Foundation, Salk is constantly searching for scientific initiatives in which a little financial fertilization might cause a major breakthrough or give birth to a new scientific discipline. Neuroscience, cognitive neuroscience, and computational neuroscience, all regarded by biologists as potential gateways to mental health, are of enduring interest to MacArthur and to the Howard Hughes Medical Institute (HHMI), the Lucille Markey Charitable Trust, the James McDonnell, Whitaker, and other foundations. At the moment, they are of minimal interest to government funders. "Foundations are untrammeled by large bureaucracy," observes Hughes vice president Maxwell Cowan, "so they can be responsive to new initiatives and developments, and can be focused at critical times in a field or institution."[42]

Although the federal budget for biomedical research remains impressive, leading-edge biologists have recently found more encouraging support from the HHMI, a medical research organization with an endowment of over $12.9 billion. Were HHMI a foundation it would be the second or third largest in the United States. It is organized, however, more like an operating foundation; using the income from its endowment to support its own research programs, it also, in keeping with an agreement with the IRS, makes external grants. It has filled the research-funding gap for laboratories at fifty-one academic institutions where over fifteen hundred postdoctoral scientists are working in neuroscience, cell biology, immunology, structural biology, and genetics. By 1990 HHMI was granting over $200 million a year to medical research and training at American universities—about 10 percent of the total NIH budget. In 1999 its internal and external investment in medical research totaled over $350 million. While no foundation can match the influence over science the Rockefeller exerted in its early years, HHMI has come closer than any other.

Bold and Cautious

Philanthropic money must keep moving in its search for creative destiny.
—Fred Powledge, The Nation Institute

The foundations; strategy remains essentially what it was at the beginning of the century. Provide funding in an unabashedly elitist fashion. Single out innovative, interdisciplinary, high-risk projects that state and federal governments won't touch, and accelerate them a little. If the federal government discovers the value of the work and begins to support it, step aside and find another emerging discipline with cross-disciplinary potential. "We cannot be the life blood of any field," says McDonnell Foundation Program Director John Bruer. "We are the venture capitalists."

Energetic investigators, starting their careers and exploring speculative, leading edge-projects are still favored by the foundations. "Nobels are of no interest to us," one foundation trustee told me in confidence. "They're lazy and conceited. We want hungry young post-docs willing to work eighteen-hour days to discover a particle, solve an equation or find a cure."

Though foundations are still willing to take risks that government isn't, the financial risks are in fact small; grants range from $15,000 to $100,000 for a promising researcher. "We focus on people with a track record, at a time when they would like to take some risk in their science, but can't afford to," says Pew executive director Rebecca Rimel of the Pew Scholars program. "We call [those grants] an insurance policy for risk taking."

A criticism of foundations heard throughout the nonprofit sector is echoed at higher volume in the scientific community. Foundations, complain some researchers, are flighty and mercurial. They tend to abandon promising developments at the mere whiff of failure or, worse, upon the appearance of a sexier scientist with a hotter project. They push promising research to the back burner before it has had a reasonable chance to prove a hypothesis or develop a product. There is certainly some truth in these allegations. Large foundations do occasionally shift their science funding from one entire area (molecular embryology) to another (cognitive neuroscience) without adequate warning to grantees, who are frequently abandoned in the middle of an experiment.

A commonly cited example is MacArthur's sudden pullout from parasitology, leaving eleven research centers suddenly hunting for new money. Denis Prager, director of health programs at MacArthur, defended the decision. "We've done what we set out to do," he told *Science* magazine. "We attracted new people to the field, and they are now publishing in good journals." Nina Agabian, who headed one of the abandoned parasitology labs, says: "That's crazy. The cutback will only serve to discourage good researchers from entering the field."[43] Sensitive to such criticism, the Lucille Markey Foundation recently instituted the policy of funding new projects for up eight years.

The contemporary art of raising science money from private philanthropy involves drawing attention to oneself. Hot topics excite funders, as do paradigmatic theories and breakthrough scientists. Thus the most visible, vocal, investigators are favored while scientists of equal stature with mundane workaday projects are often ignored. Lower-profile scientists grumble about the foundations' obsession with novelty. Program officers counter that they are the ones who must go out on limbs no one else will approach; if they do not seek out the innovative pioneers, innovation itself will disappear. If the Alfred P. Sloan Foundation hadn't supported neurobiology in the early 1970s, goes the argument—or Rockefeller hadn't invested in molecular biology or Keck in neuropeptide expression in the brain—molecular neurobiology might never have achieved its triumphs. In fact, it might never have appeared as a scientific discipline at all.

So private foundations continue to fund science as they always have, at once boldly and cautiously. They will retain their leading role in shaping America into a science-oriented, technocratic society by supporting educational institutions that train the leadership of industrial society. Within the boundaries of science itself, risks will be taken, disciplines will be blended, and scientists reaching for the outer limits of knowledge will be funded. But in areas where science relates to society at large, particularly to matters economic, philanthrocrats will, as they always have, take great care not to offend the sensibilities of their trustees or threaten the system that makes foundations possible in the first place.

4
Health

Public health is purchasable. Within natural limitations a community can determine its own death rate.
—Herman M. Biggs, New York City Health Commissioner, 1911

Whether measured in dollars or grants, health is—and almost always has been—the American foundations' second-largest interest, after education. From their earliest beginnings the foundations have made large grants for medical research and education, health care, and public health. Yet one might reasonably question what many philanthropists have meant by *health*, as they have consistently given the category of public health their lowest funding priority.

Both John D. Rockefeller and Andrew Carnegie were convinced early on that scientific medicine would lead, ipso facto, to public health. And, as in so many fields, their early initiatives in health philanthropy set an example followed by thousands of other, newer foundations. Five foundations—the Commonwealth Fund, the Henry J. Kaiser Family Foundation, the Robert Wood Johnson, Milbank Memorial, and the Howard Hughes Medical Institute—have even made health and medicine their sole philanthropic interest.

It should be noted, however, that the Milbank and Commonwealth foundations ignored the example set by Rockefeller and Carnegie and took an early interest in public health. In the 1920s Commonwealth and Milbank created demonstration projects in various American communities, large and small, to show that community investments in health education and prevention would pay off in less communicable disease, lower health care costs, and a generally healthier population. Public health, they sought to prove, was purchasable. Though strongly resisted by private

practitioners and the American Medical Association, which quite naturally preferred a physician-centered approach to public health, their efforts still provide inspiration for the current "healthy communities"
movement. Indeed, the early officers and trustees of both foundations
frequently alluded to "the building of better communities" as one of the
purposes of public health.[1] (See chapter 10 for more on the "Healthy
Communities" initiatives.)

By 1997, $3.2 billion (16.7 percent) of the $19.5 billion granted by all
foundations that year was donated to hospitals, universities, laboratories,
and other institutions working in one way or another to advance the
health of the nation. Subcategories of health reported by the Foundation
Center included hospitals, reproductive health, medical research, specific
diseases, and public health. Hospitals took the lion's share of 1997 foundation largesse—31 percent of the total health outlay. Public health received 7 percent.

While it is likely to remain high on the list of American philanthropic
priorities, the nature of health grantmaking has altered in recent years,
mostly in response to sea changes in the structure of American health
care delivery systems, a third of which are now supported by federal and
state government agencies. The advent of managed care and the massive
privatization of that solid, century-old institution of civil society—the
nonprofit charity hospital—have also had a major impact on foundations' funding decisions. Most recently, a handful of new "conversion
foundations" have become major players in the field of health philanthropy. Yet even the seeds of this exciting, but yet to be realized, potential
were sown by professional philanthropists working for Rockefeller and
Carnegie in the first quarter of the twentieth century.

The Medical Model

*Formerly, when religion was strong and science weak, men mistook magic for
medicine; now when science is strong and religion is weak, men mistake medicine
for magic.*
—Thomas Szasz

Although they championed and supported projects in disease prevention
and public health, early American philanthropists consistently saw scientific medicine as the royal road to national health. The putative motives

for their choice are ambiguous and hotly debated by historians; they range from protection of the rich from plagues of the poor to the creation of a healthy industrial workforce. The literature also mentions the advancement of science and the strengthening of corporate capitalism, as well as genuine charitable and humanitarian impulses. All these motives could no doubt be found in varying degrees in the hearts and minds of the thousands of donors, trustees, presidents, and program officers who supported health initiatives during the past century. Even within individual foundations, motives and priorities shifted over time as staff members and trustees came and went. In any case, we may surely conclude that—whatever the ferment of religious and utilitarian motives—original donors all believed a complex society could only advance in the world if its people were healthy.[2] And a healthy populace was most likely to result from institutionalized professional medicine.

We do know that Frederick Gates, philanthropic advisor to the enigmatic John D. Rockefeller and architect of the Rockefeller medical foundations, held to this view. And he insisted on many occasions that medicine could only keep a nation healthy if it served all of society and not just the interests of one class or the medical profession. That was the only way to improve worker productivity and ensure the survival of corporate capitalism. (Of course, we have no way of knowing whether he believed that or simply said it to please his boss.)

Either way, assuring the health of all classes was no easy task. Even with Rockefeller's vast fortune behind him, Gates had to fight the American Medical Association and other institutions of organized medicine. In those days, of course, the AMA was small and poor, a weak force when faced with the power behind a massive endowment. But it grew rapidly in size and influence, in great part, ironically, because Rockefeller and Carnegie lent it legitimacy by favoring professional medicine as the fastest route to public health.

The contest between the AMA and the foundations over the structure and practice of medicine has persisted for almost a century. It has produced a system of medical specialists (e.g., oncologists, cardiologists, nephrologists, dermatologists), wonder drugs, and bold technologies that serve a gradually shrinking portion of American society. Allopathic physicians are the high-status professionals of our civilization in great part because Abraham Flexner, in a 1912 report to the Carnegie Corporation, argued that only those who pursued a healing approach grounded in clinical research should be allowed to practice. All other healing modalities were marginalized as germ theory and the allopathic model of medicine came to dominate western health care.[3]

In the first century of American health philanthropy almost everything was tried and funded. Only two areas have remained unchallenged by foundations. One is the preeminent role of hospitals in health care; the other is the resistance to a single-payer health care system or national health plan. While every other country in the developed world has found ways to assure some health care to most of its citizens, about 44 million Americans remain uncovered, languishing helplessly between the extremely poor and aged who are covered by Medicare and Medicaid and those who are either employed with generous benefits or affluent enough to buy their own costly health insurance.

To some degree this situation is a result of actions taken by American foundations—not because they have aggressively opposed a national health plan but because their funding of systems research and the development of health care delivery models quite deliberately excludes anything that sounds like socialized medicine. As the 1993–94 debates over Bill Clinton's health reform initiatives made clear, the insurance industry, the AMA, and their friends in Congress seem capable of sensing socialism in almost any reform of the system.

Physicians for a National Health Program have been turned down by almost every foundation to which they have applied for support. They have received some small grants—from the Veatch Foundation, the Alberlin Family Fund, the Public Welfare Foundation (which stipulated that their grant was "not to be used for single-payer work"), and a few individual philanthropists. Neighbor to Neighbor, Public Citizen, and other organizations advocating single-payer systems have been similarly rebuffed. Although the Robert Wood Johnson Foundation is widely regarded as the most progressive health funder and has refrained from opposing a national health plan, it has routinely sponsored conferences hostile to single-payer options.

Johnson hosted two such conferences in the mid-1990s. At "Administrative Costs in Medicine" and "Medicare Reform" only proponents of for-profit medicine and managed care made presentations. Single-payer activists like Dr. David Himmelstein and Stephie Woolhandler were invited to attend but could only listen as their opponents attacked them.[4] Meanwhile, the National Center for Policy Analysis and the Heritage Foundation have received generous foundation support for programs opposing health care systems similar to those of Canada and Germany.

When George Soros, who had already distinguished himself as a maverick philanthropist, realized that money was having a corrupting influence on medicine, he created a project called "Medicine as a Profession." "There is unanimity among doctors, deans, historians and health economists that money has never been more in the forefront of medicine or potentially so powerful in determining medical decisions," declared Soros upon launching the project with a $15-million grant. "We have never more needed professional ethics to stand out against marketplace forces than now."[5]

The aim of Soros's program is to bring medical and consumer organizations together to monitor and improve health care systems and ensure that ethical as well as financial considerations govern patient care. It plans to teach young health professionals "how to serve and how to advocate for their patients, particularly patients coming from underserved communities." Although Soros bemoans "the prominence in medicine of for-profit health maintenance organizations," he skates cautiously around the single-payer issue. Yet his project clearly illuminates the strongest argument for a national health plan—the clear failure of managed care to reach millions of citizens.

Since the 1930s, new forces and the tremendous growth of the health care economy have noticeably weakened the foundations' influence over medicine and public health. Their approximately $1-billion-dollar injection into a trillion-dollar health care economy is but another pebble in the Mississippi. Government, which at all levels picks up a third of the nation's health bill—and an even higher portion of the health research budget—is today far more influential than any foundation. Even though some foundations support research into the design and improvement of government systems, it is legislatures and health bureaucracies that call the shots.

Band-Aid Philanthropy

When in the late 1960s the Robert Wood Johnson Foundation appeared committed to funding a broad range of health-oriented projects, observers in health philanthropy were unconvinced. Some feared that conflicts of interest would plague any foundation created from the profits of medicine and health products. Others pointed to the preponderance of Johnson & Johnson executives and other trustees with cozy ties to the medical establishment. The Lilly Foundation, skeptics noted, had deliberately avoided funding medical and health research to escape any perception of conflict. Robert Wood Johnson, they predicted, would soon fall into lockstep with the deeply self-interested fee-for-service medical monopoly. They couldn't have been more wrong.

By 1968, when a $300-million endowment was transferred to the foundation from the estate of Robert Johnson (it was worth $1.3 billion by 1999), the government had become such a major player in medical research and health care financing that even large foundations like Rockefeller, Commonwealth, Kaiser, Milbank, Hartford, and Markle were marginalized. Johnson's trustees, however, predicted that the participation of the state in the nation's health care would create larger, unanticipated problems. Desiring to make the new foundation a force for change, they hired seasoned activist David Rogers from Johns Hopkins University to run RWJ, as it came to be known.

Rogers, who was deeply concerned about the social and economic inequities of American health care, acquired the virtually inactive health policy section of the Carnegie Corporation, placed it under RWJ control, and set out to reform what he saw as an essentially unfair system. Avoiding the perennial clichés of American health philanthropy—hospital wings, biomedical laboratories, and cancer research—RWJ committed most of its $45-million annual outlay to making health care available to high-risk youth, the handicapped, the elderly, rural infants, and others slipping through the Medicare/Medicaid nets. It was a challenging and controversial task that is still far from complete.

During the Reagan years, when access to medical care was gradually restricted to fewer and fewer people, RWJ became an active ombudsman for indigent patients, including the growing number of America's homeless. Even so, like other foundations, RWJ has avoided advocating the single-payer/national health plan solution as politically unpalatable.

More than any other foundation, Johnson has invested heavily in public health, which, its program officers believe, is the only aspect of national health that belongs solidly in the public sector. Their "Turning Point Initiative" makes grants to state health departments to examine the coordination of their work with other, related departments. RWJ has been particularly imaginative in defining nonmedical health problems like teen violence, substance abuse, and unwanted pregnancy as national health problems.

In 1987 foundation chronicler and acerbic critic of traditional philanthropy Waldemar Nielsen singled out RWJ for special praise: "Judged by the standards normally applicable to foundations," he wrote, "the Johnson Foundation is virtually in the class by itself. In the intellectual power that has governed its strategy and grantmaking, in the social sensitivity and political skills by which its programs have been shaped, in the able and creative way in which they have been managed, and in the general qualities of integrity and independence that have characterized all that it has done, RWJ is the best of the big foundations today."[6]

This was not a view shared by those on either the Right or the Left of the American political spectrum; the Right resented any interference with medical profiteering, and the Left wanted Johnson to stop tinkering with the system and help create a national health plan. But, like so many large foundations, RWJ has remained assiduously centrist on controversial health issues. With the help of the Rand Corporation and other national think tanks, it has sought ways to "build capacity among consumers, health care providers, managed care organizations, and state agencies to make managed care work for vulnerable populations."[7] All its efforts, it would seem, are geared toward obviating the need for a national plan. It would perhaps be unfair to call RWJ a drag anchor on health care or health philanthropy; yet the beneficial influence it could so easily have exerted on progress toward universal coverage has failed to materialize.

War on Cancer

Imaginative philanthropy has been practiced by other health foundations, but most have been on the initiative of venturesome individuals like

George Soros and Mary Lasker. As early as the 1930s and 1940s, Lasker, the widow of Albert Lasker, the advertising tycoon who handled the American Tobacco account and coined the slogan "Reach for a Lucky instead of a sweet," saw the massive health problem presented by cancer and sought to solve it with money. (Her choice was particularly appropriate, given her husband's clear contribution to its incidence.) Aware of the enormity and virulence of the disease, Lasker was convinced that cancer could only be defeated by putting enough money behind enough good minds. "We are so close to a cure for cancer," she wrote in a 1970 full-page ad in the *New York Times*, "We lack only the will and the kind of money and comprehensive planning that went into putting a man on the moon. Why don't we try to conquer cancer by America's 200th birthday?"

Lasker knew, however, that there were not enough assets in her foundation, or for that matter in all the foundations, to tackle cancer. To make even a dent in the 265 diseases then called cancer would require billions of dollars, and years—more money and time than most foundations would commit to one problem. The federal government would have to be involved, deeply involved, for a decade or more.

Fortunately, Mary Lasker's skills as a lobbyist surpassed even her philanthropic acumen. Mixing charm, media savvy, and direct political pressure, she pleaded her case to Congress and the executive branch, eventually obtaining an audience with Richard Nixon in the Oval Office. No one knows what she said to the president in that meeting, but she got quick results. In 1971, while signing a $233-million special NIH appropriation creating the separate and autonomous National Cancer Institute, Nixon declared war on a disease that was striking down three-quarters of a million Americans every year.

Because the war Nixon declared was almost exclusively medical and virtually ignored the environmental etiology of many cancers, the age-adjusted incidence of cancer among Americans has risen almost 55 percent since 1971. And, despite a current federal annual outlay of $2.5 billion, cancer remains the only large-scale killing disease in America whose rate of incidence is rising. Nonetheless, people with cancer are living longer than they did earlier, mostly because of chemotherapy and radiation. Yet more people (one in every three) are getting some form of cancer, and more are dying from it than ever (one in four).

Can we blame this failure on Mary Lasker, or upon any philanthropist for that matter? Certainly not. In fact, we cannot place the onus for defeat in this war on anyone who fought in it, whether in a hospital, the laboratory, or the foundation. The problem is that the whole strategy, the strategy of war, was wrong from the start. What has been learned about cancer after a national expenditure of hundreds of billions of dollars is that the disease cannot be defeated. It can only be prevented. Despite that rather obvious conclusion, the warlike search for a cure continues pretty much as Mary Lasker conceived it and Richard Nixon defined it. The only significant difference is that the battleground has shifted from the cellular to the molecular level.

The lessons that philanthropists can learn from Mary Lasker's venture are legion, but perhaps the most vital one is the clear folly of letting philanthropists or scientists assume strategic control over complex initiatives. It is a lesson not easily learned by the trustees and program officers of large foundations, as ensuing chapters will demonstrate.

Conversions

We need to recognize that these foundations are diminishing the amount of health care services that are available to the indigent
—Mary Boland, Catholic Charities, Archdiocese of Denver

In 1984 three top officials of the Greater Delaware Valley Health Care Center in Pennsylvania bought the center from its nonprofit owner for $100,000. Claiming that its value derived from its nonprofit status, state regulators required the new owners to pay the entire purchase price to other nonprofit health facilities in the area. Two years later the owners sold the then for-profit company on the open market for $20 million.

The next year the officers and doctors affiliated with Group Health of St. Louis, a nonprofit HMO, bought it for $4 million and issued themselves stock valued at thirty-three cents a share. They, too, dutifully donated the $4 million to charitable organizations providing health care in the St. Louis area. A year later, a mere quarter of the new company's stock was sold for $10 million ($14.28 a share, almost forty-five times the original price).

In both these cases, the real value of the original nonprofit organization went to shareholders, not, as one might expect, into services originally provided by Group Health or Greater Delaware Valley Health Care.[8] Eventually, however, these and other similar incidents came to the attention of the Consumer's Union, which convinced the Internal Revenue Service and state governments nationwide that the *full* value of such nonprofit-to-for-profit conversions should be turned into new philanthropic entities called "conversion foundations." Turning "economic capital into social capital," is how one plan executive described it.

However, it takes a good deal more public pressure and government oversight to get full value from health conversions. In 1991 HealthNet, a nine-hundred-thousand-member HMO in California, decided to convert and valued itself at $104 million. Not nearly enough, protested Consumer's Union, which persuaded state regulators to jack up the price to $300 million plus 80 percent of the stock in the new for-profit company. Today the resultant Wellness Foundation endowment is worth almost a billion dollars.

There are presently 134 conversion foundations in the country with combined assets of $16.3 billion. Together they pump over $800 million annually into American health programs—over 40 percent of overall health grantmaking.[9] More than twenty of them hold assets in excess of $100 million; three (all in California) have over $1 billion. These "conversions," as they are called, are changing the face of health care in America, and a few are becoming models of democratic philanthropy.

Conversions are the byproduct of a profound transformation in American health care—the transfer from public to private, from nonprofit to for-profit enterprise—an equity shift that has resulted in the largest and fastest transfer of charitable assets in history.[10] And the new foundations, several of them among the fifty largest foundations in the country, are among the most exciting players in health philanthropy. Not only do they fund long-neglected areas like health promotion, disease prevention, and public health, but they are also increasingly directed by trustees from the communities they serve rather than by overnight millionaires and the managers of new for-profit entities (as earlier conversions were).

Most of these new foundations are better informed, more imaginative, and more responsive to community needs than traditional health foundations. Whereas the latter are unlikely to fund programs in children's health and health services for the working poor, such projects are the perennial favorites of many conversions. Several conversion foundations have created hospitals that differ markedly from those evolved from health plans and HMOs. Such hospitals have earmarked, in accordance with state regulation of conversions, considerable funds for indigent care and for other services not offered by new for-profit institutions. These investments are particularly vital to communities struggling to fill the gap in needed services created by the devolution of government welfare programs. Conversion foundations of all types have, in fact, played a central role in the massive readjustments required of state and local governments saddled with responsibilities abdicated by Washington. Nonetheless, despite conservative protestations to the contrary, such foundations will never be large enough, or wealthy enough, to fill the gap left by devolution.

However, if nonprofit-to-for-profit conversions continue and state governments persist in requiring that the full value of each transaction inure to the benefit of the public, conversion foundations could soon surpass traditional foundations as health grantmakers. Only 15 percent of the nation's fifty-two hundred hospitals are presently for-profit institutions. The rest—with an estimated asset value of close to $200 billion—are potential candidates for conversion. Moreover, the net worth of the nation's nonprofit health insurers (including the unconverted "Blues") is estimated at $92 billion.[11] Their combined total is close to the asset value of all existing private foundations.

The question, then, seems clear. Should those assets be maintained as tax-exempt institutions dedicated to serving the medical needs of local communities and indigent people? Or should the hospitals, HMOs, and insurance carriers be converted into for-profit, tax-paying companies while their assets are transferred to foundations dedicated to improving the health care and health delivery systems of all Americans. Some advocates for conversion have suggested that the taxes paid by for-profit conversions should also be captured and earmarked for community health projects.

Studies attempting to ascertain whether conversions have been good or bad for health and health care have been inconclusive. Some show increased efficiency among the new entities; others point to reduced services. Many observers find it difficult to believe that large, national for-profit corporations beholden primarily to shareholders can ever deliver adequate and equitable health care to the same populations served by the nonprofit entities they replaced. "The culture of health care used to value the care of the vulnerable," observes Judith Bell; "now it is increasingly devoted to the care of shareholders."[12]

The Consumer's Union, in particular, has questioned whether important, but possibly unprofitable health services ranging from trauma to prenatal care will remain in place when a nonprofit organization becomes a business whose goals is to make a profit.[13] And who will ensure that insurance is available to people other companies will not cover? Will indigent patients be cared for? Will teaching hospitals survive, along with health care research? In short, is the question of social equity being addressed?

The jury remains out on that issue, and on the question of whether competition between nonprofit and for-profit organizations has a salutary effect. Is the whole process of conversion, now almost a decade underway, truly in the public interest? The answer will rest in part on the effectiveness of conversion foundations.

And that effectiveness will depend largely on government oversight of their work. A certain amount of regulation of these exciting new entities will be required, not only to be certain that assets are fully valued and transferred in their entirety to the conversion foundation, but also to ensure that the resulting foundation remains faithful to the original purposes of the nonprofit corporation. As a resolution of the National Association of Attorneys General states, "the proposed uses of the proceeds of the transaction should be consistent with the charitable purpose for which the assets are held by the nonprofit health care entity."[14]

Without such oversight there is nothing to prevent a conversion foundation from misspending its resources. Recently the Jackson (Tennessee) Foundation (a conversion from Goldlark Medical Center) purchased two airplanes for a high school flight-training program and contracted with Mississippi State University to build model space shuttles for space and aeronautic training. And the Venice (Florida) Foundation used its income to buy batting cages for the Venice Little League.[15] "With careful over-sight and monitoring," asserts the Consumers Union, such abuses can be avoided, and conversion "transactions can occur while the public's inter-ests are protected."[16]

Meanwhile conversions continue, and, despite closer regulation, hand-some profits are still being made from the process. In 1992 HealthNet, the California HMO mentioned above, became Health Systems Interna-tional. Twenty percent of the new entity was purchased by thirty-three executives for $1.5 million. Four years later their shares were worth over $300 million. Former HealthNet CEO Roger Greaves provides an example of the profits that can still be made from conversions. His $300,000 investment has grown to over $30 million—a 10,000-percent gain.

Of course, not every deal works out quite that well for participants. In 1994 Columbia-HCA Healthcare, the nation's largest for-profit hospital chain, announced plans to purchase up to five hundred more hospitals. The following year it began joint-venture discussions with forty-one non-profit hospitals. Then, in March of 1996, it revealed its intention to form a joint venture with Blue Cross and Blue Shield Mutual of Ohio, that state's largest nonprofit health insurer.

The Blues proposed to sell 85 percent of their assets to Columbia for $299.5 million: $19 million of the sum would go to Blue Cross executives, trustees, and attorneys for "consultation" and for concluding noncompe-tition agreements. When Blue Cross policyholders sued against those pro-visions, the Ohio attorney general opposed the deal and the national Blue Cross/Blue Shield Association revoked the Ohio organization's license. Subsequently, a federal judge ruled that the new entity could not use the Blue Cross or Blue Shield trademarks.

Finally, exactly a year after negotiations began, the Ohio Depart-ment of Insurance rejected the merger. The case sent a strong signal throughout the nonprofit and for-profit health care sectors: consumers, legislators, and the courts are all carefully watching the largest redeploy-ment of charitable assets in history. That watchfulness can only spell good news for the future of conversion foundations and for the poten-tial of democratized philanthropies to serve the interests of public health.

The End of Health

Ill health is not solely caused by germs, nor is good health only brought by doctors and drugs.
—David Hunter, Former President, The Stern Fund

Postmodern America is on the cusp of many alleged endings. With the exception of racism and poverty, the demise of almost everything addressed in this book has either been declared or predicted in widely discussed essays entitled "The End of _____." Under that title history, nature, childhood, agriculture, manhood, evolution, philosophy, education, and even sex have all been declared dead, finished, canceled, washed up, adjourned. We live, it seems, in an age of terminations.

There is a nihilistic resonance to these pronouncements, which, on close examination, seems undeserved; for in completion there can be achievement, and in ending accomplishment. This is certainly true of health. The accomplishments of the human health care system are impressive, particularly for those of us who thrive in the western world. We are living much longer than we were a century ago. Far fewer of our children are dying (though too many are still malnourished); several hideous diseases have been all but eliminated; and, with the notable exception of cancer, the incidence of most diseases is either stable or in decline. Many of these accomplishments have been supported by foundation philanthropy.

So why entitle a section of a book about philanthropy "The End of Health"? Quite simply because all the achievements in public health and medicine could soon be rendered moot by global biospheric threats— not only to human life but to millions of other species. And organized philanthropy has yet to rise to the occasion.

Global threats to health are speculative, of course, and there is no shortage of skeptics and contrarians who insist that the planet has never been in better health. They may be right, although there are enough signs, enough evidence that climate is becoming chaotic, hormones are being disrupted, viruses are crossing species barriers, and the planet's temperature is rising to suggest, at the very least, that foundations should be funding exploratory research into the extent of these threats. For most of them are anthropogenic, and remediable.

Why, a reader might ask, are matters so clearly environmental being discussed in a chapter about health and medicine? Quite simply because environment is a matter of health, and medical science needs to reach beyond the well-being of individual humans, beyond human diseases and their cures, and treat the planet as if it were a living organism—which a growing number of scientists believe it is.

Contemporary medicine is designed to protect human life, to make us live longer, to let us fulfill our lives, and to destroy or neutralize all nonhuman adversaries in nature. Our concepts of medical progress assume that the world will be better if more humans survive, live vital active lives, travel more, learn more, earn more. Philanthropy acts on the same beliefs. But medicine ignores the impact the human species is having on other life. So does most philanthropy.

If medicine is to succeed as a pro-human science it must acknowledge, sooner rather than later, the interconnectedness of human and nonhuman life and recognize the environmental threat to human health. Veterinary medicine should not be regarded as a completely separate practice from human medicine; nor should, botany, ethnobotany, wildlife biology, toxicology, geography, or ecology.

More immediately, but no less crucially, the end of health is becoming increasingly real to millions of Americans (about 44 million to be more precise). Their experiences are linked directly to the ongoing privatization of health care, which has been both supported and opposed by American foundations. The saddest part of that development is that the concurrent demise of nonprofit charity hospitals could spell the beginning of the end for civil society itself, burdening foundations with a challenge for which they are unprepared and unequipped.

5

Environment

If a foundation has a large interest in Alaska and a lot of money, you definitely have a large interest in Alaska.
—Bill Turnage, Former Director, The Wilderness Society

Although regarded by conservative essayist and sociologist Robert Nisbet as the most significant social movement of the twentieth century, the century-old, uniquely American phenomenon known as the environmental movement is frequently overlooked—and at times derided—by advocates and philosophers of civil society. And it is ignored by most foundations. Of this mosaic of approximately fifteen thousand largely volunteer-based grassroots organizations, fewer than fifty are national in scope. Yet it is, "the nationals"—the Sierra Club, the Wilderness Society, the Environmental Defense Fund, the National Wildlife Federation, and the Audubon Society—that the media identify as the major players and agenda setters of American environmentalism. These "well-branded" nationals spend about 70 percent of the total funds devoted to nonprofit environmental advocacy and protection. Most of them carefully avoid challenging the power structures and relationships that have the most profound environmental impacts. It is therefore not surprising that the few mainstream American foundations willing to make large grants to environmental causes favor these organizations.

Despite a century of quite respectable activism, most foundation trustees see environmental groups as too adversarial, too confrontational to rank alongside family, neighborhood, church, and palliative charities as legitimate institutions of civil society. Even conservative philanthropists who accept the need for environmental activism bridle at government regulation, which most greens support, and at the militancy displayed by some of the movement's adherents. Most are unwilling to fund organizations that advocate state intervention in industrial processes or calls for support public actions against polluters. An extreme minority of trustees consider environmentalists pagan nature worshippers intent on undermining the Judeo-Christian ethic.

Of the almost fifty thousand foundations in America—private, community, and corporate—only 213 consider protection of the environment a serious enough cause to join an affinity group called Environmental Grantmakers Association (EGA). This organization evolved from a 1987 breakfast meeting held in Washington where the few environmental funders were attending a Council of Foundations conference. They met subsequently to discuss common interests and strategy and are now headquartered in the New York offices of the Rockefeller Family Fund. The organization keeps and publishes a directory of its membership, plans and coordinates an annual national meeting and several regional meetings, and holds special briefings for environmental fundraisers throughout the year.[1] The combined assets of EGA members total approximately $80 billion, of which about $500 million annually, about six-tenths of one percent (0.625 percent), is granted to a varied array of environmental projects.[2]

Environmental grantmakers seem to love affinity groups. They have also broken up into an array of such sub-affinity groups as the Consultative Group on Biodiversity, which is itself broken up into sub-sub-affinity groups: the Systemic Contaminants Working Group (toxics), the Marines (oceanic issues), and the Biodiversity Education Working Group, which communicates the findings of the various groups to each other.

Although there is no scarcity of controversial environmental issues, both scientific and political, to address, the question that appears to preoccupy EGA is its membership. About once a year a disagreement arises, usually over allowing a corporation or corporate foundation to join. In 1991, when Waste Management Inc. (now WMX) applied, several representatives of greener, mostly private foundations opposed admitting it; they argued that WMX was an environment scofflaw with a long list of infractions and several large fines from the Environmental Protection Agency to prove it. But because WMX had given generous grants to several environmental organizations, others wanted to let them in. "They're only trying to greenwash themselves," argued the opponents. "So what?"

responded WMX's champions, "if we let them in, we can keep on eye on them."

After a short period of indecision—during which WMX was first in, then out—the EGA membership committee relented and accepted the firm. Eventually WMX's adversaries grew accustomed to is presence, if not to the idea of corporate membership in general. There are currently 14 corporate members in EGA. Whenever a debate arises over something like funding organizations that question the ecological wisdom of genetic engineering, several corporations usually line up with the more permissive foundation members

The "big tent" principle of EGA membership thus risks making the words *environmental grantmaking* a meaningless label. In fact, that risk has already been realized and is reflected in the grants list of many "environmental" foundations. Such funders frequently favor organizations like the Environmental Defense Fund, which negotiates compromise bargains with polluting corporations while less-accommodating (more-litigious or confrontational) groups such as Greenpeace and the Native Forest Council look on in horror.

Meanwhile, as environmentalists and their adversaries debate the successes and failures of American environmentalism—a parlor game in green circles—assays of human and wildlife adipose (fatty) tissue continue to reveal significant residues of recognized carcinogens, mutagens, teratogenic agents, and (more recently) endocrine-disrupting organohalogens and phthalates. Of all the measures used by scientists and historians to determine the success or failure of environmentalism, what could be more significant or revealing than a tissue survey? Mass extinctions of species, perhaps?—which do appear to be occurring, although they are subject to more debate than the presence of synthetic chemicals in human and animal bodies. Nevertheless, many politicians and corporate officials have already declared victory and heralded the environmental movement as an American success story—a tribute to the strength of our civil society. And, if granting priorities are a fair indicator, many foundations seem to agree that environmentalism has triumphed and our problems are solved.

Despite the clear and well-documented impact of three centuries of environmental degradation, combined with a host of new global threats, the environment remains but a minor issue for American foundations, large and small. Last year just over $4 billion, or 2.7 percent of the $150 billion donated from all sources, went to environmental causes (including animal rights and land trusts). Foundations were proportionately more generous—4.3 percent of their grants in 1995 went to environmental organizations, up from 1 percent in 1980. (Before then, "Environment" wasn't even a category in the Foundation Center's annual report of giving.)

EGA states one of its primary purposes as promoting "recognition that the environment and its inhabitants are endangered by unsustainable human activities." Its most active internal working groups address topics such as sustainable agriculture, toxics, transportation, and environmental justice. Nonetheless, about sixty cents of every foundation dollar contributed to environmental causes in 1998 went to "natural resource protection," a category almost entirely devoted to land trusts. Such trusts buy conservation easements and open land and deed them permanently on behalf of some vague concept of "nature." In fact, the largest single environmental grant made since Rockefeller family money created national parks in the Tetons, Maine, and the Virgin Islands was a David and Lucille Packard Foundation pledge of $175 million to protect California's rapidly shrinking open space from development. This sum will be leveraged through The Nature Conservancy (TNC) and the Trust for Public Land (TPL).

To be sure, urban sprawl, which threatens the habitats of an increasing number of vital plant and animal species, is a serious problem, though few activists see it as central to the cause of environmental protection. The Nature Conservancy, TPL, and the American Farmland Trust have protected millions of acres nationwide; yet their beneficial effect on the environment does little to avert the assaults on land, air, and water wrought by industrial and technological culture. Moreover, protection of the environment is rarely a landowner's motive for selling a development easement, as deeding land for conservation purposes is often a tax or business strategy rather than a gift to nature. In other words, the main selling point of conservation easements is financial, not ecological.

Other categories of environmental philanthropy also reveal the limits of foundations' interests. About 10 percent of their environmental grants in 1998 went to pollution control research, 8 percent to botanical and horticultural programs, and barely 5 percent each to policy advocacy, other research areas, and education programs. An almost immeasurably small sum is granted every year to advocates of environmental justice, although the disproportionate pollution of areas in and near communities of color has been well documented. Even more revealing than those statistics is the sad fact that of EGA's 213 member foundations, only 34 have endorsed a set of principles entitled "Philanthropy as Stewardship," which recommends practices for operating foundations in an environmentally responsible manner. What seems to bother the vast majority of member foundations that declined to sign the principles was the attempt to establish procedures for conducting foundation operations in "an environmentally sound manner." This constraint, to the evident horror of fiduciaries, includes a proscription against investing in corporations that threaten the environment. (See Appendix for more on foundation investments.)

As paltry as the dollars and grants dedicated to the environment are, they still stir consternation on the left and right. Those on the left deplores foundations' tendency to quell activism in the environmental movement by supporting polite, respectful organizations quick to join industry in the search for market-based solutions and to tout incremental improvements as triumphs. On the right, old-line conservatives complain that industrial wealth is being contributed to a cause that costs industry money; while newer advocates of the reactionary "Wise Use Movement" see a "cartel of eco-money" supporting the foes of private property. To a degree, they're all correct. Yet neither side should feel threatened by the foundations' current minimal support of environmentalism.[3]

Although foundations provide only about 7 percent of the total budgets of nonprofit environmental organizations, they exercise considerable influence over their activities and strategies. Not surprisingly, groups that rely more heavily on foundation support tend to be more centrist, more inclined to follow the "soft path" of environmental reform. Organizations like the Environmental Defense Fund, the National Audubon Society, the National Wildlife Federation, the Natural Resource Defense Council, the Sierra Club, and the Wilderness Society show up on the funding list of most environmental grantmakers. They are safe havens for foundation philanthropy, for their directors are sensitive to the economic orthodoxies that lead to the formation of foundations and careful not to do anything that might diminish the benefactor's endowment. In a social movement in which the antagonist is so often private enterprise, that sensitivity constitutes a limiting edict—one which most of the aforementioned groups are handsomely rewarded for obeying.

The clear, though rarely uttered message from the largest environmental grantmakers is this: be cautious reformers, challenge specific violators, take the worst of them to court, lobby for environmental regulations, educate the public, but don't rock (or knock) the industrial boat if you intend to rely on significant foundation funding. (For more on this theme, see chapter 7.)

The rewards of following this course are more and larger grants, which simply reinforce the worst tendencies of reform environmentalism—most notably the urge to compromise. The resultant polite political movement fails to confront some of the most environmentally abusive companies in American industry—even those that are not members of EGA or represented on national foundation boards. Thus the presidents and staffs of foundations that make environmental grants can play it safe; they do not need to defend controversial grants to their trustees, to whom market incentives, lobbying, and not-too-aggressive litigation are a fairly easy sell.

Because environmental grantmakers lean toward project-specific funding, money from foundations tends to have a lot more policy leverage than money derived from memberships, which is generally allocated to operational support. (Only a handful of sizable foundations—most notably the Joyce-Mertz Gilmore, Jessie Smith Noyes, and Turner—regularly provide general operating support to environmental groups.)

Moreover, although the direct mailings of environmental organizations often solicit contributions for general strategies and specific projects, they are not contractually obliged to carry them out. Not so with foundation money. Foundation officers concerned about "accountability" seek specific quantifiable results and impose constant oversight, often insisting on detailed reports, on-site visits, and detailed audits. In some cases, foundations officers place themselves or their representatives directly on the boards of organizations they support (see chapter 7).

The problem with this kind of active participation in environmental programs is that foundations are not organized to solve environmental problems. Even though the expansion of the environmental movement has been facilitated by organized philanthropy, none of the most impressive triumphs of American environmentalism have resulted from foundation funding. It was uncompromising activism that led to outright bans and immediate eliminations of specific practices, pollutants, and technologies. That kind of militancy very few foundation trustees will support—whether in environmentalism or in education, health, science, and the arts.

Proactivity

Nevertheless, some of the largest environmental grantmakers have become intensely proactive, and highly controversial among environmental activists. Foundations like the Pew Charitable Trusts and the Rockefeller Family Fund, these environmentalist contend, have squandered resources on the expansion of bureaucratic reform environmentalism, which has then faltered in the face of a more powerful, better-financed industrial lobby.

The kind of proactive grantmaking, in which solutions to social, environmental, and scientific problems are devised by foundation program officers, paid experts, or consultants—rather than in the reports and proposals of potential grantees—is becoming increasingly common. And it is resulting in a shift of power, problem solving, and decision making from the nonprofit to the foundation sector. Money has always talked, of course; but under a regime of proactive grantmaking it more often tends to dictate. It needn't be that way, but until foundations are more democratically structured, it is more likely than not to be the case.

Michael Lerner, president of the Jennifer Altman Foundation, has written extensively on the pros and cons of proactive philanthropy, which he differentiates from "receptive philanthropy," which tends to result when foundation executives listen for and respond to good ideas. "I am inclined to believe that it is characteristic of our aggressively masculine culture that proactive philanthropy is valued over receptive philanthropy."[4] Lerner sees value in both approaches but believes that a balance between the two creates the best philanthropy.

Pew Foundation president Rebecca Rimel, who presides over one of the most proactive of all large foundations, acknowledges the problem. "One of the dangers of this kind of funding is that foundations have this wonderful way of not knowing what the world's problems are but how to solve them. Pew's board members," she claims, "were very concerned that buried in this proactivity or strategic thinking would be an arrogance, a sense that we didn't know how to listen. We weren't going to be responsive to grantees, not only to their needs but also to their expertise and that it was going to be our way or no way."[5]

Yet proactive funding isn't necessarily a bad thing, and philanthrocrats should not be limited to writing checks for the best-sounding proposals that happen to cross their desks. But the best grantmaking tends to come from open dialogue and cooperation between grantor and grantee. When foundation officials assert control, limitations, and rigid conditions on grantees, resentment arises and projects fail. And when they do, program officers rarely admit failure, and even fewer accept blame.

However, when foundations are imaginatively guided, by fair-minded, collegial, and visionary leadership, proactive funding can work . In these circumstances foundations become instigators of progress and a major force in the renewal and strengthening of civil society. But when proactive grantmaking carries with it a we-know-better attitude or tone the result is rarely constructive, as the following section demonstrates.

Tenant Activism

People rarely argue with you when you're handing out money.
—John Gardner

In the early 1990s, convinced that the environmental movement was drifting away from what they conceived of as its mission, Pew, the Rockefeller Family Fund, MacArthur, and a few other foundations began designing new strategies and tactics and offering national organizations money to carry them out. By combining forces and money with other large foundations, Joshua Reichert, Pew's environmental program officer and an anthropologist, has become a major player in the movement. With a sizable staff to design and oversee multimillion-dollar megaprojects, he is, in essence, a kingmaker. "Reichert's ideas have a way of becoming reality," according to *Boston Globe* writer Scott Allen.[6] His initiatives have restructured national debates on endangered species, public land forestry, and energy deregulation, invariably by pushing militant environmentalists toward the center and withholding funds from uncompromising activists.

Mainstream environmental organizations desperate for resources have risen to the bait, with minimal concern that money is shaping their policies and their strategy. In 1990 the Sierra Club, which has historically received very little of its revenue from foundations, accepted a $275,000 grant from the Frank Weeden Foundation to perform work—as prescribed by Weeden—on population issues. Overnight, population research and advocacy became the highest-funded activity of the Sierra Club. And, sadly, the Club was drawn into a national controversy over immigration control; it culminated in a divisive ballot initiative brought before the full membership in April of 1998. To Weeden's dismay, the club's members voted overwhelmingly to remain neutral on the issue of immigration.

That didn't, however, silence the sirens of proactive grantmaking, or forewarn a movement fast becoming addicted to foundation largesse. In 1993, when the W. Alton Jones Foundation declared that "grassroots organizing" (or at least their definition of it) was the future, national organizations that hadn't spent a minute organizing locally stepped up to the window; their proposals embraced the foundation's definition of grassroots organizing and read as if they were fully prepared to undertake it.

The same year, Josh Reichert circulated a proposal to three other large foundations asking them to join Pew in funding a new institution called Environmental Strategies. Its mission, Reichert said, would be "to assist environmental organizations to conduct public education campaigns on priority national environmental issues." Implicit in its design was a critique of the environmental establishment's own communications and lobbying ability and an assumption that Reichert, his trustees, and the trustees of three other foundations knew better how to "identify public policy issues that are of greatest mutual concern and importance."

Reichert's stated aim was to create a new, collaborative organization based in Washington "to improve the campaigning skills of national, regional and local environmental groups and to help see to it that those skills are employed to the best effect on priority national issues." Reichert's associate, Tom Wathen, expounded the strategy in a co-authored critical appraisal of past "environmental issue campaigns" prepared for the foundations that Pew hoped would join in the new venture.

"For considerable sums of money, public opinion can be molded, constituents mobilized, issues researched, and public officials buttonholed, all in a symphonic arrangement," Wathen wrote in the coauthored report. "While business and industry have made extensive use of them, environmentalists have been slow to employ and, equally important to coordinate the new political arts. As a result environmentalism has fallen behind in a political arms race that requires even higher levels of organized constituent involvement to influence officials and engender administrative and legislative action."[7]

Although Wathen and his coauthors never state explicitly who will determine the priority issues, they point out that "foundations play an integral role in the planning and execution of issues campaigns because, as often the sole source of funds for broad public outreach, grantmaking becomes the focal point for inter-organizational cooperation. Consequently, unless foundations take the initiative in collaborating with national and local environmental organizations, little improvement can be made in campaigning on national environmental issues."[8] Josh Reichert added, with emphasis, that Pew would "*never* ask an environmental organization to change its agenda." He does acknowledge, however, that such groups might very well do so to get the money dangled before them.[9]

To many environmentalists the most troubling aspect of Pew's initiative was its provision that the board of Environmental Strategies be composed of both environmentalists *and* grantmakers. It is true that when foundation executives sit on the boards of the nonprofits they fund, they are generally quiet and respectful of the organization's wisdom and independence. But their very presence at board meetings is intimidating. Money may not be talking, per se, but it's watching. Even when grantmakers do not utter a word, or suggest a single tactic, they make tenant activists of their grantees, rendering them hostages to whatever strategy or action the funders choose. "The tendency for funders to create new organizations that are intended to speak for all of us, but which are accountable only to the funders who established them, is a very disturbing trend," according to Stephen Viederman former president of the Jessie Smith Noyes Foundation.[10]

Reichert's Environmental Strategies initiative, which has twice changed its name, is now called the National Environmental Trust. It has turned out to be a reasonably successful venture, not—as some foundation officials might claim—because they are on the board but because it is run by a talented, energetic director named Phil Clapp. Thus far Clapp has been able to stand up to Reichert and the other funders. The depth of his independence from the other foundations has, however, yet to be seriously tested. It will most likely be challenged if he attempts a genuine foray into grassroots politics.

So, though the directors of environmental organizations privately bemoan the intrusion of philanthrocrats into their business, they line up for the money being offered by the meddling foundations, which report that grant proposals flood their offices whenever they so much as hint at a new idea or strategy. Grantmaker faddism, sometimes called "mission drift" is, incidentally, not unique to the environmental movement. It happens in funding for education, science, health, and the arts where, for close to a century, foundation trustees and program officers have set, mediated, and massaged the agendas and policies of grantees simply by changing their minds about an issue or strategy.

When foundations lost interest in Alaska, so did many of their grantees. Some became passionate about forests, with good reason: there was money in the air. When Josh Reichert began talking about a national campaign to save the remaining 5 percent of uncut, old-growth forests in the United States, his office was inundated with grant proposals. According to Reichert, most of them proposed doing exactly what he said needed to be done. "It was as if he had thrown a huge steak into a den of starving lions," recalls Tim Hermack of the Oregon-based Native Forest Council. "The lions pounced on it, even though it was laced with arsenic."[11]

The very existence of a few million dollars earmarked for forestry reform caused a donnybrook between reform-minded organizations like the National Wildlife Federation, Audubon, and the Sierra Club, which are all comfortable with small incremental improvements, and less-compromising ("zero cut") groups like the Native Forest Council. The grassroots groups feared that proactive funding would tip the forest-management debate in favor of the incrementalists who were endorsing bureaucratic "ecosystem management" schemes to permit controlled logging in national forests.

And that is exactly what happened with the old-growth forest coalition, providing yet another example of how foundation funding moderates public policy on behalf of corporate interests. According to Goddard University professor Brian Tokar, who has researched environmental grantmaking for a decade or more, "Pew expressed little interest in aiding ongoing efforts at grassroots organizing, public education or legal intervention by the member groups."[12] As they dangled millions of dollars in front of starving organizations, the funding group led by Josh Reichert stipulated that no one advocating zero cut, criticizing corporations by name, or producing ads that did so would be eligible for membership in the forest coalition—or for funding. In addition, he insisted that the coalition be run by the Natural Resources Defense Council (NRDC), an organization that very few grassroots activists trust or admire (see chapter 7).

"Foundation money behind a compromise position tempts nonprofits to moderate their hard-line stance or risk being left out in the cold," remarks Tim Hermack, who advocates a zero-cut policy in all public forests.[13] His organization, the Native Forest Council, one of the most effective grassroots groups in the movement, was left out in the cold.

Andy Mahler, director of Indiana-based Heartwood, served briefly as chair of the forest coalition, a position he quickly grew to regret. "Pew was only interested in funding a campaign focused on legislation passed by a Democratic Congress, and that Clinton would sign," Mahler told Brian Tokar in September of 1996. He said he was happy to have people "talking about uniting the movement, but it became a money chase . . . and put incredible strains on the forest movement that it has not recovered from to this day."[14] As national unity dissipated, Reichert shifted his strategy to fund a series of regional initiatives, the most prominent of which was the Northern Forest Alliance in New England.

The Pew Trusts' 1994 annual report describes how the foundation created the alliance and imposed order through a team of lawyers, scientists, and consultants who, Reichert said, would "play a key role integrating many of the ideas behind the programs we support, participating with colleagues from the environmental community in defining the goals and objectives of these programs, designing their operating structures, hiring key staff and, in some cases being directly involved in program execution."[15]

Reichert intervened directly in environmental movement activity once again in September of 1995. In his view, another coalition of national and grassroots organizations, this one led by former Congressman Jim Jontz (D-Ind.) to protect the Endangered Species Act (ESA), was faltering. Jontz and his colleagues were demanding more than Reichert thought was reasonable. The latter's response was to offer the nationals in the coalition $1.5 million, with the proviso that they fire Jontz and his lieutenants and hire the National Environmental Trust's Phil Clapp. They agreed. Jontz was dumped, and Clapp took control.

At that point the struggle to protect endangered species ceased being a grassroots initiative and became an extension of Washington electoral politics. Democratic party regulars were hired by the campaign, the coalition's position on reform of the ESA was moderated, and a compromise solution was offered to all sides. It was classic preelection politicking, and it paid off for those willing to sell out a few threatened species.

The main problem with such foundation-created coalitions is that they rarely survive long past their funding period. "Synthetic alliances deteriorate into bureaucracies," observes Oregon forest activist Jim Britell. "And they create dependency on foundations, which allow them to disregard grassroots organizing. Their money is too easy."[16]

Foundations, like the general public, are fickle, and at times even more subject to the herd mentality. So when a handful of large foundation program officers like Josh Reichert, Wade Green (Rockefeller), and Peter Myers (W. Alton Jones) decide that one environmental strategy is more worthy than another, a significant number of their colleagues tend to follow. If they or any six high-profile foundations were to pull their philanthropy from the mainstream environmental movement altogether and shift it to the grassroots level—funding communications infrastructure, organizational development, special training, or whatever they perceive at the moment to be vital—the character and energy of American environmentalism would change overnight. Of course, they are unlikely to do that; the century-old tendency of foundations to favor and fund the moderating forces in all social movements remains intact, as does the drag-anchor effect it creates. And, lamentably, this phenomenon is true of foundation behavior in most of the fields they fund.

Yet proactive grantmakers like Reichert are right about one thing. The American environmental movement lacks vision and strong leadership. How else could such a well-established, well-financed movement supported by so many millions of voters have become so ineffectual?

Nonetheless, are large, mainly conservative foundations the right institutions to redirect the movement in more imaginative and strategic directions? Is money the answer? And if it is, are the nationals the best conduit for it? What about the fifteen thousand or so other organizations working in local communities and watersheds against environmental degradations of every sort, alongside community development groups with sustainability uppermost in mind? It is from those organizations that imaginative new ideas and strategies seem to arise, not from those that have established themselves as willing players in the Washington game of reform environmentalism, or in corporate strategies for energy efficiency.

Throughout the 1990s the federal government was gradually abandoning its civil authority over the environment—largely because national politicians finally realized that the Washington-based groups on which they relied never had the grassroots support they claimed. At this juncture, then, foundations truly committed to environmental philanthropy might be well advised to stop placing so much faith and money in the relatively docile national groups and instead make more grants to regional and local organizations on the true front lines of the movement. As Steve Viederman told the 1999 annual meeting of EGA, "Lasting change will not come from yet another grant to a national environmental organization. Lasting change *will* come from supporting people committed to place, who see the environment in the broad context of their communities, who organize to seize power and achieve greater control of their lives."[17] They all heard it, but few of the environmental grantmakers in the audience seem likely to follow that advice in the near future.

Yet a $200-million shift in resources from the mainstream to the grassroots of American environmentalism—about what foundations contributed to environmental activism in 1995—would go a long way toward strengthening the social movement that at least one essayist has predicted would become the most significant of the twentieth century. Such a prophecy is unlikely to be fulfilled without imagination and a little risk. Some of that risk could be taken by grantmakers willing to assume a higher moral ground than their own trustees. Failing that unlikely development, our land, air, and water must await greener trustees who will realize that only the kind of massive, front-end funding that Irene Diamond made for AIDS research can solve our most serious environmental problems.

As a younger, more imaginative generation of donors like Paul Brainerd, Wren Wirth, Richard Goldman, the Packard children, and program officers like the Hewlett Foundation's Michael Fischer enter the philanthropic domain, the environment may soon receive more foundation support and attention. Packard, Brainerd, Hewlett, and other new foundations, mostly located in the western states, have announced their intention of expanding environmental grantmaking. Packard has followed through with some interesting nine-figure grants. But will they improve the situation? Will the expansion of support strengthen the movement and improve the environment, or will it simply bloat the coffers of the accommodating, brand-name environmental nobility of New York, San Francisco, and Washington? And will the next generation of environmental grantmakers regard industrial, biotechnologically driven agriculture as a serious environmental threat? We explore that question the next chapter.

6

Food

When foundations aren't doing significant things, it's probably because they aren't listening.
—John Gardner, Former President, The Carnegie Corporation

Championing the massive global restructuring of agriculture known as the Green Revolution is perhaps American philanthropy's single most ambitious international undertaking. This initiative, instigated primarily by the staff and trustees of the Rockefeller Foundation, was later taken up by Ford and several other foundations.

The program was vast, technically complex, and in many ways truly revolutionary. Yet its goal was simple: Feed the world. The strategy, given its creators, was quite predictable: to transfer Western scientific agricultural technologies to "undeveloped" countries, thereby increasing worldwide yields of basic food crops and ending hunger.

It is worth taking a close, critical look at the Green Revolution, not only because it is the single largest and longest-lasting initiative of the American foundations, but also because it illuminates so many of philanthropy's best and worst aspects. New philanthropists wishing to learn about the pitfalls of large-scale grantmaking would be wise to study the fifty-year history of this project. Meticulously documented in the archives of the Rockefeller and Ford foundations are all the planning, strategizing, idealism, imagination, conceit, and unbounded hubris of large-scale philanthropy. The story of this massive undertaking is a valuable case study of an earnest, long-term philanthropic effort to solve a complex, seemingly intractable problem without addressing the fundamental reasons for its existence.

On any list of the greatest grants—Philanthropy at its Best, the Triumphs of American Grantmaking, Ten Grants That Changed the

World—the Green Revolution would rank in the top five. That rank-ing—if its social and ecological consequences are ignored—is well de-served. Although hunger has not been ended by the revolution, it has been reduced; enough food is now produced, year after year, to feed the world—with some to spare.

However, for reasons officers, trustees, and scientists of the Rockefeller Foundation did not foresee, and later ignored, there are still about 800 million hungry people in the world and 185 million seriously malnour-ished preschool children.[1] Thirty years ago, when the initiative was still germinating, there were an estimated 950,000 underfed people on the planet. So, proportionately, there is now less hunger on the planet than there was then. Yet, with food enough to feed the world, 800 million people staring at starvation is hardly a triumph of science or philan-thropy. How could this happen? A close look at the history of the Green Revolution offers some answers. More importantly, it offers to future philanthropists, whatever their interests, some indispensable lessons.

Surplus and Poverty

It is axiomatic that a well-fed world is a peaceful world.
—J. George Harrar, Rockefeller Foundation

The Green Revolution was seeded in 1941 with a small Rockefeller grant to begin maize research in Mexico. Mexico was the natural place for a Rockefeller-funded agricultural science project and 1941 was an appro-priate year. The country had a new president, Avilo Camacho, a man American business leaders perceived as far more amenable to private property and free enterprise than his predecessor, Lazaro Cardenas. Three years earlier Cardenas had nationalized all Standard Oil assets and operations in Mexico and instituted sweeping land reforms that strongly favored the peasantry. Cardenas's program was immediately abandoned by Camacho in favor of a modernization strategy benefiting private farm-ers and neglecting the *ejidataros* (small landowners) and campesinos.

Despite the loss of vast economic assets, there remained a strong geo-political incentive for Rockefeller trustees to do everything possible to stabilize Camacho's government by promoting a productive agriculture industry predicated on private land ownership and the free market. The *Cardenistas* were out of power, but agriculture was still not producing enough to feed the country, a condition that existed in most countries of Latin America. Throughout the region, the Rockefeller family's massive investments made them vulnerable to the kind of instability that results from a hungry populace.

By 1943 researchers in the Rockefeller's Mexican Agriculture Program (MAP) were studying the science of corn propagation and teaching Mexican agronomists what they had learned. The project expanded rapidly to other Latin American countries—Colombia, Chile, Peru—and to other food crops—beans, forage, wheat, and rice. The program in Mexico attracted agriculture students from throughout South and Central America. Early reports from Rockefeller scientists described huge mounds of wheat and beans stacked in Mexican village schoolyards—the result of unprecedented crop yields from surrounding farms. To Rockefeller trustees those mountains of food represented an authentic triumph of science over ignorance.

From its beginning, the Rockefeller trusts were always more likely than most other foundations to employ science in pursuit of political goals. John D. Rockefeller's founding of the Rockefeller Institute for Medical Research in 1901 had inaugurated three decades of support for an international technical assistance mission that reshaped medicine and medical research worldwide. Since then, as we saw in chapter 4, scientific medicine had incorporated most other approaches to healing and had come to dominate Western medicine. In much the same way as they had earlier depoliticized medicine, the Rockefeller trustees sought in the 1940s to depoliticize agriculture. It would prove an impossible task.

When in 1905 the Reverend Frederick Gates had advised John D. Rockefeller to create a series of "great corporate philanthropies," he had placed "scientific agriculture "at the top of a list of proposed programs. The following year the Rockefeller's General Education Board began an eight-year project that granted $1 million to domestic agricultural research. So by 1941, when Rockefeller made its first international agriculture grant in Mexico, the foundation was already well endowed with agricultural expertise.

The Rockefeller Foundation itself was created in 1913 "to serve the welfare of mankind throughout the world." The new foundation's programs reflected the era's deep and abiding faith in science and in its ability to transform society, allay misery, and bring order into a chaotic world. "All important fields of activity, from the breeding of bees to the administration of empire, call for an understanding of the spirit and technique of modern science," wrote Rockefeller officer Wickliffe Rose in 1924. "Promoting the development of science in a country is germinal," he added. "It affects the entire system of education and carries with it the remaking of a civilization."[2] Subsequently, remaking civilizations in the developing world became a central Rockefeller enterprise. It began, however, with the advancement of America's own agricultural practices.

When the foundation was reorganized in 1928, its new divisions were oriented around specific fields of science: social science, medical science, and natural science. The Natural Sciences division headed by Warren Weaver included agriculture as well as biology and physiological psychology. From the start the agricultural scientists asserted their independence from the social sciences, a separation that lasted well into the 1960s. Moreover, the early agronomists of the Green Revolution paid scant heed to the natural environment. It is thus not surprising that the lasting detrimental effects of the Green Revolution have stemmed from lack of attention to the social and ecological impacts of its agricultural practices.

Earlier, during its first year of operation, the Rockefeller Foundation had opened a public health mission in Mexico. Shortly thereafter, foundation officials and the Mexican minister of agriculture met to discuss creating an agricultural mission, and the foundation offered to train Mexican agronomists in the United States. But, primarily because of the instability of the Cardenas administration, the proposed mission was not was formalized until Cardenas was replaced by the more accommodating Camacho.

Shortly after returning from a visit to Mexico in 1940, U.S. Vice President Henry Wallace had a chance encounter with Rockefeller President Raymond Fosdick. "If the Rockefeller Foundation would undertake to help the Mexican people increase the yield per acre of corn and beans," he told Fosdick, "it would mean more to the future of Mexico than anything else that government or philanthropy could devise."[3]

In the weeks following that encounter, young Nelson Rockefeller, who at the time chaired the International Development Advisory Board (IADB), held extensive meetings with Wallace and Fosdick. The political stability of Mexico and the burgeoning population of India were as important topics of discussion as beans, corn, and agricultural science.[4] The IADB had already recommended cooperation "with these countries [Mexico, India, etc.] in a vigorous food production drive that would break the back of famine and hunger" and, in the process, stabilize their governments.[5]

It was Henry Wallace, though, who pushed hardest for the Mexican initiative.[6] Himself a prosperous farmer and a committed progressive, Wallace, who later became U.S. secretary of agriculture, regarded himself as "the father of industrial agriculture."[7] He based this claim largely on his founding of the Pioneer Hybrid Seed Company and the rather small role he played in forming MAP.[8] (In 1960 the latter was phased into the International Maize and Wheat Improvement Center in Mexico and is now known by its Spanish acronym, CIMMYT.)

CIMMYT (pronounced *simmit*) became the model for similar centers throughout the developing world, most notably in India. Collectively, they have transformed the entire field of agricultural research and altered farming practices throughout the Third World. Whether for better or for worse remains to this day a matter of heated debate.

The Mexico projects were directed by plant pathologist George "Dutch" Harrar, who later succeeded Dean Rusk as president of the Rockefeller Foundation. If anyone deserves the title Father of Industrial Agriculture, it is Harrar. In test plots at thirteen International Agricultural Research Centers scattered around the planet, Harrar and his scientists developed new crop varieties that vastly increased yields of basic food stocks, particularly wheat. By the early 1950s the goal of feeding a fast-growing Mexican population plagued by famine and undernourishment seemed in sight. As Harrar wrote to his colleagues, "the Rockefeller-Mexico program has demonstrated that a mere handful of well trained scientists can, in an amazingly short time, catalyze the agricultural economy of a nation."[9]

In 1956 the program was taken to India, where the twin global crises of population explosion and a communist insurgency added urgency to the challenge of feeding the hungry. In fact, a reading of the documents in the Rockefeller Archives indicates clearly that Cold War geopolitics and population growth were as much on the mind of foundation trustees as feeding the masses. "Rockefeller Foundation staff and trustees saw

India as an overpopulated nation, caught in a Malthusian trap and teetering on the brink of communism," writes agricultural historian John Perkins.[10] Even Rockefeller breeding geneticist Norman Borlaug came to regard his seed research in India as "buying time" against the "population monster."

Perkins believes that postwar concern for national security, as much as humanitarian motives, were the ultimate driving force of the Green Revolution. That's only one historian's perspective, of course; still, agronomists and others concerned about hunger and conservation did frequently use the security argument to capture the attention of government leaders. Without the vast resources of the federal government, they knew, their revolution could never succeed.

The archives also reveal that Rockefeller President Raymond Fosdick's concern about population was a direct response to a widespread criticism of the foundation's international public health programs: that they helped increase the populations of Third World countries unable to feed them. Fosdick agreed with critics who said that such policy was essentially unethical, because it led inexorably to worldwide famine. In 1947 John D. Rockefeller III, the most influential of the trustees, responded to Fosdick's concern, proposing that the foundation conduct internal research on the interrelationships among human fertility, demography, economics, and culture in the Green Revolution areas.

The resulting report caused an uproar at Rockefeller, mostly over the process that produced it and the propriety of having one powerful trustee, even a Rockefeller, direct a study on an issue so central to the foundation's operations. Few of the report's readers seemed equally bothered by its overweening tone of paternalism and disrespect for Indian village life. Here, for example, is its aerial view of the Indian countryside:

The villages are as uniform as so many ant hills. Indeed, from the air, where a number of villages can be seen simultaneously, they have the appearance of structures built by creatures motivated by inherited animal instincts, and devoid of any inclination to depart from a fixed hereditary pattern. The inheritance in this instance, of course, is social.

The villages maintain themselves on a subsistence level with respect to food, but do not produce a surplus for the cities. India had reached a point where the practice of agriculture no longer serves the traditional and important purpose of providing leisure for the development of the creative aspects of culture, the arts, the sciences and religion.[11]

"If one sees another culture as overabundant, hungry insects, one might well conclude that the only issue is how much food does it take to keep them alive and tranquil," John Perkins believes. "This is not to say that physical supplies of food are not important, but unfortunately the Rockefeller Foundation's heavy emphasis on overpopulation as the cause of hunger created a situation in which Foundation staff could not see and appreciate other dimensions of hunger, especially distribution to people without access to land or money."[12]

As a consequence of this rather basic oversight, the civil societies of a dozen or more large countries were fundamentally and permanently transformed. An agricultural system around which village life and livelihoods had revolved for thousands of years was virtually destroyed. Faith in knowledge triumphed. Biological science prevailed over social science, and industry trumped culture.

While foundation staff and trustees eventually came to agree that population growth, communist agitation, and agriculture were inextricably linked, the funding and operation of Green Revolution research maintained its singular obsession with plant genetics and crop yields. Warren Weaver, a mathematician by profession, was particularly insistent; he saw scientific research as indispensable to India's stability and argued that agroscience institutions similar to the U.S. land grant universities should be created there and elsewhere. Industrialization of agriculture, he was convinced, would lead to industrialization of agrarian societies, and, ipso facto, to lower population growth. Yet, as food production grew exponentially as a result of the Green Revolution, so did population. Even so, many soldiers in the revolution persisted in believing that they were winning and continued to recruit more combatants.

During the late 1950s Dutch Harrar rode the commuter train to New York with a former Saskatchewan farmer named Forrest ("Frosty") Hill. Hill, an agricultural economist and former provost of Cornell University, was working in the Ford Foundation's fledgling agriculture division. At the time, Ford was sitting on millions of dollars with no idea of how to spend it. Harrar spent many trips down the Hudson trying, through Hill, to siphon off a few of those millions for the food-production initiative Rockefeller had begun almost twenty years before.

In 1959 the Ford Foundation signed on with a $7-million grant to the International Rice Research Institute (IRRI) in the Philippines. About that time, Ford Vice President W. H. "Ping" Ferry coined the phrase *Green Revolution*. The media loved it and offered up a spate of glowing stories about the immanent conquest of world hunger. The publicity, which ignored social and ecological quandaries, encouraged Ford trustees to pump more money into the initiative. Before long the Ford Foundation had become a major player in the quest to feed the world.

Ford's interest in the revolution seemed even more closely linked to Cold War anxieties than the Rockefeller's. "If our aid to [undeveloped countries] is lacking or wasteful, the Communists will do the job on their own, to the irreparable loss of the West and the United States" reads an internal memorandum written in 1954, two years before Ford made its first contribution to the Green Revolution. It continues:

From the point of view of the West and the preservation of its most cherished values it is of utmost importance whether, in their current efforts to modernize, the underdeveloped countries will lean toward the West, adapting its technology and political ideas to suit their special needs, or instead, accept the Communist promises and eventually the Communist system.[13]

Meanwhile Congress, according to Ford trustees, was moving too slowly to remedy social conditions that were leading to unrest in rural areas, particularly in India. Foundation President Paul Hoffman was determined to stop that country from going the way of China. As Congress was sitting on its hands, he believed, the foundation should take the initiative to keep the Soviets and Chinese from fomenting insurgency among the vast peasant populations of southern Asia. Food would be the counterweapon; science, the savior.

Ford rapidly increased its investment in agroscience, eventually becoming an equal though, qualitatively unique, warrior in the Green Revolution. Unlike the Rockefeller Foundation, Ford saw clearly that "a program cannot concentrate on some particular element of development without running the risk that it may be rendered useless by failure to carry on parallel developments in other fields."[14] Thus Ford, more than Rockefeller, integrated its support of agricultural science with sociological and anthropological research in an attempt to understand the social consequences of modernizing agriculture.

Before long, however, the challenge of feeding the world became too expensive for even the largest private foundations in America. In the early 1960s Rockefeller and Ford officials began lobbying the federal government to provide a budget for the Agency for International Development (A.I.D.) to support the agricultural initiative. They succeeded. For the next eight years A.I.D. was the central banker of the Green Revolution.

When less than a decade later A.I.D. began to back away from the program, agronomists at Rockefeller persuaded the World Bank to take its place. The bank joined the revolution with great generosity, making credit available to farmers for advanced machinery, farm chemicals, seeds, and livestock. But, as ethnobotanist and World Bank historian Catherine Caufield points out, "credit approval was often conditional on farmers' adopting new techniques, switching to particular crops, buying insurance, and selling to a specific buyer who would deduct the loan payments from the farmer's earnings."[15] It was a formula that enriched the rich farmer and further impoverished the poor. The foundations offered no resistance as the bank pursued its established practice of expanding wealth by providing assistance to the wealthy.

By the mid-1960s Rockefeller and Ford had also coaxed the Milbank Memorial and Kellogg foundations into the funding pool. With the World Bank providing credit, over $3 billion a year was pumped into the development of new agricultural infrastructure in the Third World— more pesticide and fertilizer factories, larger commodity exchanges, huge meat-packing plants, grain silos, and canneries. The revolution spread quickly to almost every food-deficient country of the world. Measured in gross tonnage and per unit of human labor, the yields of staple food crops—grains, pulses, forage, and root crops—grew impressively.

The premise of the revolution shared by scientists, development experts, and philanthropists was that abundant foodstuffs would find their way to hungry mouths and assure peace. When food scarcity was reduced or eliminated, according to this logic, primitive agrarian societies would advance into the modern world. Yield per acre became the ultimate standard of social progress, and yield per capita a measure of national stability. And stability was still regarded by Cold War strategists, politicians, and foundation trustees as the antidote to insurgency.

The Green Revolution thus became a techno-political fix for a potential communist revolution. As historian Keith Griffin put it, "technical progress was regarded as an alternative to land reform."[16] Ironically, the Soviet Union, which was promoting and supporting rural land reform along with revolutionary "wars of national liberation" throughout the world, was also pressing a structurally similar initiative—centralized (state-owned) farms, mechanization, heavy chemical usage, and "miracle" seed stocks—with ecological and social consequences not unlike those of the American experiment.

In 1968 the Rockefeller Foundation began sponsoring international meetings of agronomists and other scientists at their posh retreat in Bellagio, Italy. Two years later foundation officers proposed a worldwide network of agricultural research centers under a permanent secretariat. In 1971 the Consultative Group on International Agricultural Research (CGIAR) was formed; by 1983 there were thirteen research centers under the CGIAR umbrella, with a combined annual budget exceeding $100 million.

Not long after CGIAR's creation, the Green Revolution met its goal of producing a global harvest of basic foodstuffs sufficient to feed the world. In 1971 Rockefeller Foundation scientist Norman Borlaug won the Nobel Peace Prize for his breeding of high-yield dwarf varieties of wheat. To many contemporary agronomists, including Robert Herdt, currently vice president for agricultural sciences at the Rockefeller Foundation, "the Green Revolution was over in 1971." Science had triumphed.[17] To Brian O'Connell, a tireless booster of American philanthropy, the revolution spawned by Borlaug and Rockefeller was "the prototype of efforts to relieve human misery."[18] But was it? Did it? How much human misery has actually been relieved? And how much was created by the Green Revolution?

In 1971, the putative year of triumph, officers at the Ford Foundation were asking themselves the same question. In a speech to southwestern American farmers and agronomists, Ford's agriculture program director, Lowell Hardin, told his audience that "a truly widespread green revolution [was] a promise, not a reality." He saw a "danger of rhetorical overkill concerning the achievements of the Green Revolution" and asserted that "technology alone cannot do the job." For the first time, a foundation executive publicly admitted that "the green revolution is exerting a destabilizing influence on traditional social and political institutions. . . . Increased output is not necessarily associated with positive social change," Hardin added. "How the change takes place has much to do with who shares in its fruits."[19] Yet even this remarkable admission from an architect of the revolution—a sign that the external critique of the thirty-year old initiative had finally reached the ears of someone inside a foundation—skirted the central issue.

Population

American philanthropy reflects both our genius and our wound. It illuminates both our extraordinary entrepreneurial spirit and our systematic lack of commitment to caring for people and their environment.
—Michael Lerner, President, Jennifer Altman Foundation[20]

At the heart of the Green Revolution, though all too rarely discussed by its adherents, is the matter of human population. "Much of the conflict that has occurred in the world during the past decades has been the result of population pressure,"[21] George Harrar acknowledged in a 1951 memo to his associates. Yet even scientists like Harrar who did address the population question seemed to share the faith in the so-called Malthusian transition that says "reductions in human fertility follow economic development rather than precede it."[22] In most instances, however, expanding agricultural production and global food supplies was a way to avoid addressing the more controversial issue of population control, which so often begets indictments of racism, imperialism, economic privilege, and Euro-American hegemony.

When Lowell Hardin made his landmark speech in Tulsa the world's population was 3.5 billion, three times what it was a century earlier. Today it's approaching twice that size. Hardin mentioned the numbers and spoke of holding back famine for ten to twenty years, a goal he described himself as "cautiously optimistic" of meeting. Recent events, particularly in sub-Saharan Africa, have added even more reasons for caution.

Eventually, all the principal foundations supporting the Green Revolution became involved in population control. Rockefeller has a sizable population control program, as does Ford. But lengthy or serious discussions of the population question are rare in the agriculture archives of either foundation, even though the two issues are intimately linked.[23]

A 1974 memorandum from R. G. Anderson, associate director of Ford's wheat program, to Lowell Hardin illustrates the hazards of discussing population in the context of food and agriculture. "What are the problems facing man?" Anderson asks. "What are the needs, and what tools do we have to attack the various problems, be they biologic, input supply or economic adjustments?"

Anderson mentions "the population problem" but immediately apologizes for doing so. "It may seem peculiar to start a paper on crop production with the population problem," he writes. "However this is not only basic to the problem of food, it is an historical event unknown before." The Green Revolution was, according to Anderson, "never meant to be anything but an attempt to provide breathing space in which to bring population into balance with resources. The effort was never designed to create utopia or to cure all the social problems in the countries to which it has been exported." Contemporary participants in the revolution still accept that rationale, but most would part ways with Anderson over his solution to the problem. In the same memo, he goes on to quote a colleague, who says:

It is an ethical imperative to feed the starving and to feed them well, even if it were proven beyond a shadow of a doubt that a hundred years hence we shall run into a Malthusian limit. But it is equally imperative that those born a hundred years hence shall not starve. The conflict can only be solved by lacing the food with sterilizing agents, or by other means to the same effect. If this is rejected as interfering with sovereignty or racial insult, there may be no solution.

"Responsible scientists say we can buy a little time," Anderson adds, "but it is going to become increasingly expensive to produce food."[24] Anderson's memo beautifully illustrates the hazards of addressing population control: the topic leads inexorably to just the kind of controversy that foundations have historically sought to avoid. Economics is safer; science, safer still.

Supply sans Demand

Destructive negativism in the social sciences and naive optimism in the technical sciences are luxuries which poor rural people cannot afford.
—Robert Chambers, Ford Foundation

There can be no denying that hundreds of millions of tons of additional grain, rice, and legumes have been harvested since the Green Revolution began. But have they reached those most in need of them? No. The best that can be said is that the number of people who are underfed and under-nourished has declined slightly. So, while as a percentage of world population the proportion of people being fed has increased, starvation, malnutrition, and disease exacerbated by hunger persist—despite a global food supply sufficient to feed them all.

As *Business Week* acknowledged in a 1994 report from India, the revolution had succeeded in reducing grain imports and creating a surplus, but it had failed to allay the very crisis it addressed. "Even though Indian granaries are overflowing," the article reads, grain was rotting in storage as "five thousand children die each day of malnutrition, and one third of India's 900 million people remain poverty stricken."[25] How could this happen?

The problem with the strategy chosen by Rockefeller and Ford was that it dealt primarily with supply and ignored the demand side of the agricultural equation. Supply, as it turns out, is only half the problem, and thus half the solution. Demand for food is everywhere and is persistent, but without purchasing power in the hands of the hungry, demand is useless. As any freshman economics student could have explained to foundation trustees, food will not move toward hunger without economic incentive. Enrich the hungry with just enough to afford a few beans, rice, legumes, or basic grains and produce will begin to move to where it is needed most. But that is a matter of economic justice, not science. Science was something with which Rockefeller trustees felt completely comfortable. Economic justice, on the other hand, suggested socialism.

So for the first forty years of the Green Revolution, the growing surplus of food barely moved to where it was needed most—not because the government and nongovernmental international agencies weren't trying to improve the economic lot of the poor. They simply couldn't do so fast enough to compensate for the large numbers of subsistence farmers and their families who were being pushed off the land and impoverished by industrial agriculture. It was a political challenge that lay beyond the scope, interest, or ability of the foundations that had fomented the Green Revolution.

The designers and bankers of the revolution had failed to anticipate that larger landowners would be able to afford the new seeds sooner than small farmers, and thus would be the first to reap the higher yields. This advantage was particularly inequitable in Latin America where, under the latifundio system, half of all the arable land was owned by 2 percent of the people. So, while the lower food prices that resulted from increased harvests clearly benefited low-income urban consumers, they became an insurmountable barrier to farmers with smaller yields. Millions of small farmers—lacking adequate credit to purchase the seeds, tractors, fertilizer, and pesticides that would have made them competitive—went belly up. Forced to sell their land, they become farm laborers or moved to urban barrios in search of work.

Throughout the underdeveloped world, thousands of farms were foreclosed, their owners driven into a diaspora of cheap labor working for those wealthy enough to buy their land, or for the Western corporations that built fertilizer and pesticide factories in rural areas. This "proletarianization" of the peasantry was particularly hard on women, who were even less likely than their male peers to own land. Those unable to find jobs in the countryside moved reluctantly into crowded cities, where many resorted to prostitution.

Meanwhile the cities were expanding outward, expropriating some of the best agricultural land. Urban sprawl also increased the energy requirements for food and fiber as crops had to be shipped that much farther to markets. Twenty-five years into the Green Revolution, the downside of a supply-driven Cold War strategy had become all too clear.

As the revolution progressed it became increasingly evident that even technologies that improved the lot of small farmers benefited large farmers even more. Thus the inequities grew. A few social scientists realized that genuine improvement would come only when laws and policies concerning land tenure, credit, prices, and other factors disproportionately affecting the poor were addressed. But, like population control, these were considered politically risky issues, particularly in countries where landholding interests were strongly represented in national legislatures.

"Focusing narrowly on increased production cannot alleviate hunger," Institute for Food and Development co-founder Frances Moore Lappé and colleagues reminded philanthropists, "because it fails to alter the tightly concentrated distribution of economic power, especially access to land and purchasing power. If you don't have the land on which to grow food or the money to buy it, you go hungry, no matter how dramatically technology pushes up food production."[26]

Small farmers in dry areas worked under an extra hardship, for designers of the revolution had deliberately developed their seeds for areas endowed with ample irrigation—land that, naturally, tended to be owned by wealthier farmers. Not only was the experiment more likely to succeed on well-irrigated land, but many of the new crops required more water than traditional varieties. Moreover, hybrid varieties produced in the new agriculture centers required farmers to purchase new seeds every year; this was a further disadvantage for peasant farmers, who preferred "open-pollinated" strains that allowed them to save seeds from their own crops for the next growing season.

Rockefeller scientists made a number of attempts to bring their technologies to the peasantry. In 1967 CIMMYT tried to recruit Mexican *campesinos* into the Green Revolution through the "Plan Puebla." But the inability of modern agronomists to understand their languages and their farming practices—as well, as peasant resistance to the use of chemical fertilizers and pesticides—led to immediate failure.

Of course, there were bound to be mistakes and oversights in a project as vast and ambitious as the Green Revolution. Many of them could be fixed or remedied, through either existing institutions or new ones created to address the problem. And there was plenty of money for small fixes. But the one intractable problem foundations seemed unwilling to address throughout the Cold War—economic inequity—severely limited the success of the experiment.

Gradually, class divisions widened in agricultural communities throughout the developing world. "It now appears that in the agro-economic environment of the countryside, high rates of economic development may actually exacerbate social tensions and ultimately undermine the foundations of rural political stability," wrote political scientist Francine Frankel in 1968. She was prescient. Armed conflict erupted shortly thereafter in Tamil Nadu, India, where forty-three people were killed. The following year the Indian home ministry reported an increase from nineteen cases of agrarian conflict in 1968 to forty-one in 1969. Most, led by landless peasants against wealthy landowners, concerned wages, tenure, crop share, and land distribution.[27]

"One bad agricultural season could lead to an explosive situation in the rural areas," warned the home ministry in 1969.[28] That happened in the Punjab, where by the late 1980s fifteen thousand people had lost their lives in a much larger, protracted insurrection. More recent Zapatista uprisings in Chiapas, Mexico, appear to have had similar roots, as they were instigated by subsistence farmers unable to compete with large-scale corporate agriculture.

A 1995 retrospective review of more than three hundred research studies of the Green Revolution published over thirty years found that 80 percent of the researchers who had investigated the matter found increased economic inequity.[29] Even researchers favorable to the revolution, including many whose work was funded by the Rockefeller and Ford foundations, found economic imbalance to be a problem, although they tended to downplay its significance. The attitude of Donald Winkelman, a CIMMYT scientist, was typical; when asked by historian Bruce Jennings why he did not consider socioeconomic studies relevant to agricultural science, he replied, "I am not interested in theories of how the rich screw the poor."[30]

Skeptics Ignored

It is as though philanthropy exists for its own sake, rather than for the communities it is intended to serve.
—Pablo Eisenberg

There were a number of skeptics of a purely science-driven, supply-side strategy both inside and outside the Rockefeller Foundation, but little heed was paid to their forebodings. One of the external critics was University of California geographer Carl Sauer, who was invited to comment on the foundation's plans shortly after the initiative was launched in 1944. In a handwritten evaluation copied to Rockefeller President Raymond Fosdick, Sauer warned that the U.S. model of agriculture could destroy the vital diversity of Mexico's corn seed stock and seriously compromise the nutrition of the country's campesinos.

Aggressive agronomists and plant breeders could ruin the native resources for good and all by pushing their commercial stocks. . . . Mexican agriculture cannot be pointed toward standardization on a few commercial types without upsetting native economy and culture hopelessly. The example of Iowa is about the most dangerous for Mexico. Unless the Americans understand that, they'd better keep out of this country entirely, this thing must be approached from an appreciation of the native economies being basically sound.

In a separate memo written the same year, Sauer reminded the foundation of the recent soil damage to Puerto Rican farms caused by "the hasty introduction of American tools and methods. Only the exceptional American agricultural scientist will see the hazards of cultural destruction," he wrote. "But he will be under pressure for quick results, and as an alien to a strange situation, might overlook the fact that native practices represent real solutions to local problems. . . . Mexicans must build on the preservation and rationalization of their own experience with slow and careful additions from the outside."[31]

In February of 1945, after traveling through Mexico with two Rockefeller agronomists, Sauer issued another warning; he wrote to the foundation's director of social sciences to disparage "natural scientists who remain unaware of the cultural medium in which they are working."[32] He argued that social and agricultural scientists should work together on the project and protested forcefully against the cultivation of wheat in Mexico, Peru, and Chile, where malnourished peasants were in far greater need of legumes.

Nor was Sauer the only person to predict dire social consequences from Rockefeller's agricultural strategy. In fact, at about the same time, the foundation's own International Health Division completed two studies concurring with Sauer's critique and documenting the dietary shortcomings of the new system. Even trustee John Dickey, president of Dartmouth College, predicted after a visit to MAP sites in Mexico that "within three to five years the program will raise some very acute problems with respect to the political control of [the program's] benefits." In his opinion, "these very benefits may introduce fresh economic disparities within the Mexican economy."[33]

In 1949 Warren Weaver, a strong proponent of interdisciplinary studies, wrote to Rockefeller Foundation President Chester Barnard, urging him to form a joint committee of biological and social scientists to oversee the Mexican initiative. Barnard rejected the idea, saying that as Harrar was running the program he should have the sole power to bring in other disciplines.

As chance would have it, that same year William Myers, a longtime member of the Rockefeller Foundation's General Education Board, contacted Harrar directly to suggest that he include sociological research in the retrospective review of the Mexican program. In a terse memo to

Weaver, Harrar dismissed the whole idea of "entering the field of applied sociology," regardless of the status or qualification of those suggesting it.[34] So at the highest staff level of the foundation, Sauer, Weaver, Dickey, Meyers, and anyone who raised social or political concerns about the agriculture program was summarily rejected. On several occasions in the years that followed, questions of equity and social fallout were raised again, only to be dismissed or ignored by Rockefeller officials.

A similar pattern developed inside the Ford Foundation. The archives contain a spate of memoranda acknowledging the "Appalachia effect" of industrial agriculture (creation of communities of "sharecroppers and landless laborers unable to find either land to rent or jobs") but arguing that "few rural people have been made worse off absolutely" and that "citizens at large have been made considerably better off because food prices are somewhat lower than would likely have been the case had there been no Green Revolution."[35]

Thus no coherent social critique of the Green Revolution was developed until the early 1960s, when the negative impact of its grantmaking and strategy had become so patently obvious that even Rockefeller scientists couldn't ignore it. It was, in fact one of their own, Donald Freebairn, a staffer at CIMMYT, who first raised questions of equity and land tenure in a voice that earned attention. Nonetheless, Freebairn's request for permission to attend a 1959 Montevideo conference on land problems was denied. "We appreciate the importance of these problems in the Latin American countries," reads the response from Freebairn's superior, A. H. Moseman. "But it would seem desirable for members of our staff to avoid becoming directly involved in these fields in a manner that might impair the effectiveness of our cooperative activities."[36]

Freebairn was not the only Rockefeller scientist aware of the social situation in developing countries. In a 1961 address to the Weed Association of America, foundation agronomist Ed Wellhausen described the poverty and hunger experienced by about half the people of Latin America, where most of the crops grown on the latifundia were exported and most of the revenues from their sale was hoarded in banks outside the continent. "Reform is needed," Wellhausen asserted. "Unless some immediate attempts are made to alleviate social grievances, violent revolutions are highly probable." More food was not enough, he insisted. Better government, universal education, progressive taxation, and more efficient use of natural resources were all required. But food, he acknowledged, had to come first. "Starving people generally won't wait for long term solutions."[37]

Ten years later, as head of Rockefeller's economic unit, Freebairn struck again, this time in a special internal report entitled "The Dichotomy of Prosperity and Poverty in Mexican Agriculture." He argued that agricultural research could not remain strictly scientific or technical, that it must also address questions of "land and liberty," "equity and justice," and "social welfare."[38] Rockefeller officers and trustees ignored Freebairn, just as they had Wellhausen. But officials in A.I.D. and the United Nations Development Project, who were sent a copies of the Freebairn memorandum, took particular notice of his concern for social equity.

Rockefeller-funded wheat scientists within CIMMYT remained hostile to their colleagues' reform proposals for at least another decade. The goal of productivity, they argued, would be compromised by addressing concerns about social welfare. Equity was someone else's problem. They rejected outright the notion that pressing for yield maximization at any cost was causing the inequities their colleagues observed.

Meanwhile, critics in the Third World began to speak out, contending that centralization of production had led to centralization of political power, cultural uniformity, and increased militarization of the state. Science, they complained, had been placed above society and the social consequences were proving disastrous. In many countries, India in particular, village autonomy had given way to bureaucracy, and debt dependence was compromising the security of small farmers. In short, critics alleged, the Green Revolution had planted a gigantic land mine in the Third World, where the whole project was just as often regarded a failure as a success.

In much of the undeveloped world, the Green Revolution was seen, not as a program to end world hunger but as a Western imperial response to peasant insurrections like the Chinese revolution. From Beijing, Mao Tse Dung was encouraging peasants everywhere in the world to confront their landlords. By combining science and politics under western guidance, a well-armed global bulwark was built against communist insurrection and wrapped in the noble cause of ending world hunger. To critics in the developed world, too, the episode illustrated the mindset of Cold War corporatism transferred to philanthropy.

It was a harsh criticism, and by no means shared by everyone in the Third World. But even moderate observers agreed that the revolution was a mixed blessing. "The poor benefit from the Green Revolution," according to D. P. Singh, architect of India's Green Revolution, "but not proportionately." He points out that the revolution favored large land-owners with access to irrigation, credit, and economies of scale in both the sale of crops and the purchase of fertilizers, pesticides, and farm equipment. The gulf between rich and poor farmers, Singh contends, "widens in absolute as well as relative terms."[39]

"Without a strategy for change that addresses the powerlessness of the poor, the tragic result will be more food and yet more hunger," predicted Lappé and colleagues in 1978.[40] Even the World Bank, which contributed massively to the project, eventually saw the limits of a supply-side strategy. Hunger, a 1986 bank report concluded, can only be reduced by "redistributing purchasing power and resources toward those who are undernourished."[41]

The reasons for Rockefeller's failure to grasp the equity issue, or acknowledge the importance of distribution, are deeply buried in its history. "The Rockefeller Foundation was founded upon the immense wealth of one American," historian Perkins reminds us.

Although the Rockefeller family lost direct control over this wealth, the people selected to be the first trustees were not inclined to question or criticize the legitimacy of the foundation's resources. Subsequent trustees and officers were of the same inclination. Warren Weaver [particularly] fell into a long tradition of personnel who presumed that class and wealth were not interesting issues, if they even existed. It is thus doubtful that [he] thought deeply about the caste structure of India and its relation to agriculture, food and hunger. . . . And given that the most important agricultural advisors to the Foundation during the formative years of [the Green Revolution] were a plant breeder, a soil scientist and a plant pathologist, it was not surprising that the programs were insensitive to the complexities of distribution.[42]

Long before the Rockefeller Foundation awoke to the crisis it was fostering, the Ford Foundation took an interest in the political aspects of agriculture, putting social scientists to work directly in the project and heeding their advice. Social scientists tend to be more pessimistic than their physical or biological brethren; they are quicker to see who is gaining or losing from a program or initiative and to find ways to ameliorate the problem. As Robert Chambers advised the Ford Foundation in 1983, things work best "when physical and biological scientists work together with social scientists. The outcome can be a sort of practical political economy of technological change."[43] He might also have advised that the scientists consult with those most immediately affected by the Green Revolution—small farmers. But that is a lesson most foundations have yet to learn.

Social scientists, wrote Chambers, provide "an analysis of power and interests, of who stands to gain and who to lose, which can both inform and change styles and priorities in technical research . . . and improve the chances that poorer people will benefit." If the trustees of the foundations supporting the Green Revolution recognize this, he believes, "the next generation of biological technology should better fit the resources of small farmers and the needs of the landless and make things better for them than they would otherwise have been."[44]

Rockefeller trustees clearly perceived a threat of socialist revolution in that sort of thinking. But Ford's seemed to heed Chambers, who believed that "many of the changes that can benefit the rural poor are not revolutionary in the normal sense, but require small and painstaking steps taken resolutely in a consistent direction. The revolution needed here is professional: a turning around to face the other way, to put first the resources, technology, crops and animals of the poor and give them more priority."[45]

Environmental Impacts

Science and technology made their first advances by rejecting the idea of miracles in the natural world.
—Angus Wright, *Innocents Abroad* (1984)

The agricultural imperative not only subsumed cultural considerations and ignored economic reality, it ran roughshod over the environment. Green Revolution scientists and proponents have assumed from its inception that nature was the source of scarcity, and that nature-induced scarcity could be defeated by technology. From that reductionist perspective, soil becomes an inert "factor of production" and ecosystems are seen as "resources." In that context, agricultural scientists work in highly specialized fields of research searching for the perfect germ plasm of single crops like rice.

It should be said in fairness to the agronomists, soil scientists, plant breeders, and entomologists who shaped the Green Revolution that the concept of sustainability didn't exist in its early years. Nor were genetic diversity and monocropping recognized as ecological antagonists, even in India where, in less than fifty years, the thirty thousand rice varieties traditionally cultivated were reduced to fewer than ten. Scientists are wiser now, partly because of their experiences in the Green Revolution and partly, ironically, because of the revolution's successes.

Today even the most ardent champions of industrial agriculture acknowledge the global hazard of growing only fifteen varieties of food plants to provide 90 percent of the calories needed to feed the world. They express alarm at the fact that 75 percent of the genetic diversity of the world's food crops has been lost since the beginning of the century.[46] A few even admit that by persistently supporting industrial farming we are closing the door on the potential for sustainable agriculture.

But in their haste to praise their programs in terms of increased yields and decreased labor, early boosters of the Green Revolution denied or ignored the destructive effects of monocultural agriculture long after they had become evident. The havoc wrought to land and water and the other very real threats to the natural and human environment were glossed over. Epidemics of new pests like the green leafhopper and the brown planthopper, which ravaged rice crops in Asia during the 1970s, were seen as mere technical setbacks to be remedied by spraying with ever more potent pesticides.

Not until 1975 was integrated pest management—the use of insects to control insects—even considered by the foundation-funded agriculture research centers of IRRI and CIMMYT. And not for several years after that did they begin to breed crops for resistance to insects and disease or focus on biological methods of pest control.

By then, the widespread spraying of toxic herbicides, insecticides, and fungicides were creating human and animal health problems unanticipated by managers of the Green Revolution. The combination of excessive irrigation, crop monoculture, and harsh chemicals began to affect the health of farmers and farm workers. Groundwater reserves were also depleted and contaminated, effectively sterilizing millions of acres of arable land throughout much of the Third World. Even on land still in production, yields began to decline. By some estimates, almost half the world's supply of topsoil has been lost to the waterlogging and salinization caused by industrial agriculture. This loss is particularly ironic in light of claims made by champions of the revolution, who sought to reassure environmentalists that increased yields would mean less land under cultivation and, therefore, more room for wildlife and nature preserves. A few myopic Greens, notably the Sierra Club's Carl Pope, evidently bought into the argument, perhaps only to please potential funders.

In addition, the new technologies of the Green Revolution required vast inputs of energy, particularly for the "miracle" varieties of rice and wheat. In addition to millions of barrels of oil to fuel tractors, trucks, and combines, petroleum was needed to manufacture nitrogen fertilizer and other agrochemicals. In India the amount of chemical fertilizer used per acre rose by a factor of six, leading some critics to call the whole initiative a fertilizer revolution, rather than a seed revolution.[47] In Asia the rate of application has increased to forty times the yield of rice.[48] According to Cambridge University geographer Tim Bayliss-Smith, traditional rice farming produced ten times more energy in food than was expended to grow it. In fully industrialized farming the gain is zero.[49]

Advocates of the revolution have recently acknowledged the ecological risks inherent in chemical-intensive monocrop farming. But they have not responded by exploring traditional, and sustainable, methods, many of which have fed billions of people for centuries. Quite predictably, the response of Rockefeller's scientists has been a technological one—a *bio*technological fix.

Gene Revolution

Genetically modified organisms are the future. And while we shouldn't embrace them blindly, without safeguards, we have to recognize their extraordinary potential to feed a hungry world.
—Dan Glickman, U.S. Secretary of Agriculture

The invention of gene-splicing allows laboratory scientists to create transgenic varieties, in which traits are transplanted from one species to another—even across the plant-animal barrier. Gene-splicing has created such enormous economic potential that transgenic germ plasms are now being patented by large chemical and pharmaceutical companies like Monsanto, Novartis, Calgene, and AgrEvo, which are gradually cornering the market on bioengineered seeds. This privatization of science and life forms does not seem to bother the Rockefeller Foundation, which provides seven-figure grants for biotech research.

Some seeds are engineered to work only with specific chemicals—with both seed and chemical produced, of course, by the same manufacturer, be it Monsanto, Calgene, or AgrEvo. So biotechnology forces buyers of Monsanto's seeds to purchase a package of Monsanto's pesticide: the only one that will protect their crop from pests. Monsanto also genetically engineers crops to resist Roundup, the number one chemical herbicide in the world, which is also manufactured by Monsanto. Calgene calls the process "built-in management"; others prefer to call it "ecological agriculture." In fact, genetic modification has created major management hassles for many of its practitioners.

In 1973 scientists at IRRI successfully developed, with Rockefeller funding, a rice seed genetically resistant to the brown planthopper. It was planted in the Philippines and for two years seemed to have solved the problem. However, in 1975 a new strain of planthopper appeared, in defiance of the resistant gene. The new bug spread rapidly throughout the Philippines and eventually migrated to Indonesia, where it wiped out hundreds of thousands of acres of rice.[50] IRRI quickly developed a new resistant strain, which worked for three years before yet another variant planthopper evolved to override its resistance. On this occasion, even intensive pesticide spraying failed to wipe out the new strain, though, ironically, it killed insects that preyed on the planthopper.

In 1996 Monsanto introduced a patented cottonseed containing genes that produced *Bacillus thuringiensis* (Bt), a natural insecticide that kills beetles and moths. Nonetheless, after almost two million acres were planted with the transgenic seed in five southern states, there was a heavy bollworm infestation. Farmers had to resort to heavy spraying to save their crops. The following May Monsanto was forced to recall sixty thousand bags of "Round-up ready" canola seeds, which somehow had not been tested for human consumption.

In the late 1970s the planthopper experience in the Philippines and Indonesia prompted some Green Revolution scientists to consider pursuing research in integrated pest management (IPM). Using benign insects to control destructive insects seemed far preferable to poisoning land, water, and farm workers with toxic chemicals. "Field schools" to teach IPM to local farmers have since been opened in Indonesia, India, China, Malaysia, Bangladesh, Vietnam, Thailand, and Sri Lanka. In all locations, both pests and pesticide use have been greatly reduced.

This outcome might suggest that the ability to reform the system and rectify serious errors is somehow built into the institutions of the Green Revolution. But the process is painfully slow, and resistance to the idea that much of the social and ecological damage could have been avoided by a less-reflexive reliance on advanced chemical technologies is still prevalent. Moreover, the episode painfully illustrates how the drag-anchor effect of large-scale philanthropy can delay reform and slow progress.

Although genetic engineering is neither a product or an invention of organized philanthropy, the foundations, including some that actively support environmental activism, have remained remarkably sanguine about its potential to diminish biodiversity, in some cases irreversibly, and to weaken farmers' defense against weeds and insects. Whereas genetically modified organisms have been widely discussed in scientific and ethical circles for twenty-five years or more, research programs and think tanks that assess or challenge the impact of biotechnology have had great difficulty obtaining foundation support—even from sources they expected to fund their work. Theories and explanations for this reticence abound, some more conspiratorial than others. But at bottom, it seems, lies that undying faith in scientific authority, high technology, and American ingenuity that has been part of foundation culture since the days of John D. Rockefeller and Andrew Carnegie.

It was that faith, no doubt that prompted the MacArthur Foundation in 1994 to begin funding what they euphemistically called *bioprospecting,* the collection of seeds, organisms, and germ plasms from around the world. MacArthur's literature for the next five years spoke of "exploiting charismatic ecosystems" and "mining indigenous knowledge." When environmentalists and indigenous tribal leaders complained about both the practice and the language, saying that *biopiracy* was a more appropriate term, MacArthur changed the language but continued to support the practice.

There are signs of change, however. At the 1998 annual meeting of the Environmental Grantmakers Association in Houston, there was a call to create a special interest affinity group, the Funders Working Group on Biotechnology. This network of program officers, directors, and trustees of over seventy foundations has an office in San Francisco and is working hard to bring critical thinking to bear on the benefits and threats of biotechnology, particularly as applied to agriculture.

Most members of the group appear to have joined to become better informed about the methods and safety of biotechnology. However, a sense of urgency seems to be emerging among members and—to the delight of those interested in a more cautionary approach to agricultural biotechnology—the Rockefeller Foundation became a paying member of the group in 1999.

Denial

Dollars are little or nothing without wisdom.
—Philip Stern

Until quite recently the foundations that initiated and funded the Green Revolution have been remarkably defensive about its outcome, and most remain in quiet denial about the lasting social and environmental impacts of their philanthropy. While they have admitted to problems and negative impacts along the way, they continue to believe them to be unavoidable but fixable.

As for the revolution's negative political consequences, their defense rests largely on the claim that unjust social orders existed in Third World societies long before the Green Revolution began. Private American foundations, say the philanthropists, have neither the right nor the responsibility to change the social order of another culture. Few are willing to admit that the way the Green Revolution is structured exacerbates existing cultural inequities and does nothing to remedy them—by, for example, offering low-interest credit to small farmers. Nor have the foundations addressed the question of whether they had the right or responsibility to *prevent* changes in the culture's social order of another culture—the kind of changes, some argue, that have resulted from the Green Revolution.

Not until the late 1980s, about the time that the U.N. Food and Agriculture Organization reported that rice yields were beginning to decline throughout Asia, did the creators and funders of the Green Revolution begin to respond forthrightly to criticisms of their invention.[51] However, instead of questioning the central scientific premise of the revolution or disrupting its agricultural strategy, they simply found ways to make its technologies more available to poor farmers. Thus the environmental damage resulting from chemical-based farming became even more widespread.

In their literature, if not in the privacy of their boardrooms, the Rockefeller and other foundations remain unwilling to face the real downside of the revolution they have spawned. Firmly focused on the undeniable triumph of larger yields, they persist in minimizing the social and ecological consequences of mass, centralized, mechanized chemical agriculture for sensitive lands and cultures. "It is an example of how contemporary scientific enterprise is politically and socially created, how it builds its immunity and blocks its social evaluation," writes Vandana Shiva, director of the Research Foundation for Science, Technology and Natural Resource Policy in Dehra Dun, India. "It is [also] an example," Shiva says, "of how science takes credit for successes and absolves itself from all responsibility for failures."[52]

Even the Rockefeller's few skeptical trustees were eventually won over by the persistent cheering of Green Revolution partisans. Frances Fitzgerald, a journalist and for ten years a Rockefeller trustee, says she had been particularly concerned about the social disruptions she saw occurring in Green Revolution areas. But after junkets to India and Africa hosted by Rockefeller program officers, Fitzgerald was eventually persuaded that whatever the negatives, they were outweighed by the benefits of increased crop yields. In a 1998 interview in New York, she admitted to being a complete convert and ardent supporter of the Green Revolution." To the precautionary note, "it will not feed the world forever," she added, "And of course it's far easier to grow more stuff than it is to deal with the population issue."[53]

Without actually admitting failure, the Rockefeller and Ford foundations have tried to integrate the critique of the Green Revolution into their funding. Ford has been particularly sensitive to the social consequences of high-tech agriculture. It has recently made grants for projects in integrated pest management, natural resource conservation, small farm participatory research, and agricultural ecology.

Even the World Bank which now chairs CGIAR, has admitted publicly that its lending policies have at times been counterproductive. "Research over the last four or five years has shown that continuous application of fertilizers and pesticides does not lead to a continuous increase in yields," accedes World Bank Vice president Visvanathan Rajgopalan. "In fact some decline has been noted."[54] Yet, although there has been a good deal of promotional hoopla about subsequent changes in both bank lending and foundation funding, the money spent on social research and techniques such as IPM and sustainable agriculture has been paltry compared to the increasing support for biotechnology and the other trappings of the gene revolution. Of the funds donated by the Rockefeller Foundation to rice research between 1984 and 1996, $74.5 million was spent on "advanced biological research" (biotechnology) and $3.4 million on related social science research.[55] Thus, while Rockefeller biologists are seeking alternatives to chemical-intensive farming and studying the impact of high-tech agriculture on indigenous cultures, the central goal of the Green Revolution—feed the world through high-yield production—has not changed.

Sustainability

Get big or get out.
—Earl Butz, 1982, U.S. Secretary of Agriculture

As Hegel taught us, all great ideas irrepressibly breed their opposites. Thus in the early 1990s, a few American foundations—recognizing the shortcomings of mechanized, chemical agriculture—began to take an active interest in "sustainable agriculture" and the emerging sciences of biodynamics and agroecology. Unlike supporters of the Green Revolution, most of these newcomers acknowledge that agricultural science should be based on the farmer's experience, because that is where all of agriculture's best innovations have come from. Moreover, they believe that ecologically sound agriculture is not, as many of its critics contend, a return to unproductive hardscrabble subsistence farming.

Agroecology applies new agricultural science to traditional farming methods: small-scale production, multicrop farming, crop rotation. Rather than increased production, the goal of agroecology is the enhancement of biodiversity and protection of the ecological neighborhoods in which humans live and farm. In the long run, of course, the success of sustainable agriculture depends on humanity's ability to control it own fertility. Yet there is no indication that both cannot be achieved at once.

Agroecology takes into account *all* the ecological downsides of high-tech, high-yield farming. It is now well known, for example, that the very same technologies that have so successfully increased grain yields damage the aquatic ecologies in which fish procreate. This is a fact that is rarely discussed in the literature of the Green Revolution, or acknowledged in foundation reports on the subject. So "do we really increase food production when we increase wheat and rice yields at the expense of seafood?" asks American organic farmer Frederick Kirschenmann.[56]

By 1994 even the International Rice Research Institute had recognized that increased rice yields had not produced the desired effect. "Years of teaching were in effect wrong," admitted IRRI's deputy director Ken Fisher on a National Public Radio broadcast aired in July of 1994. Fisher admitted that pests had become resistant to pesticides, which themselves had caused serious health problems in the Green Revolution's target areas. But even more telling than Fisher's admissions was the question IRRI scientists were asking: had the process that increased rice yield three and fourfold in fact *lowered* total food supplies by killing fish and the honeybees that pollinated the fruit trees planted around rice paddies? Some Green revolutionaries have even acknowledged the threat to biodiversity created by replacing indigenous varieties with bioengineered seeds.

In the last decade of the twentieth century about a dozen U.S. foundations, most notably the Jesse Smith Noyes, Pew, Mott, and even Rockefeller, began to provide support to sustainable agriculture research and practice. With crop yields from Green Revolution seeds dropping noticeably and production from agroecological, biodynamic, and organic farming increasing, there is hope for a future of productive, nonpolluting agriculture. But that hope will not be realized without a lot of patience and long-term research. Forgetting that the Green Revolution required decades to produce results, two key foundations, Pew and Mott, have recently backed away from their funding of sustainable agriculture. "This is a real setback for the movement," according to Vic De Luca, recently appointed president of the Noyes Foundation, which is in for the long haul.[57]

The End of Agriculture?

Isn't it time to put the culture back in agriculture?
—G. K. Chesterton

There is much to be learned from the Green Revolution about the philanthropic imagination, the art of grantmaking, and agriculture. The revolution's fifty-year history illustrates how stubborn some philanthrocrats can be, and how slow their trustees are to pull back from a misguided strategy or immanent failure. The problem is worsened, of course, when foundations rely solely on their own research—or on research they have funded—and ignore the findings or opinions of independent observers and, even worse, the views of the people affected by an initiative.

By the time a problem is researched, documented, and published, it is so thoroughly entrenched that solving it requires a massive, heavily funded correction and an embarrassing acknowledgment that detractors' criticisms were correct—two actions foundation trustees are loath to take. When foundations do admit to the shortcomings of their projects, they do so slowly and euphemistically. "This has been a most informative program," or "the outcome of this undertaking stemmed from factors of uncertainty and unpredictability" are often a close as philanthrocrats get to admitting failure.

Thus solutions, if they occur, do so only after considerable damage has been done. "Here is the dilemma of research that hopes to be useful," write Peter Marris and Martin Rein in a preface to their Ford Foundation–funded evaluation of the foundation's vast and highly controversial Gray Areas Program. "The longer it takes, the more thorough the knowledge. But by then the events it describes are long since past, the context of decisions may have changed, and its insight is of only historical interest." [58]

Has Ford—or any other foundation that has read this report—reformed its processes to allow for a change of course when faced with negative consequences? Had research on the social and ecological effects been available sooner, would the scientists and philanthropists of the Green Revolution have responded rapidly? John Perkins, who observed the project closely for years, is not certain it would have made a difference—at least not to trustees of the Rockefeller Foundation.

Even if a substantial body of empirical and theoretical work had existed on the issues of sustainability and equity, it is not clear that the Rockefeller Foundation would have considered them. Foundation officers and trustees were deeply committed to concerns of geopolitical and military significance. Keeping Mexico friendly to the United States and preventing the possible "loss" of India to communism were the frameworks within which the Foundation laid the groundwork for development assistance. Their theories of the purpose and means of development probably would have made it impossible for them to foresee any problems with sustainability and equity.[59]

Perkins is not the only historian to observe that foundations and the scientists they support have difficulty learning from their mistakes. Bruce Jennings of the University of California–Berkeley observes that

In spite of the promise of a science-based utopia, the authority exercised by communities of scientists has proven insufficient to eliminate hunger, illness, and other conditions opposed to life. While observers are divided as to why these problems do not get solved, their continued presence is nevertheless used by various institutions and their leaders to extend certain kinds of science for organizing both state and society. The kinds of science that have emerged and the reasons for their emergence explain the relations between science, society and politics. One of the best illustrations of this situation is the rise of agricultural science to a position of political authority on a global scale.[60]

An even deeper lesson can be learned by looking back to a memo written by renowned development expert Wolf Ladejinsky in 1954—*two years before Ford joined the Green Revolution*. Ladejinsky was addressing his remarks to the Ford Foundation's director of overseas development, Ken Iverson. Ladejinsky is primarily concerned with "what constitutes human welfare and how to advance its cause"; in that regard, he saw clearly something that had completely escaped the biological scientists at Rockefeller. Quoting from an earlier report to the trustees of the Ford Foundation, Ladejinsky wrote: "The problems and opportunities of our time arise out of man's relationship to man, rather than to his relations to the physical world."[61] To which he added:

Not all realities are economic, and in the underdeveloped countries many of the motivations behind the drive for improvement are social, political, and psychological. There is no gainsaying the importance of a rise in agricultural output, but it does not by itself meet the needs and it is not at all certain that achievements in technical assistance will automatically or necessarily insure a greater sharing of economic welfare, greater sharing of political power, free public schools, the emergence of representative government and other developments which denote progress in democracy."[62]

It is impossible, of course, to assess the damage that would have been avoided had the trustees of Ford and Rockefeller heeded the simple advise of Ladejinsky in 1954.

Indonesia would almost certainly not be in the state it is today. In 1984 Indonesia was deemed by the Food and Agriculture Organization (FAO) of the United Nations to be "food self-sufficient." The country's leaders were praised for having embraced the Green Revolution. The FAO assessment was based on rice, the surplus of which was interpreted as food sufficiency. In truth, the Green Revolution had forced millions of Indonesians who had survived previously on corn, roots, and other staples to rely almost solely on rice. Moreover, farmers were compelled to adopt wetland rice cultivation in regions unsuitable to that type of farming. Differences in nutritional needs were glossed over, along with environmental consequences. "Paradoxically," reports a 1999 study released by the Institute for Food and Development Policy, "food and ecological insecurity worsened in parts of the country, even as more rice was produced." The report continues: "Thirty years of 'Green Revolution' has left many farmers dependent on expensive external inputs of seeds, fertilizers and pesticides, the tragic result of which became stark with the onset of the Asian financial crisis of 1997."[63] When these inputs were limited for lack of foreign exchange and fertilizer subsidies were withdrawn, agricultural productivity was seriously impaired. Indonesia's farmers were further imperiled by an influx of cheap or free emergency food aid, which did nothing to encourage them to revive its own agriculture without again succumbing to chemical-intensive monoculture farming.

There are signs that this critique of the Green Revolution has finally reached the inner sanctum of Rockefeller. The most recent overview of its Agricultural Sciences Program acknowledges most of the problems detractors of the program have cited for decades. "Modern high yield agriculture of the kind long supported by the Foundation has been attacked on a number of fronts over the years," reads the report. "In the officers' view such attacks have not carried the day and they remain convinced that high yield seeds and fertilizers are essential. Admittedly, however, some elements of the past high yield systems, especially pesticide use and continuous cropping, may result in long term failing yields while giving higher yields and incomes in the first few years of use."[64]

That passage is about as close as any foundation involved with the Green Revolution has ever come to admitting failure or folly; it is accompanied by an understated comment that the Rockefeller Foundation is "devoting a small portion of its resources to a third issue now globally important—whether systems being developed and used are sustainable." The authors of the report recommend that foundation trustees earmark 7 percent of the $17,275,000 budgeted for agricultural science for "measuring sustainability." They also recommend giving a small grant to a project called "Initiatives for Development and Equity in African Agriculture" (IDEA), which is "designed to address institutional and equity questions." Overall, they propose to spend 57 percent of the agriculture budget for "knowledge (research)," 26 percent for "building capacity," and 14 percent for "field and program management." In other words, they recommend more of the same: high-yield strategy, neutrality on land reform, virtual neglect of cultural factors, undying faith in scientific authority, advanced biotechnological research, and utilizing science to achieve geopolitical goals.

Yet all may not be lost. In 1999 critics of the revolution, domestic and foreign, took heart in the appointment of academic ecologist Gordon Conway as head of the Rockefeller Foundation. Though hiring Conway is a clear signal that Rockefeller trustees intend to continue the Green Revolution, he will steer it in a decidedly different direction, one in which farm policy is based on farmers, not on commodities, and in which relationship to the land is as important as relationship to labor.

Conway expects that by 2020 there will be 2.5 billion more mouths to feed on the planet, and he is convinced that they cannot be fed without genetically modifying food production. He believes that European worries about the healthfulness of bioengineered crops are overstated, although he shares critics' concerns that a few large Western companies may corner seed and crop patents and render them unaffordable in poorer countries. Rockefeller, he says, needs to seek ways to protect the intellectual property of developing countries represented by their traditional seed stocks.

Many of the Green Revolution's most outspoken critics studied with Conway at Sussex University and know him to be deeply concerned about the social inequities and ecological perturbations created by industrial agriculture. While working in Borneo, he was one of the first scientists to realize that pesticides were killing the natural predators of borers and bagworms, and to advocate integrated pest management.

In his recently released book, *The Doubly Green Revolution,* Conway asserts that the next phase of the revolution must not only provide farmers with the wherewithal to produce more food; it must also address the economic concerns of producers and the environmental impact of chemical-drenched agriculture, which, he readily admits, has been a disaster. He believes that Rockefeller should cease supporting research into chemically dependent crops, like "Round-Up Ready" beans (which are altered to allow herbicide application without damaging the crop) but continue to seek ways to engineer pest resistance directly into plants' DNA. Moreover, until biotechnological research creates pest-resistant crops, Conway remains an enthusiastic supporter of integrated pest management.

When he discusses the broad topic of agriculture, he tends to speak of feeding the hungry more than of promoting technology. Whereas his predecessor, Peter Goldmark, was concerned with feeding the 2.5 billion people expected to be born in Asia and Africa over the next generation, Conway is focused on the 800 million who today live in hunger. "If the Green Revolution was a fantastic success, we wouldn't have 800 million poor people," he told a reporter in late 1999.[65] He is deeply interested in what creates poverty and what philanthropy can do to end it. In fact, within weeks of beginning his new job at Rockefeller, he had changed the name of the Agriculture Sciences Division to Food Security.

Critics of the revolution might be even more enthusiastic had they read a long paper Conway wrote for the Ford Foundation in 1987. I found "Helping Poor Farmers," a fifty-page critique of the Green Revolution as it had evolved over the previous thirty-five years, buried in the Ford archives. In it, Conway makes the very point critics had been shouting at the architects and scientists of the Green Revolution for twenty-five years or more.

Increases in agricultural productivity, whether measured in terms of land, labor or capital, cannot of themselves solve the problems of the poor. Producing more food is a necessary, but not sufficient condition for alleviating poverty. . . . There is now enough food in the world so that no one need, in theory, go hungry. Yet malnutrition and poverty persist in developing country and the family farm remains a precarious form of livelihood in the West.

But Conway had more to say.

Increased productivity needs also to be sustainable in both ecological and socio-economic terms. Farming systems reliant on techniques that are polluting or degrading of soil and water, or are dependent on subsidized inputs, carry their own seeds of disaster. Sustainability is threatened too by technologies that prove insensitive to traditional social and cultural values. . . . For the poor to benefit from the potential agricultural technology they have to gain greater control over the institutions, both formal and informal, that govern access to resources and inputs and the distribution of harvests.[66]

This was new and decidedly radical advice, even for the Ford Foundation, which has historically valued the social sciences more than the Rockefeller has. While both foundations have tended to remain defensive about social criticism of the revolution and intent upon a biological approach to ending hunger, exciting changes seem possible with Gordon Conway running the Rockefeller Foundation, given his cautionary attitude toward agricultural biotechnology.

In June of 1999, Conway addressed a special meeting of the board of directors of the Monsanto Corporation, by then the leading international player in commercial plant biotechnology. The gathering was held in secret at the Willard Hotel, a few blocks from the White House. The directors were expecting a friendly visit from the gracious Mr. Conway. Instead they received a tongue-lashing. The industry, Conway maintained, had rushed too many controversial products to market and created a backlash against itself. Monsanto, the main target of the backlash, had recently acquired a smaller seed company that owned the patent on a genetic technology that rendered seeds sterile.

The so called terminator gene was designed to prevent farmers from collecting seeds from their own crops without paying the seed's patent owner a royalty. With dead seeds, farmers would have no choice but to buy new seeds from the patent owner (Monsanto) every season. In an impassioned speech, Conway implored Monsanto to abandon the terminator technology, stop opposing labeling laws, and consider the real needs of farmers in the developing world. In light of recent protests in Europe and India over the whole matter of genetically modified organisms, Conway feared that the growing backlash against Monsanto over the terminator seed would spill over and damage public support for all crop biotechnology. "We have a lot of people to feed," he said, "and biotechnology is one of the answers."[67]

"Admit that you do not have all the answers," he told the stunned but furious directors, who included international bankers, Harvard academics, former Secretary of Commerce Mickey Kantor, and the former heads of the U.S. Social Security system and the Environmental Protection Agency. "Commit yourselves to prompt, full and honest sharing of data," he scolded. "This is not the time for a new PR offensive but for a new relationship based on honesty, full disclosure, and a very uncertain shared future."[68]

There can be few other instances in the history of American philanthropy when a major corporate board has heard such a frank rebuke from a foundation president. And few such rebukes gained such a prompt response. On October 4, 1999, Monsanto publicly abandoned research in terminator seeds and withdrew all relevant products from the market.

And in December of 1999 the Rockefeller Foundation formally announced its new global strategy for all grantmaking: feeding the poor without harming the environment. "Globalization can make the rich richer and the poor poorer, or it can make everybody better off," Conway told the Chronicle of Philanthropy while describing the foundation's commitment of $23.4 million to agricultural programs that benefit the poor and take account of their views. He also announced a smaller grant of $3 million to a program created to gather corporate executives, scientists, government officials, and other leaders to discuss the appropriate use of biotechnology in food production. He cautioned that the Rockefeller Foundation was no longer simply "interested in biotechnology per se. We're interested in poor people getting enough food."[69]

Conclusion

As a new century dawns, humanity is offered a choice between two diverging ways of feeding itself. Both are complex, and both require separate but equally advanced inputs of scientific knowledge. One relies on chemical and genetic technologies, the other on a profound understanding of natural and ecological systems. This is not an easy choice. And though biochemical and sustainable agriculture are not mutually exclusive technologies, it is virtually certain that the one favored by the corporate and philanthropic participants in economic globalization will prevail. The definition of food and the health of the natural world both hang in the balance.

7
Energy

The free market has problems, but it also has great power.
—Hal Harvey, Executive Director, The Energy Foundation, 1991

Laissez-faire economics cannot solve our energy problems.
—Hal Harvey, Executive Director, The Energy Foundation, 1991

When they founded the Energy Foundation in 1991 Adele Simmons, Rebecca Rimel, and Peter Goldmark—heads, respectively, of the MacArthur, Pew, and Rockefeller Foundations—issued the following statement about their mission:

America's independent foundations—at their best—can serve in four distinct ways: First they can identify nascent dangers and alert the public before such dangers reach a grave level. Second, foundations can spark initiatives to respond to these dangers. This work usually entails an examination of the root causes of problems, rather than their symptoms. Third, foundations can support those who are not well represented in the mainstream of political and social discourse, ensuring that their voices are better heard. Finally, foundations can bring together the energies and talents of many diverse—sometimes even adversarial—groups to build new solutions to problems.[1]

That statement, and the eight years that followed its publication in the Energy Foundation's first annual report, reflect better than almost any episode in American philanthropical history the lofty ambitions of proactive grantmakers. The record of those years illuminates, too, the calamities that can result from bold philanthropic initiatives taken in the absence of democratic processes.

In few cases has the leverage of foundations over the activities and policies of nonprofit organizations been less evident, but more real, than in the creation of the Energy Foundation. At its opening in January 1991, the new foundation's stated goal was "to assist in the nation's transition to a sustainable energy future by promoting energy efficiency and renewable energy."

The foundation was a noble and environmentally critical initiative and an appropriate response to government devolution. Both the federal and many state governments had drastically cut back research on renewable energy during the Reagan era; and nationwide renewable capacity (solar, wind, and geothermal) was shrinking along with government. Then the Gulf War demonstrated, once again, the depth of America's dependence on fossil fuel. It was a good time to launch an aggressive program to promote and fund renewable energy projects.

The Energy Foundation began operations in 1991 with a $20-million promissory grant from the John D. and Catherine T. MacArthur Foundation, the Pew Charitable Trusts, and the Rockefeller Foundation. Today it is the largest of a new breed of grantmaker known as a *passthrough foundation*. Its primary function is to pass through its books money that might just as easily be granted directly by its donor foundations—which now also include the Joyce Mertz-Gilmore, McKnight, and Packard foundations. Among the fifteen members of its board are five who represent the foundations, including four from the donor foundations. Although the Energy Foundation passes along in excess of 90 percent of what it receives, it spends a small portion of the annual cash flow on seminars, conferences, and independent research. It also promotes a number of specific national policies its director believes will lead to sustainable energy production.

Because California had long been the nation's leader in energy innovation and a global pioneer in renewable investments, the foundation's headquarters are located in the San Francisco Presidio. It is headed by two engineers—both of whom hold bachelors and masters degrees in energy planning from Stanford University. Hal Harvey, an amiable passive-solar home builder, had earlier worked with Hunter and Amory Lovins's Rocky Mountain Institute, an energy-conservation think tank in Colorado. Eric Heitz, a civil engineer, was an old college friend of Harvey's.

Both came to the new foundation with a solid grounding in energy systems and renewable technologies. However, under the guidance of his benefactors, Harvey has been distracted by more mundane and less productive interests. According to people close to the foundation, he tends to be preoccupied with such "upstream matters" as where the money is coming from. In that capacity, he spends more time than Heitz visiting East Coast foundations and attending meetings as a trustee of the Joyce Mertz-Gilmore Foundation. Heitz looks "downstream" (where the money is going) and is regarded by grantees as "the enforcer" of the Energy Foundation's complex, controversial, and at times contradictory agenda. Regardless of their diverging duties, both leaders of the Energy Foundation are engineers and share the can-do, nuts-and-bolts, faith-in-the-technological-fix outlook of that profession.

Although the originating foundations promised only $20 million and a three-year run, by 1998 they had contributed more than $100 million to the Energy Foundation, which by then had an annual budget in excess of $13 million. Although there is a sunset provision set for the end of the year 2000, few of those close to the action believe the sun will ever set on the Energy Foundation. Only the Rockefeller Foundation has said it will suspend its $2.5-million annual contribution and consider support on a project-by-project basis. The MacArthur, Pew, McKnight, and Mertz-Gilmore foundations seem impressed with the work accomplished thus far and likely to continue their regular contributions. Moreover, the huge new David and Lucille Packard Foundation of California made a $6.75-million grant to the foundation for 1999—to be used in part to open an office in China.

Creating a new and separate foundation to address extremely complex scientific and political issues like those surrounding energy was heralded by some as a brilliant idea. Rimel, Goldmark, and Simmons must be credited with an invention that obviates an enormous duplication of effort by individual foundations attempting to solve America's energy problems. It is undeniable that the Energy Foundation has saved scarce resources that would otherwise have been wasted on redundant bureaucracies. And, from the grant seekers' perspective, the ability to shop at one source—rather than making the same pitch three or more times—is a blessing.

On the other hand, concentrating so much leverage in one funding body could create serious power problems, as well as an orthodoxy that, if misguided, would be difficult to challenge. Though aware of these risks, the Energy Foundation's founders were willing to shoulder them.

Strange Brew

Churches have to compete for supplicants. Foundations have no such problem.
—Waldemar Nielsen

In the first decade of its existence the Energy Foundation performed some constructive tasks and supported many worthy ideas and projects, particularly in the area of energy efficiency. In fact, the path to energy sustainability exists in the work of the organizations on its grants list, groups like the following:

• The Worldwatch Institute, which received $50,000 to promote a vision of a sustainable energy future relying on efficient and renewable energy technologies.
• The American Council for an Energy Efficient Economy, granted $90,000 to promote energy-efficient mortgage programs and home-energy rating systems.
• The Citizen's Conservation Corporation of Boston, which received $50,000 to advocate the purchase of energy-efficient appliances and equipment in public housing.
• The Island Press, granted $30,000 to publish a definitive book about the relationship between energy and the environment.
• The Bicycle Federation of America, recipient of $300,000 to help make the bicycle a viable mode of transportation throughout the country.
• And, perhaps most significant of all—in light of point three of the founders' lofty preamble—a $36,000 grant to Earth Island Institute (1) to study the range and depth of the adverse impact of current energy policy on low-income and minority residents in the inner city, and (2) to explore mechanisms for including them in the policymaking process. More than any other, this grant gives hope to residential communities and small power consumers that their needs and views will be considered seriously in the inevitable restructuring of America's energy systems.

The foundation has made many other admirable contributions to the development and promotion of fuel-efficient transportation, building technologies, and renewable energy systems. Its 1998 annual report proposes ten national policy changes that, Harvey is convinced, would "cut U.S. carbon emissions in 2010 by approximately 462 million metric tons—95 percent of what is required under the Kyoto Accord."

Nonetheless, a close examination of the foundation's total grant list, particularly its extraordinary generosity to a few select recipients, reveals a strong bias toward lawyers, free market economics, shareholders of fossil fuel corporations, public utilities, and the investment bankers who underwrite utility securities. The largest recipients of Energy Foundation largess are three mainline environmental organizations: the Natural Resources Defense Council (NRDC), the Conservation Law Foundation (CLF), and the Environmental Defense Fund (EDF). The foundation-funded work of these nonprofits counters, at times even undermines, the efforts of smaller grantees by promoting an approach to energy restructuring that could easily have been hatched in the boardroom of any private utility in the country—and in at least one case actually was. Within the nonprofit sector, opposition to their chosen course of action, which has become virtually a national strategy, is hushed—muffled, perhaps unintentionally, by small grants from the Energy Foundation.

A list of the projects that the Energy Foundation will *not* fund is as revealing as what they do support. Application guidelines set a number of limitations, for example, no R&D. "Too expensive," says Harvey. "Besides, the Energy Department does a pretty good job." Funding of local projects, technology research and development, and demonstration projects (model solar homes) are all out, as are grants to establish or support community energy projects. These restrictions force a host of worthy energy projects to seek support elsewhere, a task made more difficult by the existence of an energy foundation that gives away $12 million dollars a year. Smaller foundations can ask grant seekers, in effect, "Why should we give you money, when the Energy Foundation has all that cash to support energy work?"

The Energy Foundation's very largest grants go to the Natural Resources Defense Council, an environmental law firm created in 1970 by the Ford Foundation. To restrain the underpaid idealists hired to litigate for NRDC, Ford originally placed the new organization under the close supervision of a committee of five Wall Street lawyers ("the five gurus") led by Whitney North Seymour Jr. All but one were Republicans, and their role was simply to prevent zealous young lawyers from taking hard-line positions against such sacred cows as the public utilities. Although the watchdog committee has long since been disbanded, NRDC trustees remain sensitive to the interests of Wall Street. That loyalty was most recently demonstrated in the positions they are taking on the deregulation and restructuring of the nation's last legal monopoly, its most heavily capitalized industry, and the nation's leading industrial polluter: the electrical utilities.

In 1991 the Energy Foundation pledged $1.5 million to NRDC, most of it to be spent over the next three years "to promote regulatory reform in the West and to work collaboratively with consumer advocates, utilities, and utility commissions to design and implement cost-effective energy efficiency programs for all customer sectors."[2] Although consumer advocates and energy customers could hardly be pleased with NRDC's positions, or the fate of California energy deregulation, trustees of the Energy Foundation and its beneficiaries seem satisfied—if grants are a fair indication. NRDC received $1.9 million from the Energy Foundation in 1997 and $1.15 million in 1998. And, if continued funding of the Energy Foundation itself is a realistic indicator, the original benefactors are pleased as well. On top of the $3.75 million the Energy Foundation granted NRDC between 1991 and 1998, the Pew donated a separate $1.3 million to the nonprofit's energy initiatives.

In accordance with Energy Foundation guidelines, NRDC's attorney Ralph Cavanagh used the funds to develop a set of principles called the California Collaborative Process, which he asked all stakeholders (except labor unions) to endorse. Although Cavanagh later said he regretted using the term *collaboration,* because it "still has overtones of Vichy France," he remains insistent about the principles—in spite of his own deviations from them (the consequences of which we explore below).

An early indication of Cavanagh's brand of reform came shortly after NRDC received its first Energy Foundation grant. The issue was an Oregon ballot proposition that would have assigned the costs of decommissioning the disastrously designed Trojan nuclear power plant to utility shareholders, who had assumed the risks of nuclear power by investing in it. Cavanagh opposed the proposition. "Utilities won't do the right thing," he argued, "if you inflict the fiscal equivalent of capital punishment on them." Equating reduced dividends with a death sentence would became Cavanagh's mantra and NRDC's strategic premise in the nationwide debate over energy deregulation that ensued. Throughout the process, funds for NRDC's leadership in the battle continued to flow through the Energy Foundation. Meanwhile, energy activists in Oregon have asked Cavanagh to stay in California.

Being on a first-name basis with the CEO's of America's largest utilities, Cavanagh socializes with them frequently at "powwows" convened and sponsored by the Energy Foundation. He also makes frequent trips to Chicago, New York, and Philadelphia to visit energy program officers and key trustees at MacArthur, Rockefeller, and Pew—often in the company of Hal Harvey. At the top of his list of industry friends is John Bryson, a former chairman of the California Public Utilities Commissioner (CPUC) and now CEO of Edison International, which owns and operates Southern California Edison, the largest utility in California. Bryson is also a cofounder of NRDC.

When Bryson was at NRDC, and later at the CPUC, renewable energy advocates regarded him as "the prince of light." "He pushed through everything we wanted," recalls former wind-energy executive Alvin Duskin. But all that changed when Bryson went to work for Edison. Through its international subsidiary, Mission Energy, Edison is building massive high carbon coal–fired power plants in Australia, Indonesia, Thailand, and elsewhere. Its attempt to build one on the Mexico–United States border was successfully thwarted by American environmentalists who had once considered Bryson a colleague. He is now viewed as a leading antagonist of the entire renewable energy initiative in California. Yet he remains close with the Energy Foundation's favored grantee, Ralph Cavanagh, who defends Mission Energy's purchase of the Homer City, Pennsylvania, coal plant, one of the dirtiest in the East.

Shortly after he created the collaborative, Cavanagh persuaded Bryson and California's two other major utilities to consider a concept called Demand Side Management (DSM). It attempts and purports to reduce demand for electricity created by inefficient and wasteful technologies like electric heating. Cavanagh's benefactors, quite naturally, approve of this noble cause. In addition to its contribution to the Energy Foundation budget, the Pew Charitable Trusts has given NRDC $6 million to encourage DSM efforts nationwide. For utilities and environmentalists alike, it would have been money well spent for a win-win solution—if John Bryson and his colleagues had genuinely embraced the concept of energy efficiency and been sincere about reducing consumption.

Instead, financial analysts persuaded them that there was more profit in building new power plants than in encouraging energy efficiency; the cost benefits of efficiency would, they argued, accrue principally to energy consumers, not producers. Thus, from the perspective of energy efficiency, allowing utilities to influence the demand side of the energy equation was rather like asking Philip Morris to voluntarily pay for an anti-smoking campaign. It was clearly not in the interests of a provider to reduce net demand when the path to higher profits lay in increasing capacity.

Although a good deal of publicity surrounded the effort to reduce electrical demand, particularly at peak periods, reductions have been minimal. In California, they have also been accomplished at great expense to energy consumers, given the compensation paid for lost revenues and shareholder incentives provided by the state deregulation legislation. Thus DSM, as designed by Energy Foundation grantees, thus provides little more than free public relations for utilities that consumer organizations had only a few years earlier chastised for promoting energy-intensive technologies. ("Don't Be A Dishwasher, Buy One," a Pacific Gas & Electric billboard advertisement had urged in the 1980s.)

Eugene Coyle, an economist who consults for utility ratepayer organizations, was among the first to spot the flaw in DSM logic; the scheme, he said, was like "driving with one foot on the gas and one on the brake." Coyle blames Energy Foundation grantees, who "tried to persuade the utilities that it's possible to disconnect profits from sales by offering rebates to customers if they'll replace old model refrigerators with new, more efficient models. Sounds great, but the new models are giants and have ice makers in the doors and what-not, so they use more electricity than the older, 'less efficient' models."[3]

"The clean energy movement," Coyle continues, "has been damaged by a top-down, anti-democratic, funder-led set of objectives developed by assessing what the enemy will accept, and then selling that accommodating framework." That approach "at best ameliorates a bad structure." He adds that energy consumers "can no longer afford to wait for what they want because someone with 'access' assures them it is beyond their grasp. Any [initiative] should be opposed until it can show that there are benefits for the environment and small customers resulting from deregulation."[4]

Shortly after Coyle testified to that effect before the CPUC, the office of The Utility Reform Network (TURN), a power-consumer's group that employs his services, received a visit from Eric Heitz of the Energy Foundation. Heitz, who had processed a grant of $120,000 to TURN, was concerned, he said in a follow-up letter, that Coyle's "DSM related testimony is not focused on the goal spelled out in your proposal: To insure that the collaborative will succeed." TURN refused to muzzle Coyle and was not re-funded. "They didn't apply," according to Hal Harvey, who claims to have great affection for the organization.[5] Coyle's recollection is that the Energy Foundation completed its then-current commitment to TURN and made it clear that applying for another grant would be a waste of time.[6]

Behind the NRDC's California Collaborative Process lay the unexpressed objective of preserving the century-old and wildly profitable symbiosis between investment banks and utilities. Energy Foundation grantees working with the electric utility sector, which controls 25 percent of all invested capital in the United States, soon came to realize that the bottom lines of large private utilities were inviolate. Neither investors nor investment bankers could be saddled with the inevitable costs of energy restructuring. As long as they understood that clearly, Cavanagh and his colleagues were free to talk tough. About as tough as Cavanagh talked, however, was to call the utilities' unwillingness to invest in energy conservation "a crime without villains."

Holding over the utility industry the specter of litigation and a proposal for increased regulation, Cavanagh asked the CPUC to accept the outcome of the collaborative process. It was agreed that in California all decisions would be made by consensus, that a set meeting schedule would be adhered to, and that the proceeding would not be used to undercut any participant's interests. All stakeholders in the collaboration—utilities, industry users, consumer organizations, and NRDC—promised to see the collaborative process through and, at least in public, to speak in one voice. The invalid assumption behind Cavanaugh's request to CPUC is that public utility commissions exist to protect the public, whereas they more often act to shield the utility industry from its own actions and, indirectly, to protect the massive national investment in electrical generation. Thus shareholders, not consumers, are the primary concern of PUCs.

Eventually, the collaborative brought the utilities further into the alleged reform process and Cavanagh into a more influential role. This pleased the Energy Foundation, which continued to fund NRDC generously even as California utilities abandoned most of Cavanagh's efficiency programs and started building new plants. Few in the environmental community took note of the fact that engineers were running the energy industry, and that only engineers were running the Energy Foundation.

At Cavanagh's request, the CPUC agreed to stay out of the process while he sold stakeholders on a shareholder-incentive scheme that would essentially guarantee utilities a profit regardless of whether the process led to more or less consumption. The request eventually spilled over into statewide debates over deregulation of the energy industry, in which the assets stranded by deregulation became a major obsession of the utilities.

The NRDC proposed that *stranded assets*—that is, generation or transmission systems that would be uneconomical in a competitive market—be amortized, either directly by ratepayers or indirectly through a bond issued by a state trust. The proceeds of the bond issue would be used to retire the utility industry's $28-billion investment in nuclear and alternative-energy power plants. The bonds would be repaid over a ten-year period by a special assessment on consumers' energy bills. So, either way, the ratepayer was saddled with the stranded costs. California was an important early battleground over stranded assets, which nationwide are estimated at between $200 and $300 billion. In 1996, when the bond issue came before the state legislature, all eyes were on Sacramento.

When they crunched the numbers, ratepayer advocates and consumer economists soon realized that the 10-percent rate reduction promised by deregulators would be more than eliminated by the new bond assessment. Particularly hard hit would be small residential consumers. Large industrial users, who had had a hand in designing deregulation, would fare much better. When that point was raised at meetings of environmental and consumer groups formerly in the collaborative, Cavanagh dismissed their alternative; passing *any* fraction of stranded costs on to shareholders, he asserted, was politically unfeasible.

No doubt John Bryson and other utility executives had told Cavanagh that if the bonded debt scheme were threatened, the credit rating of the entire utility industry, perhaps the whole state, would be jeopardized; and that the resultant anger of millions of widows and pensioners who held shares in PG&E and Edison made the idea of shifting the burden of stranded costs onto shareholders even more politically unfeasible. That argument may well have been valid, but it didn't mean that alleged proponents of public benefit should give up without a fight—or at least an attempt at compromise.

"I have never seen anyone give away so much and get so little in return," recalls ratepayer advocate Lenny Goldberg. When Goldberg and others proposed a scheme that would reduce consumers' liability for stranded costs, Cavanagh argued against anything less than full recovery. Whatever leverage environmental or consumer organizations might have had was lost by his unconditional support of the electric utilities and their interests. When complaints about their most-favored grantee poured into the Energy Foundation, they were ignored.

Eventually it became clear to electricity consumers' organizations that in a deregulated environment they would have no say about how power was generated. They also realized that they were being asked to cover investors' losses as a trade-off for a rate reduction rendered meaningless by the deal. It was equally clear to them that Energy Foundation grantees had done nothing that would affect the value of their benefactor's endowments, which are substantially invested in oil, natural gas, and fossil fuel–dependent utilities.

Hal Harvey told local newspapers that he personally thought the bailout of nuclear power was a rotten deal for ratepayers. "From a consumer point of view, the companies that made those mistakes should pay for them," he told one newspaper. "But we didn't have a dog in that fight." In fact, he had a good fighting dog in TURN, an early grantee of his foundation. The problem was that TURN was attacked by two pit bulls—NRDC and the Environmental Defense Fund (EDF), both of which continued to receive generous funding from the Energy Foundation. "We were not tooled up to fight the equity battle," Harvey admits. "On the other hand, we are not the 'Equity Foundation,' we are the Energy Foundation."[7] And, indeed, Harvey and the Energy Foundation have kept the equity groups on a very short leash.

Had California consumer activists been watching the nationwide activities of the Energy Foundation, they would not have been so baffled by Harvey's equivocation nor Ralph Cavanagh's duplicity in California. In 1993 the Energy Foundation had granted $155,000 to Environmental Action (EA) in Takoma Park, Maryland. EA was arguing with the Federal Energy Regulatory Commission (FERC) over the recovery of stranded costs at the national level. When EA took a stand on behalf of consumers, NRDC once again stepped in on behalf of the utilities. "The best approach to stranded costs is to recover them through charges paid by all customers of a utility that remain physically within its service territory and retain connections to the integrated grid," read a NRDC comment filed with FERC in 1995. In August of that same year EA countered that FERC's pro-shareholder stand on recovered costs was "not based on legal or public policy grounds" and should be withdrawn.[8]

At about the same time, EA staffer David Lapp wrote and circulated a controversial article entitled "The Demanding Side of Utility Conservation Programs." In it he argued that demand-side management, still vigorously defended by NRDC, was unfair to the ordinary consumers to whom lost-revenue costs were being passed. In addition, he noted, DSM programs were often little more than public relations fluff fed to the public by utilities who had with no interest in reduced consumption. "Reducing energy consumption through efficiency programs," Lapp pointed out, "goes against the inherent interest in expanding sales."

Although the Energy Foundation disapproved of EA's position and Lapp's communications, they did not terminate his grant as they had TURN's. Instead, it created and funded a new organization called Project for a Sustainable Energy Policy, placing it under the management of an NRDC staffer and presenting it to FERC as the true voice of the national environmental movement. The new organization's position, forcefully stated, was that utilities nationwide should be allowed to pass the investment losses from stranded assets on to consumers.

Another East Coast Energy Foundation grantee, who spoke on background for fear of losing his funding, described the role played by the Conservation Law Foundation—"a member of the Energy Foundation's brain trust"—during the FERC negotiations. "CLF's strategy," he recalls, "was to give the utilities stranded costs in exchange for a few small environmental improvements. We said: 'But we can get more.' They disagreed, and in chorus with Ralph Cavanagh argued that stranded costs were 'inevitable . . . they cannot be stopped.'" After a pause, he added: "If we didn't have the Energy Foundation in this battle, we'd be much further along. They are using their money to support an agenda, not to build a lasting progressive movement for clean energy."

Meanwhile, back in California, the agreement finally reached between NRDC and Pacific Gas & Electric was announced in an ad PG&E ran in several daily papers in 1996–97. It quotes Ralph Cavanagh in praise of the largest utility in northern California: "PG&E programs benefit every sector of the economy," he said. "The farmer, the factory owner, or the family of four can save money and improve the environment through PG&E's various energy-saving efforts."

And, even though automobile and oil companies had strongly resisted more stringent state emission and mileage standards, the ad also praised General Motors, Shell, and Chevron "for helping develop the first generation of cleaner burning natural gas vehicles and the stations to refuel them." The fact that natural gas is just another fossil fuel, albeit one that burns cleaner than coal or oil, and that the domestic auto manufacturers have fought California clean air standards tooth and claw did not seem to offend Cavanagh's environmental sensibilities. It seems strange, and quite lacking in insight, for a foundation whose stated mission is to assist a "transition to sustainable energy future" to be supporting a switch from one fossil fuel to another while existing wind, solar, geothermal, and hydro companies wait patiently for capital and an opportunity to become competitive.

The sad fact is that while the intentions and motives of Energy Foundation officials may be above reproach, their entire effort to encourage renewable energy systems in California has failed. There is less, not more renewable capacity in the state today than there was when the foundation opened its doors in 1991. Hal Harvey, Eric Heitz, and their trustees are not, of course, solely to blame for this situation; in the past decade, the cost of fossil fuel generation has dropped more dramatically than the cost per kilowatt hour of wind and solar technologies.

Nonetheless, the Energy Foundation and its major grantees deserve, and receive, ridicule for placing so much trust in the alleged good faith of monopoly power companies while overlooking the obvious fact that CPUC commissioners (particularly their president) are no friends of energy efficiency or renewable energy. The foundation's entire strategy was based on the flawed assumption that deregulation was inevitable and could only be achieved by unconditionally accommodating its policies to the interests of electric utilities.

A Model for the World

Given the conditions of contemporary life, any foundation that operates by traditional wisdom will simply be irrelevant.
—Peter Schragg

California is critical to any quest for sustainable energy, not only because it's $23-billion energy market is the largest in the country and its renewable capacity is still far higher than any other state's, but because its deregulation schemes are being mimicked in one form or another in about the half the states in the union and are being watched closely by the rest of the world. Thus in 1996 it was national news when the California Assembly unanimously passed Assembly Bill 1890 (AB 1890), which deregulated retail sales of electricity. It had the strong support of NRDC, EDF, and the Center for Energy Efficiency and Renewable Technologies—another Energy Foundation grantee based in Sacramento and cochaired by Ralph Cavanagh.

An early version of AB 1890 was crafted in the offices of Southern California Edison. Edison's restructuring scheme for the industry was unconditionally championed by CPUC President Daniel Fessler, the commissioner least enthusiastic about renewable energy generation. The price of the industry's support of the bill, which mandated a 10-percent rate reduction for residential power consumers, was release from the additional stranded costs they would face in a newly competitive market. Under deregulation, when hydro power came on line, along with cheap new natural gas plants—and when "green consumers" had began power from renewable sources—some utilities would be left short of revenues needed to amortize their investments in old coal-fired plants and nuclear generators.

Therefore, NRDC and EDF—acting as virtual spokesmen for the utilities—advised the legislators drafting the bill that the industry required that the bond issue be attached to the bill, thus passing on to small-scale energy consumers the obligation to pay the bonded debt and interest. Large users operating under the acronym CLECA [California Large Energy Consumer's Association] had already negotiated generous rate reductions in return for their support. "Big dogs eat first," quipped Amory Lovins, Hal Harvey's former employer and mentor. Though Harvey claims that he and the Energy Foundation were opposed to AB 1890, they did nothing to restrain their own grantees who were spending Energy Foundation money to defend it.[9]

When they realized its objectionable consequences, consumer and ratepayer organizations that had earlier been neutral on the bill quickly reversed their position. By mid-1998 a ballot initiative had surfaced. It would shift the bond liability from ratepayers back to utility shareholders who, as the initiative's authors argued, had assumed the risk of capital investment in the first place. Environmentalists, energy activists, and consumer advocates who drafted and supported the initiative hoped NRDC and EDF might recognize this one essential shortcoming of AB 1890 and endorse the referendum, or at least remain neutral.

They did not. On May 22, 1998, the two organizations issued a joint press release stating their support for AB 1890 as passed; while acknowledging their friendship with the initiative's supporters and expressing respect for their "sincerity," the two nonprofits opposed the referendum. Its enactment, said the release, "would invite paralysis in an industry where change is urgently needed" and "lead to years of litigation and delay." Ralph Cavanagh issued a separate communiqué expressing "respect [for] the integrity and intentions of Proposition 9's sponsors [and] regret [for] this rare disagreement among friends." On the NRDC web site, he posted a claim that "California's Proposition 9 is trying to fix something that isn't broken." He claimed that the referendum, if passed, would threaten the development of renewable capacity—though he didn't explain how. And, instead of leaving the utilities to defend their own interests, Cavanagh argued vigorously against the referendum on public radio. Outspent 40 to 1 by a utility industry conveniently greenwashed by two prominent environmental organizations, Proposition 9 was soundly defeated.

Cavanagh has no regrets. "Someone who had so much to do with working out the settlement that led to AB 1890 had very little choice but to oppose Proposition 9, whose purpose was to overturn our settlement," he told me a year later. And Cavanagh remains steadfastly behind the legislation. "On efficiency and low income services, I'll hold it up to any restructuring bill in the country."[10] But what about the prospects for renewable capacity, the putative central purpose of the foundation supporting Cavanagh's work?

A reasonable compromise between utilities and public interest groups representing environmentalists and consumers would have been to delay the bond until public utility commissions were assured that power consumers would at least receive a truly competitive market in exchange for it. That arrangement, written into the 1996 Telecommunications Act, has worked for all sides in the deregulation of the telephone industry. Why not try it with electrical energy? "It does not protect investors," is the answer most frequently offered by utility executives, with the apparent concurrence of the Energy Foundation's largest grantees.

Since 1950 investors in almost every utility in the United States have received a return on investments that is more than adequate to compensate them for losses from stranded costs. Why give them more? In a free enterprise system isn't the risk of capital investment supposed to be borne by investors? Why exempt the shareholders of private utilities, who are already clearly benefiting from the terms of restructuring? And why should an energy foundation and environmentalist nonprofits defend that exception?

The inaccurate claim that AB 1890 represents "a mutually acceptable formula," and the fact that the word *nuclear* was never mentioned in the NRDC-EDF press release, was a clear signal to the environmental community: two of its most powerful national organizations had been clipped to a short leash held by an agent of three of the nation's largest charitable trusts—two of which were created from fortunes derived from nonrenewable fuels and are still heavily invested in oil- and gas-dependent technologies.

Perhaps it is not significant, only interesting, that the combined Pew Charitable Trusts, one of the largest environmental funders in the country, every year earn more than twice as much in dividends from extractive corporations such as Weyerhaeuser, Phelps Dodge, and Atlantic Richfield as it grants to organizations like the Energy Foundation.[11] Pew officials adamantly claim that that fact is irrelevant and has absolutely no effect on the environmental policy or direction of the Energy Foundation or Pew's funding of it. Nor, they say, has it influenced the active role played by the Energy Foundation and its largest single grantee in California's energy deregulation, a process they expected to encourage the expansion of nonpolluting energy systems.

It has not been lost on knowledgeable Greens that in the year the NRDC was negotiating the details of AB 1890 (1996) the amount of carbon dioxide emitted by American electrical plants actually increased by 4.7 percent. Nor are they unaware that the stock of Edison International soared 25 percent in the four-month period after the bill was signed into law. However, few participants in the debate over California energy deregulation expected that PG&E, operating under a different corporate name, would use proceeds from the bailout to purchase two of the dirtiest fossil-fueled power plants in Massachusetts, where they are allowed to operate, as is, for another twenty-five years.

Hal Harvey seemed disappointed but unfazed by that event when I discussed it with him, despite his acknowledgment that PG&E would undoubtedly crank both plants up to full capacity and pump tons of carbon dioxide and other global-warming gasses into the atmosphere. Nor did he seem terribly concerned that the endowments of his benefactors are heavily invested in fossil fuel technologies, or that some of their directors, as well as leaders at NRDC, have large stakes in the energy status quo.

If for no other reason, the fact that NRDC's de facto CEO, Frances Beineke, is married into the public utility industry should induce the organization to recuse itself from discussions of utility restructuring, or of any process that could affect utility investors. And a tax-protected institution like the Energy Foundation should find an alternative source for its philanthropy. Had it done so in the early 1990s, energy deregulation nationwide might be taking a very different turn.

It would be easy enough to build a conspiracy theory around the fact that Pew's and Rockefeller's investments are clearly being protected by the positions taken by the Energy Foundation's largest grantees. In fact, others have tried to make the case, more than once and with unconvincing results. Twenty years from now when Rockefeller's "Energy Foundation" archives are open to the public, researchers may find evidence to substantiate such a theory. At present, it seems sufficient to note the massive dissonance evident in cooperation between fiduciaries concerned about the dividends of oil and gas corporations and grantmakers who publicly express a passion for sustainable energy.

Retail Wheeling

Philanthropy appears to have become the refuge of people who want to annoy their fellow creatures.
—Oscar Wilde, *An Ideal Husband*

At the core of an argument backed by millions of dollars of private foundation money is Ralph Cavanagh's assertion that environmentalists will never persuade governments to deny support for one source of energy while providing it to another. This, of course, is a specious reading of history. Since the Atoms for Peace program of the 1950s, the federal government has provided hundreds of billion of dollars in direct and indirect subsidies to nuclear energy; yet, except for a few paltry tax breaks offered during the late 1970s for wind and solar installation, renewable technologies have been left to compete for market share on their own.

California's AB 1890 does provide $540 million to support renewal energy expansion during the four-year "transition to competition." That is not even enough, most energy economists agree, to replace the capacity that will be lost as older renewable resources go off line for lack of capital to sustain or replace them. And, as the provision ends four years after passage of AB 1890, it has already expired. Renewable investors simply cannot compete with declining fossil fuel prices and the low capital costs of natural gas–fired plants. Wall Street is therefore taking a dim view of renewable technologies like solar, wind, and geothermal, as evidenced by the current ratio of planned fossil fuel-to-renewable generation capacity—about 118 to 1. (It's only about 50 to 1 in California, despite the AB 1890 subsidies.)

Ralph Cavanagh now claims that "AB 1890 has been good for the state's environment because it allows customers to choose green power." But he knows as well as anyone that nearly all green marketers in California are selling as "renewable energy" power produced by existing plants, thus reselling energy that often had already been sold to other customers from capacity that existed before green marketing was initiated. And he knows that *retail wheeling,* an industry term for the right of residential energy consumers' to choose their power source, is essentially a fiction.

In fact, he said so himself in an eloquent 1994 article entitled "The Great Retail Wheeling Illusion." In it he asserted that "retail wheeling is not deregulation . . . and calling it 'competition' is really an exercise in benefiting the few at the expense of the many."[12] That sounded like the sentiments of someone who is leading the charge against retail competition. At the time, Cavanagh was joined by Armond Cohen, a senior attorney at CLF, who offered his own blistering critique of retail wheeling's false promise of lower rates to residential consumers "Driven by the desire to escape embedded capacity [stranded] costs, retail wheeling proponents are essentially fighting the last war—the war over nuclear imprudence," wrote Cohen.[13]

In October 1994 the Energy Foundation too took up the cudgel against retail wheeling. Harvey and Heitz described it as "a particularly dangerous deregulation of the electric utility system. . . . a bad way to implement competition. The overall economic, environmental and equity impacts," they predicted, "could be staggering."[14] All four authors rejected the utility industry's claim that retail wheeling was inevitable.

That same year, Cavanagh and Cohen helped organize a coalition of fifty-six public interest, labor, and consumer groups to sign a "Joint Declaration on the Electric Utility Industry" opposing retail wheeling. That practice, it alleges, "encourages utilities to ignore making investments that will lower utility costs and environmental impacts over the long run. Among the losers would be those who consume relatively small quantities of electricity (most of us) and those with a stake in improved environmental quality (all of us)."

Although he eventually abandoned the grassroots coalition he had helped create and supported industrial proponents of retail competition, Cavanagh says he "remains a confirmed skeptic about the environmental benefits of retail wheeling." He admits that "green marketing has resulted in way less than one tenth of the [meager] renewable capacity added in California since passage of AB 1890."[15]

At the Energy Foundation, Harvey and Heitz were busy revising their position on retail wheeling. Their 1995 briefing paper on the subject makes no mention whatsoever of equity issues. "A year ago, utility advocates knew only that certain reforms like 'industrial strength' retail competition for large customers would be a disaster for consumers and the environment," the report reads. "Now, as new models of the utility industry take shape in California and New England, new levers to push energy efficiency and renewable energy are emerging as well."[16] Seemingly, the problems that had a year earlier made retail wheeling ("green marketing") a disaster for consumers had simply vanished.

Cavanagh knows that even if green marketing were to grow, there would still be a pitifully small demand for additional capacity and, therefore, little capital generated to expand renewable capacity. Nationwide, renewable capacity (excluding that from large hydro projects) has remained virtually unchanged, at 2 percent, since the mid-1980s, due principally to the ineffectiveness of the 1978 Public Utility Regulatory Policies Act (PURPA), which encouraged public utilities to purchase power from renewable and cogeneration facilities. PURPA failed dismally to achieve its purpose.

What is clearly needed, but deemed unpalatable by utility executives and big industrial consumers, is a regulatory mandate (federal, state, or both) that *requires* retail sellers of power to purchase a specified percentage of their power from renewable ("green") sources. The Energy Foundation proposed just such a policy in its 1998 annual report: "A national renewable energy portfolio standard requiring that 10 percent of our total energy production be from renewable power sources by 2010 would greatly boost the nascent wind, solar, and bioenergy power industries."[17]

Such a Renewable Portfolio Standard (RPS) could create an additional 100 gigawatts of renewable power capacity at a cost of less than $1.50 per household per month; it would also cut carbon emissions by over fifty million metric tons, a substantial step toward meeting the standards set by the Kyoto Treaty. Although the foundation's major grantees do not oppose RPSs, they will not fall on their swords to achieve them, for fear of losing the access to utility executives they earned in the battle over deregulation.

In 1997, when California renewable energy advocate Nancy Rader, a consultant to the American Wind Energy Association, first proposed a RPS, NRDC and EDF found it "too radical," and "politically unfeasible." Instead they championed a temporary and politically vulnerable 3.3 percent utility-bill tax called a "Systems Benefits Charge" (SBC). The tax later became the central plank of NRDC's energy strategy and was actually written into AB 1890 (lowered to 2.3 percent in deference to large energy consumers), along with a stipulation that the California Public Utility Commission (CPUC) could not collect the portion of the tax earmarked for renewables until after 2001). That provision rendered the whole strategy totally inadequate as support for renewable capacity, purportedly its intended purpose.

When she first proposed RPS, Rader "assumed that the environmental groups—NRDC, EDF and the Sierra Club—would be my allies in aggressively promoting renewable energy. I assumed we would be a team. I was wrong. Instead they told me that RPS didn't have a chance, that we might as well give it up before even starting. It was the most frustrating experience of my life."[18]

To the great surprise of NRDC, EDF, and their friends in the utility industry, the CPUC separately endorsed a renewable portfolio standard, as did Republican Representative Dan Shaefer. The latter wrote an RPS provision into his otherwise weak federal restructuring bill. His lead was followed by a host of Democratic legislators, half a dozen state legislatures, and the Clinton administration, which in April of 1999 proposed a 7.5 percent renewable portfolio standard for all retail sellers in the United

States. By then the Energy Foundation had joined the chorus and advised its grantees to cease arguing that RPSs were politically unfeasible. Ralph Cavanagh obeyed but proceeded immediately to negotiate versions of the standards that would be acceptable to public utilities, thus weakening a key bargaining chip for the ultimate deal. Other Energy Foundation grantees, however, refused to support RPS at all.

At one point an Energy Foundation program officer (unidentified) called the Conservation Law Foundation (CLF) in Boston and ordered it to stop opposing the RPS in a Massachusetts restructuring bill. The order was disobeyed, and CLF, which had received $1.1 million from the Energy Foundation in 1997, received zero in 1998. It was, in fact, fortuitous timing, as CLF had begun to transform itself from an environmental advocacy group to a commercial venture and fee-for-service organization. Having its grant money in CLF's bank account could have created serious problems for the Energy Foundation, as it almost certainly will for CLF if it continues to wander toward profit-making activities.

When CPUC invited proponents of RPS to help develop an implementation plan for the RPS, various groups offered their suggestions. EDF proposed instead a weak systems benefit charge (SBC) for renewables that would raise about $100 million a year, 25 percent less than what legislation already on the books would produce and far less than an RPS would have generated. EDF's proposal was, predictably, endorsed by California's three largest investor-owned utilities. EDF actively lobbied other environmental and consumer groups to support the proposal and oppose RPS. The Environmental Defense Fund, which in 1997 received $300,000 from the Energy Foundation for its utility work, received zero in 1998. The foundation was sticking by its policy. In spite of Hal Harvey's public claim that "we leave the choice of tactics to local groups,"[19] the Energy Foundation has, in fact, withdrawn its benefactions from grantees who oppose their stated policies.

The withdrawals are selective, however. Harvey asserts that he and his trustees "did not support AB 1890. Only our grantees did." Nonetheless, the foundation evidently did not consider the difference great enough to consider defunding NRDC. "Yes, we give NRDC a lot of money," Harvey admits. "It's because they have the strongest energy program in the United States and the most competitive proposals."[20] By contrast, no organizations that oppose stranded costs, or even wish to use them as a bargaining chip, receive support from the Energy Foundation. The Massachusetts Public Interest Research Group (Mass PIRG) obtained grants from the foundation until they started beating the stranded-costs drum. Mass PIRG activists believe that stranded costs are the only thing utilities really care about in the deregulation battle. Thus, strategically, they are a good provision to hold out on. The Energy Foundation evidently disagrees.

When Ralph Cavanagh saw that his most generous funder was troubled by his opposition to RPS, he began (as noted above) negotiating RPS provisions acceptable to the utilities—over the objections of the Union of Concerned Scientists and the American Wind Energy Association, who believed he was once again asking for too little. In deference to an industry that would prefer to let the market find its own way to renewables, Cavanagh and his camp switched course and re-endorsed politically vulnerable tax incentives, all the while insisting that marginally ethical green marketing would lead inexorably to clean and sustainable energy production.

Hal Harvey disagrees. "I have never been a fan of green marketing." Even if it worked, he said, it would only serve as "a modest supplement of green citizenship." However, Harvey's quarrel with Cavanagh over this vital aspect of energy deregulation does not appear to affect his respect for NRDC, even though the latter opposes the "unreasonable," "impractical," and "radical" strategies of about 75 percent of the foundation's other grantees. The alternative strategy it supported was to give entire loaves of concession to private utilities, break off a few crumbs, toss them to renewable energy advocates, and declare victory.

Even though NRDC and EDF are trying very hard to be political players, they are simply not very good at it. They lack savvy and frequently behave as if they were serving other interests, or have invisible conflicts. And—because of a lack of grassroots support—they necessarily bargain from a position of weakness. Thus they cave in too soon, as NRDC did in California. According to Cavanagh, "It [AB 1890] is the best we could get."[21] Nonetheless, the Energy Foundation continues to reward their strategy with millions of dollars in grants, and the California episode—which should be regarded as a learning experience, an object lesson, and a case study in political naiveté—has, in the minds of the Energy Foundation and its favored grantees, become a model for energy restructuring.

Competition and the Fine Art of Program Direction

Overall, fewer than one in twenty foundation proposals are approved for funding, and even those that are eventually funded are denied scores of times before they hit pay dirt. So competition for foundation largesse is fierce. It exists on three levels. There is relatively polite macrolevel competition between fields like education, health, science, human welfare, environment, international affairs, and the arts. It is manifested in cautious reports, essays, white papers, and opinion editorials arguing for the importance to our civilization of a particular field—and pointing to the dire consequences of diminishing private support for it.

Within each field, competitors become a little more testy. One art form, (opera for example) attempts to persuade foundations it is somehow more deserving of support than symphony orchestras, or modern art museums claim that they are more relevant than collections of classical art. In every field this sort of argument is endemic: prevention versus cure; supply side versus demand side; basic versus applied science; higher versus lower and public versus private education.

But it is within each field that these contests can and often do become petulant and ad hominem, as symphony conductors compete directly with each other for scarce resources and professional fundraisers attempt to win Foundation X away from Doctor Y.

Competition for funding is a positive force in organized philanthropy. Behind the constant preening, exaggeration, and burnishing of images is a compulsion to offer new solutions to serious social and cultural problems. From this ferment of braggadocio, a shrewd program officer can sift good ideas and, with money, encourage promising pioneers and activists to run with them.

In facing the challenge of deregulation, had the creators, trustees, and grantees of the Energy Foundation respected democratic processes, things might have turned out very differently. If—instead of deferring to the industry responsible for two-thirds of the acid rain emissions, one-third of all carbon dioxide emissions, and half of all nuclear waste—they had sought and implemented policies to bring the capital costs of renewable energy in line with fossil fuels, and had built a movement to promote cost-effective efficiency through entities other than utilities, America might now be well on its way to a sustainable energy economy.

Lessons Unlearned

If there is self-criticism in the foundation industry it is remarkably muted.
—Pablo Eisenberg

It's difficult to define or categorize what the Pew, MacArthur, Rockefeller, and Joyce Mertz-Gilmore foundations have accomplished with the $100 million they have routed through the Energy Foundation since 1991. But the largest portions of it given to NRDC, EDF, and CLF can hardly be called "environmental grantmaking," though that's what they call it. It's an ironic category, because sound environmental practices call for diversity, and diversity was lost when five different foundations, with five different philosophies, decided to pass all of their grants through a single foundation run by two engineers educated at the same university. So the ultimate question is thus not whether this is environmental philanthropy but whether or not it is good philanthropy.

Can selling out consumers and forestalling the development of renewable energy reasonably be considered successful policy? Or, in the field of electrical energy where old companies and huge industries stand to suffer from any fundamental reform, shouldn't the Energy Foundation and its benefactors acknowledge their incompetence and change course? If they were truly candid, they might also admit defeat, or at very least acknowledge that they had advocated and supported a seriously misguided public policy that was encoded into bad law. But even in the face of deregulatory failure, characterized by superinflationary energy prices, they won't admit they were wrong. Foundations and their grantees rarely do.

Although it is difficult to believe that sophisticated program officers in the supporting foundations could consider their investments in the deregulation wars money well spent, all but one continued to renew their commitments to the Energy Foundation years after a major flop became obvious. Only one of the six foundations that support the initiative, Rockefeller, has pulled out after donating a total of $21.9 million. Gordon Conway, Rockefeller's new president, says they did so because the Energy Foundation is now self-sufficient. Of course, if all its beneficiaries believed that, it wouldn't be true. We can only assume that the loyal remaining foundations approve of the Energy Foundation's choice of grantees and of their policy positions. Or perhaps they aren't paying enough attention?

Conclusion

It is time for a new social contract between the independent sector and the rest of society.
—Michael Lerner, President, Jennifer Altman Foundation

While observing the work of organized philanthropy in search of the true intent of its trustees, it is often instructive to look first at a foundation's largest grantees. The Energy Foundation makes this an easy task, as their grants to three relatively conservative nonprofit law firms subverted much of what was accomplished by hundreds of its other grantees. The lesson here is that seven-figure grants have a way of reinforcing lunacy, and big funders can be unwitting enablers of terrible tendencies and misguided policies. Smaller grantees, observing the folly and lamenting it in private, can only stand and wait for their own next grant.

Yet the Energy Foundation and its benefactors have moved even beyond that pale of reason. By continuing to support agents of capitulation and deferring to free market arguments made by people who haven't spent a day of their lives in the free market—meanwhile throwing mere crumbs to energy visionaries, renewable activists, and consumer advocates—well-meaning philanthropists have once again become drag anchors on social progress. At a time when federal support of renewable energy sources has dwindled away, foundation support is more critical than ever. It's the worst possible time to behave like a drag anchor.

From a broader perspective, the whole episode is symptomatic of a malady that has plagued organized philanthropy since its earliest days, when men like Andrew Carnegie and John D. Rockefeller deemed knowledge and expertise sufficient ingredients of change and rejected a role for social agitation. There is no indication that the Energy Foundation or its major grantees have learned anything about the value of public advocacy or democratic processes. Whether the large foundations that have supported the experiment from the beginning—placing enormous trust in engineers while ignoring public advocates—have learned anything about democracy remains to be seen. What is clear is that by creating a separate foundation to tackle a controversial challenge they can effectively insulate themselves from challenge and controversy.

8

Art

Convert pork into porcelain, grain and produce into priceless pottery, the rude ores of commerce into sculptured marble, and railroad shares and mining stocks—things which perish without the using, and which in the next financial panic shall surely shrivel like parched scrolls—into the glorified canvas of the world's masters. Convert your useless gold into things of living beauty that shall be a joy to the whole people for a thousand years.
—Joseph Choate, at the opening of the Metropolitan Museum, 1894

In America today, creativity in the arts and humanities is devalued, regarded increasingly as a luxurious pastime, an elitist pursuit, or a traffic generator for chambers of commerce. Almost lost is the sense of art as a vital adjunct to science, a sustainer of achievement and beauty, and—perhaps most important in any civilization—a mirror of the human condition. The consequences of this outlook are becoming all too evident.

Once admired as a wellspring of robust cultural innovation, an incubator of artistic genius, the United States is now most often esteemed for its adventure movies, nihilistic music, bimbo tv sitcoms, advertising commercials, and stand-up comedy. These so-called art forms are nothing to sneer at in economic terms: entertainment is one of the very few industries in the country that maintain a positive balance of trade. And within the context of each form, Americans produce excellent work, especially in filmmaking, poetry, jazz, photography, and modern dance.

But does the most powerful nation in history make a notable contribution to global culture? Does America's most profitable export reflect the legacy of a great civilization? And can philanthropy, as it has in the past, find a way to revitalize the creative environment that produced Winslow Homer, Herman Melville, Mary Cassatt, Carl Sandberg, Maria Tallchief,

Tennessee Williams, Alexander Calder, Georgia O'Keefe, Edward Hop-
per, Alice Walker, Orson Wells, Martha Graham, and Charlie Parker.

"The arts are not a frill," Ernest Boyer told the 27th Annual Conference
of the Western Alliance of Arts Administrators in 1995. We are only "beginning, as a nation, to recognize that the quality of a culture and the quality
of the arts are inextricably interlocked. And we are beginning to understand
that if we do not educate our children in the symbol system we call art, we
will lose not only our civility, but our humanity as well."[1] Are the philanthropists listening? A few perhaps, but their grantmaking does not suggest
that they are rallying to the losing cause of artistic creativity.

While legislators shift their discourse on cultural appropriations from
"how little?" to whether to fund the arts at all and cultural critics bemoan
the lack of support for the humanities, foundations are gradually reducing their support of the creative process. Perceiving a grim financial outlook for most arts groups, trustees have become hesitant to continue their
support. Even though the share of grant dollars for the arts increased
slightly between 1998 and 2000 from 12 to 12.7 percent of the total
foundation outlay, the longer-term trend is down from the high of over
15 percent in the 1980s. Moreover, within the arts and humanities grant
category, there is a disturbing shift away from funding the work of creative artists toward grants that reflect a philanthropic view of the arts as
a "civic enterprise."

Most of the increase in arts funding are the result of large one-time
gifts to traditional arts institutions for special projects—acquisition of a
particular work of art, a special exhibition, or a specific theatrical production. Few observers believe that such grants are good news for the arts
or humanities, particularly for performance institutions desperate for
general support. Operating grants to arts organizations have declined
from over 30 percent to about 16 percent of total arts funding.[2]

Among champions of culture, there is some concern about the decline
of foundation support for the arts, but it lacks a sense of crisis. "We
affirm that a healthy cultural life is vital to a democratic society," John
Brademas, president emeritus of New York University and chair of the
President's Committee on Arts and Humanities, wrote in a solemn but
alarming letter to President Clinton. "A great nation must invest in its
cultural development just as it supports scientific discovery and protects
natural resources." That is a true and well-expressed sentiment, but it is

hardly new; nor is it often heeded by those in the federal government. Yet many arts lobbyists consider government arts funding vital to the future of American creativity, even though it provides less than 1 percent of total national contributions to the arts.

About half of the revenue for nonprofit arts is derived from admission fees and sales of such items as CDs, prints and replicas, and commemorative programs. The rest comes from patronage. Overall, nonprofit arts institutions obtain 12 percent of their income from foundation grants— about two and a half times the amount received from the National Endowment for the Arts and all the state arts councils combined. Of the almost $10 billion donated to the arts in America in 1995, however, about $8.7 billion came from individuals. Next to that sum, the National Endowment for the Arts' $99 million is chump change, and the total corporate gifts of $114 million are not much more.

All these components of cultural patronage in the United States are interdependent and synergistic. Earned income, philanthropy, and government support are each vital to the nonprofit arts economy. Pull off one leg and the whole arts enterprise could collapse, or at least return to the relative insignificance it had before 1960. An alarming number of government leaders either don't believe in that theory or care so little about the arts that they are willing to test it. The same can be said, unfortunately, for too many philanthrocrats; for even as financial markets boom and more money becomes available, foundation funding of the arts and humanities continues its gradual decline.

The Evangelist

Money is like manure. Keep it in a pot and it stinks; spread it around and it grows things.
—Kenneth Langone, Founder, Home Depot

Although foundations were the first institutional source of support for the nonprofit arts community—Mssrs. Rockefeller, Carnegie, and Mellon having recognized the wisdom of fostering culture—the massive and influential art grant as we know it was unknown until around 1957, when the Ford Foundation stepped into cultural philanthropy with both feet.

The Carnegie Corporation under President Frederick Keppel, the John Simon Guggenheim Memorial Foundation, and a few other smaller foundations had dabbled in what they called "the aesthetics" through the early part of the century, mostly with the joint aim of encouraging a wider appreciation of high culture—of strictly European origins, of course—and defining the American parameters of "fine art." Nonetheless, the early creators of organized philanthropy, most of them self-made industrialists, were more interested in science than in art and far more committed to improving society and strengthening the workforce than in patronizing culture. The utilitarian value of the arts escaped them, so their funding was small, idiosyncratic, and more concerned with arts literacy and appreciation than with encouragement of artistic creativity. Before 1920 less than 1 percent of total foundation philanthropy went to the arts; by 1930 the share had risen to 2.7 percent.[3]

In 1943 the Carnegie Corporation ceased funding the arts altogether. Between then and 1960, less than 3 percent of all foundation funding went to the arts. At midcentury corporations discovered the expediency of funding the elite arts in their headquarter cities, and while politicians talked a lot about cultural patronage, neither federal nor local governments had yet offered a penny to the arts.

In 1960, however, the philistine culture of the 1950s personified in the presidential candidacy of Richard M. Nixon was suddenly superseded by the artistic taste and style of his vanquisher, John F. Kennedy—and even more so of America's highbrow first lady, Jacqueline Bouvier Kennedy.

President Kennedy became a champion of cultural philanthropy. While pressing for public support of the arts, he liked to tell a story about Abe Lincoln, who ordered work to proceed on the Capitol dome at the height of the Civil War. When political opponents protested, Lincoln said, "If the people see the Capitol going on, it is a sign that we intend this Union shall go on." Franklin Roosevelt quoted Lincoln in 1941 when, with much of the world at war, he dedicated the National Gallery in Washington. In 1962 Kennedy said that Lincoln and Roosevelt "understood that the life of the arts, far from being an interruption or distraction in the life of the nation, is very close to the center of a nation's purpose—and is a test of the quality of a nation's civilization."[4]

Almost overnight, classical culture and fine art became de rigueur, inside and outside the White House. At the Ford Foundation an unusually creative grantmaker named W. MacNeil Lowry was hired as the first vice president for the arts. Mac Lowry came to Ford at a fortuitous moment;

it was then by far the largest foundation in the world with assets approaching $4 billion. Flush with cash, it was still uncertain about how to spend it.

Lowry was an evangelist and knew how to work an audience, most importantly the audience in the boardroom of the Ford Foundation. In less than twenty years he managed, through sheer ardor for art and patient persuasion, to wangle over $400 million from Ford's trustees for the revitalization of American arts and humanities. The arts in America would thrive and improve, Lowry told his board, only if imaginative philanthropists invested in the institutions of art and in artists themselves—in both production and creation.

Lowry offered documented support for his pitch in the form of alarming reports funded by two other foundations: *The Performing Arts: Problems and Prospects* by the Rockefeller Brothers' Fund, and *Performing Arts: The Economic Dilemma,* a product of the Twentieth Century Fund. Both reports prophesied doom for American arts and cultural institutions, which were then suffering from low wages, high deficits, and pressure to inflate ticket prices out of the reach of all but the wealthiest citizens—hardly the formula for a vibrant national culture.

By 1962, and for many years thereafter, the Ford Foundation was the largest private source of funding for art and culture. The country was primed for a cultural revolution characterized by a shift from elitism to cultural pluralism, and Lowry believed that without a prospering nonprofit arts community a civilization's culture would never reflect its finest values. In America, that meant nourishing Latino choreographers, African American playwrights, Asian sculptors, and angry Beat poets as well as classical composers, concert pianists, art museums, and opera divas. "We have to find and support the oddball creative fanatics,"[5] Mac Lowry wrote in one memo to the trustees. The institutions that apprenticed and employed artists and artisans also had to be supported. With that mindset, Lowry proceeded to virtually invent new fields of art and to place the nonprofit art sector at the very center of American cultural development.

Ford granted millions of dollars, not only to promising talent and the creative process, but also to debt retirement, endowments, building construction, and the creation of new dance and theater companies to train and encourage the next generation of performers. But perhaps the most imaginative of all his initiatives was Lowry's attempt to direct the bulk of artistic philanthropy away from New York City and toward other areas of the nation where, he knew from his own travels, a wellspring of creative genius was languishing unnoticed by the culture mavens of Manhattan. (He only partly succeeded. New York still leads all other states in art grants received. In fact, cultural organizations in four states—New York, California, Pennsylvania, Texas—plus the District of Columbia receive 55 percent of all foundation giving to the arts and humanities.)[6]

Lowry encouraged the growth of strong regional performing arts institutions, particularly dance and theater companies, which had not attracted the attention of other foundations. Grants were made for audience development and management training as well as to advance artistic professionalism and creative development. Minority theater groups in midwestern cities like Detroit, Chicago, and Cleveland were spawned and supported until they had local followings large enough to survive on their own.

According to historian Stanley Katz, "Ford invested enormous sums of money, and not in a random way. It wasn't just that the leadership had a set of ideas, but [that] the whole domestic policy side of the Ford Foundation had a set of ideas about how cultural and social development were linked. It is one of the great examples of private social planning in American history and we are still living with the consequences of it."[7]

The regionalization of the arts fostered by Lowry and Ford was based on the faith that if more Americans were involved in the arts, more would support them. New artists would appear and art would flourish. For the first time, arts grantmakers were thinking in ecological terms. Art institutions, artists, and audiences were all seen as interdependent, symbiotic species in a modern arts ecosystem. Good art could not thrive without strong institutions, which would wither without good art. The loss of either would lead to a loss of audience, without which the economic base would be lost. It was an ingenious principle and effective while it lasted, but the ecosystem Lowry envisioned now faces collapse—a casualty of the culture wars that rage through the American body politic.

Under Lowry, Ford applied the art of leverage, demanding matching grants and other preconditions designed to assure the continuity and sound financial management of all arts institutions, whether large conservatories or tiny art schools. "Ford's influence on the arts can be likened to a chain reaction," writes San Francisco Foundation arts program director John Kreidler. Gradually other foundations, some intentionally others unwittingly, began to emulate the nation's largest trust, albeit on a much smaller scale. Between 1955 and 1970, large national foundations increased their annual number of arts grants from under five hundred to over two thousand. The proportion of foundation dollars reaching the arts increased during the same period from 10 to 20 percent.

By 1966 the foundations were providing almost 60 percent of the unearned income of nonprofit arts organizations. Only 7 percent was coming from state and federal sources.[8] By the early 1980s corporations and their foundations, eager for the public goodwill that arts funding clearly brought, followed suit. Exxon, Mobil, Phillip Morris, Texaco, Hallmark, and AT&T became household names in the cultural world. Yet arts funding seems to have been a fad that corporations found they could avoid; most have pulled back from all but the most high-profile arts projects in favor of education, which is arguably in a worse crisis than the arts in America—and has a more immediate and utilitarian impact on corporations.

It should be noted that even at the apex of what is now called the Ford Era of arts philanthropy, very few foundations—Rockefeller being the main exception—followed Mac Lowry's precise example: that is, investment in creative development by taking risks with avant-garde artists and companies or supporting new art forms and performance media. Despite their alleged innovativeness and flexibility, most family and community foundations made their cultural grants to safe and established institutions like art museums, ballet companies, and symphony orchestras, all of which received large endowments, new buildings, and operational support.

Arts historian Paul DiMaggio explains the disconnect between rhetoric and action by pointing to the "embeddedness of private foundations in local leadership networks . . . networks of reciprocity that reinforce aesthetic conservatism and impel foundations to assist the most powerful and traditional institutions."[9] Against that indictment, even Ford has no defense. In 1962 its trustees granted $6 million to opera and $8 million to ballet, and in 1966 it made its largest single arts outlay—$80 million—to retire the debt and enhance the financial stability of sixty-one symphony orchestras across the country. Meanwhile it upheld its populist reputation by offering four- and five-figure grants to a wide array of promising painters, poets, playwrights, sculptors, choreographers, and musicians.

Lowry acknowledged, and defended, the foundation's massive investment in orchestras. It is true, he said in a memo to Ford trustees, "the program far exceeds in size and scope anything which has ever been done for the arts. And only two agencies in the United States—the federal government and the Ford Foundation—could contemplate it."[10] From a strictly managerial standpoint, it was a more creative grant than it seemed; $25 million was given outright, in cash, mostly to retire debt, but the rest came in Ford Motor Company stock. The latter was accompanied by a covenant that allowed orchestras to sell the stock slowly in the future; the arrangement permitted the foundation to divest itself of its only security, as the law required, without driving down the stock's market value. If Ford prospered (and it did), American symphonies would too.

However, for no fault of Lowry's, the symphony gambit failed, because musicians and their unions found ways to cannibalize the newfound endowments. Lowry's brilliant response was to create the National Arts Stabilization Fund, which served the same purpose as internal endowments but kept the corpus of money away from the musicians.

Since 1980 and the departure of Mac Lowry, the Ford Foundation has lost its preeminent position as America's arts funder. It has been replaced by the J. Paul Getty Trust, a $4.5-billion endowment whose $250 million in annual arts grants exceed the combined donations of all fifty state arts councils. Following far behind is the Lila Wallace–Readers Digest Foundation, which has on occasion granted over $50 million a year to the arts; the Mellon Foundation, which occasionally exceeds $30 million in a year; and the Pew and MacArthur foundations, which provide just under $20 million (most of it to the Philadelphia and Chicago arts communities, respectively). By 1992 Ford had shrunk from the largest arts foundation the to to ninth; that same year, over 40 percent of arts funding came from the twenty-five largest foundations in the United States. Nonetheless, historians of culture and philanthropy will long remember the Ford Foundation as the superpower that brought the big trusts permanently into the world of arts, and Mac Lowry as the philanthrocrat who created the intellectual paradigm around which arts philanthropy still dances.

Ford's leadership was also instrumental in the formation of the National Endowment for the Arts (NEA), although the central roles were played by the Rockefeller Foundation and the Twentieth Century Fund. Conceived in the Kennedy administration and inaugurated by Lyndon Johnson in 1965, the NEA modeled its grantmaking on practices originated by Lowry, especially requiring matching grants from states and other patrons as a condition for funding artists and institutions. By 1968 NEA's leverage ratio had reached 1 to 3. For every dollar the endowment granted three came in from other sources. Leverage became a persuasive selling point for arts lobbyists and foundation program directors alike. Other government arts agencies, including the Institute for Museum Services, the National Trust for Historic Preservation, the Corporation for Public Broadcasting, and the National Endowment for the Humanities were also catalyzed by the trusts—notably the Rockefeller and Mellon foundations, the Carnegie Corporation, and the Twentieth Century Fund.

The NEA quickly became the driving force behind cultural pluralism and the democratization of American art, a fact that bothered some of its critics as much as Robert Mapplethorpe's photographs and the infamous Richard Serra sculpture bothered others. Although at the height of Ford's push, the total of nonprofit arts organization funding derived from the foundations barely surpassed 7 percent, the leverage they applied brought millions more into the arts. Moreover, the thousands of minority artists given employment made the foundations star performers in a multipolar cultural system that included, besides the NEA, state and federal arts agencies, the American Council for the Arts, and the President's Committee for the Arts and Humanities.

But more significant than their popularity is the fact that Ford and its imitators were able to create, through leverage, a vast nonprofit community that stood side by side and competed aggressively with the strictly proprietary arts industry that existed before the Ford initiative. John Kreidler offers this example from the San Francisco Bay Area, where "only twenty or thirty nonprofit arts organizations were in existence in the 1950s, whereas a far greater number of theaters, musical ensembles, performing arts presenters, and galleries were operating on a for-profit basis. By the late 1980's, the end of the Ford era, the Bay Area contained approximately one thousand nonprofit arts organizations, and far fewer proprietary operations continued to exist." [11]

The consequences of foundation dominance in arts funding has not pleased everyone, particularly those who resent what they call the "coercive philanthropy" practiced by some large foundations: Robert Brustein, artistic director of the American Repertory Theater, claims that foundations "force theater to think of social ends instead of excellence."[12] Brustein cites as an example the goals of the Lila Wallace–Reader's Digest Fund: "To expand their marketing efforts, mount new plays, broaden the ethnic makeup of their management, experiment with colorblind casting, increase community outreach activity and sponsor programs designed to integrate theaters into their communities." Of course, if Brustein doesn't like the guidelines of a foundation he needn't apply to it for funding. On the other hand, the Lila Wallace Fund has committed $45 million to achieve its goals—a sum hard to resist for the sake of a principle.

Supply versus Demand

I have grown weary of saying "I have grown weary of saying that culture should be supported," to people who have never lived in communities that create the poems and stories and songs that are such a part of our culture.
—Jane Sapp, Mississippi blues singer

In the last years of the twentieth century the arts funding community became sharply divided over the question of whether to support artists, artistic processes, or audience development. Supply-siders say, "Fund the arts, improve talent, encourage creativity, train performers" with the aim of creating excellence. That excellence will bring the audience. Demand-siders disagree. There has been enough "production," they say. Only audience development, a subset of traditional marketing research, will create a commercial demand for the arts that will be filled, ipso facto, by talented dancers, musicians, painters, actors, and sculptors. Create a demand, they argue, and a supply to fill it will appear. That's traditional market economics, but it's yet to be proven in the arts. Nonetheless, most large foundations seem to have faith in the theory, although a handful—the Jerome, Bush, Pew, Rauchenberg, Koret, and the Creative Capital Fund—still offer small grants to individual artists.

Under demand-side management, civic leaders eventually come to regard the arts as a competitive advantage over other cities and states. Marketing firms like KPMG Peat Marwick perform studies for clients to quantify the economic impact of the "the arts industry." In a study for the California Arts Council, for example, Peat Marwick found that impact to be "surprisingly robust." It reported that "non profit arts organizations add $2.159 billion to the California economy, create 155,000 jobs and generate $77 million in state and local tax revenue. . . . A survey of out-of-state visitors also shows that the arts are a strong magnet for cultural tourists, who spent $288 million on in-state transportation and lodging, generating $158 million in income and 4,200 jobs." Such is the rhetoric of demand-side art patrons.

While there are strong partisans for each side of the supply–demand debate, and most foundation officers see things both ways, there has been a noticeable shift toward the art-as-civic-enterprise model. This, of course, is consistent with the foundations' tendency to favor production over creation and to see their role not as protecting art per se but as promoting art in service to community.

Lila Wallace–Reader's Digest, until recently the largest arts funder in New York, leans toward demand-side funding. Although at reduced rates, they continue to fund the red carpet institutions they have always supported—the New York City Opera, Metropolitan Museum, New York Philharmonic Orchestra, Lincoln Center, and Chamber Music Society. Recently, however, the foundation initiated a challenge-grant program with a dozen community foundations; its announced aim was to strengthen local foundations' capacity to act as point-institutions for audience development in their regions in order "to foster art as civic enterprise."

Dennis Collins, president of the Irvine Foundation in San Francisco, likes the Lila Wallace approach. He, too, sees the arts as "a powerful engine for economic development, attracting tourism, creating jobs, and generating tax revenues." It is possible that in saying so he is simply playing to his conservative trustees—and he has a few. Yet Collins also sees tremendous value in the creative and educational potential for the arts, though even in that regard his pitch is unabashedly utilitarian. "We know that students who participate in the arts do better on standardized tests. And we know that the arts impart values and skills that employers seek such as the ability to work as part of a team, and to devise creative solutions to problems." Art thus becomes a catalyst of industrial enterprise.

A visible manifestation of the art-as-enterprise approach to grant-making is the urban arts center, over a thousand of which have been built in American cities during the past two decades. Usually constructed (or retrofitted into abandoned structures) in depressed inner cities at costs ranging from $30 to $200 million, the centers are often conceived and promoted by downtown commercial and real estate interests as economic catalysts for urban renewal. And, although corporations and wealthy individuals have provided important support, the foundations have pumped millions of dollars for purchase and construction costs into new centers and complexes like Philadelphia's Avenue of the Arts.

By providing facilities for a wide range of cultural expression—the visual and performance arts ranging from opera, ballet, and symphony all the way across the cultural spectrum to beauty pageants and bodybuilding competitions—these centers have had an unexpected impact on the arts. "These buildings don't just house culture," Edward Rothstein recently wrote in the *New York Times;* "they alter it."[13] They have created an "arts center culture" that boasts of its classical programs to the philanthropic elite and its popular offerings to the middle-brow audiences who buy the bulk of tickets. "A new urban logic is created," according to Rothstein. "The arts don't grow out of the city; the city will grow out of the arts—or rather, out of the upper income demographics associated with [the arts]."

The $65-million Bass Performance Center in Fort Worth Texas, for example, was pitched to foundations as a performing arts center for orchestra, ballet, and musical theater. Unmentioned in the initial proposal were Judy Collins, Milton Berle, the Flying Karamazov Brothers, and an ice skating extravaganza, all booked the first year. Gradually, at Bass and elsewhere throughout the country, while the bodybuilders, bar mitzvahs, and pop musicians pack the houses, rows of symphony seats remain empty. The commercial imperative of urban arts centers, which are often grossly overbuilt, pushes them farther and farther from the commitment to nonprofit arts originally described to foundation philanthropists. Arts that turn a profit are favored over those that require ongoing philanthropic support, and *culture* is redefined—though not always for the worse. Arts centers in most cities serve a diverse audience from the city's various communities. Indeed, some have encouraged and reinforced excellence in performing arts that might not otherwise have found an audience—for example, gospel music and modern dance.

The sad fact is, however, that with federal, foundation, and corporate support for the arts either static or shrinking, art institutions have little choice but to embrace the demand-side position and rely on marketing strategies—outreach programs, increased ticket prices, and related product sales (e.g., books, CDs, and reproductions). In this environment art can too easily be commodified, becoming a commercial "product" to be either supplied or demanded, depending on your perspective. Almost lost, on either side, is the intrinsic value of art—"art for art's sake"—and its contribution to (and challenges of) national culture, to aesthetic sensibilities, and to a deeper understanding of ourselves. It becomes no more than another economic entity, a magnet for commerce. Not since the demise of the WPA has there been a golden age of creative patronage in the United States—a patronage that asks for nothing but stubborn commitment to an artistic vision.

In a demand-obsessed context, art grantmaking has become fad-driven. Foundation guidelines and statements of purpose change annually, even semiannually, to reflect the trend du jour in art marketing. One year *innovation* is the buzzword, next year it's *interdisciplinary,* then *multicultural, community-based, community-directed,* or *experimental.* Grant writers call it "mission creep." Only the most agile can keep up. When too many fund-raisers have the rap down cold and scores of applications have to be turned away for every one approved, foundations rephrase their objectives and guidelines. The most successful grant seekers (some call them "mercenaries") are the few who learn the new rhetoric as fast as its churned out and layer the buzzword or concept of the week into grant proposals rewritten quickly enough to meet the next deadline.

Art grantsmanship has thus become a process in which adaptation is more valuable than creativity, rhetorical agility more useful than talent, and "spin" is the ultimate skill. Mission creep is not, incidentally, unique to arts funding; nor are shifting winds of patronage new to foundation grantmaking. But both appear to be more common in the arts and humanities than in other funding categories. Or perhaps arts fund-raisers just complain more openly than their counterparts in other fields.

The important point, however, is not the complaints of fund-raisers. Grantee bitterness is endemic to the nonprofit world. What is of essence is the fact that foundations, as Brustein noted above, have interjected themselves between nonprofit arts institutions and their audience. Art producers now play to foundations; they no longer compete for audiences but for the attention of funders. And, according to Melanie Beene, consultant to nonprofit administrators, "very few of them have the moral courage to be honest with funders." [14]

With their newfound influence and historical leverage, foundations can mediate culture very easily with a mere change of interest or rhetoric. If an opera company hears that the Rockefeller Foundation is emphasizing "cultural diversity" next year, it might well postpone plans to stage Puccini for a season and schedule instead an Anthony Davis opera. Same opera company, different culture. Something very similar happened at the Public Broadcasting System (PBS) in 1988, when producers there heard that program officers at several foundations were losing interest in women's issues and focusing their attention on race. PBS suspended production on a ten-part history of women in America that was already well underway; the next year its grant-funded miniseries were *Eyes on The Prize, With God on Our Side,* and *Blacks and Jews.* Public broadcasting produced what Rockefeller and other foundations—not the creative talent at PBS or independent producers—thought was vital.

Of course, patrons have been dictating art since the dawn of patronage. The Medicis paid for what they wanted and got what they paid for. Mozart worked for the archbishop of Salzburg, literally eating with the servants, and wrote music for the Austrian royal court. And after the French Revolution, when art patrons were either beheaded or bankrupted, the state became the patron, a practice that eventually spread throughout western Europe, where today artistic expression is mediated extensively by bureaucratic patronage supported, quite willingly, by taxpayers. (Each French taxpayer contributes $32 a year to the arts; the comparable American figure is 32 cents—and American taxpayers complain far more about government arts agencies than the French do.)

Art as a civic enterprise remained the hot button in the late 1990s. Art as social service and art for art's sake are out, for the time being; art as traffic generator to inner cities is in. Unfortunately, the divide created by the foundations' changing preferences tends to run along color lines; white avant-garde artists are inadvertently favored over artists of color, simply because they are more likely to think like marketers, rather than creators.

"Markets are wonderful, powerful things," observes cultural essayist Arlene Goldblatt, " but they can no more function as the primary protector and generator of cultural resources than they can create other social goods such as education, healthcare and public safety." She adds a suggestion useful to foundation grantmakers in the arts: "With the overwhelming social trend toward privatization and commercialization, an underlying principle of cultural policies should be to create protected public space[s] in culture, analogous to nature preserves as protected public land. . . . Just as public libraries can function as part of our cultural commonwealth, every community should have the cultural infrastructure to sustain a lively, multi-directional, creative climate."[15]

Conclusion

What gives me hope in troubled times?
Mozart and quantum mechanics.
—Victor Weisskopf

In November 1996 Brown University hosted a symposium entitled "American Creativity at Risk." Keynote speaker Robert MacNeil, former coanchor of the MacNeil-Lehrer News Hour, explained why a great nation needs artists: "To continue telling the country its story, its unfolding narrative," he said. "To help metabolize rapid changes in mores, in manners, in attitudes to gender and race . . . to sharpen our moral conscience. . . . To gratify the nonmaterial spirits in the land of unprecedented material appetites. . . . To restore our frayed sense of community. . . . To stimulate sensitivity to beauty . . . and in Milton's phrase 'to justify the ways of God to man.'. . . In short, America needs its artists to help it obey that most basic of admonitions, to know thyself." And to his jeremiad, MacNeil added: "America is creative or it is nothing."

The conference occurred at a time of deep cynicism and indifference toward the arts and their value in a pluralistic democracy. Political attacks on multiculturalism, Hollywood, and the National Endowment for the Arts are all expressions of a deeply held distrust, even fear, of artistic expression. Suspended, it seems is Benjamin Barber's belief that "the arts and humanities are civil society's driving engine, the key to its creativity, its diversity, its imagination and hence its spontaneity and liberty." Instead, artistic creativity is seen as the spawning ground of socially corrosive ideas—postmodernism, nihilism, and cultural relativism—which *Philanthropy* publisher John P. Walters describes as "acids that dissolve all elevated arguments for the arts."[16]

Perhaps because our indigenous culture is so popular, so commercial, and so diverse, Americans have never clearly understood the public purposes of art articulated by MacNeil. So much about American culture seems not only unartistic but at times contrary to any positive public purpose. Commercial advertising, tabloid journalism, and gangsta-rap music come to mind.

Foundations are in a unique position to contemplate the public purposes of the arts and to seek ways to help artists pursue constructive and high-minded aspirations. To do so, philanthropists would probably have to create a new category of research- and policy-related grant that, unfortunately, might siphon money away from the creative processes, at least for a while. But such a thoughtful consideration of art's purposes and values seems essential if organized philanthropy is to play a positive role in stimulating the growth and evolution of constructive cultural expressions.

As a countermeasure to their own overwhelming fiduciary control, foundation officers might consider offering arts institutions some of the alternative investment instruments now made available to community and economic development projects: program-related investments (PRIs), venture capital, low-interest loans, and loan guarantees. A few small foundations—notably the Dayton Hudson Foundation, J. M. Kaplan Fund, and Dade County and New Haven community foundations—have dabbled in arts PRIs, but larger foundations have yet to show an interest.

Another lasting problem is described by Paul DiMaggio. Despite the estimable intentions of a few small foundations, "few grants support access to and participation in the arts for the poor and working poor; conservation or preservation of performances in dance, theater, or improvisational music; or assistance for innovative artists and arts organizations. Nor are there many that support programs and organizations promoting the values of pluralism and diversity through genres like jazz and dance. . . . The resources of the relatively few foundations that do support such activities are stretched extremely thin."[17]

It's not a new sentiment, nor has it escaped the attention of prominent philanthropists. "The arts are not for the privileged few but for the many," John D. Rockefeller III proclaimed in 1963. "Their place is not on the periphery of daily life, but at its center." Nonetheless, measured in dollars or in number of grants, the high-brow arts of European origin are still most favored by the foundations.

In an age when the market is fast becoming the final judge and arbiter of everything, including excellence, it will be interesting to observe its long-term effect on the arts. Can a creative community relying almost solely on demand produce a renaissance? Will America again become a globally respected source of art forms besides popular film, ads, rap, and country music? Does it really matter? Is America's role in the world primarily, alas, an economic one, its main contribution technological, and its future that of a reliable supplier of whatever the market demands?

And will foundations intent upon strengthening democracy change course, and as they did in the 1960s and 1970s, to regard robust arts and humanities as an essential force in civil society? Will grantmakers become more mindful of the wider context and treat the arts world as an active ecosystem that must be nourished in its entirety to survive? And will contemporary discourse on cultural philanthropy rise above seeing the arts as a commercial magnet, providing "competitive advantage" for one tourist market over another?

Finally, will they also come to question the influence in a democratic society of patronized art created for a mass audience? When patronage derives from private wealth and is controlled by private citizens in private chambers, does not the power of that patronage approach that of plutocracy?

9

Civility

Many many good things have I bought!
Many many bad things have I fought!
—Elliot Rosewater

Kurt Vonnegut's *God Bless You, Mr. Rosewater,* subtitled *"Pearls before Swine,"* is perhaps the only American novel written about a foundation. It is also a testament to the philanthropic imagination and a good a way to begin and end a chapter about "civil society"—a popular though ill-defined idiom of contemporary philanthropic discourse.

The novel's young hero, the athletic, handsome, and Harvard-educated Elliot Rosewater, is a hopeless lush. Early in the book he is placed in charge of the family foundation and opens lavishly decorated offices in the Empire State Building—"headquarters for all the beautiful, compassionate and scientific things I hope to do."

At first Elliot takes the foundation quite seriously. "Rosewater dollars fought cancer and mental illness and race prejudice and police brutality and countless other mysteries, encouraged college professors to look for truth, bought beauty at any price," writes Vonnegut. But eventually booze gets the best of young Rosewater, and things take a turn toward weirdness.

Concerned about Elliot's drinking and his somewhat eccentric lifestyle, Norman Mushari, a young lawyer in the family law firm, plots to oust him and place the Rosewater Foundation in the conservative and sober hands of a distant cousin in Providence, Rhode Island. To accomplish this transfer Mushari must prove Elliot insane. Rosewater provides him with ample evidence, written and unwritten. He finally drops out of his life in New York (including his marriage) and moves the foundation to Rosewater County, Indiana, the family's old home territory. The county is in economic and social ruin, having been abandoned by the same company that created the Rosewater Foundation.

When Elliot's soon-to-be-deserted wife asks him what he intends to do there, he replies, "I'm going to care for these people." The residents of Rosewater County, Elliot says, "can't even take care of themselves any more—because they have no use. The factory, the farms, the mine across the river—they're all completely automatic now. And America doesn't need these people for war any more. Sylvia, I'm going to be an artist."

"An artist?"

"I'm gong to love these discarded Americans, even though they are useless and unattractive. *That* is going to be my work of art."[1]

Installed in a second-story walkup in the seamiest part of a town, Elliot sleeps in a cot and runs the Rosewater Foundation as a private welfare agency for the town's neediest citizens: among them, down-and-out drunks, floozies, and other reprobates. "This is the Rosewater Foundation. How may I help you?" Elliot inquires as he answers the phone. He rescues poor people from penury, one small grant at a time.

Senator Rosewater, Elliot's sanctimonious right-wing father, is horrified by his son's behavior and his concept of philanthropy. But when he finds out that the scheming Mushari has left the family firm and is representing Fred Rosewater's attempt to seize control of the foundation through the courts, the senator reluctantly sides with Elliot. The defense argues that as mankind is capable of compassionate love for the totally worthless, supporting them is a legitimate and noble cause of foundation philanthropy.

This defense, of course, lies at the very heart of the most central question about charitable philanthropy: Who deserves it? It also challenges the legitimate role and purpose of private foundations and raises questions about what we really mean by phrases like *civil society*.

Bowling Alone

The central project of the progressive liberal state is to eradicate civil society and transfer its functions to government.
—William Schambra, Bradley Foundation

In America more people bowl than vote, and most people who bowl, bowl alone. Harvard's Robert Putnam weaves those two facts together into a trenchant essay about the sorry state of American civil society, "Bowling Alone: America's Declining Social Capital." For Putnam, *social capital* means the "features of social organization such as networks, norms, and social trust that facilitate coordination and cooperation for mutual benefit, and enable participants to act together more effectively in pursuit of shared objectives."[2] Whether or not such shared goals are praiseworthy is, according to Putnam "entirely another matter." Generally, the more social capital a society possesses—in the form of trust, reciprocity, tolerance, and inclusion—the better it functions. The government works better, the economy runs better, and people are happier.

Although Putnam contrasts these features with physical and human capital ("the tools and training that enhance individual productivity"), neither he nor other champions of the good society believe that a strong and civil nation can be created or maintained without both kinds of capital. Unlike physical capital, however, new social capital requires a deliberate restructuring and revitalization of civil society—a transformation that money cannot buy. Civic renewal is thus a moral as well as a philanthropic process. Philanthropy's role is to supply the human capital to staff and operate the renovated institutions of civil society. That is not the end of its responsibility, however. According to Putnam, philanthropy should also play a vital role in designing the new civil society, as will be evident below.

A bowling league, most proponents of civil society would agree, is an association of civil society. For Putnam the decline in bowling leagues is emblematic of more perilous erosions, particularly in, for example, church attendance, union membership, and volunteering with the Red Cross and Scouts. (Champions of democracy would also mention the decline in voter participation.) To advocates of a new civil society, whom I call *civil societarians,* these signs are indications of a social meltdown, a prelude to America's descent into moral chaos.

These critics see civil society as the vast collection of associations or mediating institutions that exist outside of government and the business community. According to Don Eberly, director of the Civil Society Project in Harrisburg Pennsylvania, and a prolific writer on the topic, it is "a distinct social realm consisting of families, churches, charities and voluntary association, where we meet each other voluntarily, work toward common purposes and learn the essential democratic habits of collaboration and trust."[3]

Without millions of such associations, assert Eberly, Putnam, and their followers, the very fabric of a society begins to unravel and civilization dissolves. There are ample signs of that denouement in America, giving credence to the fears of civil societarians. The indicators they most frequently cite are the rapid growth of one-parent families, teen pregnancies, violent crime, and "radical individualism." "Reclaiming the American dream will require a transformation that is fundamentally moral and cultural—namely the recovery of moral society," says Eberly.[4]

Civil societarians often invoke Alexis de Tocqueville, the twenty-six-year-old French social philosopher and author of *Democracy in America*. After traveling through the United States in the 1820s, he accurately predicted that the American model of political democracy would soon replace the aristocratic institutions of Europe. Tocqueville was especially enthusiastic about the vigorous volunteerism and the almost-countless community groups he found in the United States: "Nothing in my view deserves more attention than the intellectual and moral associations in America." Putnam bemoans the loss of what the young Frenchman saw as Americans' willingness to step forward without command or payment for tasks "religious, moral, serious, futile, general or restricted, enormous or diminutive."

Yet, for some reason, Putnam and most of his admirers forget to celebrate the concomitant "loss," since Tocqueville's time, of slavery, limited suffrage, debtor's prison, vigilante justice, lynching, and the ethnic cleansing of the frontier—the demise of which are certainly triumphs of civil society. And if they must bemoan losses, why not the loss of fresh air and clean water? The movement formed to protect air and water during the twentieth century is rarely mentioned by proponents of civil society; nor are the civil rights, peace, women's, and human rights movements. The salient comparison of American civil society should probably not be between America in 1826 and America in 2000; it should be between America and the rest of the world today.

Putnam's "Bowling Alone," originally published in the relatively obscure *Journal of Democracy,* has been reprinted and republished many times and is now a book. It has become a virtual manifesto for the emerging civil society movement, which itself has developed into a cause celebre for higher-profile political conservatives like William Bennett, Lamar Alexander, and former Georgia Senator Sam Nunn. Unfortunately, the issues surrounding civil society have gone barely noticed, until quite recently, by philosophers, politicians, and philanthropists to the left of Nunn.

Political scientist Benjamin Barber, who could best be described as a moderate on the subject, believes that "after the Civil War, civil society began rapidly losing ground to nascent corporations with an appetite for expansion and a tendency toward monopoly. Market forces soon began to encroach on and crush civil society. Government responded with an aggressive campaign on behalf of the public weal." Barber neglects to mention the role played by the foundations in this campaign—foundations created by the same corporate wealth that was to co-opt so many of the functions of civil society.

"In assuming the powers it needed to confront corporations," Barber continues, "government inadvertently encroached on and crushed civil society from the opposite direction. Squeezed between the warring and ever expanding public and private sectors, civil society began disappearing from American life. Sometime between the two Roosevelts it disappeared altogether."[5]

"Although American government today is neither colonial nor totalitarian, it has usurped the space of civil society," Barber laments. Don Eberly agrees. "The primary reason civil society has atrophied," he claims, after bemoaning the corrosive effects of secular modernity on our moral and social ecology, "is that government has supplanted many of its functions."[6]

"A widespread tendency toward passive reliance on the state" is how Putnam describes it, although he cites as contributing factors the movement of women into the work force, residential instability, fewer marriages, more divorces, fewer children, and lower real wages.[7] William Schambra, director of general programs at the Harry and Lynde Bradley Foundation, which was created "to strengthen democratic capitalism and the institutions that sustain and nurture it," speaks of "the tyranny of the therapeutic state"; he proposes that Americans renounce "the idea of national community . . . which has proven in political practice to be this century's greatest disappointment." Ignoring twentieth-century advances in civil rights, social security, universal suffrage, and labor law—all initiatives of the national government—Schambra simply recommends "the restoration of the strength and moral authority of local community institutions."[8]

It was this essential distrust in government that drove the recent Republican party initiative to dismantle the welfare state and withdraw financial support for other social programs, in the process imploring foundations that had designed the welfare state to pick up the bill. "Civil society is about a human order that is larger and richer than the state," Eberly proclaims, "one that the state is better at destroying than renewing."[9]

Eberly is cautious, however, and less extreme than Schambra about the political solution. "The mistake of the Democratic majority was in believing it could create the good society by merely building government up. The danger for the Republican majority may be in believing that it can create the good society merely by tearing the government down."[10]

It is clear that not all observers of civil society are of one mind—not even all conservatives, most of whom are despondent and pessimistic. There are other scholars, like Boston College's Alan Wolfe, who do not see community life in America as endangered. "What we are witnessing is not a decline in community," according to Wolfe, but "the emergence of a new form of community. Down deep there is a tremendous sense of optimism in American life; and Americans are not accepting the idea that the world in which we live is deteriorating." Contrary to Putnam and Eberly, Wolfe concludes from his research that "this is a country of deep social involvement and it remains so. People may be involved in fewer organizations," he says, "but they are more active."

Michael Schudson at the University of California San Diego seems to agree. He finds evidence of increased citizenship in the growth of rights movements—something that conservative civil societarians generally dismiss as evidence of individualistic obsessions. In 1935 only 2 of the 185 cases that came before the Supreme Court dealt with rights. In 1989, the ratio was 66 of 132, a clear reflection, Schudson believes, of citizen participation in the protection of basic human and civil rights.[11]

From the standpoint of philanthropy, the key issue about civil society is not where it belongs—completely within the state, completely outside the state, or somewhere in between. That's a quandary for political scientists, philosophers, and active citizens. The relevant question for foundation trustees and officers is how should the functioning institutions of civil society be financed—publicly, privately, commercially, individually, or by a combination of all four? Clearly the latter is the status quo and should probably remain so. But what is a healthy ratio between private and public support, between individual and institutional support? And who should fund what, and what powers should funding confer on the givers? And, to focus our attention even more sharply on the topic of this chapter, what role should foundations play in the future of civil society?

The traditional narrative of organized philanthropy—accepted as a matter of faith—is that foundations strengthen civil society. The truth, however, is that some do and some don't. Of course, all foundations believe they do, according to a definition of civil society that suits their own particular politics and purposes. Yet if foundations are so good for civil society, why, we must ask them, is the society with the largest philanthropic sector in the world civilly weak in so many ways? Why does the United States have some of the most intractable social problems in the developed world? And some of the worst statistics for murder, crime, infant mortality, single parenthood, prison population, and voter turnout? And why is there so much injustice?

History suggests that societies do not become more civil because they are wealthy or well endowed with philanthropists. In fact, the opposite appears to be true. Societies become wealthy because they are civil. In other words, the associations of civil society precede wealth and private philanthropy, not the reverse. In fact, there is some question as to whether wealth itself—disproportionate or excessive wealth—may not hasten the demise of civil society.

"Is it possible," asks Michael Lerner, Jennifer Altman Foundation president, "that philanthropy may in important respects contribute to, as well as alleviate the problems of the United States?"[12] That heretical question, rarely broached by philanthrocrats, illuminates the central contradiction of foundation philanthropy: because foundations are dependent on an unequal distribution of wealth, they will not directly address the injustices created by disproportionate wealth. They may design and fund impressive programs to ameliorate poverty—like the Annie E. Casey Foundation's recently launched $500-million, ten-year initiative to strengthen poor families in twenty-two American cities—while ignoring the fact that the assets of the wealthiest people (and foundations) in those same cities are growing exponentially. Thus foundations are to some degree passively complicitous in the imbalance of wealth in America and, if Lerner's question is valid, in the deterioration of civil society.

In fact, his is a particularly pressing question today as the welfare state retreats and governments at all levels abdicate ("devolve" is the politicians' word) their financial commitments to social institutions. Of course, it's not the role or responsibility of the foundations to fill in for the state; nor should they organize citizens to pressure the state to protect the commonweal. But it would strengthen civil society greatly if philanthropy funded the organizations that do so.

The Bradley Solution

There is inherited wealth in this country, and also inherited poverty.
—Ben Franklin

Organized philanthropy is giving with an attitude.
—John Bruer, James S. McDonnell Foundation

Complaining about what he calls the "hypercentralism" of American government, perennial presidential aspirant and foundation creator Lamar Alexander joins the chorus of civil societarians by citing the damage that "Progressive" (he really means liberal) programs have had on family, school, church, and neighborhood associations. Though his claims are often exaggerated and apocalyptic in tone, there is some truth to the complaint that the bureaucratic meddling that goes with most government programs is counterproductive. That doesn't mean that the philanthropic intent of these mostly foundation-designed social programs is illegitimate, or that they should not be continued under a less-intrusive bureaucracy.

Nevertheless Alexander claims that "the moral authority of the Progressive [*sic*] vision of government has slowly eroded away, but the institutions it created are still standing, waiting to be replaced."[13] Most of the initiatives Alexander indicts—undertakings of the New Deal, the New Frontier, and the Great Society—were designed by foundations or foundation-funded think tanks like Brookings and the Urban Institute. Therefore, Alexander and his colleagues argue, the private foundations should get us out of the mess they have created. They should do so by underwriting and supporting new, independent social programs established completely outside the state, free of bureaucratic control, and, preferably, operated by "faith-based" institutions. Few foundations have risen to this challenge, largely because of the inherent hypocrisy of the proposal.

In 1997 Lamar Alexander accepted the chair of the National Commission on Philanthropy and Civic Renewal (NCPCR), a creation of the Harry and Lynde Bradley Foundation of Madison, Wisconsin. NCPCR would almost certainly have been nicknamed the Alexander Commission had not for the chairman earlier used another hastily formed nonprofit entity—a foundation formed to accept otherwise illegal six-figure campaign contributions—during his 1996 primary bid for the Republican presidential nomination. The $5.5 million Alexander raised through this private operating foundation financed a national closed-circuit television campaign to recruit Republican check writers to his cause. When it was over, he described the whole apparatus to the *New York Times* as "a lot better than a PAC."[14] To avoid the taint of scandal associated with Alexander's project, the NCPCR quite sensibly dubbed itself the Bradley Commission.[15]

In an array of essays and op-ed pieces published before the commission was formed, Bradley Foundation President Michael Joyce had made quite clear his conviction that the misfortunes of society's disadvantaged are not the result of racism, sexism, or other forms of discrimination but of their own lack of will, discipline, spiritual character, and family values. "We understand serious social problems as rooted in the imperfect choices confronting humans with limited natures and insufficient knowledge," Joyce proclaimed in a 1996 speech defining "Conservative Philanthropy" to the Heritage Foundation. "For the amelioration of these evils and the promotion of progress, conservative philanthropists rely on certain social processes such as moral traditions, the marketplace and the family."

The Bradley Commission's 130-page report, *Giving Better, Giving Smarter: Renewing Philanthropy in America,* was released in late 1997. Its recommendations were quite predictable, given its sole funding source. No one acquainted with Joyce's views could have been surprised by its observation that "private foundations and philanthropies are engaged in too much study." Yet it was a strange opening statement for a foundation report based on nineteen assigned papers, two public surveys, and a national profile of organizations and arguing that "foundations provide too little direct service, and too little hard-nosed evaluation of what they get for their money." That, too, is an interesting observation from a foundation that had just spent over a million dollars on the very report that

contained it. The commission went on to complain that "large foundations had started to act like government, that they spent too much time
talking to one another, rather than addressing problems directly . . . [and
that] established philanthropy prefers the grand theory—and abstract
cause—over the simple solution to a tangible problem."[16]

The report offers a "road map" for philanthropists, who, it says,
should become "civic entrepreneurs . . . as exacting in . . . giving as in
other areas of life." Local organizations should be favored over nationals,
and beneficiaries should be "entrepreneurial." Worthy charities are those
that accept "little or no" government support and are run, preferably,
by faith-based institutions.[17]

The commission's strongest recommendation to philanthrocrats is not
to fund organizations that pursue the "root causes" of social problems
or that advocate on behalf of the people they serve. This advice would
deny support to most of the mainstream foundations themselves, their
trustees, and, posthumously, most of their founders—including John D.
Rockefeller (Sr. and Jr.) and Andrew Carnegie, all of whom both believed
passionately that organized philanthropy should seek the root causes of
social problems and crises and not merely provide alms for the poor and
dispossessed.

Funding local charities and eschewing root causes are particularly curious recommendations from a commission funded and created by a foundation that between 1980 and 1990 increased its support of conservative
public policy think tanks from 2.5 percent of its total grants to 60 percent,
a proportion it sustained through most of the nineties. Between 1992
and 1995 Bradley donated over $25 million to the American Enterprise
Institute, the Free Congress Research and Educational Fund, the Hudson
Institute, and the Heritage Foundation. Heritage alone received $4 mil-
lion, partly to advocate for a bill sponsored by Representative Tom Doo-
little (R-Texas) that would have restricted the ability of charities that
receive government funding to lobby Congress. At the root of the Bradley
Commission's recommendations is a belief shared by its commissioners
and benefactor that "to remain effective, philanthropy and volunteerism
must be shielded from government's sometimes fatal embrace."[18]

Ordinarily there would be little reason to question the credentials, ideological or otherwise, of a national commission, which is generally comprised of a balanced mix of Democrats, Republicans, and nonpartisan

specialists. In the case of the Bradley Commission, however, prior intimacy with the Bradley Foundation seems to have been a requirement for membership. No fewer than six of the NCPCR's eleven commissioner were grantees; a seventh, Vice Chairman Reed Coleman, was an influential trustee of the Bradley Foundation.

Commissioner Mary Elayne Bennett was also unlikely to buck the Bradley line on philanthropy. She was not only the recipient of generous Bradley support—for *Best Friends,* her sex, drugs, and pregnancy counseling program for teenage girls—but so was her husband, former Secretary of Education William Bennett. Through his sponsor, the Heritage Foundation, Bennett received $275,000 from a Bradley-inspired consortium of foundations.

Predictable, too, was commissioner Chester Finn, the John M. Olin fellow at the Hudson Institute mentioned in chapter 2. Finn brought impressive credentials to the mission, foremost of which was his association with Olin, one of very few American institutions to be found to the political right of the Bradley. Both foundations generously support Finn's employer, the Hudson Institute, an Indianapolis-based brain trust that has had a decided influence on the political philosophies of Dan and Marilyn Quayle. (The former vice president is a trustee of Hudson.)

Another member, Kimberly Dennis, brought her talents to the commission from the Philanthropy Roundtable. This group was formed in 1983 from an insurrection of angry trustees and philanthrocrats who bolted from the Council on Foundations after the latter adopted standards calling for racial and gender diversity on foundation boards. Dennis's résumé includes recent employment as a public policy grantmaker at the Olin Foundation, as well as membership on the boards of the archconservative Political Economy Research Center and the New York–based Donner Foundation, a generous funder of right-wing policy think tanks and universities.

Consulting for the commission was a swarm of academics and policy wonks dear to the Bradley Foundation, many of them from other Bradley-funded organizations. James Q. Wilson from the University of California-Los Angeles, the Hudson Institute's Leslie Lenkowsky, and Gertrude Himmelfarb from City University of New York provided background research and essays for the project. Their work was directed by Bruno V. Manno, another loaner from the Hudson Institute. Manno wasted no time assigning the keynote policy paper blasting New Deal and Great Society programs to Bradley Foundation President Michael Joyce. In 1993 Joyce, with conservative editor William Kristol at his side, co-founded the Project for the Republican Future—in which Lamar Alexander hopes to be a major player, with a boost from, of course, the Bradley Commission.

The commission's prescription for America was a risky gambit at a time, in the late 1990s, when everything seemed so prosperous possible, and easy. That may be why few other foundations have paid heed to it, although they all seem equally dedicated to discussing, defining, and lamenting the sorry state of civil society. Post-devolutionary America's ability to be truly civil, it seems clear, will not be tested until harder times cause millions of the working poor to fall into the safety nets woven by neighborhood associations and palliative charities supported by faith-based institutions and financed, one supposes, by private foundations. Conservative civil societarians believe that there is enough compassion and financial wherewithal to save them. Only time will tell.

Another foundation, the Pew Charitable Trusts, has also taken an extraordinary interest in civil society. In 1996 it made a $947,000 grant to William Bennett and former Senator Sam Nunn to create another commission, the National Commission on Civic Renewal (NCCR). The central question the NCCR addressed was put by Bennett: "How is it that we have experienced unprecedented economic growth and prosperity, and yet many believe we have become coarser, more alienated, less civil?" Bennett suggested that "examining empirical research should help shed some light on these questions and better equip us to formulate the next steps in addressing these problems."

Typically, Pew not only wrote a check, but also had members of its Public Policy Program participate in selecting NCCR commissioners. The commission, which had a slight preponderance of conservative members, met three times over two years. Through the Institute for Philosophy and Public Policy at the University of Maryland, it conducted and studied surveys documenting Americans' loss of trust in their fellow citizens, their dissatisfaction with contemporary values, and their conviction that "the United States is in a long term moral decline." Bennett's co-chair, Sam Nunn, found "the research truly enlightening. Unfortunately it confirms the diminished trust that many Americans feel, but it also furthers my belief that we must work hard to find solutions."

As promised, in 1998 the commission compiled and released *A Nation of Spectators,* a report lamenting the fact that fewer Americans than ever are involved in civic affairs, It called, predictably, for civic renewal. After meeting and studying the state of civil society for three years, the commissioners concluded that "there is no blueprint for civic success, but there is a surefire recipe for civic failure—disengagement from the enterprises that help define the common good. We therefore close where we began, with a call to citizenship—acts and traits of character that create the possibility of self-government but that no government can enforce."[19] Pew granted the commission an additional $200,000 to disseminate that finding, even though nothing in the report hadn't been said and published over and over by the Bradley Commission, Robert Putnam, Don Eberly, and a host of other civil societarians.

However, an interesting difference between the Bradley Commission and the Bennett–Nunn Commission is the readiness of Bennett, Don Eberly, and fellow commissioners to blame capitalism for some of society's most intractable problems. "Unbridled capitalism is a problem," Bennett told the National Press Club in November 1996. "It may not be a problem for production, but it's a problem for human beings. And it's a problem for that whole dimension of things we call the realm of values and human relationships."

Don Eberly, too, weighed in against the free market view of his Republican colleagues. "It really is absurd to absolve the marketplace for the kind of cultural decadence that everyone decries these days. Decadence is brought to us by the marketplace," laments Eberly, who describes himself as being "anti-Wal-Mart" because they and other mall chains are destroying Main Street village life in America. "Conservatives have begun to see that big business is as problematic as big government," agrees William Schambra.

Finding social problems imbedded in capitalism is not a difficult task for observers right, left, or center. Economic systems of any persuasion create social pathologies. The challenge to foundations—which would not even exist without capitalism—is to find remedies that leave the system that spawned them intact: in medical terms, to destroy the pathogen without destroying the host.

Foundation executives have employed germ theory and viral meta-
phors for a century or more, but the unexpressed belief behind all their
nostrums seems to lie in an idea most recently expressed by James Gibson
of the Urban Institute: poverty is "organic to capitalism" and therefore
not subject to "cure." The problem with this thinking—and it is central
to any evaluation of organized philanthropy—is that foundations consider it good grantmaking to fund research projects that document social
pathologies and to recommend ways to study them further, perhaps even
ameliorate them , all the while protecting corporate capitalism.

Social Movements

*Foundations should do things that make contemporaries uncomfortable. That's
the only way change can occur.*
—Peter Goldmark, former president, Rockefeller Foundation

Never has so much money led to so few changes.
—Ralph Nader

Conservatives are eager to invoke Tocqueville and to call for the return
of a society of dedicated volunteers with an infinite variety of "religious,
moral, serious and futile," interests and tastes. Yet they are less tolerant
of associations whose goals and tendencies are inimical, even repugnant
to their own political or moral sensibilities. Some are unwilling, for example, to accept militant environmental organizations as legitimate participants in civil society; others reject radical political parties, reproductive
rights organizations, labor unions, civil rights activists, and gay liberation
groups.[20] These conservatives seem bent on silencing unwanted movements and stifling their advocacy while letting Judeo-Christian institutions and private corporation advocate whatever they please.

History suggests that the health of civil society will not improve unless
those with broader definitions of it are given a voice. And that is unlikely
to happen until all the mainstream foundations immerse themselves even
more deeply in the public debate over the definition and complexion of
civil society, then support organizations working for racial and gender
equality, prison reform, and peace, alongside civil and human rights.
How civil can any society be without these voices? How could apartheid
have been defeated in South Africa, suffrage have come to women in
Kuwait, parliamentary democracy been restored in Scotland, and com-

munist regimes have been defeated in Central Europe without well-organized citizens' groups pushing peacefully, though at times militantly, for social change?

The activist elements of civil society are literally changing the world. They are "reshaping politics and economics at both the domestic and global levels," according to Lester Salamon, director of the Center for Civil Society Studies at Johns Hopkins University. "I believe it is as important a development to the latter part of the twentieth century as the rise of the nation state was at the end of the nineteenth century."[21] Citizen initiatives are generally conceived by visionaries like Mahatma Gandhi, Florence Nightingale, Muhammad Yunus, and Ralph Nader, whose ideas are then expressed in organizations seeded by philanthropists, singular or organized. Once established, the organizations they fashion tend to become self-sufficient, supported by the very citizens they are created to serve. The process is one of experimentation, leading first to activism and then to the engineering of nonviolent social change.

The United States has been since its inception the global laboratory for social experimentation. At any given moment in its history, a considerable portion of the myriad associations of civil society have been experimental in nature. Almost every social theory and model has been, if not thoroughly tested, at least studied, debated, or attempted by a small group, workplace association, or community somewhere in the country. Over three centuries Americans have tried slavery, limited suffrage, universal suffrage, racial segregation, integration, producer cooperatives, consumer cooperatives, intentional communities, gated communities, suburbs, communes, closed shops, open shops, hierarchical workplaces, democratic management, and worker collectives. Also tested has been every imaginable way to educate, employ, punish, reward, heal, protect, and inspire the citizenry. America has tried harder than most civilizations—and suffered through some painful political movements, even a civil war—to maintain and defend "liberty and justice for all."

And foundation money, although a minuscule portion of organized philanthropy, has been a significant, though not always welcome, source of support and influence for social experimentation and social action. Yet, with the single exception of civil rights, foundation interests in America's signature social movements—for women's rights, peace, environment, environmental justice, students, gay liberation, and particularly labor—has been parsimonious, hesitant, late, and at times counter-productive. And if the number and size of grants is a fair indicator, foundations have generally favored middle-class over lower-class social movements.

If there is a central motive behind social-movement philanthropy as it is practiced in America it is to strengthen democracy by encouraging concerned citizens to struggle outside the government domain, between elections if you will, for their rights and freedoms. "Grassrooting the system" is the way Ohio State University Sociologist Craig Jenkins describes it. Jenkins has made a lifelong study of social-movement philanthropy, which

has become an institutional force in American society and contributed to the grassrooting of the system by fueling the growth of movements . . . and pursuing an enlarged definition of citizenship as a central goal. . . . Social movement philanthropy has been guided by a general "rights" framework . . . that emphasizes the importance of political representation, and the extension of civil, political and social rights to all groups. It has attempted to realize the model of pluralistic democracy where all groups and interests are politically represented. This has created and incorporated a variety of previously excluded and unorganized groups. [22]

Few trends or initiatives have stimulated as much divisiveness or debate within the philanthropic community as foundation funding of social and political movements. From the time in the 1960s when a handful of tiny foundations (Field, Weibolt, Norman, Taconic, Ottinger, Stern, and the New York Community Trust) initiated support for organizing and litigation projects to advance civil rights, the central question has been: Is this a proper use of tax-protected private philanthropy or surplus wealth?

Those questions persist, of course, but the debate has moved far beyond them to ask whether foundation grants to social movements have been sufficient, timely, and effective? Is foundation support of minority causes a noble investment in civil society or a deluded dose of noblesse oblige? Has it strengthened or weakened social movements? Eventually the debate circles around to the ultimate question: Who is winning in the increasingly vigorous philanthropic battle between conservative and liberal foundations attempting to shape American politics through strategic grantmaking?

In 1970 sixty-five foundations made 311 grants totaling $11 million to social activists. It was a small investment but over thirty times the amount given in the same category a decade earlier. Since 1960 a handful of large foundations had entered the game, notably Ford, Carnegie, Rockefeller, Sloan, and Lilly. In 1970 Carnegie granted Ralph Nader $55,000 to open the Center for the Study of Responsive Law; by the end of the decade, over fifty national organizations, with budgets totaling in the millions, were associated with the center. John Gardner received $20,000 to launch Common Cause; the Ford Foundation made generous grants to the NAACP; and the Field Foundation funded the Center for Defense Information and the Center for National Security Studies—from which Admiral Gene LaRocque and former intelligence agent Morton Halperin fed vital nonclassified military data to the antiwar movement.[23]

The 1970s were the heyday of progressive movement philanthropy. Support of political activism not only increased, it also began to be noticed outside the world of organized philanthropy, though the attention was not always welcomed. Active funders grew to over 125; in 1980 they gave $22.8 million to movement organizations, a 20 percent drop from the decade's high point in 1977 but still a strong increase over the preceding decades.[24]

During the 1970s a profusion of small and quite deliberately radical foundations were created, many of them by wealthy young heirs who chose philanthropy as their mode of protest against the system that allowed them to be rich. Besides committing themselves to economic justice, these new philanthropists broke a century-old American tradition by not naming their foundations after themselves or their parents. Thus names like Vanguard, Haymarket, Third World, Liberty Hill, Bread and Roses, North Star, and New World, began to appear, not in the *Foundation Directory* at first, but on the membership roster of progressive coalitions like the Funding Exchange and the National Network of Grantmakers. It wasn't the end of philanthropic narcissism, of course, but it was a clear statement against it.

These small funds have experimented with new modes and methods of giving money, and in the process shattered several more hallowed conventions and shibboleths of modern philanthropy. Leaders from targeted movements, for example, were placed on foundation boards; and generous grants were made for the operational support of rape crisis centers, tenants' rights groups, antinuclear protesters, farm worker unions, homeless advocates, childrens' rights litigators, conscientious objectors, and prison-reform organizations—none of whom had ever before been able to interest foundations in their work. "Small progressive funders have to be audacious," says former Veatch Fund director Daniel Cantor, "because our bigger cousins can't and won't do what's necessary."[25]

Intrafoundation networking and collaboration were also encouraged. Flow funding—that is, passing money through accomplished activists to promising new activists—was tried. (See chapter 10 for more on this type of funding.) Funding cooperatives of small donor-directed funds with names like Tides, Threshold, and the Funding Exchange were instituted. Together with other quaintly named foundations, the funding coops sowed the first seeds of foundation democracy (see chapter 11).

Another innovation, *volunteer funding boards,* was the invention of the Haymarket Fund. These committees, made up entirely of local movement leaders, addressed activists' concerns that social-movement funding was empowering donors to shape social change and coopt movement activity. Funding boards meet face to face with donors, who share equally in funding decisions.[26] The model, which signaled a major power shift in organized philanthropy, was eventually adopted by other progressive funders and, in various forms, is gradually working its way into larger foundations; in the latter, the division between "rich givers and poor recipients" remains more pronounced and hierarchies of class, race, and gender persist.[27]

Support of social movements grew rapidly through the 1980s, partly in response to the emergence of a conservative and decidedly antiprogressive backlash against the surging and at times militant social movements of the 1960s and 1970s. Conservative critics, many of whom regard private foundations as repositories of hostile un-American values, contended that social-movement philanthropy constituted a tax subsidy for political expression and that it encouraged public disrespect for authority. The backlash, incidentally, was also generously supported by private foundations, albeit those from the opposite end of the political spectrum. The result was a fairly high turnover among foundations willing to support activist organizations. Fortunately, more foundations entered the fray than left it, and the new ones tended to make larger grants.

In 1990, 146 foundations gave $88 million to advocacy projects. The mean grant exceeded $25,000, and the number of grants given that year approached thirty-five hundred.[28] Both of these numbers represent tenfold increases over 1970 giving. Moreover, for the first time ever, social-movement funding surpassed 1 percent of total foundation giving. While it has since remained small, it is a reliable function of private philanthropy and provides some highly leveraged risk capital.

It should be noted, however, that funds to organizations representing the poor and disadvantaged have always been dwarfed by more and larger grants to public interest research groups and highly professionalized middle-class reform organizations created to protect the environment, press for government accountability, and advance consumer rights.

Within social movements themselves there is a running debate over the impact of foundation support. Some argue that foundation patronage "has had a corrosive influence on democratic society."[29] Others claim that the dominant motive behind most movement philanthropy is social control; in their view money is granted to moderate movement leaders to discourage militancy and demobilize grassroots confrontation. Craig Jenkins refines that theory when he writes that "foundation patronage is overwhelmingly reactive to indigenously based protest activity, the major recipients being professional social movement organizations." The purpose, Jenkins says, is "to channel movements into institutionalized actions."[30]

Though he does not deny the existence of co-optation motives, Jenkins nonetheless believes that channeling often "provided the means for implementing major movement gains." Unfortunately, it also "reduced the incentive for movement leaders to engage in time consuming grassroots organizing, which eventually blunted the movement and thus reduced its impact."[31]

Jenkins's research shows this phenomenon to be more noticeable in some movements than in others. In child advocacy, for example, it is not much in evidence; but within the mainstream environmental movement, where over 70 percent of foundation support goes to professional organizations, it is blatantly obvious. Most of the funding goes to groups that are the creations of the large foundations, while less than 7 percent is given to grassroots activists.[32]

Toward antipoverty initiatives foundations have been much less enthusiastic. "Even foundations that claim anti-poverty activities as a priority program area remain unwilling to support the organizing and advocacy that are so crucial to the elimination of poverty," complains Pablo

Eisenberg, vice chairman of the National Committee for Responsive Philanthropy and former executive director of the Center for Community Change. Eisenberg believes that foundation support for community organizing, advocacy, and public policy work are more essential than ever in the wake of government devolution and welfare reform. "If more foundations are not willing to come up with the necessary funds to support those efforts they will have to bear the responsibility for failing to strengthen our democracy at a crucial time in our history."[33]

This issue, of course, raises again the drag-anchor question. If the effect of funding cautious professional activists is to quell violence and stifle unproductive militancy, all the better. But if its consequences are to deny a social movement the achievement of legitimate goals, to limit equal opportunity to a minority, or to withhold justice from a whole class of citizens, then it would be fair to say that foundation philanthropy, as practiced, has been a drag anchor on social progress. The civil rights movement offers a good arena in which to test this proposition.

Civil Rights

Two nations, between whom there is no intercourse and no sympathy; who are as ignorant of each other's habits, thoughts, feelings, as if they were dwellers in different zones, or inhabitants of different planets.
—Benjamin Disraeli, *Sybil, or The Two Nations,* 1845

Choose your rut carefully. You'll be in it for another 500 miles.
—Proverbial advice to wagon-train drivers headed west

"We look back in amazement at how many years this country tolerated the denial of constitutional rights," marveled plenary speaker David Hunter at the 1975 annual meeting of the Council of Foundations. "Can anyone point with pride to the timeliness and leadership that the great majority of foundations played in exposing the situation?" It was a call to conscience from a man who had recently left the Ford Foundation to become executive director of the Stern Family Fund, a small but decidedly activist foundation created by the descendants of Julius Rosenwald, founder of Sears Roebuck.

At Ford Hunter had distinguished himself as a creative program officer specializing in antipoverty work. Yet for years he had been frustrated in his attempts to move the giant foundation more aggressively toward universal suffrage and civil rights—two challenges to American democracy that few other mainstream philanthrocrats then believed private foundations could or should address. Most of the Stern family, on the other hand, lived in New Orleans, where they had witnessed bus boycotts and lunch counter sit-ins since the 1950s and 1960s. They had been immersed for a full generation in the discourse of racial segregation and agreed with Hunter that civil rights was a cause private foundations should support. Though some members of the family still questioned the wisdom of integration, and others disliked the tactics of direct confrontation, the family consensus was that Jim Crow had to go.

After long conversations with family matriarch and foundation chair Edith Stern, Hunter was convinced that a majority of her trustees could be persuaded to support voter registration drives and foster civil rights, particularly in the South, where the New Orleans–based foundation had done most of its earlier grantmaking in civil rights. By 1960 other small foundations had made a few small grants to the cause of universal franchise, and the ground was still fertile. The family's hope was that real progress could grow from small seed grants. Hunter, however, knew that they wouldn't be enough. The movement would eventually need far more support than one small foundation could provide. But if a southern family pitched in and was effective, Hunter reasoned, he could eventually persuade his colleagues at Ford and other large foundations to come in behind them with some real money.

The Stern Fund should "support institutional or social change in an attempt to get at and correct the root causes of social pathology and to foster a more human, open and egalitarian society," wrote Hunter in a draft of proposed guidelines for the fund. He later routed a copy of the message to former associates at the Ford Foundation. At the time Hunter, wasn't the only person lobbying Ford but was part of a chorus that struck a chord during the early 1970s. Ford trustees poured millions of dollars in grants into the civil rights movement, some say too little, others say too late. Their actions were not too late, however, to provoke a massive right-wing assault on the foundation. It culminated in 1977 in the bitter resignation of Henry Ford II, who not only publicly scolded his staff and fellow directors but privately called the foundation a "madhouse."

Dean Rusk, watching from his office at the Rockefeller Foundation, called the Ford Foundation "the fat boy in the canoe," because what it does "makes a difference to everybody else." When "the fat boy" signed on to civil rights in the late 1960s, its peers sat by the sidelines while minority people remained marginalized and disenfranchised. "Not enough foundations are close enough to critical and fundamental issues of our society," Hunter rebuked members of the Council on Foundations in 1975. "You're not aggressive enough, you're too distant from the controversies that pervade our public discourse. . . . If foundations do not rise to this challenge, they expose themselves to the charge that they only represent the established order and are incapable of moving beyond their genesis."[34]

Foundation trustees and officials had never heard anything quite like Hunter's reprimand from one of their own. Yet, Hunter remembers, refusing to take any credit for the achievements of the civil rights movement, it was "not until the victims of discrimination raised their own voices" that most large foundations really begin to fund civil rights.[35] Here again belated and cautious foundation funding raises questions about the drag-anchor effect.

Between 1953 and 1980 civil rights philanthropy was equally divided between public advocacy, grassroots activism, and technical support. Without dating the flow of funds, it could be argued that each dollar had equal value, whether it went for grassroots, advocacy, or technical support. But timing is everything in a social movement. When direct confrontation   sit ins, boycotts, protest demonstrations—are reaping rewards for a movement, why fund a moderating process?

When the large foundations finally did make their move, the political extremes once again weighed in. No sooner had the NAACP received its first grant than the Left began impugning the motives of elite philanthropists, whom they accused of seeking private control and the moderation of social movements that could otherwise lead to substantial social and economic change. Leftist critics also contended that allowing the wealthy to promote their own definitions of justice through philanthropy was courting plutocracy. Foundation trustees' motives, they argued, were simply not to be trusted.

The Right claimed, and still claims that foundation support of civil rights was a tax subsidy for political expression and that it contributed to the erosion of law and order. A recent American Conservative Union report entitled *Financiers of Revolution* blames the Ford Foundation for urban and student turmoil. Heather MacDonald, a prolific and outspoken critic of liberal foundations, complained in 1996 that "they have used litigation to create and expand the iron trap of bilingual education." In an appeal to conservative blacks she asserted that liberal foundations "have funded the perversion of the Voting Rights Act into a costly instrument of apartheid; and they lie behind the transformation of due process rights into an impediment to, rather than a guarantor of justice."[36] Of course, the Voting Rights Act had long since ended the political careers of many of Heather MacDonald's legislative heroes, who were defeated in districts where, for the first time since Emancipation, blacks were able to reach the polls.

But more central to the debate than right/left differences is the question later posed by Craig Jenkins: "Is upper class patronage of social movements compatible with America's conception of democratic government and politics?"[37] The trustees of Ford and a dozen or so other large- and medium-sized foundations clearly thought so. Civil rights philanthropists defend their patronage as a force that strengthened democratic institutions by giving voice to the disenfranchised.

The real philanthropic motive for funding civil rights has been a mystery to observers since it began, and will likely remain so forever. Although theories about it are exchanged in heated debates, they only prove that the intentions of a foundation's board of trustees are as inscrutable as the aims of a founding donor—for deliberations on such sensitive matters are conducted behind a veil of privacy. Even if we could read the minutes of all those Ford Foundation board meetings in which voting rights and Mexican American legal rights were discussed—as they surely were at great length—we would probably not be able to discern a given trustee's true motive, which he or she would probably not express, even in the company of trusted colleagues.

Who can say for sure what lay in the collective mind of one or even a dozen or so foundations that helped fund the civil rights movement at a time of national strife in the 1960s and early 1970s, when it was clear that something had to be done? Was social control the aim? Were the rich fearful of violent revolution? Were they out to demobilize radicals within the movement? Or is civil rights philanthropy no different from any other altruistic impulse, motivated by a mixture of compassion, guilt, and a timid sense of justice?

Individual programs, grants, and their timing can be interpreted in a way that supports almost any theory. Conceivably, two or more of the above sentiments could coexist on the same board of trustees. One might prevail with one grant or series of grants; but at any given time the philanthropy of a single foundation might reflect hegemony, fear, and subversion—all three suspect motives. And, motives aside, critics contend that because people with upper-class backgrounds are unable to identify with the interests of the poor and disenfranchised, they will always favor safe, professional projects that employ the educated elite, leaving the gritty grassroots organizations to support themselves with bake sales and door-to-door canvasses.

As early as 1962 journalist Louis Lomax accused the "white angels" who funded voter-registration drives of being "out to de-fang the civil rights movement." Others, Jenkins writes, complained that by encouraging professional advocacy, foundations were creating "a corporatist system of representation which allows the elite to control who represents the unrepresented, while simultaneously making the system seem responsive, thereby blunting dissent."[38]

There is no question that overt radical activity and rhetoric preceded the creation and funding of the Voter Education Project by the Taconic, Stern, Norman, Field, and New York foundations (later joined by Ford and others); or that the Congress of Racial Equality (CORE) and the Student Nonviolent Coordinating Committee (SNCC) were left out in the cold by these foundations, which routinely abandoned organizations that projected black power sentiments. Even so, these facts do not support the allegation that the funding of moderate professionals stifled dissent or hurt the entire civil rights movement.

In fact, Craig Jenkins believes, quite to the contrary that on some occasions, particularly during the civil rights era, "professionalism led to significant movement successes, [as] it worked to consolidate gains that were initiated by indigenous organizing and protest." After passage of the Civil Rights Acts of 1964 and 1965, for example, mainstream foundations movd to attack the still intact Jim Crow system by generously funding the Voter Education Project.

"A more sophisticated criticism of social movement philanthropy," according to Jenkins, "is that foundation patronage has reduced the incentives for movement leaders to pursue indigenous organizing and thus indirectly weakened the movements."[39] This was certainly true of the women's movement in the 1970s, which received over $30 million from the Ford, Rockefeller, Carnegie, Mott, Mellon, and other large foundations. It paid for some useful legal victories, but it left the movement bereft of grassroots energy—a serious liability later in the decade when passage of the Equal Rights Amendment was effectively blocked by better-organized conservatives.

A similar situation arose in the late 1960s after Ford decided to create "an NAACP for Mexican Americans" and underwrote the Mexican American Legal Defense Fund (MALDEF) and the national council of La Raza. When the two organizations began organizing "brown power" along the Mexican border and challenging entrenched politicians like Henry Gonzales (D-Texas), Ford was accused of meddling in electoral politics. Its response was to move MALDEF's headquarters to Washington and La Raza's to San Francisco, thereby eviscerating the legal support for Mexican Americans where they needed it most.

David Garrow, professor of political science at City University of New York, has studied the emerging debate over civil rights funding and finds a "nascent consensus" among sociologists and historians who have deconstructed the civil rights grantmaking of the 1950s and 1960s. The consensus "essentially concludes that philanthropy was 'bad' for the civil rights movement, while internal radicalism was 'good.' " Garrow explains:

External assistance . . . was not only not necessary for the southern movement's initial emergence in the 1950s or for its most significant local achievements during the 1960s, but it oftentimes was downright harmful to the movement's progress and development—both because competition for outside funds and support became a debilitating dynamic in the intra-movement relations between civil rights organizations, and because . . . external philanthropic support had the effect of bolstering the movement's most "moderate" groups—such as the Urban League and the NAACP—at the expense of those on the more "radical" cutting edge of the movement, whose popular and indigenous appeal within grassroots black communities, rural and urban, gave the freedom struggle most of its political strength and media appeal.[40]

One undeniable effect of foundation funding of civil rights was the creation and strengthening of professional organizations within the movement. Whether or not that's an entirely good thing is the essence of an ongoing debate about all social-movement philanthropy. Grassroots activists and those who value their role resent the foundations' tendency to favor well-educated, well-behaved professionals like Whitney Young,

Bayard Rustin, and Vernon Jordan, leaving the Stokely Carmichaels, Cesar Chavezes, and Rap Browns to fend for themselves. Grassroots partisans tend to embrace the social control theory, which sees foundation philanthropy as an attempt by liberal elites to temper the depth and direction of social change by rewarding moderates and starving the radicals.

That is not to suggest that Young and Jordan themselves didn't value the radical fringe. They did. It gave them respectability and legitimacy. Through what sociologist Herbert Haines calls the "radical flank effect," the high visibility of black power proponents shouting "burn, baby, burn" as one city after another was torched through the late-1960s, stimulated a substantial increase in foundation support for "responsible" organizations. Foundation program officers from Ford and other mainstream foundations sought them out, knowing that they although their trustees could never be persuaded to support a troublemaker like Martin Luther King, they would think highly of a well-dressed, moderate lawyer like Thurgood Marshall. Not long after Marshall publicly called King "a rabble rouser . . . a boy on a man's mission . . . an opportunist," the NAACP Legal Defense Fund, where Marshall was working at the time, received several million-dollar grants from a half dozen or more foundations.

Whatever the hidden motives of civil right philanthropists, it is clear that their grantmaking was inherently reactive in nature. Foundation trustees were not responding to their own consciences or to a love of justice but to the objective realities in American cities—blazing slums, inflammatory rhetoric, and social statistics that documented a deep institutional racism.

In any case, all foundation support for social movements—whether civil rights, environmentalism, women's rights, peace, or consumer protection—remains small potatoes any way it's measured. And, as a portion of total foundation giving, support for civil rights has been immeasurably smaller. It has never even been a line item in the Foundation Center's annual report of giving. The share of the combined civil rights organizations' budget contributed by the foundations has never exceeded 30 percent, even at the height of the movement; and no single organization received more 50 percent of its budget from foundation sources.[41] Nonetheless, the nature of the grants and the leverage they can generate have made foundations a defining force in some social movements—and a source of continuing controversy in them all.

Not that all foundations *should* necessarily finance social movements, or even be the central bank of civil society. There is so much else to be funded. Besides, as we have seen in this and earlier chapters, organizations that rely totally on foundation largesse are generally far less effective than those that garner a healthy portion of their budgets from public or membership support. Still, as quasi-public trusts, social entrepreneurs, and putative associations of the independent sector, foundations do bear considerable responsibility for renewing and strengthening the vast and diverse mosaic of organizations that comprise American civil society, including organizations whose aims may not be in the best interest of wealth-based institutions like the foundations themselves.

Right—Left—Center

America works best when it receives a roughly equal infusion of ideas from the right and the left.
—Jean Stephanic and Richard Delgado, University of Colorado

The profusion and success of American social movements has sharpened a controversy in political circles about the proper role of philanthropy. Not surprisingly, that argument has spilled over into philanthropic circles and prompted an increasingly heated consideration of the function of foundations in civil society. The assault has come from both sides. "From C. Wright Mills to Barry Goldwater, voices on the left and right have protested that America is run by an elite," writes David Samuels, "an elite whose members include the leadership of both parties, the Rockefeller family, the Joint Chiefs of Staff, bankers, academics and the press."[43] And behind them all, allegedly, are the foundations.

As the discussion of civil rights reveals, the Left has been suspicious of philanthropic motives for at least a century and has generally regarded foundations as the engines of plutocracy. On occasion, spokespeople for the Left quote Karl Marx's allegation that "a part of the bourgeoisie is desirous of reducing social grievances, in order to secure the continued existence of bourgeois society."[43] A handful of American scholars, most prominently Professor Joan Roelofs at Keene State University in New Hampshire, have studied the political influence of the foundations and find themselves in general agreement with Marx on that point.

"The large foundation contributes to amusement, to placation of artists, to biochemical research, and to routine charity," writes Roelofs, "but perhaps their most interesting endeavors are in directing social reform, [wherein] they and their creations supply the ideas for political change." Roelofs and her peers on the left see the foundations, a creation of the Progressive Era, as a response not so much to that period's corporate excesses and machine politics as to the rise of populist and socialist impulses. "When foundations took an interest in reform organizations, progressivism began to transmit all evidence of class struggle into 'social problems' and tasks for social scientists," Roelofs charges. "And even more urgent than ameliorating the lot of the masses was the need to co-opt intellectuals, as the political culture of the opinion leaders was strong in socialist sympathies."[44]

Roelofs and other leftists believe that the funding of social movements that began in earnest during the 1960s was similarly designed to steer activist organizations toward "reasonable, pragmatic goals." The ulterior aim was "to support forms of activism which do not seriously challenge the power structure."[45] Fearing that African Americans would regard themselves as part of Africa's anticolonial uprisings, large foundations poured funds into moderate organizations like the National Urban League, the NAACP, and Community Development Corporations. The goal, according to Roelofs, was to defuse black militancy and champion "black capitalism."

There is evidence to support her view. In 1969, Ford Foundation President MacGeorge Bundy appeared before the House Finance Committee chaired by Wright Patman, who had been aggressively investigating foundations for ten years. When asked why Ford was supporting "radical organizations," Bundy calmly replied:

For institutions and organizations which are young and which are not fully shaped as to their direction, it can make a great deal of difference as to the degree and way in which they develop if they have a responsible and constructive proposal for which they can find support.

If they cannot find such support, those within the organization who may be tempted to move in paths of disruption, discord and even violence, may be confirmed in their view that American society doesn't care about their needs.

On the other hand, if they do have a good project constructively put forward, and they get help for it and run it responsibly, and it works, then those who feel that kind of activity makes sense may be encouraged.[46]

Comparing the voices of the Right and Left describing the foundations makes one wonder whether they could possibly be examining the same phenomenon. "Once an agent for social good," writes Manhattan Institute scholar Heather MacDonald in the *Wall Street Journal,* "the biggest U.S. foundations have become a political battering ram targeted at American society." According to MacDonald, everything changed in the 1960s when the Ford Foundation "flowered into an activist socially conscious philanthropy, [and] pioneered the idea that foundations would improve the lot of mankind not by building lasting institutions but by challenging existing ones." These "liberal leviathans" conceived of themselves as "laboratories for the welfare state" and bankrolled the "massive affirmative action machine" that imposed racial quotas throughout American society, leaving the country with an array of troublesome institutions. "The NAACP," MacDonald alleges, "would be nowhere without foundation support."[47]

"Big philanthropy in this country has had little if anything to do with good works as that term is generally understood," Chester Finn writes to Microsoft Chairman Bill Gates, "and still less to do with buttressing the institutions and values of a free society. Instead, much philanthropic activity is engaged in subverting those institutions and values."[48] Finn forewarns the budding philanthropist, who had then placed only about $5 billion of his vast fortune into foundation endowments, that "foundations have become smug, self-referential and ossified." They are, Finn charges, "caught in a hammer lock of political correctness." (Gates's contributions would eventually surpass even those of the Wellcome Trust of England to create the largest foundation endowment in the world.)

Finn illustrates his argument with a random sampling of four- and five-figure grants from the Ford and Rockefeller foundations for projects that "provide an ongoing discussion of gender sexuality and the justice system," fund "a web site about the Zapatista uprising in Chiapas, Mexico," support "a community conference on environmental racism," underwrite "a documentary about women's' sexual awareness and self-esteem," and assemble "an interactive installation based on an Iroquois prayer." Finn does not point out that the combined grants for all these projects barely equal the travel budget of Finn's employer, the Hudson Institute; nor do they represent the central mission of either Ford or Rockefeller. Yet he describes them as "typical" expressions of a multiculturalist dogma infesting the entire foundation community.[49]

Before closing his letter to Gates with a predictable pitch for educational vouchers and charter schools, Finn pours cold water on a few of Gates's own philanthropic gestures—particularly his grant to a teachers' union administering a high school technological-training program. He advises Gates to seek out and support "islets of civil society . . . faith-based social services that care for the ill, feed the hungry, wean the addicted and teach the young"—all causes the large foundations shun "because they stress responsibilities rather than rights."[50]

When foundations began underwriting social protest, even less-reactionary conservatives in and out of Congress challenged the propriety of spending tax-exempt surplus industrial wealth on what they saw as an effort to "remake America" in the "progressive image" of the foundations.[51] Stirring up baseless grievances against corporations, banks, and other institutions of free enterprise, they said, was self-defeating, as was any activity that encouraged government regulation of industry.

This complaint is not new. It is essentially the same indictment that has been blasted against "progressives" and most philanthropists since the turn of the century. What is relatively new is that sometime in the late-1960s the Right borrowed a stratagem from the Left: it began to combat "progressivism" with its own philanthropy. Among the tactics emulated in creating what Paul Weyrich calls "the new conservative labyrinth" was the use of strategically placed foundation grants to foster and promote political ends. The Reagan revolution was substantially, though not completely, foundation-funded.

The labyrinth has created an ideological base and organizational infrastructure for the rise of conservative power since 1980. Its think tanks, legal centers, and new media outlets workin concert to project a basic conservative message—smaller government and freer markets—to American voters. The labyrinth is funded by a dozen medium-sized, virtually unknown foundations that abandoned their earlier disapproval of political activism and began committing major funds (in some cases their entire funding budget) to combat the welfare state, public education, affirmative action, environmental regulation, homosexuality, and a host of other cultural expressions they perceived as disruptive of the values of the nuclear family.[52] With combined assets of just over $1 billion, the "dangerous dozen," as they are described by some liberals, donated about $300 million between 1992 and 1994, about 70 percent of it to conservative political causes and institutions.

Conservative foundations have also borrowed from liberal foundations the practice of collaboration, and have used it far more effectively. They have a clearly articulated vision in which they invest wisely and as one. In fact the Bradley Foundation works so closely with the Olin, Scaife, and Smith Richardson foundations that they are known in funding circles as the "four sisters." Together, the sisters helped found and have for a quarter century or more faithfully supported such established institutions of the Right as the Heritage Foundation, the Cato Institute, the American Enterprise Institute, the Federalist Society, Free Congress Research and Education, Citizens for a Sound Economy, the Hoover Institution, and the Manhattan and Hudson institutes.

In addition, they have contributed consistently and generously to the Washington, Pacific, Atlantic, New England, and Southeastern Legal foundations, all of which are very conservative. Their media favorites include *Human Events, Weekly Standard, New Criterion, Commentary, American Spectator, National Interest,* and National Empowerment Television, which now reaches eleven million homes. Future journalists and editors for these and other conservative outlets are trained in the "Collegiate Network" of conservative student newspapers supported by the Olin, Scaife, Bradley, and Smith Richardson foundations. The latter also make generous six-figure grants to such perennial conservative commentators as Samuel Huntington, Irving Kristol, William Bennett, James Q. Wilson, Robert Bork, Charles Murray, Dinesh D'Souza, Allan Bloom, and Chester Finn.

What mainly differentiates the "four sisters" and their brethren on the philanthropic Right from the philanthropic Left is their steadfast loyalty to a core group of institutions that have inspired and driven the conservative revolution since before the first election of Ronald Reagan. "Like good capitalists, conservative philanthropists conceive of grantmaking as an investment in people and institutions," observes author Karen Paget. "Like good bondholders, they are in it for the long haul."[53] This single-mindedness could not be more different from the mainstream foundations' unpredictable issue-du-jour, three-years-and-you're-out approach to grantmaking.

The twenty-fifth anniversary dinner of the Heritage Foundation held in New York in 1997 bore witness to Paget's observations. There fifteen hundred formally clad supplicants raised toast after toast to philanthropists (all present) who had written big checks in 1977 and were still writing big checks to support the people who drafted "Mandate for Leadership," the manifesto of the Reagan revolution. These same check writers now have the eye and ear of almost every legislator in the country. During the evening the Heritage Foundation announced that—in addition to its $28.7 million annual budget—it had already taken in $25 million of the $85 million it intended to raise to form a permanent endowment.

Hoisting their glasses were intellectuals, political scientists, communicators, and politicians, all loyal cadre of the conservative uprising. Some of them had been grant recipients of the same philanthropists since college days, when they were discovered and mentored by program officers who knew the power of ideas and sought out the talent to develop them. Millions of dollars have been donated by conservative foundations to train young intellectuals, communicators, and activists in American colleges and universities.

At the other end of the conservative strategy is a foundation-driven restructuring of the American think tank. Gone is the drab office full of tweedy wonks pumping out turgid white papers that no one reads. *Communications, marketing, grassroots mobilization,* and *constituency development* are departmental functions of the new conservative think tanks housed in suites of offices rivaling those of a Fortune-500 corporation. "The unique thing we have done is to combine the serious, high quality research of a traditional think tank like the Hoover Institution or the Brooking Institute with the intense marketing and issue management capabilities of an activist organization," says Stuart Butler, vice president of the Heritage Foundation.[54]

Discouraged liberals complain that "progressive" foundations aren't matching the amount of money their conservative counterparts are spending on political initiatives. In fact, the amount has little to do with success. "It's the way conservatives have spent the money that has made the difference," according to Paget, who asserts that conservative grants "are focused on building institutions, not programs. And since conservatives don't continually shift program priorities, conservative organizations don't have to repackage their agenda or scramble to replace old funding with new"—a perpetual dilemma for activist organizations faced with a much larger but more mercurial, less strategically oriented, and chronically unfocused field of funders. [55]

Another factor that differentiates conservative from liberal foundations is the latter's tendency to favor traditional institutions of higher learning over freer and more flexible think tanks. Because universities tend to stifle critiques of existing institutions, they are no longer suitable environments in which to challenge prevailing beliefs or foster political revolutions. Thus the think tanks have become the Right's academies, where they are not restrained from creating their new orthodoxies. And, ironically, they offer their academies the very intellectual freedoms they so vigorously sought to deny American universities during the 1960s and 1970s.

Left-liberal observers note with considerable envy the sums flowing into the conservative think tanks—about four times the amount flowing the other way. Michael Shuman, a former fundraiser for the Institute for Policy Studies (IPS), a small and relatively ineffectual left-wing think tank in Washington, complains that "progressive foundations . . . give too little to too many" organizations. He argues that the thousands of small grants scattered around grassroots organizations could be more effectively invested in a few large think tanks like—one might presume—IPS. Admitting to a "combination of dismay and envy," Shuman points out that IPS's annual budget of $1.5 million "could run the Heritage Foundation for about thirteen working days."[56]

Aside from his naive devaluation of grassroots power (the Right could not have prevailed without the street-level activism of the Christian Coalition), where Shuman's logic wavers is in characterizing large foundations like Ford, Rockefeller, Pew, Kellogg, and MacArthur as "progressive." While there are progressive people on the staffs and boards of these and most other large foundations, they are either balanced off or overwhelmed by an equal number of their political opposites. The Ford Foundation board of trustees, for example, contains nonprofit leaders from India, Ecuador, and South Africa; but they sit across the table from executives from Lucent Technologies, Xerox, and Levi Strauss and a couple of high-powered Wall Street lawyers.

"I would be hard pressed, even with a gun to my head, to say that we were conservative or liberal," says Rockefeller Foundation's communications director, Denise Gray-Felder. Conservative foundations "have deliberately gone out and created institutions, trained scholars and worked with editorial boards to push an ideological agenda, and that's not what we're really about."[57]

"Ideological agenda" is the operative phrase in that remark. "I don't see any grantmaker who considers themselves progressive or liberal articulating what a progressive future would look like," Margaret Ayers of the Robert Sterling Clark Foundation told the *Chronicle of Philanthropy*. Jessie Smith Noyes Foundation President Steve Viederman concurs. "Any analysis of philanthropy comes down to power," he says. "Foundations have it. Progressive foundations regret it. And they are wary of taking the offensive."[58]

So, while grants may be made to an occasional "progressive" think tank like IPS, or to organizations active in an array of single interests—for example, biodiversity, public health, nuclear proliferation, women's rights, civil liberties—they tend to be neutralized by equal and opposite grants made by the same foundations to counterparts on the Right. The same year that the MacArthur Foundation made a grant to IPS, for example, they also gave generously to the Hoover Institution and the Olin School of Business.

Moreover, large foundations, no matter how liberal they may be perceived to be by conservatives like Heather MacDonald or Chester Finn, do not harbor ambitious political strategies; nor do they seek to fundamentally restructure society. "Mainline foundations tend to take a bland, neutral stance on most of these issues," comments Waldemar Nielsen. "It represents a lack of courage," he adds, "an unwillingness to get into controversy. It's a kind of hiding out from reality."[59]

The fact is that mainline foundations are not in the philanthropy game to win hearts and minds or to create new orthodoxies—both central objectives of the consistently ideological foundations of the Right whose trustees and staffs are of one mind and pretty much of one class. Politically balanced boards of trustees create politically neutral foundations. Thus most American foundations are centrist, and their philanthropy is cautious and apolitical.

Conclusion

If America ever ceases to be a good country, it will also cease being a great country.
—Alexis de Tocqueville, 1835

From the melding of the civic habits and benevolent traditions of America's tribes there emerged a new civilization, unique in the world and characterized by a distinct and still undefined concept of civil society. The search for an American definition of civil society will continue indefinitely, and foundations will remain in the fray, as some support and others oppose descriptions that fit or don't fit the intentions of their original donors and the politics of their trustees.

If one political camp or another were to prevail, the entire independent sector of American life might well be thrown out of balance. The country can only hope that the Right will come to see value in diversity and minority rights and that the Left will accept the notion that family, church, neighborhoods, and bowling leagues are as vital to civil society as any of its own activist associations. Each side, of course, will forever have its favorites. But if the Right and Left could agree on a broad, inclusive, and tolerant definition of civil society, their relentless competition over other matters of public policy might diminish.

Meanwhile, if private and community foundations are to become the venture philanthropists and central bankers of civil society, the tax laws need to be altered to encourage the formation of new foundations, enhance their growth, maximize their payouts, and accelerate the democratization of their decision making. In the following two chapters I explore how these and other reforms could make organized philanthropy a valued institution of civil society in the new century.

A Closing Argument

If you would help another man, you must do so in minute particulars.
—William Blake

It's important to include ourselves in the circle of those we care for.
—Slow Turtle, Wampanoag Nation medicine man

In Vonnegut's *God Bless You, Mr. Rosewater,* attorney Norman Mushari seeks to prove Elliot Rosewater insane—and therefore incompetent to head the family foundation—by producing the transcript of a extemporaneous speech Elliot had made a few years earlier. "I love you sons of bitches," he told a convention of science fiction writers whose meeting he had crashed.

You're the only ones who'll talk about the really terrific changes going on, the only ones crazy enough to know that life is a space voyage that'll last for billions of years. You're the only ones with guts enough to really care about the future, who really notice what machines do to us, what wars do to us, what cities do to us, what big simple ideas do to us, what tremendous misunderstandings, mistakes, accidents and catastrophes do to us. You're the only ones zany enough to agonize over time and distances without limit, over mysteries that will never die, over the fact that we are right now determining whether the space voyage for the next billion years or so is going to Heaven or Hell.[60]

That transcript, Mushari is convinced, is the "smoking gun" that will win his case.

In preparing for the trial, the Rosewater lawyers summon Kilgore Trout, one of the science fiction writers who heard the speech, to offer a sanity defense. They question him not about the speech but about the foundation's grants to the citizens of Rosewater County who were left destitute by the automation of the family's industrial enterprises. "What you did in Rosewater County was far from insane," Trout assures young Rosewater.

It was quite possibly the most important social experiment of our time, for it dealt on a very small scale with a problem whose queasy horrors will eventually be made world-wide by the sophistication of machines. The problem is this: How to love people who have no use?

In time, almost all men and women will become worthless as producers of goods, food, services, and more machines, as sources of practical ideas in the areas of economics, engineering and probably medicine too. So, if we can't find reasons and methods for treasuring human beings because they are *human beings,* then we might as well, as has so often been suggested, rub them out.[61]

The word *philanthropy* means, literally, love of humanity. If their work is to intersect with civil society and to aid in its reconstruction while the global economy is rendering millions of people irrelevant, it would seem wise for philanthropists to agree on a broad and reasonable definition of civil society, structure their foundations to strengthen it, and heed Trout's defense of Elliot Rosewater.

10

Imagination

The best philanthropy is constantly in search of finalities—a search for cause, an attempt to cure evils at their source.
—John D. Rockefeller

Almost anyone who anticipates having wealth beyond their immediate needs begins to imagine ways to dispose of it. Second homes, larger cars, private school tuition generally come to mind, as do stocks, bonds, country clubs, third homes, real estate trusts, polo ponies, commodities, private planes, trusts for children, and cattle ranches. Then perhaps—after the above trappings of wealth are bought and paid for—philanthropy is considered. At that point imagination becomes a vitally important element, even though the bulk of American philanthropy, whether measured in grants or in dollars, is devoid of it. In its absence grantmaking is either bland and futile or, in the worst instances, counterproductive.

Naturally, all philanthropists regard themselves imaginative, and most foundation program officers undoubtedly consider themselves creative grantmakers. Both would react indignantly to the suggestion that they or their foundations lack originality. Yet they often confuse proactive grantmaking or chic venture-capital concepts like "mezzanine financing" with genuinely innovative philanthropy. The sad fact is that a majority of America's fifty thousand or so private foundations are mindless, lawyer-ridden tax dodges that accomplish little beyond the transfer of riches to already-wealthy institutions. The exceptions, of course, deserve public acclaim—which is one of the purposes of this book.

As the preceding chapters attest, the best philanthropy begins when a truly creative person (or group) dreams up a new way to use his or her wealth to make the world a little better. But just as often the innovator is someone without money, someone, perhaps, who also lacks the ability to raise it. When a philanthropist or foundation official discovers such a person and imagination and money come together, the outcome is almost always innovation. Mix enough imagination with enough money over enough time and innovation will lead to change. And if the change leads to social or cultural progress, all the better.

Not that less-imaginative philanthropists who emulate their more-venturesome peers are wasting their money, or doing anything wrong. However, grantmakers who follow the paths blazed by others need to recognize imagination when they see it, rather than blindly writing checks to their alma maters and the S.O.B.s (symphony, opera, ballet).

Virtual Philanthropy

All the strategic thinking in the world cannot account for the wonderful opportunism of life.
—Susan Beresford, President, Ford Foundation

Because it is impossible to ascertain what portion of a nation's wealth is truly "surplus," we cannot determine how much of it will be used for philanthropic endeavors. Even though Americans are by financial measure the most generous on earth, the percentage of excess wealth that finds its way into foundation endowments remains small. Economists who anticipate an unprecedented wealth transfer over the next fifty years or so estimate that only about 10 percent of it will wind up as foundation assets. Some say the proportion could reach as high as 20 percent, which would still leave tens of trillions of dollars to be spent, taxed, invested, and kept in trust for later generations.

However, history suggests that the amount of money placed in philanthropic institutions isn't nearly as critical to America's future as the impulse that puts it there; for the activities of new foundations will be directed by their donors' imaginations, regardless of whether they are self-made billionaires, heirs to old fortunes, corporations, or contributors to donor-directed community foundations. If the original donors can envision a world, or a part of the world, made indisputably better through philanthropy—a systems analyst might call that vision "virtual philanthropy"—the foundations they create are likely to be far more effective over the ensuing generations than those operated on behalf of some such vague purpose as "the benefit of mankind."

America's early philanthropists, though they were often naive, unworldly, and downright wrong about the state of society, cannot be faulted for lack of imagination. Though Rockefeller and Carnegie were as interested in avoiding taxation as any contemporary benefactor, they seem to have believed sincerely that creative philanthropy could change the world for the better. The same can be said for our contemporary, George Soros, who may well have formed his many foundations for several reasons—including business opportunities—but who is clearly committed as well to the ideals of democracy and the values of an open society.

Bill Gates III, the visionary creator of America's largest software company and, more recently, the world's largest foundation, shows signs of becoming as adept at philanthropy as he is at business. After an early foray into what seemed to many of his detractors to be self-serving grantsmanship—the computerization of American public libraries—Gates surprised observers by creating a $1-billion endowment to provide science scholarships to minority students. That $1 billion represents over 5 percent of the annual outlay of all foundations. Though the wisdom of the program will probably be debated by educators, philanthropists, and observers for many years, Gates cannot be faulted for lack of imagination.

His scholarship initiative was, to paraphrase the donor, "philanthropy at the speed of thought," an idea not dissimilar in scale or suddenness to Ted Turner's impulsive 1998 creation of the UN Foundation. Turner was allegedly in a taxi on the way to deliver a speech at the United Nations when he cooked up this billion-dollar grant without consulting his financial advisers. In the weeks leading up to his surprising announcement, Turner had been publicly chastising fellow billionaires for their philanthropic parsimony, often mentioning Gates by name, along with Warren Buffet and other tycoons he accused of being slow to unleash their billions. Turner set an example—the huge impulsive gift—that is sure to be emulated many times in years to come.

But Gates's outreach to disenfranchised minorities—even more strongly than Turner's celebrated gesture—signals another, newer philanthropic tendency, one more typical of venture capitalists than of the ponderous, self-conscious decisionmaking of most foundations. Compare

Gates's initiative to, for example, the Annenberg Challenge described in chapter 2. Annenberg's $500-million investment in public education, which he announced spontaneously in the White House in 1993, is touted by his admirers as a milestone in imaginative philanthropy. Gates's grant, however, is not simply twice the size of Annenberg's; it goes immediately and directly to where it is needed most, instead of being filtered through a vast philanthropic bureaucracy that trickles money gradually into ostensible reform. There are many in the foundation community who wish that Gates had deliberated longer, consulted foundation professionals, and relied on education experts before throwing that much money around. But the critics' self-interest is transparent, and their own records in educational philanthropy are unimpressive. There is something to be said for "wilding" money—that is, throwing a large wad at a large problem and seeing if it sticks. Isn't that what the *venture* in venture capitalism is all about? (See box insert, "Risk.")

As venturesome as Gates seemed, he, too, was following an example set by scores of earlier philanthropists. Irene Diamond, Turner, Walter Annenberg, and George Soros imagined, respectively, worlds without AIDS, without strife, without ignorance, and without tyrants, then made massive and immediate financial efforts to make those worlds real. Their visionary impulses, writes Peter Frumkin, Harvard professor of public policy, "signal that donors of large amounts are beginning to assert themselves as never before. This new period of personal giving is challenging us to think differently about the meaning and rationale for philanthropy." Rather than second-guessing the motives and intentions of impulse donors, Frumkin says, "we should encourage a broad and active market of competing visions of the common good, while celebrating the huge wave of unfiltered pluralism that donor driven philanthropy is beginning to unleash on American society."[1]

Diversity

We live in a time between times, no longer confidently progressive in our social programs, but not sure, just yet, of our ambitions for the future.
—Susan Wisely, Lilly Foundation

The philanthropic imagination of America is as wide and varied as the nation itself. All our tastes, compassions, faiths, and political convictions

Risk

Foundation executives love to prattle on about the risks they take in their work. And they take great offense if any one accuses them of being risk averse. When program officers speak of *risk* what they generally mean is a small risk of personal embarrassment in the event a project they funded fails. So they picked a loser. Who cares? There are no shareholders to complain. No bonds in default. No bank to foreclose. Yet, despite the risk-free nature of their work, philanthrocrats love to compare themselves to venture capitalists and entrepreneurs, who in fact take tremendous risks with their own and other people's money—the risk, in fact, of total loss.

By law, foundations must give money away—at least 5 percent of their assets every year. If, say, 1 percent, or even 3 percent of that money goes to organizations that lose, squander, or otherwise waste it, who is the worse for it? The foundation still has its assets, and the program officer no doubt still has his or her job (barring an insult directed toward a trustee's spouse at a cocktail party).

So the idea that foundation program officers and executives are taking risks is ridiculous. Their own money is safe, and their jobs are not threatened by their decisions unless they take kickbacks or find other ways to embezzle funds. If a grant project fails to meet its objectives or goals, no one is laid off. It would be hard to find a program officer who was fired for granting money to an unsuccessful endeavor. The only people at real risk in the game of philanthropy are the grantees; if they don't give a program officer something to brag about, they will probably not get funded again.

are reflected somewhere in the founding charters of fifty thousand foundations. And all the pressures brought to bear on any source of wealth or power are focused on these foundations. They are lobbied just as vigorously as government is, not only by aspiring grantees but also by ideologues and activists from every reach of American life: people who bring their philosophies and needs to the attention of trustees and program officers in hopes of inducing them, through grantmaking, to head in a new direction. In many respects, these men and women are lobbying the foundations' imagination.

Because foundations are funding the future they are, unavoidably, in the change business. This intrigues partisans of every future—left, right, Christian, secular, capitalist, republican and democratic (lower and upper case), the compassionate and the social-Darwinist. Knowing that their visions cannot be realized without money, they wander through foundation offices in search of kindred spirits. And almost always, somewhere in the large and growing universe of private philanthropy, there are kindred spirits. Almost any interest group that looks carefully through *The Foundation Grants Index,* a two-thousand-page Foundation Center annual that lists all grants over $10,000, will find someone who shares its interest, if not its vision.

There are philanthropies, large and small, that fund little else but horticultural research (even specific gardens) or military research, peace activism, computer technology, biotechnology, antibiotechnology, higher education, lower education, civil rights, human rights, animal rights, gay and lesbian rights, operas, symphonies, ballet, modern dance troupes, AIDS research, AIDS hospices. There is even a $200-million endowment—twice the budget of the National Endowment for the Arts—to assure a home for every cat and dog in America. Among the 765,000 grants made last year by the fourteen thousand largest foundations, there is something for virtually every cause. Almost every figment of the American imagination receives at least a morsel of support from American foundations, which can thus be seen in their entirety as supporters of pluralism and perpetuators of diversity. This richness, of course, also reflects the diversity of imaginations to be found among American philanthropists.

Motives

A man always has two reasons for the things he does: a good reason, and the real reason.
—J. P. Morgan

We honor our great philanthropists in great part because they are such rare birds. Historically, most of America's wealthiest industrialists have been parsimonious tightwads who gave almost nothing to charity and wouldn't have dreamt of creating a foundation. And their families mostly followed suit. Little has changed. A recent study by the Community Foundation of Silicon Valley found that while ordinary citizens in America's most prosperous valley donated the national average of about 2.1 percent of their income to various causes and charities, its numerous superrich gave less than 1 percent of their income. Only 11 percent of them even named a charity in their wills.

Students of philanthropy have spent millions of hours trying to fathom the unique psychological makeup that drives the few exceptions to become philanthropists and, more rarely, to create foundations. What prompts some rich people to be generous with their money? Do they have hidden agendas? What do they imagine will happen as result of their generosity? And why do some of them create permanent trusts for charity? Theories abound. They fall under several categories: religious conviction, guilt, tax avoidance, family preservation, indoctrination of children, noblesse oblige, quest for immortality, narcissism, generosity, and of course, genuine love of humanity. But the truth is that no two philanthropists have the same motives or intentions, or, thankfully, the same imagination; yet at some level, all the above forces are at work in most of them.

In making this generalization I am not trying to avoid grappling with that essential issue of any treatise on philanthropy—individual motives. But biographers, historians, filmmakers, and other investigators have explored them thoroughly, and well. Biographers have pored through the Rockefeller archives in search of the old man's philanthropic drives. Other have studied the lives and characters of Andrew Carnegie, Julius Rosenwald, Olivia Sage, Howard Hughes, Irene Diamond, Doris Duke, the Astors, Fords, Mellons, Packards, Soros, Turners, and Gates. But I believe that there is something even more critical than motive to the outcome of philanthropy—the imagination that drives it. What do philanthropists imagine will be the end result of their giving, whatever their motive? What improvement will their money buy? What impact will it have?

So in the long run what does it matter that Howard Hughes was a narcissistic hypochondriac? Do we need to know whether John D. Rockefeller was motivated by guilt, religious conviction, or both? How important is it to determine whether Ted Turner is a loose cannon, Bill Gates an opportunist, and George Soros a market manipulator—or whether Olivia Sage was primarily bent on taunting the ghost of her tightfisted husband by creating a foundation to fund projects that would have horrified him?

The important point is that for some reason, at some moment near the end of his wretched life, Howard Hughes imagined a society made healthier by virtue of biomedical research. The result is a $19.2-billion endowment and a long list of medical breakthroughs that might never have occurred without grants from the Howard Hughes Medical Institute (HHMI). It matters little, then, that Hughes was a miserable recluse and a germ paranoiac, except to observe that hypochondria may have sparked his interest in medical research. And, in the end, what matters most about Rockefeller's money is not that he might have used it to cleanse the family of blood spilt by the militia at Ludlow but that it built a great university.

This is not to suggest that managers of HHMI haven't made some fundamental blunders, or on occasion steered the healing arts in ill-favored directions by reinforcing unfortunate tendencies in medical science. Nor has every Rockefeller Foundation grant been brilliantly conceived and executed, as the chapter on the Green Revolution attests. The point is that these contributions and the foundations that brought them into being are with us by virtue of the philanthropic imagination.

Venture Philanthropy and Social Entrepreneuring

It's not just what you're born with
But what you choose to bear,
It's not how large your share is
But how much you can share.
It's not the fights you dream of
But those you really fought
It's not just what you're given
But what you do with what you've got
—Si Kahn, "Unfinished Portraits"[2]

The most recent wave of American philanthropy is sprouting from the fortunes of high technology, which has produced more than a few billionaires and literally thousands of overnight millionaires. Combined, the high-tech rich in the Forbes 400 list of the wealthiest individuals in America are worth about $300 billion—about the same amount, coincidentally, as all foundation assets. Most of them have become venture capitalists in search of new deals and initial public offerings (IPOs), but a significant number have cashed out and are exploring philanthropy.

These are people, mostly young, who started businesses that changed the way business is done. Combining the innovative tendency with the drive and energy that made them rich, they are spawning big changes in philanthropy. Gifts are no longer seen as simple acts of charity; they are "investments" in the nonprofit sector. Thus the new breed of donors often describe themselves as "venture philanthropists," "social entrepreneurs," or "players" in the nonprofit capital market.

They also differ from their predecessors in their impatience and insistence on a level of accountability never before demanded from foundation grantees. They speak of "social return on investment" (SROI) and manage grants as if they were a portfolio of company start-ups. In this regard, the story of George Roberts, a leveraged-buyout (LBO) magnate and co-founder of the corporate-raiding partnership of Kohlberg, Kravis and Roberts (KKR), is illustrative.

Though he is not as well known or as big a donor as Turner, Soros, or Bill Gates, George Roberts's forte is imagination. Comparing him to that trio, however, is less instructive than looking at the differences between Roberts and his first cousin, Henry Kravis. The contrast illuminates the important differences between imaginative and conventional philanthropy.

Roberts and Kravis are joined only at the wallet. In every other respect they are as different as Godzilla and Bambi. Kravis is a bombastic, high-profile socialite who parties hard with Manhattan's elite, squires their decorators about town, and is a fixture of the nation's gossip columns. Roberts, who lives and works in Menlo Park California, is introverted, temperate, and reputedly much smarter than his cousin. The personality and lifestyle contrasts are reflected in their philanthropy.

Kravis's $62-million New York City Investment Fund, though steeped in the rhetoric of "job promotion," "economic growth," and "disadvantaged neighborhoods," is in fact a fairly traditional loan fund for New York industrialists and developers eager to build socially impressive projects on socially marginal real estate. The Roberts Foundation, by contrast, is a venture-philanthropy trust that finances high-risk businesses that employ and train the homeless.

By 1985, even before the notorious RJR Nabisco takeover, KKR had completed enough deals to make Kravis and Roberts both near-billionaires. (Forbes recently evaluated their wealth at $925 million each.) By then Roberts knew he had made more money than he could ever spend. It was time, he believed, to "give something back to society"—not an original impulse for millionaires. Roberts, however, became an original in a world bereft of imagination and creativity.

In 1986 Roberts and his wife Lianne established the Roberts Foundation in San Francisco. At first their grants were fairly unimaginative: they gave to the opera, museums, hospitals, children's causes, and Lianne's not-so-conventional passion, animal rights. But George soon became frustrated with conventional philanthropy and wanted to try something new, something a little riskier. "What I was looking for was something that wouldn't be done if we didn't do it," he explains.[3]

One day in 1989, on a rare and reluctant business trip to New York, Roberts happened to walk past a large number of homeless people. By that point enough men, woman, and children were living on the streets of most American cities to show anyone who could see that the nation had a crisis. But little was being done about it by either government or organized philanthropy, beyond counting the victims and dividing them into categories: veterans, deinstitutionalized mentally ill, single mothers, derelicts, junkies, ex-convicts—all of them, reputedly, "chronically unemployable."

KKR had just taken over Nabisco, and Roberts was ready to experiment with a new kind of philanthropy. Not long after returning home to San Francisco he met a burned-out social worker named Jed Emerson. Emerson had spent the previous fourteen years of his life trying to straighten out teenage prostitutes, most of them homeless. In a long conversation, Roberts tried to convince Emerson that they could use free enterprise to combat homelessness and many of the social ills it created. By then it was clear to all who had tried job-training programs (public and private) and traditional placement programs that they were doomed to fail.

Roberts believed that by starting low-skilled, labor-intensive, nonprofit businesses, organizations trying to help homeless people survive could create their own economic base while providing their clients with employment and training. Once equipped to enter the workforce, Roberts argued, most homeless men and women would soon earn enough to pay rent, and the worst of their problems would be over. When he met Emerson he was looking for someone to try out his theory. He wanted to start with single mothers, who, he believed, had the greatest desire to work. He would invest $1 million in the experiment; if it worked with the mothers he would invest more in other categories. Was Emerson interested?

"Count me out," groaned the exhausted and somewhat cynical social worker, who was fed up with nonprofits. Instead, he left the country for Greece. After a restful Mediterranean sojourn, Emerson returned to the United States to live on an Indian reservation, where, he says, "I healed myself." When he came home to San Francisco a few months later, restored and ready to work, he found a message on his answering machine from George Roberts. "Since you didn't think this was a good idea," the message said, "I am convinced you are the right person to test my theory. It's *my* idea, not yours. So I figure you won't try to sell me a bill of goods." So sure was Roberts that Emerson was the ideal manager for the project that he had waited almost a year for an answer. Emerson relented.

In 1990, with a grant of $1 million from the Roberts Foundation, Emerson, who now calls himself "a reformed social worker," started the Homeless Economic Development Fund (HEDF). He used the money to finance, one by one, businesses owned and operated by nonprofit organizations. Some failed, and some succeeded.

One that has flourished is Pedal Revolution, a bicycle repair shop that employs and trains twelve homeless kids a year. The business acquires abandoned and confiscated bicycles from the San Francisco Police Department, strips them down, rebuilds them, and sells them. But the ultimate quarry for Pedal Revolution is a steady output of trained bike technicians. In a bicycle-crazy town like San Francisco, with its scores of steep hills and thousands of potholes, there is plenty of demand for bicycle-repair skills. Pedal Revolution is one of four businesses run by Youth Industry, a local nonprofit started, and now run, by a pediatrician named Jake Sinclair. The agency employs thirty-two homeless kids at between $5.50 and $7.50 and hour. Annual sales are approaching $2 million, and at the close of last year, three of their four businesses were turning a profit.

The one in trouble was a silk-screening business named Zerolith. After thoroughly examining Zerolith's books—employing classic LBO logic learned from his benefactor—Emerson proposed a solution right out of the playbook of KKR—a merger with Ashbury Images, a T-shirt silk-screen shop across town that employed street kids and also received help from the Roberts Foundation. Negotiations were scheduled, the merger took place, and the combined operation soon turned the corner to profitability.

Roberts is often asked why, if his goal is to train and employ the virtually unemployable, he does not just support training programs in conventional existing businesses? Emerson and Roberts are both convinced, however, that nonprofit service organizations are better at employing and training the working homeless; they are familiar with the myriad personal and psychological problems their employees face and thus better equipped than for-profit managers to provide a genuinely supportive work environment. And, as Emerson points out, "the homeless never get to the door of private job-training programs. And you can't train these people in a typical thirty- to sixty-day private program with the fundamental skills they need for the job market": arriving to work on time, following basic instructions, and getting along with fellow workers. "Businesses are simply not into this kind of training. So they look to nonprofits to make it happen."[4]

Participation in Roberts's experiment is by invitation only. He does not entertain grant proposals nor mail out requests for proposals. Instead, he sends Jed Emerson out to roam the Bay Area and attend meetings of organizations and councils trying to address the problem of homelessness. Practicing what he calls "grantmaking at the margin" allows Emerson to scout programs and businesses that are unaware they are being vetted by a funder.

On occasion Emerson and Roberts look over the terrain together. When they find an organization that is starting or considering a small-scale venture to employ their people, Emerson quietly approaches its leadership to offer help. Possessing masters degrees in both business administration and social work and a rap that mixes the best of both, Emerson can get people to listen. "I have told George Roberts about your program," he tells a prospective entrepreneur, "and he would like to help you expand your business. What do you suppose it would take to get it up to a couple of dozen employees and turn a profit?"

Once a project is approved for support, Emerson and Roberts behave more like investment bankers than grantmakers. The first requirement from potential investees (not *grantees*) is not a proposal but a business plan. Using classic Business Management 101 financial projections, Roberts can assess the size and nature of a required investment, helping the grantee organization prepare for the inevitable day when it must swim alone in turbulent financial markets. "One does not, after all, take a foundation grant proposal to a bank," says Roberts. "One takes a business plan."

In November 1988, when KKR was close to completing its buyout of RJR Nabisco, Nabisco's CEO Ross Johnson pressed George Roberts for more control of the negotiations. The normally reserved Roberts was blunt and insistent. "No," he said, "we're not going to do any deal where management controls it."

"Why?" asked Johnson.

"Because we've got the money," answered Roberts. The rest is history. Within days, Roberts and his partners owned RJR Nabisco and Johnson was playing golf in Palm Beach.

Having the money is key to Roberts's investment strategy, and to his grantmaking. Though he is reserved and patient, he has been described by one of his largest grantees as "a fierce funder." He regards that comment as a compliment—not only to Roberts the venture capitalist but also to Roberts the philanthropist. In both roles, Roberts believes, he has the responsibility to intervene in the project he is supporting, although he does so more patiently with an employer of homeless workers struggling to fathom the world of free enterprise than with the managers of a takeover firm.

Roberts and Emerson say they can see many similarities between their work and traditional venture capitalism, but they also perceive sharp differences. When KKR needs to take control of a newly acquired corporation, it moves in swiftly and relentlessly. Almost anything that needs to be done to increase the return on investment (ROI) is done immediately, and with ruthless precision. With nonprofits, where ROI is irrelevant, "we are able to cut them some slack," says Emerson. But "we do keep a fairly aggressive posture with the organizations we fund, and hold them to the pursuit of specific goals." Roberts will plow money into a nonprofit venture that he would deny outright to an LBO acquisition, which he would more likely strengthen by cutting costs or downsizing middle management. "We do it," Emerson admits, "to shield them from the market"—the same market in which KKR's for-profit ventures are left to swim with competitors and predators.

Roberts believes that no matter how prosperous it becomes, twenty-first–century America will provide "fewer resources for social and community concerns." Moreover, in part because of the post-LBO restructuring of the corporate sector, workers at various levels of the employment ladder will be displaced. He doubts that many of them, especially the least skilled, will be absorbed by mainstream businesses. Under these circumstances, "the nonprofit community is uniquely positioned to provide training, transitional employment, and in some cases permanent jobs to those left out of traditional labor markets." Asked why the nonprofit community should be saddled with the task of training entry-level workers for the business community, Roberts replies, "The private sector won't do it. They're trying to make money for their shareholders. Their social role is to create jobs, not train the labor force."[5]

Traditional organized philanthropy tends to focus on broad systems by funding studies of social crises, identifying root causes, and designing nonprofit programs to address them. But Roberts, who says he "doesn't pay a lot of attention to what other philanthropists think, or do," chooses to bypass research and attack problems directly as he sees them. He does not wish to be burdened with the normal concerns of philanthropists, who, he says, obsess about accountability and evaluation and are uncomfortable with high-risk grantmaking—by which he means grants that might fail.

Pointing out that his own skills center around making investments, Roberts is also loath to waste time or money meeting with policy wonks and government bureaucrats. He prefers to collar bankers. Recently he pressed the CEOs of Citibank and Wells Fargo into investing "at the street level"—by offering loans, lines of credit, and so on to nonprofit businesses as they do in the commercial sector. According to Roberts, the two bankers seemed to agree that communities the banks would normally detour around will thrive if sound nonprofit enterprises can help homeless people enter the competitive labor market. This argument has not, however, endeared him to all bankers or business leaders, some of whom contend that subsidizing nonprofit ventures creates unfair competition for mainstream for-profit businesses.

Roberts counters by pointing out that his businesses, which pay market wages or higher, are not unfairly undercutting the labor market; and that, in any case, "the increased costs of training and supervising people whom the private business community will not employ actually creates a competitive disadvantage" for the nonprofits. In addition, because nonprofit enterprises use part of their revenues to support related social services, they bear an extra burden that for-profit competitors do not share.

It has become chic in philanthropic circles to draw parallels between foundation activity and venture capitalism. The result is a spate of hybrid terms like *venture philanthropy, high-risk grantmaking,* and *social investing.* Roberts definitely sees himself as a venturesome philanthropist but prefers to talk about *social entrepreneuring,* the process that turns people and institutions predisposed to care less about the bottom line into hard-nosed entrepreneurs like himself.

Roberts's Enterprise Development Fund is not the first philanthropic organization to experiment with supported work. Back in the early 1970s the Ford Foundation and the U.S. Labor Department created a national pilot program to test the concept on several target groups: disabled persons, drug abusers, veterans, welfare recipients, teenage drop-outs, and ex-convicts. The joint three-year project showed that providing a one-year supported work environment paid off for society—except with ex-convicts. However, neither the government nor the private sector was sufficiently enthusiastic about the project to continue it, and it died—a "constructive failure."

Although Roberts was unaware of the experiment when he created the Homeless Economic Development Fund, he was not surprised when I described its demise. He distrusts most government initiatives and can see as clearly as anyone who watches large foundations at work that they are as likely to walk away from success as they are to fund a failure.

To date Roberts has helped ten nonprofit organizations in the San Francisco Bay Area create twenty-four enterprises designed to move the homeless into the job market. They currently employ about six hundred people. Of the approximately $5 million he and Lianne give away every year, between $3 and $4 million goes to these social projects. What they seek to realize from their grantmaking is a social return on investment (SROI)—a significant and growing number of formerly homeless people who live independent lives. A retrospective study by an independent evaluator to gauge how well they are accomplishing that goal is under way. Even though Roberts is willing to invest a significant sum in each person and has no exit strategy (as most foundations do), he has his limits: "If it turns out to cost a quarter of a million dollars per job, I'll find something else to do."

In the culture of organized philanthropy, where failures are rationalized into rituals of self-justification and euphemized with phrases like "we learned a lot from this project" or "this strengthened our resolve to continue," it is refreshing to meet a philanthropist who is harshly critical of his own grantmaking. A 400-page book entitled *New Social Entrepreneurs: The Success, Challenge and Lessons of Non-Profit Enterprise Creation* (written mostly by Emerson and published by Roberts) lays bare all their foolhardy, wasteful, and counterproductive grants. Roberts offers the book free to anyone who asks for it.

Another trait uncharacteristic of other philanthropists is Roberts's reluctance to talk about his experiment until he absolutely has to. "Rather than tell people what we're doing," he says. "I prefer to show them what we have done." That approach, he believes, will make other foundations more likely to emulate him. Some of them—including many of the new foundations being formed by high-tech millionaires—are already following Roberts on the path of social entrepreneuring.

Roberts and Emerson harbor no illusions about the overall impact of social entrepreneuring. "It will not end homelessness," says Emerson, "nor will it have a noticeable effect on the welfare system." They do believe that it could make a difference in many lives. And they know from their own experience that it can move people off the streets and welfare rolls and into apartments and jobs.

There is nothing really new about venture philanthropy; it has been practiced in some form or another for fifty years or more. The number of program-related investments (PRIs) initiated by foundations has been growing steadily in recent years (see Appendix). What is unique about Roberts's ventures is his insistence that human service nonprofits not only can be involved in business but should be. When there is a thriving enterprise attached to such a program, he argues, its clients will fare much better than those served by a traditional charity.

Roberts has discovered that his kind of philanthropy is very difficult work, work that is frequently misunderstood by both private and nonprofit sectors. He finds that it requires his active attention and participation. "Raising the money is the easy part," he told his cousin Henry, who recently called to boast about the first $50 million raised for his New York Investment Fund. "The hard part is knowing what to do with it."

Following Suit

Business cannot succeed if society fails.
—Jack MacAllister, CEO, U S West

Less than a mile down Sand Hill Road from George Roberts's office in Palo Alto is the Mayfield Fund, a leading Silicon Valley venture capital firm. Mayfield general partner Gib Myers, who helped start Compaq Computers and Silicon Graphics, keeps a close watch on Roberts—not as a competitor in the capital markets but as a pioneering philanthropist. Myers is founder of the Entrepreneurs' Foundation, itself an exemplar of imaginative philanthropy.

Myers's idea was to ask fledgling Silicon Valley start-ups to donate stock certificates, stock options, and warrants to the foundation before they go public. Participating companies generally donate between .25 and .75 percent of their stock, which, if it has any value at all, is illiquid and often worthless. Myers hopes that when the firms go public and their stock price appreciates in the aftermarket, Entrepreneurs' Foundation will grow as fast as everything else in the high-tech securities market and put him in a position to make charitable contributions to the community programs that would otherwise be approaching the new ventures for support.

The brilliance of Myers's scheme is to ask the future rich to become philanthropists *before* they have scored. His usual targets are cash-poor entrepreneurs whose investors generally discourage active philanthropy, a state of affairs that has earned the Silicon Valley, and the high-tech community generally, a reputation for stinginess. Myers hopes to change all that. By mid-1999, of the thirty-six companies in the Entrepreneurs' Foundation portfolio, two had gone public and two others had been acquired. He has also persuaded over fifty individuals and fifteen other venture capital firms to contribute to the foundation. Although its endowment has yet to reach $4 million, Myers expects it to total between $100 and $200 million by 2003. That's the way money grows in high-tech industries, and no one knows that better than Gib Myers; his own three hundred start-ups are now valued at over $100 billion. The Entrepreneurs' Foundation could easily become very large, very fast.

It's a brilliant innovation in fundraising. But will the imagination that created it carry over into its grantmaking? Or will Myers's new foundation become just another proposal mill, funding community projects deemed worthy by a board of venture capitalists who haven't spent a day of their lives in the nonprofit sector? It's too soon to tell. Foundation vice president Patty Burness says that the foundation will provide the organizations they fund with what venture capitalists call *mezzanine financing*. The term is simply a venture capital buzzword to describe what about half the grants made by conventional foundations already do: finance post–start-up non-profit organizations' transition to full-scale operations.

Like venture capitalists, the foundation will place representatives on the board of each organization they fund. "We want to do everything we can to make our investment pay off," says Burness.[6] Myers and Burness never use the word *grant*. The payoff for "investments" is the "social return on investment." The winning ideas of social innovators will be rewarded, and success will be defined by quantitative standards of performance set by the foundation. This is not new thinking. In fact, it is a common approach and common rhetoric among venture philanthropists, most of whom mistakenly see the nonprofit sector through the lens of venture capitalism. What Gib Myers needs is a Jed Emerson, someone grounded in the nonprofit world who also has the know-how and imagination of a venture capitalist.

Another pioneer, Paul Brainerd, is a fairly typical high-tech millionaire but an atypical philanthropist. His rise to wealth is the classic story of the nerd in the garage who develops an indispensable piece of software. As an idealistic young journalist with a fascination for computers, Brainerd believed that every personal computer could, with a suitable application, become a printing press. The result was the Aldus Pagemaker, the progenitor of desktop publishing, which Brainerd sold to Adobe in 1996 for $525 million. His share of the deal was $130 million. He immediately made it clear that he would give it all away.

Fifty million dollars of the windfall went directly into the nascent Brainerd Foundation, with which he aims to improve and protect the environmental health of the Pacific Northwest. The foundation has made some innovative grants—most notably $3 million for the purchase of 214 acres on Bainbridge Island for an environmental-education center for Seattle-area children and a grant that helped turn eleven million acres of British Columbia wilderness into parkland. But it is in other philanthropic avenues that Brainerd has been the most imaginative.

He quickly discovered that he was not alone among novice philanthropists seeking creative ways to give away money. In Seattle, for example, so many young people have cashed out of the Microsoft Corporation that there is a regional subculture known as "Microsoft millionaires." To network with that unusual tribe of new philanthropists, Brainerd formed Social Venture Partners (SVP). "Investors," who become partners by invitation and contribute to the endowment a minimum of $5,000 a year for two years, participate actively in the selection of "investments" (again, not "grants" or "gifts"). They may also serve on the board of one or more of the nonprofits that SVP funds. Brainerd, like any venture capitalist "partnering" a start-up company, insists on "a seat at the table."

While some foundation executives question the practice of sitting on grantees' boards—"Should money have that much power?" asks Stephen Viederman, retired president of the Jessie Smith Noyes Foundation—Brainerd knows from experience that young, high-tech millionaires crave to do more than write checks to their favorite charities. "My goal is to get people engaged fifteen years earlier than they would typically get involved with philanthropy," he says, "while they still have more to give than their money." Brainerd explains that, like venture capitalists looking "for innovation and entrepreneurship, we are looking in the community to identify where the needs and solutions are. We are also trying to change the model of philanthropy."[7]

By mid-1999, SVP had 136 partners and had invested $300,000 in seven nonprofit organizations, all of them involved with children and education. The partnership also serves as an educational forum for new philanthropists, many of whom have given very little thought to the art of grantmaking. Brainerd calls these forums "Philanthropy 101": "We offer a safe environment in which they can learn a more strategic approach to giving money away."[8]

Flow Funding

May the rivers of wealth be undammed and flow freely over the Earth.
—Marion Rockefeller Weber

Alongside the venturesome philanthropists who seek new ideas and projects for their money are a few that explore new ways to give away old money. Until 1991 Marion Weber, daughter of Laurence S. Rockefeller and granddaughter of John D. Rockefeller Jr., gave away about 90 percent of her income every year. Marion, like all the young Rockefellers, was indoctrinated into the philanthropic ethic by her grandfather. Junior, as he was known to the family, instilled in them a sense of stewardship over their inherited wealth, pointing out "that wealth implied responsibility. He taught us that to whom much is given much is expected."[9] But Weber, instead of following the traditional path by sitting on the board of one Rockefeller foundation or another and channeling money into large and powerful institutions, invented *flow funding*.

Though she was considered a maverick among the Rockefeller clan from the day she left home, before 1991 her philanthropic method was traditional. "People would come to visit me or write asking for money. And they would send proposals. I became overwhelmed and fragmented by this process. I would look at a pile of proposals, take one from the pile, read it quickly. If my heart felt warm, I would fund it. If my gut felt sore I would not. I disliked this process immensely, of course. It was unhealthy. I needed more hands and eyes."

To end the paperwork and recover from burnout, Weber invited eight people whose philanthropic vision she had come to respect to each give away $20,000 of her money every year for three years. Their position is purely honorary, and they are paid no stipends or expenses. They must give the entire sum to any project or individual they choose and write a very short report. Once a year they meet to share their experiences in the Flow Fund Circle, as Weber calls the meeting. "We give as we are given," says Sukie Miller, a member of the circle, "with trust, hope, courage and the desire to learn. This is foot-to-the-floor philanthropy, and it's glorious."

Weber is pleased that her money is finding its way to the deepest roots of communities and cultures in South Africa, Peru, Russia, and New Zealand—to people and projects she could never have found on her own. "Capillary philanthropy," or flow funding, she explains, is "unimpeded by the usual obstacles of grantmaking bureaucracy . . . [and] has created a community. I am no longer isolated and overwhelmed by the work of giving, which has become more of an adventure than a duty, a creative experience that I can share with others. And instead of sitting alone in an office reading the goals and objectives of anonymous supplicants,

I invite true visionaries to join me as philanthropists every year, and I am inspired by each one."

Weber laments organized philanthropy's obsession with performance and accountability. She doesn't want to throw money away, "but nor do I want to burden visionaries with impact and accountability reports. My system is based on discernment and trust," she says. "We discuss what moves, surprises, inspires and challenges us. We are concerned with the meaning and process of our work, and deeply interested in what we can learn as a group. The money goes to places I never could have imagined, and that is the greatest joy for me."

It is unlikely that trustees and program officers of traditional foundations would place so much faith (and power) in people like Weber's visionaries. Yet doing so would undoubtedly find and ferment far more creative ideas and innovations than conventional philanthropic practices and would greatly expand any foundation's potential for imaginative philanthropy.

Place

A healthy community leads to a healthy community.
—Doug Easterling, The Colorado Trust

I could easily have fit the following discussion into one of the preceding chapters—perhaps "Health" or "Environment," or "Civility." It could equally well go in the following chapter on "Democracy," for what it describes is a form of democratic philanthropy. I placed it here because the concept of healthy communities is itself such a fine example of the philanthropic imagination at work. Healthy-communities initiatives, some of them now more than a decade old, provide an inspiring case study of ideas born far from foundation offices and boardrooms. They show that creative philanthropy can germinate anywhere. In this case the central premise came from a Berkeley, California, physician named Leonard Duhl. In 1984 in an address to a World Health Organization (WHO) meeting in Toronto, he made the rather obvious, but then-controversial, observation that there were social determinants of human health. Although American cities and foundations were slow to accept the implications of Duhl's idea, Europeans and Canadians were not. And soon after his speech, WHO embraced the practice of addressing public health community by community in a way that conceives of health more holistically than any American grantmaker had ever done.

Today, however, inside hundreds of American foundations (mostly, though not exclusively conversion foundations) the term *healthy communities* is often used to describe grantmaking aimed at improving public health and the quality of life in a defined geographical area—a city, town, rural region, or watershed—by focusing on matters that might seem to have little to do with health and medicine. The strategy common to all these projects is to involve the entire community, not just the so-called health establishment, in the process of improving and maintaining public health.

Healthy-communities grantmaking targets a broad range of factors that affect human health and well-being. A grant's purpose may be broad-based planning, or it may center on a specific project or community need: a community clinic, nutritional training program, open space planning, affordable housing, cultural development, participatory democracy, leadership training, or environmental protection. Whatever its particular focus, the goal of the grant is to improve the overall health of a community by ensuring that all citizens have access to all the determinants of good health and are, in turn, encouraged to participate in the process of providing it to the community.

While healthy-communities initiatives vary greatly from place to place, they share the belief that any healthy community

- Ensures citizens a clean and safe environment,
- Meets the basic needs of all residents,
- Has residents that respect and support one another,
- Involves the community in local government,
- Promotes and celebrates its historical and cultural heritage,
- Provides easily accessible health services,
- Has a diverse, innovative economy, and
- Rests on a sustainable ecosystem.[10]

Thus, as Duhl and those who followed him envision the healthy community, it encompasses far more than the absence of disease. It also addresses such underlying human, social, environmental, and economic factors as safe streets, affordable housing, fair wages, clean air and water, and good schools. Efforts to improve a community's total health are considered in a systemic, comprehensive context that brings together maximum citizen involvement and attention to all the factors that affect human health. Never before has the public health been seen in quite such a broad light.

And, because public health problems can only be addressed within this context, it intersects with every other aspect of civil society; for without strong, vibrant civil institutions nurtured by collaborative citizen involvement, a comprehensive health plan for a community cannot be implemented. A healthy-community project thus stimulates production of the kind of social capital that strengthens all the elements of civil society.

For the conversion foundations created, for the most part, to promote health in areas formerly served by nonprofit hospitals and health care systems, involvement in the healthy-communities movement is a natural (see chapter 4). These foundations are ideally positioned to initiate such projects by bringing all their relevant grantees together to plan for the public health. The Colorado Trust, one of first health-conversion foundations in the United States, provides a good case study.

Established in 1985 with proceeds from the sale of Presbyterian Medical Center in Denver, the trust immediately set about to fulfill its mandate "to improve the health of the people of Colorado." At first it supported such traditional public health services as prenatal care and well-baby clinics, Native American health programs, and women's shelters. But soon citizens of the twelve Colorado communities they were serving informed foundation trustees that they also needed help in building stronger families, improving transportation, and nurturing community leadership, better land-use planning, and sustainable economic development.

The trust balked. What do those things have to do with public health, they demanded? Shouldn't we be focusing on disease prevention by targeting such factors as nutrition, vaccinations, alcohol consumption, and the availability of health care? But the citizens challenged the trust to think beyond traditional grantmaking. Citing the World Health Organization's experience in European and Canadian communities, they argued that family ties and a sustainable economy were as vital to a community's health as medical services. They challenged the trust to think beyond traditional grantmaking, consider the social determinants of health, and fund new leverage points in the quest for public health.

Eventually the Colorado Trust concurred and "placed itself in the vanguard of one of the most promising, energetic movements for health improvement and community renewal in the country," writes Chris Adams a researcher retained to evaluate the Colorado Healthy Communities Initiative (CHCI).[11] Adams cites one recent study showing a link between mortality rates and the level of trust, civil engagement, and helpfulness in a community and another linking low birth weight to neighborhood social and economic conditions. "In other words," as Doug Easterling, former director of the trust puts it, "A healthy *community* leads to a *healthy* community."[12]

As for the role of foundations in furthering community health, Easterling observes that "no single organization, including a foundation, controls all the resources, behaviors, knowledge and relationships that influence health. But a foundation is in a unique position to draw out the ideas and talents that too often lie dormant when a community confronts its health threats."[13]

Conclusion

Democratic nations care little for what has been, but they are haunted by visions of what will be; in this direction their unbounded imagination grows and dilates beyond all measure.
—Alexis de Tocqueville

Behind every philanthropic impulse, regardless of the donor's philosophy or politics, is a similar intent—improvement—making the world, or some small part of it, a little better. Beauty, compassion, creativity, knowledge, and public health are all signs of improvement to a philanthropist. A few even imagine justice, albeit cautiously.

In the final analysis, the future of American philanthropy—and to some yet-unknown degree the future of America itself—depends upon the collective imagination of its philanthropists. Thus far, they have created much that we all cherish, and a little of what we most abhor about our civilization. That dichotomy won't end. In fact, it seems certain that the impact of philanthropy on our society and our lives will increase as philanthropists and philanthocrats become more proficient at leveraging their money and have more money to leverage. The products of their imaginations will continue to excite and infuriate us.

If America is to become more progressive in fact and outlook, it will be, in part, because its philanthropists seek social progress. The same applies to knowledge, health, compassion, and civility. If philanthropy nurtures them, they stand a better chance of advancing and surviving. As philanthropic resources grow, education, culture, science, and all fields that rely on foundation support for so much of their seminal research and communications will rise or decline according to the compassion and imagination of foundation practitioners. If the nation moves farther to the right, it will be because conservative foundations continue to excel at funding ideas and political strategists, as they have so imaginatively done for the past twenty-five years. If it returns to its progressive traditions, it will be because at least some large foundations regain the courage and determination to seek justice.

Imagination can also be usefully employed in formulating the definition of *philanthropy* itself, which is presently up for grabs. What does the word mean? What did it mean a century ago? Are its linguistic derivatives: *phil* = love/*anthropos* = humankind still appropriate, still relevant? Do all the activities conducted under the rubric of philanthropy truly express a love of humanity—all humanity, not just "our" humanity— American, Christian, capitalist, Democrat, Republican, Caucasian, lesbian, secular-humanist, or Native American? Is a foundation grant a gift or a strategic investment? Is a donation made to a great museum or hospital to grease the skids for an urban development project really philanthropy? Should we expand the idea of philanthropy to include a love for life itself, as in *biophilanthropy?*

While historians, ethicists, and anthropologists grapple with these questions, the philanthropic imagination will be inventing new ways to improve the world. But even now, as philanthropy approaches the status of science, even the most imaginative philanthropist continues to make disastrous and unnecessary mistakes. It has thus been a purpose of the preceding nine chapters to provide an historical assessment of America's hundred-year experience with organized philanthropy and to illuminate the pitfalls that awaited the best-intentioned efforts. As in any endeavor, history is generally the best teacher, and democracy the best solution.

11
Democracy

I'm not telling anybody anything. It's my money isn't it?
—J. Howard Pew, Trustee, Pew Memorial, 1970[1]

Things have their best chance of improvement when they rest for approval upon the informed conscience of the common man.
—Newton D. Baker, Trustee, The Carnegie Corporation, 1931–1937

Few philanthropists care more about democracy than George Soros, and few have done more to advance its cause around the world. But for Soros, democracy in Czechoslovakia is evidently quite a different matter from democracy in a foundation boardroom. This contradiction is not at all uncommon among philanthropists.

A few years back during a meeting of the trusted inner circle of the Open Society Institute (OSI)—the heart of Soros's philanthropic juggernaut—there was a protracted argument over some question. Finally, an impatient Soros exerted his authority by saying, "This is my money. We will do it my way."

"No, it isn't," objected a junior member of the staff. A hush fell over the room, and he finished the sentence in a quiet voice: "half of it is ours."

"What are you talking about?" asked Soros.

"If you hadn't placed that money in OSI or another of your twenty-five or so foundations, sir, about half of it would be in the Treasury," explained the tremulous youth. "It would be ours." Soros ignored the interruption and proceeded with the meeting. The young heretic is no longer in OSI's employ, but by all indications George Soros heard his message. Today the foundation is managed as collegially as any in the country. Still, it is by no means a democracy.

Foundations are fundamentally nondemocratic institutions. I say *non-democratic,* rather than *undemocratic* or *antidemocratic,* because American foundations make no pretense of being democratic. And few, if any, could reasonably be accused of opposing democracy. In fact, by supporting voter registration drives in Jim Crow states, many foundations distinguished themselves as champions of electoral democracy; and initiatives like the Ford Foundation's Gray Areas Program, a vast, complex urban renewal effort of the 1960s, enhanced the cause of participatory democracy nationwide. It would thus be unfair to indict foundations for a lack of, or opposition to, democratic processes. But democratic management just isn't part of foundation culture. If the word existed, it would be fair to say that foundations are *ademocratic.*

Most foundations, in fact, are chartered for the express purpose of carrying out the intent of one person only—the original donor. This person, in effect, wills his or her designs for the world to a very small number of people charged with perpetuating them as they see fit, without external oversight or pressure. No matter how wise, imaginative, or progressive subsequent trustees may be, their power is forever subordinated at some subtle level to the "original intent," sometimes referred to as *mortmain*— the dead hand of the foundation's creator. It is very difficult to legally challenge or change this ordained purpose, for very few original donors shared the insight and wisdom of Andrew Carnegie. At the first meeting of his new foundation in 1911 Carnegie told his trustees that

Conditions upon the Earth change, hence no wise man will bind Trustees forever to certain paths, causes or institutions. I disclaim any intention of doing so. On the contrary, I give my Trustees full authority to change policy or causes hitherto aided, from time to time, when this, in their opinion, has become necessary or desirable. They shall best conform to my wishes by using their own judgement.[2]

Few founders have been so flexible or so far-seeing. On the contrary, as described by Peter Goldmark, the recently retired president of the Rockefeller Foundation, the usual role of a self-perpetuating board restrained by donor intent "is to change some aspect of the larger society in accordance with a view held only by a minority or even a single person. Its job is not to reflect, protect or govern according to a majority."[3]

Nonetheless, it is sometimes possible under the legal doctrine of *cy pres* (*as near* [*as may be*]) to ask the courts for permission to change the intent or mission of a foundation, though without a very compelling reason to ignore or defy original intent the petition generally fails. The classic case cited to illustrate a successful *cy pres* alteration involves a trust created before the Civil War to harbor and aid escaped slaves. After the war the original intent of the deceased donor was clearly irrelevant, and the courts found it reasonable to change the charter and purpose of the foundation.

There was quite a different outcome in the long and expensive Buck Trust case in Marin County, California. When Beryl Buck died in 1975 she believed she was worth about $5 million; in fact, she left an estate of over $200 million to a foundation she created to assist the poor in one of the most affluent counties in the country. The trust is now worth over $1 billion. In the end, the Buck trustees were unable to convince the court that the foundation's "grantshed" (area of operations) should be expanded to cover a geographical area beyond the small, wealthy county mandated in the donor's will.

Thus foundations, bound by their charters and the law of trusts to honor and preserve the values and interests of, usually, one man or woman, are of necessity not democratic institutions. The early founders knew, too, though they rarely acknowledged it, that their philanthropy was a privilege that could exist only in an environment marked by economic inequity and social hierarchy. That is still true. The power to accumulate such wealth and distribute it as they choose would not long survive in a truly democratic society.

The idea that foundations should be democratized is not entirely new. In 1913 Jerome Greene, soon to become secretary of the Rockefeller Foundation, asked in a memo to President Wickliffe Rose, "How shall the trustees of the Rockefeller Foundation keep responsive to the will and intelligence of the people through future generations?" Greene proposed formation of a "Public Council" to run the foundation, with members appointed, one from each state, by a nominating committee at the state universities.[4] It would have been a start, and certainly a noticeable departure from the rule of the patrician boards that ran foundations at the time. But Greene's advice was ignored.

Two years later Chairman Frank Walsh of the U.S. Commission on Industrial Relations described Rockefeller's foundations as "a menace to the welfare of society."[5] Shortly after, Harvard's Charles W. Eliot advised Jerome Greene that "it is very important to add to the number of trustees of the Rockefeller Foundation persons of independent position, and known to the country as publicists, philanthropists or educators. The fundamental criticisms of the Socialists and Labor leaders can be met in no other way."[6]

Somehow the foundations endured the barbs of socialists without becoming democratic institutions; and, with exceptions that can be counted on one hand, foundation boards have been completely free from the influence of organized labor. Nonetheless, throughout their existence the matter of democracy has been at the core of assaults on foundations, whether from the left or the right. Most criticisms, however, have been about philanthropy's impact on democracy, rather than democracy's impact on philanthropy. Since Greene's proposal, the foundation community has carefully avoided the idea of applying democratic principles to the organization and practice of institutional philanthropy. Its discussions of "accountability" tend to focus on questions of government oversight and operational transparency rather than on the process by which foundations select grantees.

Accountability

The public is entitled to know the facts—all the facts—about the operation of foundations.
—Raymond Fosdick, President, Rockefeller Foundation, 1963

Who anoints foundations to do what they do?
—Alan Abramson, The Aspen Institute

To whom is a foundation legally accountable? To the public? Yes, but only in vague, minimal, and largely unenforceable ways. To its grantees? Yes, but about much as a feudal lord of the manor was accountable to his serfs. To its trustees? Yes, but only in a circular way, for as fiduciaries and guardians of donor intent, trustees are also accountable to the foundation and its charter. So, beyond paying obeisance to the few tax laws and a vague statement of purpose prescribed by mortmain, foundations are really accountable to no one. Is that right?

Progressive foundation leaders believe that the trusts should be fully accountable to the public and have said so for some time. "Since foundations are intended to enhance the public good, the public has a legitimate concern in how foundations operate," writes John Nason, "particularly in how they determine what is the public good."[7] David Truman, a trustee of the Twentieth Century Fund, heard the message: "What is at stake here is not fiduciary obligation in the usual sense of respect for the testamentary wishes of the donor, but rather the very possibility of the disposition of resources through autonomous bodies such as foundation boards. Unless the latter fully accept and are seen to accept, the 'public servant' concept, they will be destroyed or taken over by government."[8] Although resistance to such thinking within the foundation community has been fierce, Nason and Truman's views are grudgingly accepted.

Yet the case against full democratic control of philanthropy is persuasive. Being free from political oversight, it argues, allows foundations to address social issues that require immediate attention but may be too hot for government to handle. "Foundations can perform a distinctive role in society," argues Peter Frumkin, Harvard professor of public policy, "because they are free from the influence of organized constituencies and shareholders."[9]

Frumkin's assertion, which is echoed by many observers of organized philanthropy, assumes that the class of people so well represented on foundation boards are not an "organized constituency." Perhaps this is true in the strictest sense of the word *organized;* but they do share values and interests, and they network with each other as diligently as any constituency in the country. Very few foundation executives or program officers could honestly describe themselves or their work as free from the influence of their class. Nor could they argue that constituencies of women, racial minorities, artists, labor, and the poor are well represented on foundation boards.

Frumkin goes on to argue that "foundations can serve as laboratories for experimentation where new and controversial ideas can be put to the test."[10] That is true enough—though it rarely happens. He also claims that foundations have emerged "as profoundly public institutions, open and accountable to all, that work hard to build better relations with grant applicants and the public."[11] During three years of research on foundations I have met very few grant applicants who believe that any such effort to build better relations has paid off or that foundations are "profoundly public institutions." (See box insert, "Who's Who")

And while there have been occasions when a foundation or a group of foundations have stepped into a vacuum created by government inaction,

Who's Who

When a nonprofit organization applies to a foundation for support, the foundation quite sensibly requests and receives résumés of the organization's senior officers. But try to obtain background information on a foundation's executives or program officers and you'll hit a brick wall.

In early 1999 Michael Shuman and Mac MacLean of ProgressivePubs. com attempted to compile and publish a biographical directory of foundation program officers whom they considered "visionary." They planned to make the directory available to fundraisers looking for the few imaginative and "progressive" grantmakers scattered throughout the three hundred largest foundations in the United States. It would provide some basic information about them—just "the kind of rudimentary data," Shuman maintains, "that appear in *Who's Who*."[12]

He and MacLean contacted nearly a thousand program officers by phone, letter, or e-mail. For a variety of reasons, nine out of ten refused to provide résumés. In one case the president of a major national foundation ordered several program officers to withdraw their earlier agreement to participate. Another questioned the criteria for selecting the "visionaries."

"Why are foundations so resistant to helping applicants and grantees find out more about the faces behind the institutions that control the purse strings?" asks Shuman. "Like potentates of earlier historical epochs foundation executives believe their beneficent intentions raise them above the checks and balances of accountability that constrain other more pedestrian institutions. Secrecy, no matter how well-intentioned, only heightens the public's suspicion about philanthropy. The non-profit world is a public trust—one that places strong ethical responsibilities on grant seeker and grant maker alike to be especially open about who we are and what we are doing."[13] (Shuman and MacLean's "abridged" directory, *101 Visionary Program Officers,* is available through www. progressivepubs.com.)

history indicates that with rare exceptions, such as the Ford Foundation's controversial Gray Areas program, philanthropic social initiatives have been cautious, slow, and underfunded. All too often they are abandoned before they have a reasonable opportunity to succeed. Even Gray Areas, which was created by the Ford Foundation in the 1960s to confront the intractable social problems of American cities, carefully avoided ideological conflict and deliberately sidestepped the obvious but potentially explosive matter of American race relations. As University of California Historian Alice O'Connor concludes, "the Gray Area experience is best remembered not as a model of the way philanthropic activism ought to work, but as a lesson in the dangers of working within rather than challenging the boundaries established by federal government policy."[14]

Glass Pockets

The progressive nature of most national tax systems is being contravened by a concept which eludes any democratic involvement.
—Ben Whitaker

Trust no one.
—Deathbed advice of James Buchanan ("Buck") Duke to his daughter Doris.

In 1907, shortly after it was created, the Russell Sage Foundation advocated complete disclosure of all foundation activity and accounts as a preventative measure against abuse and corruption. Sage assumed the task of keeping and reporting a record of all foundation activity, a function now taken over by the Foundation Center in New York. But the records, then and now, reveal very little more than what one could ascertain from examining a foundation's tax return.

In 1939 Carnegie President Frederick Keppel confided to a friend that "if anyone looked too closely at us, we would be in real trouble." He warned his peers in philanthropy that "if the public should lose confidence in foundations as a social instrument, we will all be taxed out of existence, for there is nothing constitutional in the present exemption. Foundations," he said, "should operate with glass pockets."[15] At the time most foundations still operated in complete anonymity, with unlisted telephone numbers, post office boxes, and addresses at law firms. Three years later the U.S. Treasury ordered all foundations to file annual reports of their activities. In protest, foundation trustees filed thousands of blank or incomplete returns accompanied by contentious letters complaining that they did not have to reveal *anything* about their activities. The Treasury persisted, threatening regulatory sanctions, and one by one the foundations complied. Nonetheless, many still leave lots of official questions unanswered and file returns with huge gaps in information.

More than fifty years after Keppel's plea philanthrocrats heard an echo from a new leader. "Foundations are not living up to the affirmation and deeply held belief that they operate in the public trust when they don't welcome the public into the tent, far beyond the requirements of the law," scolded Dorothy ("Dot") Ridings, incoming president of the Council on Foundations.[16] A year later Peter Goldmark, former president of the Rockefeller Foundation, concurred in his 1997 keynote address to the council's annual meeting in Hawaii. "Foundations," he said, "function in an atmosphere which lacks the three basic chastising principles of American life: the market test, the press, and the ballot box."[17]

Not everyone in the foundation community agrees with Ridings and Goldmark. The late William Simon, former secretary of the treasury and president of the ultraconservative Olin Foundation, for example, insisted that "in a free society, the money the government appropriates is public money. The rest is private."[18] Simon's view is shared by conservative philanthropists, who argue that the "controlling power of competitive goods" provides "an adequate check on mediocre and profligate foundations." It's a silly argument, of course, as there is no marketplace in which foundation "goods" compete; they are dependent on no one for revenue, have no customers, and are subject to neither accreditation or licensing. In any case, though a few foundations still attempt to operate in secret, the availability on the Internet of IRS Forms 990 PF (now required of all foundations) makes it difficult to hide.

Although resistance to disclosure remains widespread in the foundation community, the transparency message is clear: as tax-avoidance mechanisms, foundations, because they have the power to influence public policy (including tax policy), should be more accountable to taxpayers—even more so than corporations, which are subject to the rules of full disclosure. As the young heretic reminded George Soros, at least 45 percent of his foundation's assets would have ended up in federal and state treasuries had it not been created. Should not the rightful owners of those treasuries, therefore, have a voice in the operation and direction of that foundation? And about 45 percent of the control?

Strangely enough, John D. Rockefeller, no great champion of democracy, thought so. In forming the foundation that bore his name, he invited the U. S. government to take it under its wing by giving the president, Congress, the Supreme Court, and other branches the power to appoint trustees. Suspicious of Rockefeller's motives (with some justification), Congress declined his offer. It's impossible to guess what foundations would look like today had the legislators accepted the deal and created a federal charter for national foundations. Would such bodies be more democratic than present-day foundations? More accountable? More responsive? Or, like so many other institutions of government, would they fall under the influence of money-corrupted legislatures and become partisan instruments of political patronage?

It's impossible to say, and, in a way, it's irrelevant. There are preferable ways to democratize foundations, ways that will not only empower taxpayers and assure accountability, but will also make the practice of organized philanthropy far more responsive than it is. There are also a number of practical arguments for democratizing philanthropy, which I consider after examining the moral arguments.

Moral Challenge

The central paradox of American Life is the coexistent ideals of political equality enshrined in our institutions of law and government, and the realities of unequally distributed wealth, influence and talent.
—Peter Dobkin Hall, Yale University

The moral challenge facing organized philanthropy is how best to use surplus wealth to advance civilization. Should the rich keep it and donate it as they see fit? Should we encourage them (through tax laws) to endow nonprofit institutions (including foundations)? Or should we have our government confiscate and redistribute all inheritance? A hypothetical analysis of a "yes" answer to the last question might read something like the following.

What if all the estimated $41 trillion in personal wealth expected to be transferred from one rich generation to another over the next twenty-five years or so were given, instead, directly and immediately, to the neediest Americans? It's an outrageous proposition, of course, but so is transferring the largest corpus of private wealth ever accumulated in human history to a relative handful of privileged offspring. Such a transfer to the poor would be a departure from the two prevailing philanthropic models—charitable contributions and charitable trusts—but morally it wouldn't be a bad idea. The sum in question is almost one and a half times the current GDP, twice the national debt, and about half the current value of all land and financial assets in the country. As currently budgeted, the federal government could operate for about twenty-eight years on $41 trillion.

A foundation officer would undoubtedly approach the problem with a study—probably contracted from the Brookings Institute or the Harvard Kennedy School of Public Policy—to assess the economic consequences of transferring all surplus wealth over the span of a single generation from the richest to the poorest sectors of society. The Harvard/Brookings study would show that if about $400 billion a year were evenly distributed among the thirty-eight million people in the United States who now live below the poverty line, each would receive about $10,500 a year for the next twenty-five years. Then what?

Another contract to answer this question might then be signed with the Rand Institute in Santa Monica. Once the poor had new refrigerators, dental work, and a recreation room over the garage, the preamble to the study would ask, would they be more secure than they had been before the windfall? Would their work be more fulfilling, their souls enriched? Would the social conditions that made them poor in the first place have disappeared? Would their children be better educated?[19] Probably not, Rand would conclude, referring to the Harvard/Brookings study of the overall economic consequences. For, in order to provide cash benefits for the poorest (the only kind they really need), all the investments being transferred would first have to be sold. Liquidating $41 trillion worth of real estate, securities, and other kinds of capital would not only severely depress all markets and lead to deflation, it would also eliminate capitalists as a class. Although the latter result might seem like a good idea to analysts at the New School for Social Research in New York (who would not be offered a research contract), it does requires closer examination.

What, on the other hand, if the poor decided to invest their windfall rather than spend it (an unlikely scenario) and became the new class of capitalists? Would they be any more sensitive to workers, consumers, or their community than today's capitalist class? Human nature suggests otherwise. So why bother to exchange one class of capitalists for another, particularly when the experiment seems doomed to failure. Why not do something truly imaginative with surplus capital, something between outright wealth confiscation and the reenrichment of the already rich. Why not, for example, place it in trusts committed to strengthening civil society? We're almost there today. All that is missing is a widespread commitment to democratic practices on the part of foundation trustees.

Imaginative overseers of captured wealth can do remarkable things with money, as some American foundations have already demonstrated. Hookworm was eliminated from the South by Rockefeller-funded scientists. Other foundations built public libraries, scientific institutes, minority colleges, and great museums. The civil rights movement was heavily financed with foundation philanthropy. This country has the most remarkable third sector in the world, as Tocqueville observed over 150 years ago. Much of it was seeded and is still supported by foundation philanthropy. These activities are, of course, the good deeds of philanthropy.

Much damage has also been done by foundations: the enhancement of prison labor, the loss of renewable-energy opportunities, and the worldwide social dislocation caused by the well-meaning but misguided Green Revolution are but three examples. The use of thirty-nine foundations as CIA conduits during the 1950s and 1960s did serious damage to the alleged independence of all foundations.[20] And billions have been squandered on obscenely overendowed Ivy League universities, profit-motivated science, hospitals where the rich and famous go to die, over-priced art collections, and architectural ego-spasms like "The Getty" in Los Angeles. An overall assessment of twentieth-century foundation philanthropy would grade it a C-minus, at best.

But things could improve. There are actions that could permanently diminish income disparities and eliminate social injustice. The billions wasted on failed initiatives have, after all, only come from the income on investments. The endowments themselves are still intact, and they are growing; and new foundations are being created at the rate of about three thousand a year. In 1998 people contributed the same amount of money to foundation assets as all the foundations gave away—about $17 billion. And in recent decades foundation professionals have developed the leveraging of money into a fine art. All that remains is for them to spend it right.

Of course, what *right* means is the subject of fierce debate among philanthrocrats—and that's good. What is meant by *right philanthropy*, like *right living*, needs to be reevaluated, and not only by institutions supported by surplus wealth.

The Foundations Antitrust Act

Not our money but charity's.
—Proclamation of the Council of Foundations, 1977

Non-profits must be concerned with democratic participation so that institutions function in a way that gives ordinary people an opportunity to affect the decisions that impact their lives.
—Charles Halpern, President, Nathan Cummings Foundation

It seems clear that the only way to make foundations true and effective servants of civilization instead of stewards of plutocracy is to democratize them. There are a number of ways to do that. First, we could change the tax laws to require private foundations to expand their universe of trustees beyond the family, friends, lawyers, and fiduciaries of millionaires. More community leaders and activists should be brought into the management of community foundations, and some of the folks who might benefit from corporate philanthropy should be invited into the boardroom for more than a catered lunch.

In addition, we should break up the large private foundations, much as the bloated industrial trusts of the early twentieth century were broken up by the Sherman Antitrust Act. Under a "Philanthropic Antitrust Act," no foundation could have assets over $1 billion. The new tax law would cut larger trusts into two or more smaller foundations and would also stipulate that no board of trustees could preside over more than one endowment. A philanthropist could endow as many billion-dollar foundations as he or she pleased, but each one would have to operate independently. Moreover, no one other than the founder could serve on more than one board of trustees.

Under such a rule Bill Gates's philanthropic empire would become twenty-two separate foundations, Lilly would become eleven, and Ford seven; and each would be overseen by a different board of trustees. Any foundation whose assets grew to exceed a billion dollars would have to spend the surplus value in one year.

If it were passed today, such a law would divide the thirty-nine largest trusts that currently control almost 30 percent of foundation assets into 117 new foundations, each with its own charter, fiduciaries, managers, and board of trustees. It would immediately expand the national universe of large-foundation trustees by a factor of four. As a founder, Gates could, if he chose, serve on the board of all twenty-two of his new foundations, though he would be unlikely to do so. Nor would he be apt to name all twenty-two of them after himself or family members.

It is interesting to remember that Andrew Carnegie originally designed his philanthropy in just this way, as several separate foundations. In 1911, for the sake of bureaucratic efficiency, he combined them as the Carnegie Corporation. The long-term result of that merger has been far less exciting, imaginative, and productive than the work of earlier Carnegie philanthropies.

Another way to democratize private philanthropy would be to mandate that a third of any foundation's trustees be appointed by elected officials—congressional leaders in the case of national foundations, state legislators for state-chartered foundations, and local officials for community foundations. This provision already exists for some of the latter. Trustees would serve for no more than seven years. A small family foundation (under $25 million in assets) might be exempt from public participation but would be required by statute to have on its board at least one person unrelated by blood or marriage for every family board member.

Community

Project Director: *We are convening the stakeholders in the community so they can select an action plan.*
Foundation Officer: *But what will their action plan be?*
Project Director: *We won't know until they finish their community-wide discussions.*
Foundation Officer: *But we can't let them decide. That's our responsibility.*
—Mark Gerzon

As believers in democracy we are bound to look forward to the day when the community will take over the functions performed by the foundation.
—Frederick Keppel, former president, the Carnegie Corporation

"Most foundation support for community-based programs is aimed at supporting a position the foundation believes in," says Michael Lerner, Jennifer Altman Foundation president, "not in condition-free support for civil society dialogue and community building."[21] Yet most of these same foundations claim in their published reports that they exist to build, serve, and strengthen community.

A handful of bold, though admittedly small, foundations have defied that trend: Ashoka, New World, Tides, the Flow Fund, Thresholds, Vanguard, Haymarket are a few of them. Each has taken tentative voluntary steps toward democratic philanthropy by creating advisory boards comprised of ordinary citizens. These new board members tend to be more streetwise and responsive to social or economic crises than traditional foundation trustees, most of whom are nervous about social advocacy, reluctant to initiate social change, and willing to wait a decade or more for even moderate social reforms. Many mainstream boards may appear more female and less white than they were before 1983, when the Council on Foundations adopted a resolution to recruit more women and minority trustees; but they are still populated principally by members of the academic, political, scientific, social, and economic elites.[22] Despite the resolution and the efforts of growing numbers of national foundations to diversify their boards and staffs, a Council of Foundations survey found in 2000 that 90 percent of trustees and 82 percent of staffers are white.[23]

Besides being quicker to respond to social crises and directly address injustices, democratically managed foundations would be more likely to raise the annual total of grants above the 5-percent legal requirement, especially when times are hard or when financial markets are producing double-digit returns. More trustees might even vote to spend the foundation's entire endowment in, say, twenty-five years or so, as only a handful of private foundations have done over the past century. (See box insert "Payout and Perpetuity.") While this is not a popular thought among foundation trustees or executives—obsessed as most of them are with perpetuity—they would admit that in a crisis of the magnitude of AIDS, it would probably be a good thing for a few foundations to spend their entire endowments in search of a cure—as Irene Diamond did to support David Ho's pursuit of protease inhibitors (see Epilogue).

The bottom line of the reforms I propose (back to *realekonomics!*) is that maintaining the present structure of organized philanthropy makes a certain amount of sense—moral as well as economic sense. It is true that the wealth of foundations, profits accumulated by the capitalist class, remains invested, albeit generally in land and securities and not necessarily in productive capacity, and that all too often it is used to advance enterprises that are dissonant with a foundation's declared purpose. Still, rather than liquidating all that wealth—along with the opportunity to use it for

Payout and Perpetuity

The percentage of its assets a foundation should give away every year is one of the oldest controversies in American philanthropy. The Tax Reform Act of 1969, passed after almost ten years of congressional investigation into foundation activities, mandated a 6-percent payout for all private foundations. The rate was raised briefly to 6.5 percent, then, after intense lobbying by foundation trade groups, lowered to 5 percent in 1981. Foundations are allowed to include in that 5 percent low-interest loans ("program-related investments") and the cost of doing business (all administrative expenses and trustee fees), which has risen since 1965 from about 6 percent of total payout to about 19 percent in 1999. Thus the real average payout of foundations granting the bare minimum is between 3.8 and 4.0 percent annually.

In the late 1960s, when securities prices typically advanced 6 to 8 percent a year and foundation investments were underperforming the market, 5 or 6 percent made a certain amount of sense. But in recent years, as rising stock and bond prices have helped thousands of foundations to increase their endowments by 20 percent or more every year, there has been pressure on Congress and the IRS to increase the payout requirement a percentage point or more.

The Council of Foundations, which represents an "industry" fixated on growth and perpetuity, vigorously defends the current minimum payout rate. It cites extensive research by the Internal Revenue Service, DeMarche Associates, and other financial analysts indicating that over the long run 5 or 5½ percent is an optimal payout rate. If that rate is sustained long enough, they argue, a foundation will eventually grant more than it would at a higher payout of, say, 6, 7, or 8 percent, because reinvesting more of the income will increase assets faster and provide more money for grantmaking. Thus, according to DeMarche and others, over the long haul the 5-percent rate is a boon to the nonprofit sector.

A different position is taken by the National Network of Grantmakers (NNG), "an association of more than four hundred individual and institutional funders." It believes that payout should be keyed to market performance and endowment growth and should thus have increased not decreased during last two decades of the twentieth century, when markets and foundation assets grew at more than twice the payout rate. The group has conducted its own research to prove the point.

Conducted by Columbia University economist Perry Mehrling, the NNG study shows that since 1981 the value of American foundations has tripled, while the rate of grants payout has dropped from over 8 to under 5 percent. Mehrling says that foundations could have donated 8 percent every year since 1981 and could continue to do so "without jeopardizing their long term viability." Instead they are becoming new warehouses of private wealth, exactly what the Congress was attempting to prevent with the 1969 tax code that mandated a payout rate. In 1998 the amount of new money donated to foundations approximately equaled the total amount granted by all foundations.

Few reformers propose legislating a payout increase. Even NNG prefers a voluntary "1 percent more for democracy . . . to be directed to organizations and causes working to alleviate the pressing economic and social needs of low income children, women, the elderly, and the poor in general." About half of NNG's membership supports this idea or a similar version of it. Jack Shakely, president of the California Community Foundation in Los Angeles, proposes a "community dividend"—a one-time bonus payout that foundations would provide in years when securities markets push foundation growth into two-digit strata.

A reasonable compromise between the warring partisans of payout might be to keep the minimum rate at 5 percent but to remove the expense allowance and create a tax incentive (e.g., lower excise tax on investments) for foundations that pay out more than 5 percent. Some critics of that proposal argue that removing grantmaking costs from the payout minimum would diminish the boldness and innovation of foundation work. Few of those holding this view work for foundations known for their innovativeness.

Of course, the whole payout debate is a digression from the larger issue of how the foundations' grantmaking can more effectively meet the traditional goals of organized philanthropy. And it disregards both the time value of money (i.e., the effect of future inflation) and the urgent social problems that demand immediate attention.

genuinely progressive philanthropy—would it not be sensible to encourage the formation of more democratic foundations, to tax the incomes of the uncharitable rich more heavily, and to transfer the funds collected (not the foundations' stocks, bonds, and real estate) directly to the neediest?

Conclusion

If decades of philanthropic effort to help the poor and disadvantaged have yielded growing misery, why should anyone follow that path.
—Leslie Lenkowsky, Dean, School of Philanthropy, Indiana University

It is the fate of philanthropy to be tested in our time as never before.
—Michael Lerner, President, Jennifer Altman Foundation

Conflicting views of foundations portray them, on the one extreme, as benevolent instigators of positive change, and, on the other, as sinister threats to democracy. As this book has indicated, the record provides ample evidence to support both claims about almost any foundation. But in the aggregate, neither interpretation is accurate or fair. It is closer to the truth to say that all foundations could become far more benevolent forces for positive change by simply becoming more representative of the society they were created to serve.

That's easier said than done. "I believe that we are afraid to talk about power, and to fund a dispersion of power, because we are afraid to lose it ourselves," admits Stephen Viederman, Jessie Smith Noyes Foundation president. "Whether democracy is a theory or a practice is the issue."[24] Thoughtful foundation trustees and administrators have struggled for a century with the conflict between plutocratic and democratic power, reflected as it is in the delicate balance between private ownership and public responsibility. What is the proper function of these vast reservoirs of treasure in a liberal democracy—or for that matter in any civil society? What role should they play in setting a national agenda or deciding how civil authority should be distributed? Should private wealth have any authority at all? Or should it be used to extend authority beyond the traditional reaches of power?

The ultimate question on democracy and philanthropy should not be about the rights and privileges of wealth but about whether democratic processes will make philanthropy more responsive, more effective, and more progressive. When people who have experienced economic hardship or injustice work alongside those who have not—but who for whatever reason seek justice and equality—the solutions and initiatives undertaken by foundations will be more realistic. If Third World farmers had been guiding the Green Revolution in cooperation with Rockefeller Foundation agronomists, America's largest philanthropic initiative would have been far less damaging than it was.

The moral trade-off for any institution in a democracy that wants, as foundations clearly do, to mediate public policy and help set a national agenda is the requirement to open itself, gradually but noticeably, to public review and participation. Only then can these creations of enormous wealth escape the threat of government intervention and the indictments the Right and the Left have leveled against them for a century. By becoming genuinely democratic organizations, foundations can avoid being labeled "engines of subversion" or "cultural imperialists" and will take their place as one of the constructive institutions of an open society.

Epilogue

There is no hope; but we might be wrong.
—Slogan of the Ted Turner Foundation

Love, not money, is the true currency of philanthropy.
—Robert Lehman

"The problem of our age is the proper administration of wealth, that the ties of brotherhood may still bind together the rich and poor in harmonious relationship." Thus begins the manifesto that launched a century of organized philanthropy. Written in 1889 by Andrew Carnegie under the title "Wealth," it was published in June of that year in the *North American Review*. Later another journal editor renamed it "The Gospel of Wealth," and thus it remains to this day.

Although still cited by historians and scholars of foundation philanthropy as the defining document of American generosity, the gospel according to Carnegie is badly in need of revision, for the objective realities facing philanthropy today are very different than they were 110 years ago. In fact, many of the most pressing problems America faced in the late nineteenth century have been addressed and studied—and some even solved—by the fifty thousand or so foundations created since the old prophet penned his gospel.

Not that Carnegie's manifesto is totally obsolete, or that it is bereft of lasting wisdom. It is an inspiring document that has moved many a millionaire to philanthropic purpose. And there is much in it that still applies, most notably his affirmation of Christ's admonition about the camel passing through the eye of a needle. "He who dies rich, dies disgraced" is how the sage of philanthropy worded it. His point is clear.

Anyone who gets rich in this life should give it all away "before he is called upon to lie down and rest upon the bosom of Mother Earth." For Carnegie, obviously, a foundation left in the trust of children, tax lawyers, and business associates was tantamount to giving it all away.

Though we might quarrel with that premise, it's a minor problem compared to the unease we feel reading other pronouncements of his gospel. What is in greater need of modification—and it persists in contemporary philanthropy—is Carnegie's overweening paternalism. His "man of wealth" (women are never mentioned) is "the mere trustee and agent of his poorer brethren, bringing to their service his superior wisdom, experience, and ability to administer, doing for them better than they would or could do for themselves." And Carnegie's confident social Darwinism—his belief in "the concentration of industry and commerce in the hands of a few, and the law of competition [as] . . . essential to the future progress of the race"—though not completely defunct, no longer commands universal respect.

Perhaps it was true in 1889, as Carnegie observed, that "individualism, private property, the law of accumulated wealth and competition" were "the highest result of human experience, the soil in which society has produced . . . the best of all that humanity has yet accomplished." But since then much has been accomplished that called not on individualism and the law of competition but rather on collaboration, altruism, and cooperative efforts. They have produced triumphs of science and social justice and were spawned and supported, in many cases, by philanthropic initiative.

A twenty-first-century gospel of wealth would take account of the fact that not all wealth is earned. In fact, most of the assets owned by the next generation of rich Americans will be unearned, inherited in the largest and fastest wealth transfer in world history. That transfer certainly begs for an ethos different from Carnegie's call to "the manufacturer and the merchant" to saddle himself with the burden of philanthropy.

Another verity ignored by Carnegie and most of the philanthropists who followed him is the fact that about 45 percent of any foundation's endowment really belongs to the public, whose state and federal treasuries would hold that portion of any large estate not left to a foundation. It would only seem fair, therefore, for 45 percent of a foundation's trustees to represent ordinary citizens and for a new manifesto to call for the thorough democratization of organized philanthropy. Maintaining the ratio of elites that exists on foundation boards today can only perpetuate plutocracy.

So to whom should we turn to write the new and improved "Gospel of Wealth"? Ted Turner, George Soros, Bill Gates? Probably not. In fact, most of what we have heard from them on the subject are mere sound bites—just platitudes and bravado. My candidate would be Irene Diamond, a modest but imaginative philanthropist who followed Carnegie's advice to the millionaire "to sell all that [she] hath and give it in the highest and best form to the poor by administering [her] estate for the good of [her] fellows." Seizing her deceased husband's $150-million fortune from his ill-intentioned business associates, Diamond spent it all in ten years. She left to the world the best hope yet of stopping a deadly disease that today afflicts 35 million people—AIDS. It is thus fitting to close this book with a short tribute to a woman whose work exemplifies the best of American individual and institutional philanthropy. Few lives can provide a more inspiring example of the philanthropic imagination in action.

Her husband, Aaron Diamond, was a successful New York real estate developer, a man of some controversy. He surrounded himself with colleagues who spent much of their time in court defending themselves against charges no philanthropist would want to be associated with. Shortly after he died suddenly of a heart attack in 1984, two of his associates turned up at Irene Diamond's door with a thick pile of legal papers that they wanted her to sign, immediately. But instead of signing them, she took the complex documents to W. H. ("Ping") Ferry. Ferry, a legendary philanthropist who had helped start the Ford Foundation, later developed Ford's extensive and controversial civil rights project.

Ferry counseled Irene Diamond not to sign the papers, which would convey control of the foundation created by Aaron Diamond's will to the two men who had visited her. He also introduced her to Vincent McGee, a brilliant young man who could help her set up and run a foundation she could be proud of. Not surprisingly, a brutal confrontation ensued. It was reminiscent of earlier firestorms at the MacArthur, Ford, and Robert Wood Johnson foundations, where unprincipled heirs and associates of the donor had made similar attempts to gain control of the assets. As historian Waldemar Nielsen describes the dramatic outcome of the Diamond fiasco, "philanthropic victory was snatched from the jaws of death . . . and a large foundation was saved from corruption and calamity."[1]

At one point during unpleasant negotiations, one of the participants told McGee that "Mrs. Diamond is going to participate from a distance and we'll keep her happy, but this is going to be a very big foundation and there's a lot of interesting things we can do with it." McGee, who by then had come to know Irene Diamond fairly well, knew better. "She took control," he said, "gradually, but very firmly."[2] An audit of the estate was ordered, and one of the men who had urged her to sign away control was convicted of embezzlement and sent to prison. The other was promptly removed as an executor of the estate.

Irene Diamond is an imaginative, active, and committed woman who shared her husband's passionate interests in medical research, civil rights, culture, and minority education. Hoping to bring about noticeable progress in each of those fields during her own lifetime, she followed an example set by Julius Rosenwald and a small handful of foundations creators who followed him. She decided in 1987 that the entire endowment of the Aaron Diamond Foundation would spend itself out of existence in ten years. And in 1997 the Diamond Foundation did indeed close its doors. The following year Irene Diamond received the Council of Foundations' Distinguished Grantmaker Award.

What is known as "spending out" a foundation's assets is a rare event in the philanthropic world, where fiduciaries and trade associations vigorously defend an apparently God-given right to perpetuity. Spending out is not for every foundation, as it calls for a very different philanthropic strategy than granting 5 percent of assets every year. But the results attained by Irene Diamond, which could never have been accomplished with a 5-percent payout, are inspiring testimony for anyone moved to follow Carnegie's advice literally and rid themselves of a fortune in a lifetime. There are more than spiritual rewards for such a decision.

"Knowing that we had a limited time in which to get our work done was central to our philanthropy and our mode of operation," recalls Vinny McGee. "We devoted our resources to making as big an impact as possible in a short length of time. We had the ability to look closely at a problem and not be distracted by worries over long term job security or a budding bureaucracy."[3]

Before he died, Aaron and Irene Diamond decided that his foundation should be committed 40 percent to medical research, 40 percent to minority education, and 20 percent to culture. But it will be for one initiative in medical studies—AIDS research—that Irene Diamond will be forever remembered as a fiercely dedicated grantmaker.

Commitment to a ten-year payout meant that instead of granting $6 million a year, McGee and Diamond would have $20 to $25 million to invest annually. Investing 40 percent of that sum in research on almost any virus, even one as sneaky and elusive as HIV, can make inroads. In 1987, with sixty thousand dead from AIDS in New York alone and the federal government and most large foundations dragging their heels, Irene Diamond convinced her board that the battle against AIDS should be their primary project. "I believe that foundations should provide desperately needed help that can't come to people in any other way," she later told *Foundation News and Commentary.*[4]

Diamond and McGee began by supporting a four-year postdoctoral fellowship in AIDS research at the Health Research Institute in New York. One fellowship quickly grew to twenty-five, with Diamond fellows spread strategically throughout the New York medical research establishment. Measured by the number of papers published by the hundred people who went through the program (half of them women), the fellowships were an unqualified success. In its first five years of existence, the Diamond Foundation also funded over thirty AIDS-research programs around the country.

In 1990 Diamond inaugurated the Aaron Diamond AIDS Research Center, a joint venture with the New York City Department of Health, the Public Health Research Institute, and New York University. The center became the largest laboratory of AIDS research in world and had a noticeable impact on the global pace and progress of research into biological, immunological, and pharmacological AIDS therapies.

Under Dr. David Ho, the Diamond Center took a particular interest in the mechanism of *in utero* transmission of HIV and the development of vaccines to protect the fetus against AIDS infection during pregnancy. The result was a *protease inhibitor,* a drug that effectively suppresses the virus in newborns and, in combination with other drugs, turned out to have a profound effect on adult sufferers as well. In 1996 Dr. Ho was named *Time* magazine's Man of the Year and was appointed to a professorship at Rockefeller University, now the site of the Diamond Center's main academic affiliate.

Unlike many of her peers in philanthropy, Irene Diamond never took credit for the work done in the Diamond Center labs, the discovery of protease inhibitors, or the discoveries of David Ho. "His talent is his talent," she says. Nor does she proselytize or defend the practice of spending out an endowment. "You can't make any generalizations about that," she says. "It's up to each foundation to decide. They have to work the way they see fit."[5]

At the age of eighty-nine, having spent out the foundation, Diamond remains deeply concerned about the fate of groups she started and supported while the foundation existed. "At first we tried very hard to see that they were taken care of. We called a lot of other foundations to convince them to provide support." If one of her favorites can't find funding and is in dire straits, she makes a small grant, with no strings attached, from the Irene Diamond Fund, which was created from the personal inheritance Aaron Diamond left to his wife.

Irene Diamond may not be moved to write the manifesto for the second century of American philanthropy. Yet the example of her life as a philanthropist will suffice as a substitute. She beautifully exemplifies Paul Ylvisaker's conviction, with which I opened this book, that philanthropy is "America's passing gear."

Even though organized philanthropy in America has done some demonstrable harm during the past century, Irene Diamond has proved that foundations are potentially a good thing. They can perform vital and essential functions, financing institutions, inventions, movements, science, and artistic creations that might not exist without their support. However, the full potential of private foundations has yet to be realized. It is my belief that they could have contributed much more than they have over the past century. And they could do so in the future. The infrastructure is in place, the money is there. All that is required is imagination, leadership, and faith in democracy.

Appendix
Passive, Dissonant, or Making a Difference: Which Way for Foundation Investing?

American private, corporate and community foundation assets now total about $420 billion. Floating in an $11-trillion sea of institutional assets that include pension funds, university endowments, private trusts, and mutual funds, foundations represent a fairly small ship—a lifeboat may be a more relevant metaphor. But since foundations fulfill a unique purpose and enjoy a privileged tax status, the law holds them to different standards of care than other investment pools. As a result, they possess enormous potential for thoughtful investor strategies that broadly benefit society.

However, most foundation portfolios are managed as if investments had no consequences, proxies had no value, and foundation fiduciaries were bound by the same standards of care as pension funds and personal trusts. Moreover, all but a handful of grantmakers forgo opportunities to devote even a small portion of their portfolios to community development loans, loan guarantees or other "program-related investments" (PRIs)—even though PRIs can be booked as grants and credited toward the minimum 5 percent of assets that foundations must pay out annually. According to Foundation Center data, foundation PRIs represent about 1 percent of annual grant outlays, or 0.3 percent of assets. And they are a paltry fraction of similar investments made by pension funds, churches, and insurance companies.

By law, foundation trustees bear fiduciary responsibility for their institutions' investment portfolios. But my conversations with dozens of foundation officers and directors suggest that few trustees carefully monitor the content or performance of funds in their trust. Instead, trustees tend to regard themselves primarily as program advisors, whose main role is to formulate broad grantmaking policy and philanthropic mission.

At many foundations, one or two board members sit with a few investment experts on a separate finance committee. For the remaining trustees, investment management becomes a totally separate function that takes place in another building, city, or state. In addition, many trustees are either unaware or sanguine about the fact that foundations' portfolios contain investments that contradict the very mission they are entrusted to pursue. Some grantmakers promote disarmament while remaining vested in munitions firms. Others committed to racial justice hold shares in companies with wretched equal opportunity records.

Environmental grantmakers with large holdings in oil, chemical, timber, and mining companies represent an especially striking paradox. In April 1998, the newsletter Climate Change Report analyzed the portfolios of major environmental funders such as the Pew Charitable Trust and found "a complete disconnect between their investment and grant-making portfolios. Pro-environment foundations own stock in virtually all of the corporations that sought to prevent the U.S. from committing to reduce greenhouse gas emissions."

Most grantmakers' approach to investment follows a traditional formula: more money = more grants. Never mind if the market value of a foundation's holdings in a major polluter is greater than all the funds the foundation provides to environmental organizations addressing the company's transgressions. "Sure, we take money from polluters," say trustees who are aware of the situation, "but we give it to people who are fighting them."

Most trustees, however, remain in the dark. "It's hard for a board to make sure that its investments are aligned with its mission," two foundation officials observed in the *Chronicle of Philanthropy* in October 1995. "The cultural barriers between the people who make the financial decisions and those who run the programs are usually impenetrable. Most people who run foundation grants programs have little interest or experience in investing and do not know the language of finance."

Enough Dissonance to Go Around

Discrepancies between a foundation's grantmaking mission and its investment practices may seem the natural province of liberal foundations that support organizations critical of corporate actions. In fact, there's more than enough dissonance to cover philanthropy's political spectrum.

Consider the case of the Harry and Lynde Bradley Foundation, a $500-million institution widely viewed as one of the most effective grantmakers to conservative causes. The Milwaukee-based foundation is a major supporter of both libertarian and communitarian strands of conservative activity. Its president, Michael Joyce, has become a key player in shaping the grassroots and intellectual projects that drive right-of-center politics.

On the libertarian side, Bradley provides hundreds of thousands of dollars in annual funding to organizations like the Cato Institute, a Washington think tank that has been a leading critic of corporate welfare. On the communitarian side, Bradley doles out funds to endeavors like the Civil Society Project of the Pennsylvania-based Commonwealth Foundation for Public Policy Alternatives. Bradley also makes substantial grants to conservative culture-warrior organizations such as the Foundation for Cultural Review, which publishes *New Criterion* magazine.

But Bradley's investment portfolio is profoundly at odds with all these grantmaking themes. According to its 990-PF tax filing for 1996, the foundation owned 47,250 shares of Archer Daniels Midland, one of corporate America's most prominent recipients of government welfare—largely through agricultural subsidies. It also owned 53,600 shares of Wal-Mart. And it held millions of dollars of stock in entertainment behemoths like Disney, Time Warner, Viacom, News Corporation, and Harrah's whose business lines and products routinely outrage Bradley's cultural-conservative grantees.

New Criterion may deplore entertainment companies' output, but editor Hilton Kramer says he is not interested in the investments that indirectly support the magazine. "I have no idea which foundations are invested in what," he says. "Nor does it concern me." When asked whether he was bothered by the fact that *New Criterion*'s refined aesthetic and moral traditionalism are supported by proceeds from *Married With Children* and Time Warner's gangsta rappers, Kramer refused to comment and abruptly ended the interview.

What does Don Eberly think about bankrolling his Civil Society Project with dividends from Wal-Mart stock? The former adviser to Jack Kemp says that he is deeply concerned and unalterably opposed to "the

Wal-Martization of the American marketplace, which is stripping village life from our civilization." But Eberly finds the Bradley Foundation's investment in Time-Warner even more troubling, since it is "inconsistent with their [and his] expressed interest in cultural renewal."

Distinctive Standards of Care

The clash between grantmaking and investment policy often reflects a fundamental misinterpretation of standards governing foundation investments. Those standards, rooted in federal and state statutes as well as accumulated case law and regulations, clearly require fiduciaries to earn a return on their investment portfolio and avoid self-dealing or other shady practices. But the standards also have grown increasingly hospitable to mission-friendly investment strategies.

Exhibit A is the "prudent investor rule," the granddaddy of fiduciary guideposts. In 1990, the American Law Institute incorporated a revised statement of that rule in the federal law governing private trusts (Restatement of the Third Law of Trusts, section 227). It says that a trustee's ultimate "duty to beneficiaries [is] to invest and manage the funds of the trust as a prudent investor would, in light of the purposes, terms, distribution requirements, and other circumstances of the trust" Prudence is not measured by individual investment decisions but by the totality of the trustees' investment strategy.

With its emphasis on institutional "purpose" and overall portfolio performance, the revised rule invites a different interpretation of prudent investing for foundations than it might for the management of funds whose beneficiaries are vulnerable individuals—for example, a child's trust or a pension fund. Moreover, an official comment attached to section 227 declares:

Social considerations may be taken into account in investing the funds of charitable trusts to the extent the charitable purposes would justify an expenditure of trust funds for the social issue or cause in question or to the extent the investment decision can be justified on grounds of advancing, financially or operationally, a charitable activity conducted by the trust.

According to attorney W. B. McKeown, who edits a newsletter on nonprofit law, this element of the prudent investor standard actually creates a "fiduciary responsibility" for foundation trustees "to consider the social impact of the [institution's] investments. Being true to the mission of the charity may require that the governing board address the social responsibility of its investment decisions." McKeown's interpretation of the affirmative obligation embedded in section 227 may be open to dispute, absent court decisions on the subject. But the prudent investor standard clearly encourages fiduciaries to employ investment strategies that further a foundation's program mission.

Like the stewards of private trusts and pension funds, foundation trustees are subjected to judicial supervision. Although the courts constantly discipline pension fund fiduciaries and private trust companies, foundation trustees are almost never called to the bench for breaching the prudent investor standard. A Lexis search of federal and state court cases turned up only three instances where foundation fiduciaries were accused of violating the rule or closely related standards. The best-known case, *Lynch* v. *Redfield*, dates from the 1960s. In *Lynch*, the court sensibly found that feuding foundation trustees shouldn't stick their institution's funds in a non-interest-bearing bank account for five years and shut down its grantmaking machinery.

If the investment activities of foundations were held to the same standards as private trusts, many might well have been subjected to greater scrutiny, if not outright sanction. In a landmark 1989 study of foundation investment performance sponsored by the Foundation Center, analysts Lester Salamon and Kenneth Voytek found that the median rate of return on foundation portfolios between 1979 and 1983 significantly underperformed standard market indices. Salamon and Voytek noted that the foundations' puny returns were "all the more striking in view of the generally favorable market conditions that existed" during the survey period. They laid part of the blame on "the ad hoc and somewhat lackadaisical investment approach evident among a large number of foundations." Four years later, Salamon updated the analysis with investment data for 1984–86. The results were familiar: most foundations performed appreciably worse than the market and "seem[ed] to be pursuing rather ad hoc investment approaches."

Fortunately for these ad hoc investors, foundations are held to the "business judgment rule"—a comparatively lenient standard that previously applied only to directors of business corporations. In 1974, however, a precedent-setting civil court case (*Stern* v. *Hayes*) affirmed "the modern trend to apply corporate rather than trust principles" in guiding the behavior of foundation trustees. Moreover, the Uniform Management of Institutional Funds Act, now adopted in forty-one states and the District of Columbia, stipulates that

members of a governing board of charitable institutions shall exercise ordinary business care and prudence under the facts and circumstances prevailing at the time of the action or decision. In so doing they shall consider long and short term needs of the institution in carrying out its educational, religious, charitable, or other eleemosynary purpose [alongside] its present and anticipated financial requirements, expected total return on its investments, price level trends, and general economic conditions.

Nothing in that standard seems incompatible with foundation fiduciaries screening portfolios of stocks and bonds that contradict their grantmaking programs, making mission-related investments or engaging in shareholder advocacy. Nor does the Internal Revenue Code seem to restrict mission-based investing. Section 4944 of the code bars foundations from making "jeopardizing investments"—generally defined as violations of the prudent investor rule or business judgment doctrine. However, the code explicitly exempts low-interest community development loans and other PRIs from this universe of prohibited investments.

Screening (vs. orthodoxy) advocates insist that screened portfolios need not sacrifice financial returns, even for foundations seeking to preserve perpetually the buying power of their corpus, or initial endowment. A large body of empirical literature, summarized in the winter 1997 Journal of Investing, suggests that socially screened investments provide competitive returns—including screened investments in bonds and foreign equities. As a result, growing numbers of individual and institutional investors have begun putting their money where their values are.

According to the Social Investment Forum (SIF), a trade association of financial professionals, growth in screened investment portfolios has substantially outpaced growth in the broader markets. According to SIF, investors held $529 billion in such portfolios in 1997.[1] Some asset managers, notably U.S. Trust (Boston), Trillium Research & Development, Walden Capital, Piper Jaffray, Citizens Funds, Domini, and Winslow Management will filter investments for foundations.

According to the Council on Foundations' 1996 *Foundation Management Report,* approximately one in ten foundations invests at least part of its portfolio with specific socially responsible guidelines. Small grantmakers are twice as likely as foundations with more than $100 million in assets to use such guidelines. Mid-size institutions like the Jessie Smith Noyes Foundation, the Compton Foundation, and the Educational Foundation of America rank among the most prominent users of mission-related, values-based portfolio screens.

The Council survey roughly tracks SIF's finding that "responsibly invested portfolios" account for nearly 10 percent of funds under management in the United States. However, the *Management Report* is based on a small, fairly inscrutable survey universe, and some grantmakers active in the field believe it overstates the extent of portfolio screening in philanthropy. The 1996 survey represented the Council's first attempt to gauge the extent of social investing by foundations. But instead of trying to refine those findings, a more recent Council survey on asset-management practices omitted questions about the relationship between foundation missions and investment strategies.

Historically, mainstream philanthropy has resisted portfolio screening. In 1988, economist Hazel Henderson, Don Collat of Salomon Brothers, and venture capitalist Edward Tasch (former treasurer of the Jessie Smith Noyes Foundation) formed a social venture capital firm called Commons Capital Partners. Their primary market was pension plans and foundations. "Sooner or later you are going to have to align your portfolio management with your mission," Commons Capital told prospective clients. "Let us help you start now." The group offered an investment-screening service and advice on making program-related investments. "Virtually every foundation slammed the door in our faces," remembers Henderson.

If screening mechanisms remain the exception, The Investment Fund for Foundations (TIFF) may embody the emerging strategic norm. Unlike Commons Capital Partners, TIFF had its entranceway furnished by philanthropy. Started in 1994 with funding from two dozen grantmakers, TIFF modeled itself on the Common Fund for Nonprofit Organizations, which pools investments for colleges, universities, and private schools. TIFF's initial board of directors boasted senior officials from huge institutions including the MacArthur Foundation, Rockefeller Foundation, and Duke Endowment.

On occasion, foundations ask TIFF president David Salem if he would offer a fund screened of tainted industries or corporations. Salem sends back a copyrighted one-page response saying that investment decisions made by TIFF are based solely on investment merit. Salem says that his directors have considered offering screened funds but decided such funds would unduly burden TIFF. In his communiqué Salem also challenges the claim made by some responsible-investing advocates that social restraints actually boost returns. He says their evidence is incomplete. Although, as this book went to press, Salem was revisiting the issue.

Maybe so. But investment orthodoxy hasn't always proved a reliable guide to success, either. In some respects, the establishment perspective has been strikingly shortsighted and woefully wrongheaded. Take the Council on Foundations, the most powerful trade association in philanthropy. In 1994 the Council released an "issues packet" that presented the prevailing view on foundation investment strategies. Three main themes emerged from the articles and briefings in that packet.

1. *Grantmakers need to inflation-proof their portfolios more aggressively.* No other assumption has been more pervasive among foundation establishmentarians. Council on Foundations John Edie and Morgan Guaranty Managing Director Lowell Smith warned that a "rate of return of at least 9.5 percent is necessary for most foundations to avoid the ravages of inflation." Edie and Smith acknowledged that annualized inflation averaged 3 percent for the six decades preceding 1990. But they based their 9.5 percent formula on a minimum inflation rate of 4 percent, a mandatory payout of 5 percent and management fees of 0.5 percent. As recently as late 1997, the Council was producing materials such as a four-volume Family Foundation Library Series that treated the 9.5 percent formula as holy writ.

2. *Market rates of return in the 1990s won't match the standards of the previous decade.* In a briefing paper, the consulting firm DeMarche Associates prophesied that "the 1990s likely will be a single-digit decade for the financial markets." Why? Following the theory of reversion to the mean, DeMarche argued that "since the market is again at a high level [in October 1993], future returns would be expected to be lower than the historical average."

3. *Grantmakers must jettison their little-old-lady holdings and fly high.* Assumptions about unrelenting inflation and declining market returns led the establishment to a prescription jarringly at odds with philanthropy's genteel financial sensibility. In a 1994 essay TIFF's David Salem exhorted foundation fiduciaries "not to make sure that the risks [of nontraditional investments] are sufficiently low but rather to make sure that they're sufficiently high" TIFF followed through on its advice.

Of the $210 million under management in the TIFF Investment Program during its start-up year, $114 million was invested in an emerging market fund and an international equity fund. In 1995, DeMarche Associates echoed Salem's advice in a glossy Council report that urged foundation investors to "consider asset allocations that involve higher risk."

Recent history has not been kind to these three premises. Since 1991, the United States has enjoyed the lowest sustained rate of inflation in a generation. During the past year, growing numbers of investors and analysts have contemplated the prospect of deflation, not inflation, derailing economic activity and distorting financial returns. The unprecedented bull market of the 1990s—well underway when the Council released its "issues packet"—has dwarfed the returns of the 1980s.

Moreover, market events have called into question the logic of conventional diversification strategies that encourage high-flying. For example, TIFF's early promotional materials declare that foreign investments "reduce the volatility of [investors'] overall returns [because] foreign markets and domestic markets tend to rise and fall at different times." But the more foreign portfolio investment (i.e., emerging market funds like TIFF's) fuels the interconnection of global markets, the more those markets apparently move in train—as vividly illustrated by the worldwide bond meltdown of spring 1994 and the more recent fallout from East Asia's financial woes.

Since its founding, TIFF's domestic equity funds have delivered solid returns to investors. But according to a prospectus filed with the Securities and Exchange Commission (SEC) in April 1998, TIFF's emerging market fund—now a proportionately smaller member of its mutual fund family—has registered a negative total return since its inception.

Sooner or later, rising U.S. equity markets will fall. Emerging market funds may rebound. And price instability may recur, even though the inflation of the 1970s now appears to have been a historical anomaly instead of an irreversible trend. Anyone can make mistakes, especially anyone audacious enough to categorically predict financial market behaviors. But the purveyors of grantmaking's conventional investment wisdom should be sufficiently humbled by their own fallibility to keep an open mind about asset strategies informed by program mission and less-dogmatic financial assumptions.

Shareholders Use Their Leverage

For a handful of foundations, shareholder advocacy has become part and parcel of their investment program. Rather than trying to eliminate dissonant investments, these foundations use their shares to either file or support shareholder resolutions challenging a company's egregious practices or policies. In 1994, for example, the Jessie Smith Noyes Foundation approached one of its grantees, the Southwest Organizing Project (SWOP), to see if it would like to add shareholder activism to its organizing strategey against Intel Corporation.

SWOP is an Albuquerque-based community organization with a broad social agenda, including voting rights and issues of economic and environmental justice in New Mexico. Intel, the nation's largest microchip manufacturer, was expanding a massive plant expansion in Rio Rancho, N.M. Company management had refused to meet with SWOP, which had documented problems with the expansion and expressed concerns regarding environmental and social impacts. Air and ground water, community leaders believed, would both be threatened. SWOP also criticized Intel's hiring practices and the lavish state financial incentives subsidizing its planned expansion.

As it held more than $1,000 worth of common stock in Intel, the Noyes Foundation qualified under SEC rules to file a shareholder resolution asking company management to establish a policy of allowing communities greater access to information about Intel's operations. Noyes's president, Stephen Viederman, took the matter to his trustees, all of whom supported the initiative as a way of adding value to the foundation's grant support of SWOP. (Ironically, Intel had eased through the portfolio screens used by Noyes and others, illustrating the limits of screening as a one-track approach to responsible investing).

Noyes filed a resolution for the 1995 annual meeting "to adopt a policy to make publicly available information that will allow concerned persons or organizations to assess . . . environmental and safety hazards to local communities." On the first ballot the resolution received only 5 percent of the vote. But according to SEC rules, this small proportion was enough to put the issue back on the ballot for Intel's next annual meeting.

To avoid an ongoing proxy fight and more embarrassing publicity, Intel agreed to meet with representatives of the community. After protracted discussions and a petition refiling at the 1995 annual meeting, Intel formally revised its Environmental Health and Safety Policy by adding a commitment to consult and share information with communities in which it operates. The protectors of ground water won a round.

Prior to the proxy vote, Noyes canvassed all 250 members of the Environmental Grantmakers Association to identify foundations holding Intel stock and solicit their support for the proxy. Very few responded. To Noyes's knowledge, of the large foundations only Rockefeller and MacArthur voted for the resolution. The Ford Foundation, which routinely votes all proxies, opposed it. A handful of smaller grantmakers with holdings in Intel voted with Noyes.

A few other foundations have filed similar stockholder resolutions. The tiny, California-based Rose Foundation turned a normally sedate annual meeting at Maxxam Corporation into an open forum on debt-for-nature swaps and an embarrassing examination of Chairman Charles Hurwitz's management style. Maxxam was poised to log the last privately owned stand of redwoods in California and the federal government was attempting to recover $750 million from Maxxam over a failed savings and loan. Why not swap trees for the debt to Uncle Sam, asked the Rose proxy. In 1997 one of every eight Maxxam shareholders supported the resolution, enough to place the proxy demanding a debt-for-nature swap and another seeking to elect independent directors on the following year's stockholder ballot.

Activist shareholders delivered another ringing message to Maxxam at the company's 1998 annual meeting. A resolution calling for greater management and board accountability drew 15 percent of outstanding shares, fully half of all stock not held by Maxxam chairman Hurwitz. The resolution's coauthors included CALPERS (California Public Employee Retirement System), the country's largest public pension fund. A companion resolution calling for significant reforms in Maxxam's forestry practices received 350,000 votes, just shy of the 3 percent required for automatic placement on the 1999 shareholder ballot. But a significant number of investors at the 1998 meeting said they believed a debt-for-nature swap remained a viable option.

Some foundations, rather than petitioning a company directly, grant community organizations $1,000 to buy shares and file resolutions themselves. But again, such actions are generally taken by small and mid-sized, progressive foundations like Rose and Noyes. To date none of the major foundations, some of which have substantial holdings in the country's worst-behaving corporations, have initiated shareholder resolutions. Few others follow the Ford Foundation's practice of routinely voting proxies, and, like Ford, most who do so refuse to reveal exactly how they voted on any proxy ballot. In fact, most fiduciaries simply defer to their money managers, who either toss the proxies in the wastebasket or vote the "street line," that is, with company management. Some foundation boards, claiming they cannot agree on guidelines for voting proxies, refrain from voting as a matter of policy.

Which Way?

If foundation trustees took it upon themselves to examine their vast investments in American business, they could advance their philanthropic mission with carefully executed shareholder actions that encourage companies to clean up their acts. Such actions would neither threaten return on investment nor abuse the prudent-investor rule. Indeed, research compiled by the Council of Institutional Investors demonstrates that stockholder resolutions demanding more accountable governance actually enhance the target company's stock over time. Thoughtful shareholder advocacy, as opposed to the fast-buck interventions of a Michael Price (see "Managing the Money Managers") builds long-term shareholder value.

Despite its rarity in the philanthropic world, shareholder activism has become common practice among huge, bottom line–oriented institutional investors like CALPERS and other state employee retirement plans, although they are still more likely to petition over matters of corporate governance than social issues. According to the Social Investment Forum, investors held $542 billion in assets supportive of shareholder-advocacy initiatives in 1997.

Intentionally or not, most foundations have hitched a free ride on what the *Wall Street Journal* recently termed "a surge in shareholder activism [that] appears to have spurred remarkable performance in many stocks and contributed to the overall market's gains." The Noyes Foundation has issued an invitation to grantmakers to join a new shareholder advocacy network called the Foundation Partnership in Corporate Responsibility. Noyes' chief partner is the New York–based Interfaith Council on Corporate Responsibility, the best-known practitioner of stockholder activism in the religious community. "FPCR is still in its infancy, and those who have joined tend to be small foundations," reports Noyes's president Steve Viederman. But about 120 grantmakers have signed on. In 1997 the SEC unwittingly handed the nascent network a recruiting issue when it proposed regulations drastically limiting the rights of shareholders to file resolutions against American corporations.

A diverse coalition of investor groups convinced the SEC to back off its initiative. But most foundations, save for energized FPCR members, remained on the sidelines. When the Council on Foundations was asked to take a stand, it politely passed saying it would become involved only "in those issues that affect how grantmaking organizations are regulated." Later, Council president Dorothy Ridings conceded that "the proposed rules do in some way regulate grantmaking foundations so long as foundations own publicly traded securities (and most do)." And she hinted that if more foundations showed an interest the Council would reconsider its silence. A few months later the Council's publication *Foundation News and Commentary* dedicated most of an issue to "Mission and Investment." The lead article, however, asserted that "the idea of bringing investment strategy in sync with grantmaking remains "overwhelmingly suspect to organized philanthropy."

As more socially progressive and environmentally concerned youngsters join foundation boards, they may begin breaking down those suspicions. But it probably will take years before the philanthropic community's leaders embrace the view that investment strategies are integral to their overall mission.

Viederman and Tasch of Jessie Smith Noyes want to speed up the process. "If we believe that in the coming century economic activity will create ecological and political stresses of global proportions, then it is no longer prudent to keep philanthropy and investment separate," they write." When a foundation's mission and its fiduciary responsibility are both viewed as key elements of a philanthropy's purpose, then grant making and assets management can become mutually reinforcing instruments of change." And change, most philanthropists agree, is what foundations should be all about.

Notes

Preface

1. *Millionaires and the Millennium: New Estimates of the Forthcoming Wealth Transfer and the Prospects for a Golden Age of Philanthropy*, Boston College Social Welfare Research Institute (cited in *New York Times,* October 20, 1999, B2).

Introduction

1. Michael Lerner, "A Gift Observed," p. 101 (unpublished work in progress).

2. My gratitude to Peter Goldmark and Dennis McIlnay for their help with these examples and translations.

3. Waldemar Nielsen, *The Big Foundations,* Twentieth Century Fund Study (New York: Columbia University Press, 1972).

4. The National Cancer Institute's *Cancer Statistic Review* (1998) shows increase of 55 percent in the overall incidence of all types of cancer since 1950.

5. Robert Arnove (ed.), *Philanthropy and Cultural Imperialism: The Foundations at Home and Abroad* (Boston: G. K. Hall, 1980) p. 1.

6. Ellen Condliffe Lagemann, ed., *Philanthropic Foundation: New Scholarship, New Possibilities* (Bloomington: University of Indiana Press, 1999), pp. ix–x.

Chapter One

1. Judith Sealander, *Private Wealth and Public Life* (Baltimore: Johns Hopkins University Press, 1997), p. 29.

2. Quoted in ibid.

3. I am indebted for this analysis to Susan Wisely, whose excellent essay, "A Foundation's Relationship to Its Public: Legacies and Lessons for the Lilly Endowment," was written for the 1992 annual report of what soon thereafter became the largest foundation in the country.

4. Joan Roelofs. "Foundations and the Supreme Court," *Telos* (1984–85): 60.

5. Conversation with author.

6. Quoted in Roger Williams, "Know Thy Critics," *Foundation News and Commentary* (May/June 1998): 26.

7. According to records kept by the Foundation Center, only about one in twenty grant proposals is funded.

8. In 1914 a tent colony of mine strikers in Ludlow, Colorado, was attacked by the National Guard; 11 women and 2 children were killed.

9. Frank P Walsh, "Perilous Philanthropy," *The Independent* 83 (August 1915): 262.

10. Barry D. Karl and Stanley N. Katz, "American Private Philanthropic Foundations, 1890–1930," *Minerva* 19 (1981): 253.

11. Roelofs, "Foundations and the Supreme Court," 61.

12. Karl and Katz, "American Private Philanthropic Foundations," 253.

13. Quoted in Robert H. Bremner, *American Philanthropy* (Chicago: University of Chicago Press, 1960), p. 166.

14. Willa Johnson, *Annual Report* (Washington, D.C.: Capital Research Center, 1991).

15. Quoted in Waldemar A. Nielsen, *The Golden Donors: A New Anatomy of the Great Foundations* (New York: E. P. Dutton, 1985), p. 26.

16. William E. Simon, *Time For Truth* (New York: Readers; Digest Press, 1978).

17. Michael Lerner, "A Gift Observed," p. 127 (unpublished "work in progress").

18. Katz, at the Open Society Institute seminar, New York, June 3, 1998; LaMarche, ibid.

19. LaMarche, ibid.; idem, "More Scrutiny, Please," *Foundation News and Commentary* 40 (July/August 1999).

20. Heather MacDonald, "The Billions of Dollars that Made Things Worse" *City Journal*, August 1996.

21. David Callahan, "Liberal Policy's Weak Foundations," *The Nation,* November 13, 1995; Michael Shuman, ibid.

22. Pablo Eisenberg, "Illusions of Blandeur," *Foundation News and Commentary* (July/August 1996): 30–32.

23. Sally Covington, *Moving a Public Policy Agenda: The Strategic Philanthropy of Conservative Foundations* (Washington D.C.: National Committee for Responsive Philanthropy, 1997), p. 2.

24. Karl and Katz, "American Private Philanthropic Foundations," 240.

Chapter Two

1. Council for Aid to Education, *Annual Report* 1999. Corporations, which until quite recently outspent foundations in educational philanthropy, would undoubtedly give more if university professors did not openly complain about the contrac-

tual strings attached to corporate research grants (American Association of University Professors, press release, May 17, 1999).

2. *Annual Report* (New York: Rockefeller Foundation, 1971), p. 46.

3. Frederick Rudolph. *The American College and University: A History* (New York: Alfred Knopf, 1962), p. 430.

4. Lawrence A. Cremin *American Education, The Metropolitan Experience, 1876–1980* (New York: Harper & Row, 1988), p. 650; idem, *Popular Education and Its Discontents* (New Yorker: Harper & Row, 1990), p. viii.

5. Cremin, *Popular Education and Its Discontents,* pp. 42, 39.

6. Ford Foundation, *Decade of Experiment* (New York: Ford Foundation, 1959), p. 2.

7. René Wormser, *Foundations: Their Power and Influence.* New York: Devin-Adair, 1958.

8. Ford Foundation, *Decade of Experiment,* p. 2.

9. Heather MacDonald, "The Billions of Dollars That Made Things Worse," *City Journal,* Autumn 1996, p. 26.

10. David Samuels, "Philanthropic Correctness," *New Republic,* September 18, 1995, p. 28.

11. Quoted in Meg Sommerfeld, "What Did the Money Buy?" *Chronicle of Philanthropy* 21 (no. 14): 1.

12. Walter Annenberg. White House dinner speech. December 1993.

13. National Commission on Excellence in Education, *A Nation at Risk: A Report to the Secretary of Education,* April 1983.

14. Peter Schrag, "The Near Myth of Our Failing Schools," *Atlantic Monthly* (October 1997): 72–80.

15. William Bennett and Chester Finn, "Reforming Education in Four Easy Steps," *Washington Times,* December 12, 1997.

16. Quoted in ibid.

17. Bradley also funded Charles Murray's research comparing the intellectual abilities of white and nonwhite races. It led to publication of the controversial *The Bell Curve: Intelligence and Class Structure in American Life,* Richard J. Herrnstein and Charles Murray (New York: Free Press, 1994).

18. Chester Finn, "Giving It Away: An Open Letter to Bill Gates," *Commentary* January 1998, p. 21.

19. Quoted in Marina Dunjerski and Jennifer Moore. "Debate Over Government-Paid School Vouchers Is Accelerating," *Chronicle of Philanthropy,* November 19, 1998, p. 10.

20. Finn, "Giving It Away," p. 21.

21. Author interview with Anthony Ciapolone.

22. 22. Office of the State Superintendent of Education, *Report to the California State Assembly Committee on Education,* August 1997, p. 3.

23. Author interview with Theodore Lobman.

24. Alan B. Krueger. "But Does It Work?" *New York Times,* special education section, November 20, 1999, p. 46.

25. Author interview with Roger Benjamin.

26. Ibid.

27. Theodore Lobman. "Public Education Grant Making Styles: More Money, More Vision, More Demands," *Teachers College Record* (Spring 1992): 401.

28. Sally Covington, *Moving a Public Policy Agenda: The Strategic Philanthropy of Conservative Foundations.* (Washington D.C.: National Committee for Responsive Philanthropy, July 1997).

29. Ellen Condliffe Lagemann, *The Politics of Knowledge: The Carnegie Corporation, Philanthropy, and Public Policy* (Middletown, Conn.: Wesleyan University Press, 1989), p. 256.

Chapter Three

1. Stanley Katz "Grantmaking Research in the United States, 1922–83," *Proceedings of the American Philosophical Society* 129 (1985): 2.

2. Carnegie uses the term *wordy Socialists* in *Gospel of Wealth* (New York: Century, 1900), p. 13.

3. Memorandum, Frederick Gates to John D. Rockefeller, February 2, 1910, Rockefeller Archives, record group 2 (cited in Richard Brown, *Rockefeller's Medicine Men* [Berkeley: University of California Press, 1979], p. 116).

4. Charles Warren Stiles. "Zoological Pitfalls for the Pathologist," the Middleton Goldsmith Lecture, New York Pathological Society, November 30, 1904.

5. While Rockefeller Foundation literature claimed that the hookworm was virtually eliminated, Stiles, who spearheaded the Sanitary Commissions work, profoundly disagreed. His protests went unheard and unacknowledged at the foundation.

6. Daniel Kevles, "Foundations, Universities, and Trends in Support for the Physical and Biological Sciences, 1900–1912," *Daedalus* (Fall 1992): 192.

7. Carnegie, *Gospel of Wealth.*

8. Fredrick Gates, *Chapters in My Life* (New York: Free Press, 1977), p. 186.

9. John D. Rockefeller, *Random Reminiscences of Men and Events* (Garden City, N.Y.: Doubleday, Doran, 1933), p. 177 (cited in James A. Smith, *The Idea Brokers: Think Tanks and the Rise of the New Policy Elite* [New York: Free Press, 1991] p. 38).

10. Andrew Carnegie to Simon Newcomb, January 3 1902, Simon Newcomb Papers, Library of Congress, Box 18.

11. Raymond Fosdick, *The Story of The Rockefeller Foundation* (New York: Harper and Bros., 1952), p. 146.

12. Kenneth Prewitt, *American Foundations and the Funding of Science* (Bloomington: Center For Philanthropy, Indiana University.

13. Elihu Root, "Industrial Research and National Welfare," *Science* 47 (May 1918): 221.

14. Wesley C. Mitchell, "Statistics and Government," in *The Backward Art of Spending Money,* pp. 50–51 (cited in Prewitt, *American Foundations,* p. 23).

15. Wickliffe Rose, "Three Programs and Policies of the Rockefeller Foundation," November 29, 1950, p.1, Rockefeller Archives Center, record 3/915/1/4.

16. Warren Weaver, *1933 Annual Report of the Rockefeller Foundation,* pp. 199–200.

17. Barry Karl, "Philanthropy and Social Science," *Proceedings of the American Philosophical Society.* 129(1985): 14.

18. Prewitt, *Social Sciences and Private Philanthropy: The Quest For Social Relevance.* (Bloomington: Indiana University Center on Philanthropy.

19. Prewitt, *American Foundations,* p. 3.

20. Rebecca Lowen, *Creating The Cold War University* (Berkeley: University of California Press, 1997), p. 193.

21. Rowan Gaither, "Program V Study Report to Ford Foundation Trustees," November 1949, Ford Foundation Archives.

22. Lowen, *Creating the Cold War University,* pp. 200–204.

23. *Hearings and Report, U.S. Commission on Industrial Relations,* vol. 8. (Washington, D.C.: Government Printing Office, 1915).

24. Quoted in James Weinstein, *The Corporate Ideal in the Liberal State, 1900–1918* (Boston: Beacon Press, 1968), p. 205.

25. Frank Walsh, "Are the Great Foundations Perilous?" *The Independent* 83 (1915): 262–63.

26. Prewitt, *Social Sciences and Private Philanthropy,* p. 18.

27. Raymond Fosdick, *The Rockefeller Foundation, 1913 to 1915* (New York: Harper & Bros., 1952), p. 199.

28. Fosdick, *1936 Annual Report of the Rockefeller Foundation,* p. 6.

29. Beardsley Ruml, *Final Report of the Laura Spelman Rockefeller Memorial,* 1933, p. 9 (quoted in Prewitt, *Social Sciences and Private Philanthropy,* p. 26).

30. John D. Rockefeller Sr., *Random Reminiscences,* p. 112.

31. Prewitt, *American Foundations,* p. 3.

32. Prewitt. *Social Sciences and Private Philanthropy,* p. 32.

33. Ibid. p. 33.

34. Quoted in J. L. Heilbron and Robert W. Seidel, *Lawrence and His Laboratory* (Berkeley: University of California Press, 1989), p. 219.

35. Daniel Kevles, *The Physicists: The History of a Scientific Community in Modern America* (New York: Knopf, 1998), p. 211.

36. Neils Wessell, "President's Statement," *1969 Annual Report,* Alfred P. Sloan Foundation, pp. 3–4.

37. Ibid.

38. *A Five to Seven Year Program to Advance Research and Training in the Neurosciences,* Sloan Foundation, September 1969, p. 12.

39. 1985 Sloan Foundation Report, p. 9.

40. Sloan Foundation News Release April 15, 1991.

41. Quoted in Marcia Barinaga, "The Foundations of Research," *Science* 253 (September 1991): 1200.

42. Ibid.

43. Ibid., p. 1202.

Chapter Four

1. Elizabeth Toon, *Selling the Public on Public Health* (cited in. *Philanthropic Foundations: New Scholarship, New Possibilities,* ed. Ellen Condliffe Lagemann [Bloomington: University of Indiana Press, 1999]. p. 125).

2. For the debates on the private motives of American health philanthropists, see Paul Starr *The Social Transformation of American Medicine.* (New York: Basic Books, 1982); and E. Richard Brown. *Rockefeller Medicine Men: Medicine and Capitalism in America* (Berkeley: University of California Press, 1979).

3. John D. Rockefeller Sr. was himself committed to homeopathy and demanded that it receive equal treatment with allopathic medicine. His son, John D. Jr., disagreed and respectfully guided Gates and others on the foundation staff away from what he regarded as his father's quaint obsession.

4. Author interview with David Himmelstein.

5. Open Society Institute, press release, May 28. 1999.

6. Waldemar Nielsen, *The Golden Donors* (New York: Dutton, 1987), p. 132.

7. Robert Wood Johnson prospectus, 1995.

8. Judith Bell, Harry Snyder, and Christine Tien, *The Public Interest in Conversions of Nonprofit Health Charities* (New York: Consumers Union and Milbank Memorial Fund, 1997), p. 23.

9. "Coming of Age: Findings from the 1998 Survey of Foundations Created by Health Care Conversions," *Grant Makers in Health,* February 1999, p. 1.

10. Tamar Lewin and Martin Gottlieb, "In Hospital Sales, an Overlooked Side Effect," *New York Times,* April 27, 1997, p. 1.

11. Gilbert Gaul and Neill Borowski, *Free Ride: The Tax Exempt Economy* (Kansas City, Mo.: Andrews and McMeel), p. 42.

12. Judith Bell, "Saving Their Assets," *American Prospect* (May/June 1996): 61.

13. Bell et al., *Public Interest in Conversions,* p. 12.

14. National Association of Attorneys General, spring meeting, March 19–21, 1997.

15. *Wall Street Journal,* November 6, 1996, p. 1; Domenica Marchetti. "Redefining Health Philanthropy," *Chronicle of Philanthropy,* July 24, 1997, p. 1.

16. Quoted in Bell et al., *Public Interest in Conversions,* p. 35.

Chapter Five

1. Environmental Grantmakers Association brochure.

2. Ibid.

3. Most new environmental money seems to result from a gradual intrafamily transformation as members change from exploiters to conservationists. That some wealthy families have got at least a little religion about the environment should please the greens; that very little else about their politics or religion has changed. should make conservatives happy. Even their environmental philanthropy remains respectful of free enterprise and private property.

   A mere generation ago, the fortune of the parsimonious ultra-rightwing MacArthur family was heavily invested in Florida real estate, shopping malls, and paper mills. Today the family foundations fund projects to protect the Florida Keys, the Everglades, and even clean-water initiatives that put paper mills out of business. Similar ironies can be found throughout the foundation world, where the combined portfolios of trusts like Pew (Sun Oil money), W. Alton Jones (Cities Service), and Rockefeller (Standard Oil), which include twenty-eight oil and gas development companies, support organizations that would have their founders spinning in their graves. Doubt remains, however, that the wealthy elite who remain in control of these and similar foundations can understand and direct a popular political movement.

4. Michael Lerner, "A Gift Observed," unpublished manuscript, p. 110.

5. Stephen G. Green, "Who's Driving the Environmental Movement," *Chronicle of Philanthropy,* January 25, 1994, p. 6.

6. Scott Allen, "Environmental Donors Set Tone," *Boston Globe.* October 20, 1997, p. A6.

7. Deb Callahan, Con Nugent, Donald Ross, and Tom Wathen, Ad Hoc Funder's Task Force on Environmental Issues Campaigns, *Report and Recommendations,* 1993, p. 2.

8. Ibid., p. 3

9. Author interview with Joshua Reichert

10. Speech to 1999 Annual Meeting of Environmental Grantmakers Association, Asilomar, California.

11. Author interview with Tim Hermack.

12. Brian Tokar, *Earth For Sale: Reclaiming Ecology in the Age of Corporate Greenwash* (Boston, South End Press, 1997), p. 28.

13. Interview with Tim Hermack.

14. Tokar, *Earth For Sale,* p. 28.

15. Pew Charitable Trusts, *Annual Report* 1994, p. 17 (cited by Brian Tokar in *Earth for Sale,* p. 28).

16. E-mail from Jim Britell.

17. Speech to 1999 Annual Meeting of Environmental Grantmakers Association, Asilomar, California.

Chapter Six

1. United Nations Food and Agriculture Organization figures (cited in the Rockefeller Foundation's 1997 "Agricultural Sciences Program Overview," Rockefeller Foundation Archives.

2. "History of Projects and Policies of the Rockefeller Foundation," Rockefeller Foundation Archives, R.G. 3.0, series 915, box 1, folder 4, p. 1.

3. Confidential Monthly Report, Fosdick to Rockefeller trustees, February 1944, p. 1.

4. John Perkins, "The Rockefeller Foundation and the Green Revolution, 1941–56," in *Agriculture and Human Values* (Summer/Fall 1990): 7.

5. International Development Advisory Board, *Partners in Progress* (New York: Simon and Schuster, 1951), p. 29.

6. Waldemar Nielsen. *The Big Foundations.* A Twentieth Century Fund Study (New York: Columbia University Press, 1972), p. 62.

7. Hiram Drache, "Midwest Agriculture: Changing with Technology," *Agriculture History* 50 (January 1976): 291.

8. Pioneer was recently purchased by DuPont to create a firm that will compete directly with Monsanto in the development of genetically engineered seeds.

9. George Harrar, "More Food For Our Neighbor," Rockefeller Foundation Archives, RG. 6.13, series 1.1, box 34, folder 381, pp. 11–12.

10. John Perkins, *Geopolitics and the Green Revolution: Wheat, Genes, and the Cold War* (New York: Oxford University Press, 1989), p. 15.

11. George Harrar, Paul Mangelsdorf, and Warren Weaver, "Notes on Indian Agriculture," April 11, 1952, Rockefeller Foundation Archives, RG 6.7, box 10c18a, folder IAP.

12. Perkins, *Geopolitics and the Green Revolution,* p. 17.

13. Wolf Ladejinsky to Ken Iverson, October 1954 memo, "Land Reform," Ford Foundation Archives, Record # 002593, p. 1.

14. Ladejinsky memo, p. 4.

15. Catherine Caufield, *Masters of Illusion: The World Bank and the Poverty of Nations* (New York: Henry Holt, 1996), p. 107.

16. Keith Griffin, *Alternative Strategies for Economic Development* (Basingstoke, U.K.: Macmillan in association with OECD Development Centre, 1989), p. 147.

17. Herdt interview with author, January 1999.

18. Brian O'Connell, *Philanthropy In Action* (New York: Foundation Center, 1987), p. 77.

19. Lowell Hardin, "Economic, Social, and Political Implications of the Green Revolution," paper presented to the Southwest Agriculture Forum, January 28, 1971.

20. E-mail message from Michael Lerner.

21. George Harrar, June 1, 1951, memo, "Agriculture and the Rockefeller Foundation," Rockefeller Foundation Archives, R.G. 6.13, series 1.1, box 25, folder 280.

22. Lowell Hardin to MacGeorge Bundy, memo about *Food, Population and Employment: The Impact of the Green Revolution,* ed. Thomas T. Poleman and Donald Freebairn (New York: Praeger, 1973), Ford Foundation Archives, Record # 010123, p. 2.

23. The Rockefeller Foundation had quietly made small grants for birth control research since the 1920s to, notably, Margaret Sanger. It also supported the 1927 Geneva Population Conference through a strangely named Rockefeller creation—the Bureau of Social Hygiene. The conference was organized behind the scenes by Sanger and her colleagues but attended only by scientists, many of them eugenists. An outcome of that meeting was the founding of the Union for the Scientific Investigation of Population.

24. R. G. Anderson to Lowell Hardin, "A Second Look at the Green Revolution," 1974 memo, Ford Foundation Archives, Record # 002649, p. 11.

25. John E. Pluenneke and Sharon Moshavi, "A Revolution Comes Home to Roost . . . Leaving Hunger in the Midst of Plenty," *Business Week,* November 6, 1994.

26. Peter Rosset, in *World Hunger: Twelve Myths* by Frances Moore Lappé, Joseph Collins, and Peter Rosset, with Luis Esparza, 2d. ed. (New York: Grove Press, 1998), p. 60.

27. Indian Home Ministry, "The Causes and Nature of Current Agrarian Tensions," 1969 (described in Francine R. Frankel, *India's Green Revolution: Economic Gains and Political Costs* [Princeton, N.J.: Princeton UniversityPress, 1971], p. 9).

28. Ibid., p.10.

29. Donald K. Freebairn, "Did The Green Revolution Concentrate Incomes? A Quantitative Study of Research Reports," *World Development* 23 (1995): 265–79.

30. Jennings interview with Winkelman, 1979 (cited in Bruce H. Jennings, *Foundations of International Agricultural Research: Science and Politics in Mexican Agriculture.* [Boulder, Colo.: Westview Press, 1988], p. 172).

31. Carl Sauer to Willits et al., March 12, 1941, Rockefeller Foundation Archives, RG 1.2, series 323, box 10, folder 63.

32. Ibid.

33. John Dickey to Warren Weaver and George Harrar, October 26, 1949 memo, Rockefeller Foundation Archives, R.G. 1.2, series 323, pp. 2–3.

34. Harrar to Weaver, March 16, 1949, Rockefeller Foundation Archives, R.G. 3.0, series 915, box 3, folder 17.

35. Lowell Hardin to MacGeorge Bundy, June 5, 1973, Ford Foundation Archives, Record # 010123.

36. A. H. Moseman to Ralph Richardson, memo, Rockefeller Foundation Archives.

37. Edward J. Wellhausen, "Weeds and Man in Latin America," banquet address, Fourth Annual Meeting, Weed Society of America,. St. Louis, Mo., December 13, 1961.

38. Donald K. Freebairn, *The Dichotomy of Prosperity and Poverty in Mexican Agriculture* (Ithaca, N.Y.: ca. 1969), p. 35.

39. D. P. Singh "The Impact of the Green Revolution" *Agricultural Situation in India* 13 (1980): 323 (quoted in Lappé et al., *World Hunger:*).

40. Rosset in Lappé et al., *World Hunger,* p. 60.

41. *Poverty and Hunger: Issues and Options for Food Security in Developing Countries* (Washington, D.C.: World Bank, 1986), p. 49.

42. Perkins, *Geopolitics and the Green Revolution,* pp. 14–15

43. Robert Chambers, "Beyond the Green Revolution," July 1983, internal memo, Ford Foundation Archives, Report Record #009389, pp. 16–17.

44. Ibid.

45. Ibid.

46. U.N. Food and Agriculture Organization.

47. Rosset in Lappé et al., *World Hunger,* p. 68.

48. Prabhu Pingali, Mahabub Hossain, and Roberta V. Gerpacio, *Asian Rice Bowls: The Returning Crisis?* (New York: CAB International/International Rice Research Institute, Manila, 1997), Table 4.5.

49. Quoted by Rosset in Lappé et al., *World Hunger,* p. 78.

50. Michael Hansen, *Escape From the Pesticide Treadmill: Alternatives to Pesticides in Developing Countries,* p.134.

51. In the Philippines in 1996, IRRI test plots of varieties that yielded ten tons a hectare in 1966 were producing no more than seven tons per hectare.

52. Vandana Shiva, *The Violence of the Green Revolution* (London: Zed Books, 1993), p. 23.

53. Author interview with Frances Fitzgerald.

54. Quoted in Caufield, *Masters of Illusion,* p. 112.

55. Gary H. Toenniessen, "Rice Biotechnology Capacity Building in Asia," in *Agriculture Biotechnology in International Development,* eds. C. L. Ives and B. M. Bedford. p. 203, Rockefeller Archives Library.

56. Frederick Kirschenmann, "Can Organic Agriculture Feed the World? And Is That the Right Question?" in *For All Generations: Making World Agriculture More Sustainable,* eds. J. Patrick Madden and Scott G. Chaplowe (Glendale, Calif.: OM Publishers, ca. 1997).

57. Quoted by Steven Viederman in interview with author.

58. Peter Marris and Martin Rein, *Dilemmas of Social Reform: Poverty and Community Action in the United States* (New York: Atherton Press, 1967), p. 3.

59. Perkins, *Geopolitics and the Green Revolution,* p. 36.

60. Jennings interview with Winkelman, 1979 (cited in Bruce H. Jennings, *Foundations of International Agricultural Research: Science and Politics in Mexican Agriculture.* [Boulder, Colo.: Westview Press, 1988], p. 201).

61. "Report of the Trustees of the Ford Foundation," September 27, 1950 (quoted in Wolf Ladejinsky to Ken Iverson, October 1954 memo, "Land Reform," Ford Foundation Archives, Record # 002593, p. 1).

62. Ladejinsky memo, p. 4.

63. *Indonesia: Not Your "Traditional" Famine,* Institute for Food and Development Policy, Oakland, Calif., August 1999.

64. Rockefeller Foundation, "Agricultural Sciences Program Overview."

65. Marina Dundjerski, "Rockefeller Fund: Ready to Roll Again," *Chronicle of Philanthropy,* December 16, 1999, p. 8.

66. Conway, "Helping Poor Farmers," report to Ford Foundation, 1987, Ford Foundation Archives.

67. Quoted in Scott Kilman, "Foundation Asks Monsanto to Kill 'Terminator Gene,'" *Wall Street Journal,* June 28, 1999.

68. Quoted in John Vidal, *The Guardian,* October 9, 1999 (world wide web).

69. Dundjerski, "Rockefeller Fund: Ready to Roll Again," p. 8.

Chapter Seven

1. Energy Foundation, *1991 Annual Report,* , p. 3.

2. Energy Foundation, *1992 Annual Report,* p. 19.

3. Coyle testimony before the California Public Utility Commission.

4. Ibid.

5. Author interview with Hal Harvey.

6. Author interview with Eugene Coyle.

7. Author interview with Harvey.

8. Savanaugh Blackwell, "The Private Energy Elite," *San Francisco Bay Guardian,* October 8, 1997.

9. Author interview with Harvey.

10. Author interview with Ralph Cavanagh.

11. Daniel M Berman and John T. O'Connor, *Who Owns The Sun?,* p. 114.

12. Ralph Cavanagh, *The Great Retail Wheeling Illusion—And More Productive Energy Futures,* a Strategic Issue Paper (Boulder Colo.: E Source, March 1994), p. 5.

13. Armond Cohen "The Political Economy of Retail Wheeling, or How to Fight The Last War," *Electricity Journal,* August 1994.

14. Hal Harvey and Eric Heitz, "Retail Wheeling, A Briefing for Foundations," Energy Foundation, October 1994.

15. Author interview with Cavanagh.

16. Hal Harvey and Eric Heitz, "Retail Wheeling: A Briefing for Foundations," Energy Foundation, October 1995.

17. Energy Foundation, *1998 Annual Report,* p. 24.

18. Quoted in Wallace Roberts, "Green Sellout," *American Prospect,* August 16, 1999.

19. Hal Harvey, Letter to the Editor, *San Francisco Bay Guardian,* December 3, 1997, p. 6.

20. Author interview with Harvey.

21. Author interview with Cavanagh.

Chapter Eight

1. Ernest Boyer, "Lifelong Learning in the Arts," address to the 27th Annual Conference of the Western Alliance of Arts Administrators, typed transcript.

2. Nathan Weber and Loren Renz, *Arts Funding* (New York: Foundation Center, [1997]), p. 19.

3. Paul DiMaggio. *Support for the Arts from Independent Foundations* (New Haven: Yale University Press, 1986), p. 29.

4. Nancy Hanks (former NEA director), in "America, The Arts and the Future," a 1988 lecture. She cited Arthur Schlesinger Jr. as her source.

5. W. MacNeil Lowry to Ford Foundation trustees, 1961.

6. Committee on the Arts and Humanities, *Creative America: Report to the President* (Washington, D.C.: 1997), p. 20.

7. "A Conversation With Stanley N. Katz," *National Arts Stabilization Journal* (Summer 1999): 32.

8. Kenneth L. Goody. "The Funding of the Arts and Artists in the United States," prepared for the Rockefeller Foundation, November 1983. p. 8.

9. Paul DiMaggio, ed., *Nonprofit Enterprise in the Arts: Studies in Mission and Constraint* (New York: Oxford University Press, 1986), p. 114.

10. Lowry to Ford Foundation trustees.

11. John Kreidler, *Leverage Lost: The NonProfit Arts in the Post Ford Era.* He cites Jaana Myllylumoa and Lester Salamon, *The San Francisco Bay Area Nonprofit Sector: An Update* (Baltimore: Institute for Policy Studies, Johns Hopkins University, 1992) as the source of his figures.

12. Quoted in *Newsweek,* September 29, 1997, p. 35.

13. Edward Rothstein, "A Shifting American Landscape: Downtown Theme Parks for the Arts," *New York Times,* December 6, 1998, 2:1.

14. M. Melanie Beene, "The Structural Relationship of Culture and Philanthropy: A Practitioner's Perspective," in *Alternative Futures: Challenging Designs for Arts Philanthropy.* p. 40.

15. Arlene Goldblatt, "Cultural Policy Colonization of the West, or Fattening Frogs for Snakes" (unpublished essay).

16. John P. Walter "Alec Baldwin Should Pay: Only Private Patronage Can Save the Arts," *Philanthropy* (Spring 1997): 2. (*Philanthropy* is the publication of the Philanthropy Roundtable.)

17. DiMaggio, *Nonprofit Enterprise in the Arts,* p. 114.

Chapter Nine

1. Kurt Vonnegut Jr., *God Bless You, Mr. Rosewater* (or *Pearls before Swine*) (New York: Delacourt, 1965), p. 47.

2. Robert Putnam, "Bowling Alone: America's Declining Social Capital" *Journal of Democracy* 6, no. 1 (1995) (reprinted by National Endowment for Democracy, 1995).

3. Don Eberly, "Civil Society," op-ed piece, *Harrisburg Patriot-News,* May 3 , 1996, A7.

4. Don Eberly, "Recovering Civility," *Madison Review* 1 (no. 4): 14 (reprinted in the *Wall Street Journal,* February 3, 1995.

5. Benjamin Barber, "Searching for Civil Society," *National Civic Review* (Spring 1995): 116.

6. Barber, ibid.; Eberly, "Civil Society."

7. Putnam, "Bowling Alone," p. 65.

8. William Schambra, "By the People: The Old Values of the New Citizenship," *National Civic Review* (Spring 1995): 113.

9. Eberly. "Recovering Civility," p. 14.

10. Ibid.

11. Michael Schudson, Political Paradox: The Decline of the Citizen and the Rising Tide of Citizenship (in press).

12. Michael Lerner, "A Gift Observed," p. 44 (work in progress).

13. Lamar Alexander, "Restoring the American Dream: A New Vision of Philanthropy," *Essays on Civil Society* 98 (no. 1): 3.

14. Jason de Parle, "The First Primary," *New York Times Magazine,* January 16, 1995.

15. Congressman Newt Gingrich (R-Ga.) and Senator Robert Dole (R-Kansas) also tainted their political reputations by using front foundations to accept contributions that would have been illegal if processed through normal campaign-finance channels.

16. National Commission on Philanthropy and Civic Renewal, *Giving Better, Giving Smarter: Renewing Philanthropy in America* (New York, Bradley Commission, 1997).

17. My reporting on the Bradley Commission relies on the superb research of Jon Van Til and Mark Schapiro.

18. NCPCR, *Giving Better,* p. 115.

19. National Commission on Civic Renewal, final report, A Nation of Spectators: How Civic Disengagement Weakens America and What We Can Do About It, 1997.

20. Some conservatives include the union hall in the panoply of civil society institutions because they are social meeting places. However, they rarely include labor unions themselves on their lists of the legitimate associations of civil society.

21. Quoted in David Bornstein, "A Social Force Now in the World: Citizens Flex Social Muscle," *New York Times,* July 10, 1999, A15.

22. J. Craig Jenkins and Abigail Halcli, "Grassrooting the System? The Development and Impact of Social Movement Philanthropy, 1953–1990," paper presented at the Conference on Philanthropic Foundations in History: Needs and Opportunities, New York University, November 14–15, 1996, pp. 1, 27.

23. Ibid.

24. Ibid., p. 4.

25. Daniel Cantor, "Some Thoughts on Funding for Social Change," paper presented at a meeting of the National Network of Grantmakers, February 1990.

26. Anonymous donors, who represent a considerable portion of progressive funders, are naturally excused from this process.

27. Robert Arnove, *Philanthropy and Cultural Imperialism* (Boston: G. K. Hall, 1980), p.1.

28. Jenkins and Halcli, "Grassrooting the System?" p. 7.

29. Arnove, Philanthropy and Cultural Imperialism, p. 1.

30. Jenkins and Halcli, "Grassrooting the System?" p. 17.

31. Ibid., p. 24.

32. Ibid., p. 25.

33. Author interview with Pablo Eisenberg.

34. David Hunter, Plenary Address, annual meeting of the Council on Foundations, Chicago, 1975.

35. Author interview with David Hunter, 1997.

36. Heather MacDonald, "Destructive Philanthropy, " *Wall Street Journal,* October 25, 1996, op-ed page.

37. J. Craig Jenkins, "Channeling Social Protest: Foundation Patronage of Contemporary Social Movements," in *Private Interest and the Public Good,* William Powell and Elizabeth Clemens, eds. (New Haven: Yale University Press, 1997), p. 206.

38. Ibid., p. 212. Jenkins is here characterizing the arguments of Robert Arnove, Francis Piven, Richard Cloward, Doug MacAdam, Joan Roelofs, and John Wilson. However, he separates out Piven, Cloward, and MacAdam, who believe that demobilization of the movement is an inadvertent consequence of foundation funding, whereas Roelofs and others see it as "the primary intent of the funders" (p. 212).

39. Ibid., p. 214.

40. David Garrow, "Philanthropy and the Civil Rights Movement," paper presented to the Center for the Study of Philanthropy, CUNY, October 1987, p. 1.

41. Jenkins, "Channeling Social Protest," Table 14.1.

42. David Samuels, "Philanthropic Correctness," *New Republic,* September 18, 1995, p. 36.

43. Karl Marx and Friedrich Engels. *The Communist Manifesto* (London, 1847).

44. Joan Roelofs, "Our World Grows from Foundations," paper prepared for the Socialist Scholars Conference, New York, March 1997, p. 1.

45. Roelofs, "Foundations and Social Change Organizations: The Mask of Pluralism," *Insurgent Sociologist* (Fall 1987): 37.

46. *U.S. Congressional Record,* 1969a. 371.

47. MacDonald, "Destructive Philanthropy."

48. Chester Finn Jr., "Giving It Away: An Open Letter to Bill Gates," *Commentary,* January 1998, p. 19.

49. Ibid., pp. 20–21.

50. Ibid., p. 21.

51. Samuels, "Philanthropic Correctness," p. 28.

52. In a superb study conducted for the National Committee for Responsible Philanthropy researcher Sally Covington identified the following key funders of conservative causes in America: the Adolph Coors Foundation, the Harry and Lynde Bradley Foundation, the John M Olin Foundation, the Scaife Family Foundation (Richard Mellon Scaife being the family patriarch), the Smith Richardson Foundation, the Charles G. and David H. Koch foundations, the J. M. Foundation. the Phillip M. McKenna Foundation. the Earhart Foundation, the Carthage Foundation, and the Claude R. Lambe Charitable Foundation. Covington did not include the decidedly conservative Coors Family Foundation in her study because the foundation has diversified its funding in response to boycotts that damaged beer sales.

53. Karen Paget, "Lessons of Right-Wing Philanthropy," *American Prospect,* September-October 1998. p. 90.

54. Quoted in National Committee for Responsive Philanthropy, "One Billion Dollars for Ideas: Conservative Think Tanks in the 1990s," March 1999, p. 11.

55. Paget, "Lessons of Right-Wing Philanthropy," p. 90.

56. Michael H. Shuman, "Why Do Progressive Foundations Give Too Little to Too Many," *Nation,* January 12–19, 1998, p. 11.

57. Quoted by Robin Epstein in "Shaking the Foundations," *City Limits,* October 1997, p. 15.

58. Ayers quoted by Gina Graham in "Foundation Culture," *Left Business Observer* (no. 70): 7; author interview with Steven Viederman.

59. Quoted in Epstein, "Shaking the Foundations," p. 16.

60. Vonnegut, *God Bless You, Mr. Rosewater,* pp. 26–27.

61. Ibid., p. 183.

Chapter Ten

1. Peter Frumkin, "He Who's Got It Gets to Give It," *Washington Post,* October 3, 1999, p. 5.

2. Joe Hill Music.

3. Author interview with George Roberts.

4. Author interview with Jed Emerson.

5. Author interview with Roberts.

6. Author interview with Patricia Burness.

7. Quoted in Carol Tice, "Brainerd Invests Himself in Philanthropy," *Puget Sound Business Journal,* May 28, 1999, p. 6A.

8. Quoted in "Way to Give" column, *American Benefactor,* Fall 1998, p. 32.

9. Author interview with Marion Weber.

10. Grantmakers in Health Bulletin, April 19, 1999.

11. Chris Adams, ed., *Democracy Meets Public Health: Investing in Communities to Create Health* (Denver: The Colorado Trust, n.d.), p. 2.

12. Doug Easterling, "Promoting Health by Building Community Capacity," in ibid., p. 20.

13. Ibid., p. 21.

Chapter Eleven

1. Pew made this remark when asked whether the Pew Memorial Trust (now Pew Charitable Trusts) would publish an annual report.

2. Andrew Carnegie, memorandum to the Board of Trustees, 1911, Carnegie Corporation Archives.

3. Peter Goldmark, "The Phuzzy Physics of Philanthropy," Plenary address to the Council of Foundations annual meeting, May 6, 1997.

4. Barry Karl and Stanley Katz, "Foundations and Ruling Class Elites," *Daedalus* (Winter 1987):12.

5. Quoted in Judith Sealander, *Private Wealth and Public Life* (Baltimore: Johns Hopkins University Press, 1997), p. 224.

6. Quoted in Karl and Katz, "Foundations and Ruling Class Elites," p. 12.

7. John W. Nason, *Foundation Trusteeship: Service in the Public Interest* (New York: Foundation Center, 1989), p. 13.

8. Quoted in ibid., p. 14.

9. Peter Frumkin. "Private Foundations as Public Institutions," in *Philanthropic Foundations: New Scholarship, New Possibilities,* ed. Ellen Condliffe Lagemann (Bloomington: Indiana University Press, 1999), p. 69.

10. Ibid.

11. Ibid. p. 70.

12. Michael Shuman, "Who's Who in Philanthropy: Lifting the Veil of Secrecy," *Chronicle of Philanthropy,* November 4, 1999, pp. 74–75.

13. Ibid.

14. Alice O'Connor, "The Ford Foundation and Philanthropic Activism in the 1960s," in Lagemann, ed., *Philanthropic Foundations,* p. 189.

15. Quoted in Eduard C. Lindeman, *Wealth and Culture: A Study of One Hundred Foundations and Community Trusts and Their Operation during the Decade 1921–1930* (New Brunswick N.J.: Transaction Books, 1988 [1936]), p 12.

16. Dorothy Ridings, "Message from the President," *Foundation News and Commentary,* November 1996.

17. Goldmark, "The Phuzzy Physics of Philanthropy."

18. Interview with R. M. Williams, *Foundations News* (September/October 1983): 21.

19. The redistribution of surplus wealth is not a new idea; nor has it been put forward only by socialists and communists. Midway through World War II, Yankee Republican James Conant, former president of Harvard and overseer of the nation's nuclear weapons program, called for just such a confiscatory inheritance capture. Democratic meritocracy, he averred, demanded nothing less. Inherited wealth made ruling-class children lazy and indolent. The threat of poverty would drive them to excellence, Conant believed, and democracy would thrive. He bolstered his argument with the words of Yale economist Irving Fisher, president of the American Economic Association, who in December of 1918 had called on economists to support a gradual transfer of economic ownership from the top few percent to the rest of us.

20. For a complete account of the CIA's use of foundations between 1952 and 1967, see Ben Whitaker. *The Foundations* (London: Eyer Methune, 1974), pp. 157–66.

21. Michael Lerner, "A Gift Observed," p. 62 (a work in progress).

22. After the resolution was passed, as Principle 8 of the Council's eleven-principle code of ethics, a small but vocal minority of foundations (approximately eighty) bolted from the council and formed their own organization, the Philanthropy Roundtable. The Roundtable holds annual gatherings closed to the press and publishes a conservative journal called *Philanthropy*. It does not share the council's view of foundations as public trusts, and most members were repulsed by the 1977 council proclamation that foundation endowments were "not our money but charity's."

23. Emmet D. Carson, "Grantmakers in Search of a Holy Grail," *Foundation News and Commentary* (January/February 2000): 26.

24. Speech to Environmental Grantmakers, October 1999, Asilomar, California.

Epilogue

1. Waldemar A. Nielsen, *Inside American Philanthropy: The Drama of Donorship* (Norman: Oklahoma University Press, 1996), p. 125.

2. Quotes from a recorded conversation between Vincent McGee and Susan Beresford, president of the Ford Foundation.

3. Quoted in Kenneth Danforth, "Out With a Bang," *Foundation News* (January/February 1993): 24.

4. Allan Clyde, "A Conversation With Irene Diamond," *Foundation News and Commentary* (March/April 1998): 36.

5. Ibid.

Appendix

1. That figure may be somewhat inflated, as it includes portfolios which have screened one category, tobacco for example, yet still contains holdings in companies doing business in Burma, or whose practices, products or policies would offend other investors.